DIRECTORY OF THE
WORLD'S STEAMSHIPS

DIRECTORY OF THE

WORLD'S STEAMSHIPS

ALISTAIR DEAYTON

TEMPUS

Frontispiece: Funnels of *Waverley*.

First published 2007

Tempus Publishing Limited
The Mill, Brimscombe Port,
Stroud, Gloucestershire, GL5 2QG
www.tempus-publishing.com

British Library Cataloguing in Publication Data.
A catalogue record for this book is available from the British Library.

ISBN 978 0 7524 4208 2

Typesetting and origination by Tempus Publishing Limited
Printed in Great Britain

Contents

Acknowledgements

The information on these pages has been gathered over many years and from sources too numerous to mention here. My particular thanks are due, in particular, to the following:

Bill Worden (Detroit), with whom I have cooperated on a couple of occasions for an article for *Steamboat Bill*, the magazine of the Steamship Historical Society of America and with whom I have corresponded for a many years on the subject of steamers across the globe; Roderick Smith, the editor of *Rail News Victoria* magazine, who has been of great help in supplying photographs of Australian paddlers; Michael Bor (Prague) who has been a great source of help and information about central European steamers over the years; Geoffrey Hamer and Iain Quinn who have checked various parts of the UK section of the manuscript; Jorgen Bangor, who has checked the Norwegian chapter and provided updates on various restoration efforts.

Many books have been consulted for the historical data, again too many to mention.
Can I single out:

Steamboats Today, a Pictorial Directory (Tom Rhodes and Harley Scott, 1986), which is a survey of all existing steamboats and steamships in the USA and Canada at that time.
Ships of the Inland Rivers (Ronald Parsons, 3rd edition, 1996) and *Murray Darling Riverboats* (Peter Plowman, 2005), both covering the paddle steamers of the River Murray comprehensively.
Dampfschiffe in Deutschland (Andreas Westphalen, 2003) which covers all existing German steamers at that date.
Steamboat Register (The Steamboat Association (UK), various editions) This lists all extant steamships and steamboats in the UK. The latest edition, in 2005, was published as a CD-ROM.

Max Kuhn of Interlaken, Switzerland, has maintained a list of steamers in Europe and North America for a number of years. This has now been taken over by Mario Gavazzi, of Lucerne, and is available online at www.beo-news.ch/dampf/inhalt.htm

Enthusiast magazines including *Paddle Wheels*, the magazine of the Paddle Steamer Preservation Society; *Dampfer Zeitung*, the Swiss magazine covering Swiss steamers and those of the surrounding countries; *Skärgårdsbåten*, the magazine of the Stockholm group *Stiftelsen Skärgårdsbåten*; and the aforementioned *Steamboat Bill* have been of great help.

The various websites referred to in the vessel headings are just a handful of those consulted.
My thanks must also go to Google, who have made it easy to search out details on steamers all over the world.

Introduction

The reciprocating-engined steam-powered passenger vessel dominated maritime transport from the early years of the nineteenth century, with the introduction of Robert Fulton's **North River of Clermont** of 1807 in the USA and Henry Bell's **Comet** of 1812 in Europe starting things off. The age of the commercially operated reciprocating-engined passenger steamer has now virtually ended, with the two paddle steamers on the River Lena in Siberia probably the only surviving steamers in operation outside the realms of tourism and preservation.

The steam turbine was introduced in 1901 with **King Edward** on the Clyde, although its use on excursion vessels was almost entirely confined to the Firth of Clyde and North German Coast. In 1905 the first turbine-powered liners, **Virginian** and **Victorian** of the Allan line, were built. Turbine engines dominated the world's passenger liner fleet until diesel came to the ascendancy in the 1950s. Today only a handful of turbine-powered cruise ships remain, and these are getting fewer by the year.

The last surviving smaller coastal, river and lake steamers in a particular area have, in many cases, become the objects of preservation attempts, in most cases successful in spite of the odds, although occasionally projects that have stumbled from hurdle to hurdle and never seen the steamer return to service.

This book is a survey of the world's remaining steam-powered passenger-carrying vessels, including the final few turbine-powered cruise liners. It is, in a sense, an enlarged edition of *Steam Ships of Europe* (Conway, 1988). It does not include, however, statically preserved steamships such as RMS *Queen Mary*. The Internet has meant that information about steamers in further-flung parts of the world has become easier to obtain, and it is believed to be comprehensive, although if you know of any steamer that has been missed I would be delighted to know, and will include details in a future edition.

The term 'passenger-carrying steamers' is used rather than 'passenger steamers' so as to include preserved tugs, steam launches and other non-passenger vessels which carry passengers on occasion.

Around the globe there are a large number of privately owned hobby steam launches. These have generally not been included apart from the handful that offer advertised passenger trips. It may be possible to hitch a ride on others at a steam rally. There are a large number of preserved steam tugs in Finland and in the lakes in the Dalarna region of Sweden. These have been included as regular steam rallies are held during the summer, and it is possible that passenger trips are or may be offered on the day of the rally.

Preservation and survival has taken many different forms, ranging from the small group that sees a steamer as part of local history and run and restore her on a volunteer basis, through organisations like Waverley Excursions that have their origins in enthusiast organisations, but run their steamers in a business manner, employing full-time crews and support staff, to established shipping companies like Waxholmsbolaget and the Swiss Lake operators, which are often owned by local government, and, with the support of local enthusiast organisations, have retained steamers in service.

Some preservation efforts have been successful after many years when the vessel has lain dormant, like **Medway Queen**, while others have ultimately been unsuccessful, like **Nobska**.

Steamers are also seen as part of the local tourist scene, as in the Stockholm archipelago or the Swiss Lakes, where no tourist view is complete without a white steamer in the middle, or part of an area's history, like on the Mississippi.

The main aim of reading about a preserved steamer is to sail on her, and can I encourage my readers to experience and sail on as many steamers as possible. Where sailing times and dates are quoted in the text, they are those believed to be fairly fixed. But, if travelling a distance to sail on any steamer, *please* check these details locally to avoid the possibility of making a wasted journey.

Notes on the Text

The prefixes to the vessels' names are mainly self-explanatory:

PS	paddle steamer
SS	screw steamer
TSS	twin screw steamer
SWS	stern wheel steamer
QWS	quarter wheel steamer
SL	steam launch
ST	steam tug
PL	paddle launch
PT	paddle tug

Frequency abbreviations:

F/S	Friday or Saturday
FSO	Fridays and Saturdays only
FSSuO	Fridays, Saturdays and Sundays only
FX	Fridays excepted
MFSuO	Mondays, Fridays and Sundays only
MSSuX	Mondays, Saturdays and Sundays excepted
MThO	Mondays and Thursdays only
MTWX	Mondays, Tuesdays and Wednesdays excepted
MX	Mondays excepted
SSuO	Saturdays and Sundays only
SuO	Sundays only
SuX	Sundays excepted
ThFO	Thursdays and Fridays only
ThSuO	Thursdays and Sundays only
TX	Tuesdays excepted
WSuO	Wednesdays and Sundays only
WSSuO	Wednesdays, Saturdays and Sundays only

The horsepower figures are the total horsepower, so, for a twin screw steamer, this is the total for both engines.

PART 1

EUROPE

1 United Kingdom

ENGLAND: COASTAL WATERS

Thames (tidal) and Medway

PT JOHN H. AMOS

A rusty *John H. Amos* on the slip at Chatham. (Mike Ridgard)

Length: 33.30m   **Gross tonnage:** 202
Engine type: 2 Compound Diagonal, 500hp
Built: 1931   **Passenger capacity:** originally 144
Body of water: River Medway   **Home port:** Chatham
Frequency: Awaiting restoration
Website address: www.johnhamos.org;
      www.teesships2.freeuk.com/040330johnhamos.htm
Builder: Bow McLachlan, Paisley
Owner: Medway Maritime Trust
Former names: *Hero* 1977, *John H. Amos* 1976

1931: Built as a tug/tender for the Tees Conservancy Commissioners, operating at Middlesbrough, Stockton and Hartlepool. Unusually she had two engines, one for each paddle. Her builders became bankrupt during her building and the work was completed by the liquidators using materials that were in the yard. The boilers were found not to be large enough and she could only make 11 knots instead of the intended 13 knots. Mainly used for towing barges to dredgers and the dumping grounds, and also towed dumb (unpowered) dredgers.

1967: January: Owners became the Tees and Hartlepool Port Authority, but withdrawn from service almost immediately.

1968: Donated to Middlesbrough Museum Service and moored at Stockton Quay, where she was initially maintained by a team of volunteers. Ownership later transferred to Stockton Council.

1976: 4 March: After her owners planned to scrap her, she was sold to Martin Stevens, renamed **Hero** and towed to the River Medway, Kent by the preserved steam tug **Cervia**.

1977: Returned to her original colour scheme. Regained the name **John H. Amos**. Lay at Chatham on a slipway adjacent to the Historic Dockyard, becoming derelict and flooding with every tide.

2001: Ownership transferred to the Medway Maritime Trust.

2003: March: Heritage Lottery Fund grant for £30,000 awarded for the preparation of a conservation plan. September: Funnel removed, mud removed from inside hull.

2006: June: Railway rails fixed to her sides to enable her to be lifted.

11 August: Positioned on strops to enable her to be lifted out of the water onto a pontoon for further restoration work to be done.

Work is now in hand planning for a full restoration of **John H. Amos**. This would involve an entire re-plating of the hull and would cost £4 million. It is hoped that, if and when restored, at least occasional passenger trips will be offered.

She is the only surviving paddle tug in the UK, and one of only two in the world, the other being **Eppleton Hall** at San Francisco Maritime Museum which does not feature in this book as she does not carry passengers.

PS KINGSWEAR CASTLE

Kingswear Castle leaving Strood Pier.

Length: 32.90m   **Gross tonnage:** 94
Propulsion: Paddle Steamer   **Engine type:** Compound Diagonal, 130hp
Built: 1924   **Rebuilt** (most recent): 1983
Passenger capacity: 235
Body of water: River Medway   **Home port:** Chatham
Frequency of operation: MX
Period of operation: Late April to early October
Website address: www.pskc.freeserve.co.uk
Builders: Philip & Sons, Dartmouth
Engine builder: Cox & Co., Falmouth 1904 from the earlier **Kingswear Castle**
Owner: Paddle Steamer *Kingswear Castle* Trust Ltd (Paddle Steamer Preservation Society)
Remarks: Coal-fired

1924: Built as an river excursion paddle steamer for the River Dart Steamboat Co. Operated from Dartmouth to Totnes. Was fitted with the engines and other fittings of the previous **Kingswear Castle**, dating from 1904.

1939: Requisitioned by the Admiralty. Used initially as a stores depot at Dittisham Pier.

1941-45: Chartered to the US Navy for use carrying stores and personnel at Dartmouth. Retained her peacetime livery.

1945: Returned to the river passenger service.

1961-62: winter: New boiler fitted and a number of hull plates replaced.

1965: Withdrawn from service after the summer season. Laid-up in Old Mill Creek.

1967: Purchased for preservation by Paddle Steam Navigation Ltd, a company owned by the Paddle Steamer Preservation Society.

28 August: Towed to Binfield, on the River Medina on the Isle of Wight.

1969: 8 June: Steamed for a BBC TV programme with John Betjeman. Also steamed on one other occasion in that year. Latterly while on the Isle of Wight her condition deteriorated.

1971: 16 June: Towed to Rochester, on the River Medway, for restoration work to commence. This was undertaken by Paddle Steamer Preservation Society volunteers, headed by John Megoran, now her master.

1983: 4-6 November: Steamed, on trials, for the first time since 1969.

1984: In service with a volunteer crew and without a passenger certificate, and was thus restricted to twelve passengers. About twenty all-day sailings were operated in this summer as well as five short trips and some charters.

1985: May: Passenger certificate issued for 250. Regular passenger trips started on the Medway.
 Regular Medway trips from Thunderbolt Pier, at Chatham Historical Dockyard, Rochester and Strood,
 along with some short cruises from Southend.
1986: Won the National Steam Heritage Award.
1987: Flying Bridge installed.
1995: Won first prize in the Scania Transport Trust Awards.
1999: Was included on the National Historic Ships Committee Core Collection list of ships of 'Pre-
 eminent National Significance'.
2001: Spring: New boiler fitted.
2004–05: Winter: New companionway to the fore saloon fitted.
2005: August: Strood Pier closed.

Kingswear Castle continues on her regular trips, There are several trips to Southend each summer, and an
occasional trip to Whitstable with trips from there as well. On most Sundays, Tuesdays and Wednesdays from
mid-July to the end of August she leaves Rochester at 15:00 and Chatham Historic Dockyard at 15:30 for
a cruise to Darnet Ness with upriver trips from Rochester at 15:00 on some Thursdays and Fridays and a
varying programme of day trips on Saturdays from Chatham, to Southend with time ashore, Shoeburyness,
Sheerness Docks, Whitstable or Round the Isle of Sheppey. Each September she meets up with **Waverley**
for a unique, for the UK, 'two paddle steamer trip'. In recent years, although not in 2006, she has made an
annual trip to London Bridge City Pier, with an upriver trip to Putney on the next day.

PS MEDWAY QUEEN

Medway Queen when she was in service.
(Author's collection)

Length: 54.90m   **Gross tonnage:** 316
Propulsion: Paddle Steamer   **Engine type:** Compound Diagonal
Built: 1924   **Rebuilt** (most recent): ongoing
Body of water: River Medway   **Home port:** Chatham
Frequency of operation: Undergoing restoration
Website address: www.medwayqueen.co.uk
Builders: Ailsa Shipbuilding Co., Troon
Owner: *Medway Queen* Restoration & Preservation

1924: Built for the New Medway Steam Packet Co., Rochester, for excursion service on the Thames
 and Medway.
1936: Owners taken over by the General Steam Navigation Co., although they continued as a separate
 entity.
1939: September: Requisitioned by the Admiralty. Refitted as a minesweeper, joining the 10th
 minesweeping flotilla, based at Harwich, with the pennant number *J-48*.
1940: 27 May to 3 June: Made seven trips to Dunkirk, probably rescuing an estimated 7,000 troops.
1947: Returned to service on the Medway after a complete refit at the yard of Thornycroft, Southampton.
 Her regular sailing was from Strood, with calls at Chatham, until closed in 1959, Sheerness, until closed
 in 1954, to Southend and on to Herne Bay.

1953: Attended the Coronation Naval Review at Spithead.

1957: From this year sailed to Clacton instead of Herne Bay on certain days.

1962: In her final two seasons two return trips to Southend were made on Saturdays.

1963: 8 September: Final sailing from Strood to Southend and Herne Bay. Laid-up.

1964: January: Towed to East India Dock, London. Initial preservation attempts were made.

1965: January: Towed to the River Medina, Isle of Wight.

1966: 14 May: Opened as a yacht club.

1970s: Replaced by the paddle steamer **Ryde** and moved to an anchorage in the River Medina.

1984: Moved back to the River Medway on a submersible pontoon barge. When there, no permanent berth could be secured for her and she lay at a tidal wharf, eventually settling on the mud, filling and emptying with successive tides.

1985: June: *Medway Queen* Preservation Society formed. Work began on securing the hull and removing the mud.

1987: 1 November: Towed to Damhead Creek, where preservation work has continued.

2005: National Lottery awarded a £35,900 planning grant.

2006: £1.8 million National Lottery grant awarded to rebuild the hull after several unsuccessful applications. It is reckoned that a complete rebuild will cost a further £6 million. Hull dismantled, and the engine, timber deck planking and other parts taken to Chatham Docks in a barge, while the hull, which was rotten, was scrapped.

2007: New hull to be built at A. & P. Hebburn on Tyneside.

2008: Early: Hull expected to be compleed and towed to the Medway for fitting out and installation of machinery.

The second stage of the rebuild will see the main and auxiliary engines restored, the paddle wheels rebuilt, and a new boiler fitted to ready her for service. It is to be hoped that **Medway Queen** can be fully restored. **Medway Queen**, known as 'The Heroine of Dunkirk', deserves active preservation.

TST PORTWEY

Portwey in the River Medway.

Length: 24.50m	**Gross tonnage:** 94
Propulsion: Twin Screw	**Engine type:** Compound, 330hp
Built: 1927	**Passenger capacity:** 12
Body of water: River Thames	**Home port:** West India Dock, London Docklands
	Frequency of operation: Charters
	Website address: www.stportwey.co.uk
	Builders: Harland & Wolff, Govan
	Engine builder: D. & W. Henderson & Co. Ltd, Partick
	Owner: Steam Tug Portwey Trust
	Remarks: Coal-fired

1927: Built for the Portland & Weymouth Coaling Co. Ltd. Used for the coal bunkering trade in the harbours of Portland and Weymouth, also used to supply newspapers, cigarettes, etc., to the crews of ships moored in Portland harbour, and from time to time as a salvage tug.

1927: 10 August: Launched.

1928: 28 April: Completed.

1938: Purchased by G.H. Collins & Co. Ltd, Dartmouth, still under the ownership of the previous holding company, Evans and Reid, of Wales. Moved to Dartmouth.

1941: By now working for the Channel Coaling Co. Ltd, Dartmouth, another Evans and Reid company.

1942: In Admiralty service. Based at Dartmouth, employed in harbour service and came under the Naval control of Plymouth Command.

1945: Returned to her owners. Also from now on used for pilotage duties in Tor Bay when the swell was too great for the pilot launch based at Brixham.

1951: 9 October: Sold to Falmouth Docks & Engineering Co. Ltd. Used for moving various barges, including one with a steam crane, and on other harbour duties. Steam steering engine fitted.

1959: Used in connection with the new Lizard lifeboat station at Kilcobben Cove.

1965: Sold to R.H. Dobson, Stoke Gabriel, for preservation. Moved to Stoke Gabriel.

1982: May: Steamed to St Katharine's Dock, London.

   7 June: Donated to the Maritime Trust.

1986: Moved away from St Katherine's Dock.

1994: 1 September: Steam Tug Portwey Association formed.

1995: 19 July: Long-term charter to Steam Tug Portwey Association commenced.

2000: 7 June: Sold to the Steam Tug Portwey Trust.

Portwey is now moored in the West India Dock in London Docklands and is occasionally steamed.

The former Clyde turbine steamer **Queen Mary**, ex **Queen Mary II** (1933), in service until 1977, is in static use as a pub on the Thames, although her machinery has been removed. She has recently been repainted in a version of her original Williamson-Buchanan Steamers colour scheme.

East Coast

The three former Humber paddle car ferries which operated from Hull to New Holland all survive in static roles. **Wingfield Castle** (1934), in service until 1974, has been excellently restored and is now a museum at Hartlepool; **Lincoln Castle** (1940) which was the last coal-fired steamer in commercial operation in the UK when withdrawn in 1978, is a floating pub-restaurant at Grimsby, whilst **Tattershall Castle** (1934), in service until 1972, has been considerably altered, including the removal of her paddle wheels, and is now a bar-restaurant in central London on the Thames.

South Coast

SL GALLANT

Gallant at Fowey (from an advertising flyer).

Length: 9.10m

Propulsion: Single Screw   **Engine type:** Compound V-shaped, 12hp

Built: *c.*1900   Rebuilt (most recent): 1988
Passenger capacity: 12
Body of water: River Fowey   Home port: Fowey
Frequency of operation: Daily
Website address: www.cornwall-information.co.uk/details.asp?listid=81
Builders: Unknown   Engine builder: Owner, 1988, Semple design
Owner: C. Lee, Fowey

*c.*1900: Hull built as an open motor boat.

1988: Hull acquired in derelict condition by the present owner, who restored it, and fitted it with a home-built engine and boiler.

1989: June: First steamed. Has been used every summer since then on passenger trips at Fowey.

Gallant offers 45-minute trips on the River Fowey. Times are locally advertised on a chalked board.

TSS SHIELDHALL

Shieldhall passing the Hook of Holland on her return from *Dordt in Stoom*, 1996.

Length: 81.69m   Gross tonnage: 1,753
Propulsion: Twin Screw   Engine type: 2 Triple Expansion, 1,600hp
Built: 1955   Rebuilt (most recent): 1990
Passenger capacity: 100
Body of water: Solent   Home port: Southampton
Frequency of operation: Most SSuO mid-July to early Sept
Period of operation: Mid-July to mid-September
Website address: www.ss-shieldhall.co.uk
Builders: Lobnitz, Renfrew
Owner: The Solent S P Co.

1955: Built for Glasgow Corporation as a sludge steamer, carrying treated sewage from the sewage works at Shieldhall and Dalmuir to the dumping ground a few miles south of Garroch Head, the most southerly point of the island of Bute. Passengers were carried, normally from community groups, sponsored by Glasgow City Councillors (originally the passengers carried on the sludge steamers were ex-servicemen from the First World War). Occasionally an enthusiast party was carried, e.g. from the Clyde River Steamer Club.

7 July: Launched.

20 October: Entered service.

1977: Sold to Southern Water Authority, Southampton.

4 November: left Lamont's yard, Greenock, for Southampton, painted with a blue funnel bearing the SWA logo.

1980: 9 June: Entered service, carrying sewage sludge from Millbrook Sewage Treatment Works to The Nab, off the Isle of Wight. By this time her funnel was back to the original buff with a black top.

1985: 5 April: Withdrawn from service and laid-up.

1988: Purchased for preservation by the Solent Steam Packet Ltd.

1991: 9 June: First voyage under preservation.

1995: First voyage away from Southampton, to Poole.

1996: May: Visited the Festival of the Sea at Bristol, then sailed directly to the Netherlands for the *Dordt in Stoom* Steam Festival at Dordrecht Holland, which she revisited in 2000, 2002 and 2004.

1999: Used in the film *Angela's Ashes*, and also in the Brazilian TV film *Terra Nuestra*.

2002: Included in the Core Collection of the National Historic Ships Register.

2005: July: Visited the Clyde for two weeks as part of her Golden Jubilee celebrations.

Shieldhall is a unique survivor of a passenger-cargo steamer. She operates with a volunteer crew on a variety of trips out of Southampton, including special events such as Cowes Week and the International Festival of the Sea at Portsmouth, in addition to day trips to Poole and Weymouth.

The former Southern Railway paddle steamer **Ryde** (1937) survives in parlous condition at Binfield Creek on the River Medina on the Isle of Wight. She was in service until 1969, and was used for various roles at her present location. There have been various efforts made to restore her and return her to service, but her hull condition and location, trapped in a man-made pond, make this almost impossible. More information is available on www.psryde.co.uk.

Bristol Channel

ST MAYFLOWER

Mayflower at her berth in Bristol.

Length: 19.30m   Gross tonnage: 32
Propulsion: Single Screw   Engine type: Compound, 180hp
Built: 1861   Rebuilt (most recent): 1987
Passenger capacity: 12
Body of water: Bristol harbour   Home port: Bristol
Frequency of operation: certain SSuO
Period of operation: Easter to late October
Website address: www.bristol-city.gov.uk/ccm/content/Leisure-Culture/Arts-Entertainment/whats-on.en?XSL=eventdetail&VenueId=Oo&EventId=14251&AllRecords=true
Builders: Stothert & Marten, Bristol
Engine builder: Sisson, Gloucester 1898
Owner: Bristol Industrial Museum
Remarks: Coal-fired

1861: Built as the tug **Mayflower** for Timothy Hadley, towage contractor for the Gloucester and Berkeley Canal Co., used between Sharpness and Gloucester Docks, replacing the horses previously used.

1874: Purchased by Sharpness New Docks & Gloucester & Birmingham Navigation Co.

1899: Single-cylinder engine replaced by the present compound engine. New boiler and funnel fitted by Sissons & Co. at Gloucester. Steering position moved forward of the funnel, and waist-high iron steering shelter added to give the helmsman some protection.

1907: Additionally used on the River Severn from Gloucester to Worcester from this date.

1909: Again re-boilered. Funnel altered to a hinged one.

1922: Deck raised by about 30cm, bulwarks cut down and replaced with stanchions.

c.1930: Boiler again replaced.

Late 1930s: Wooden wheelhouse replaced the steering shelter.

1948: Came under the ownership of the British Waterways Board. Now used for towing mud-filled hopper barges from a dredging point to the dumping ground.

1962-63: Winter: Again used for ship towing during a cold winter when other tugs' diesel fuel froze.

1963: Laid-up: Occasionally used for tank cleaning at Gloucester.

1967: Sold to T. Morgan for scrap, continued laid-up.

c.1972: Sold to K.T. Donaghy.

1981: Purchased by Bristol City Museum and Art Gallery for preservation. Towed to Bristol where restoration started to return her to the appearance of a mid-nineteenth-century tug.

1987: Returned to steam.

1988: Early: Steamed back to Gloucester for a courtesy visit.

Mayflower is regularly in steam on selected summer weekends, making trips round Bristol Floating Harbour from her base at Bristol Industrial Museum.

Mersey

ST DANIEL ADAMSON

Daniel Adamson at the Boat Museum, Ellesmere Port, 1987.

Length: 33.53m
Propulsion: Single Screw   **Engine type:** Compound, 500hp
Built: 1903   **Passenger capacity:** 100
Body of water: River Mersey   **Home port:** Liverpool
Frequency of operation: Undergoing restoration
Website address: www.danieladamson.com
Builders: Tranmere Bay Development Co.
Engine builder: J. Jones & Son, Liverpool
Owner: *Daniel Adamson* Preservation Society
Former names: *Ralph Brocklebank* 1936

1903: Built as the tug-tender **Ralph Brocklebank** for the Shropshire Union Railway & Canal Co. Used in a barge-towing service between Ellesmere Port and Liverpool, also carried passengers.

1915: From this date operated as a tug only.

1921: Sold to the Manchester Ship Canal Co. Used as a canal tug, but also operated passenger cruises from Manchester to Eastham.

1929: Removable awnings added to the bridge and stern decks.

1936: Major rebuild. Bridge raised to present level. Passenger accommodation upgraded, with the interior finished in wood laminates and light fittings in the then contemporary art deco style. Renamed **Daniel Adamson**. Operated both as a tug and as the company directors' inspection vessel and venue for corporate hospitality functions.

1986: Laid-up at the ship dock at the Boat Museum, Ellesmere Port.

2004: February: After it was announced she was to be scrapped, the *Daniel Adamson* Preservation Society was founded to preserve her.

10 April: Towed to Liverpool.

20 May: Moved to Clarence Graving Dock, Liverpool for hull survey, sandblasting and painting.

6 June: Came out of dry dock and was moved to the Salisbury dock, where restoration work has continued.

2006: 27 April to 15 May: Dry-docked at Birkenhead for a full survey, funded by the Heritage Lottery Fund.

The *Daniel Adamson* Preservation Society is planning to restore **Daniel Adamson** to active service carrying passengers.

INLAND WATERWAYS

Canals

SNB PRESIDENT

President near Braunston. (Nigel Wood)

Length: 21.80m   **Gross tonnage:** 15
Propulsion: Single Screw   **Engine type:** 1-cylinder simple expansion
Built: 1909   **Rebuilt** (most recent): 1977
Body of water: Dudley Canal   **Home port:** Dudley
Frequency of operation: Rallies, charters
Period of operation: Easter to early October
Website address: www.nb-president.co.uk
Builders: Fellows, Morton & Clayton, Saltley
Engine builder: Sissons, 1950s, fitted 2002
Owner: Black Country Museum, Dudley, assisted by 'The Friends of President'.
Remarks: Coal-fired

1909: Built as a steam cargo-carrying narrow boat for the fleet of her builders, Fellows, Morton and Clayton Ltd, Saltley. Worked on the English canals, mainly on the express or 'fly' service between London, Birmingham, Leicester and Nottingham. Built with iron sides and an elm bottom. Originally had a vertical tandem compound steam engine built by her builders/owners under licence to W.H. & H. Haines Ltd of Birmingham.

1925: Steam engine replaced with a Bolinder diesel. After she was motorised was also probably used from Birmingham to Ellesmere Port, Liverpool and Manchester.

1946: Sold to Ernest Thomas, a Walsall coal merchant and director of Fellows, Morton and Clayton.

1948: Sold to George and Matthews of Wolverhampton to carry coal. Later became part of the British Waterways Northern Maintenance Fleet, based at Northwich, working on the Trent and Mersey, Macclesfield, and Shropshire Union Canals.

1973: Derelict by this time, purchased by Nicholas Bostock and Malcolm E. Braine, Walsall.

1974: Towed from Northwich, where she lay half-sunk, to Norton Canes Dock where restoration started. Hull was repaired including replacing the elm bottom, and a replica cabin and boiler room were fitted.

1977: Two-cylinder Worthington-Simpson steam engine dating from about the same time as **President**, and 1928 boiler from **Leviathan**, owned by the Kennet and Avon Canal Trust, purchased and installed. Boatman's cabin fitted out.

1978: August: Returned to steam for the President Steamer Co.

1983: January: Acquired by the Black Country Museum, Dudley.

1984: October: Support group Friends of President formed.

1990: Boiler replaced.

1992: Steamed 1,002 miles in ninety-two days round the English canal system.

2001: 27 January to 23 March 2003: Major refit with present engine and new cabin fitted and major hull repairs. The engine was built as a training engine for a Merchant Navy College.

President makes a wide variety of trips on the canal network, although, as she was built as a cargo boat, and has been restored to appear as such, she does not normally carry passengers. She is present at many special events and rallies, and is berthed at the Black Country Museum when not on tour. It is not beyond the bound of possibility that the odd passenger may be carried at one of the rallies.

SNB SIDNEY

Sidney on the Trent & Mersey Canal. (T. Pavitt)

Length: 16.76m
Propulsion: Single Screw   Engine type: 2-cylinder simple expansion
Built: 1993
Body of water: Trent & Mersey Canal
Frequency of operation: Charters
Builders: Kingfisher Marine, Leeds
Engine builder: Severn-Lamb Ltd, Stratford on Avon 1974
Owner: T. Pavitt
Remarks: Narrowboat

1993: Hull built. Fitted with a 1974-built engine formerly in a steamboat named **Grace Under Pressure** and a war-built ex-US Army boiler.

1994: March: First Steamed.

1995: May: Used as a mobile catering unit in a Country Park and also used for charters.

Lake District

SS GONDOLA

Gondola on Coniston Water.

Length: 27.40m   **Gross tonnage:** 42

Propulsion: Single Screw

Engine type: 2-cylinder simple expansion V-shaped oscillating, 16hp

Built: 1859   **Rebuilt** (most recent): 1979

Passenger capacity: 86

Body of water: Coniston Water   **Home port:** Coniston

Frequency of operation: Daily

Period of operation: 1 April to 31 October

Website address: www.nationaltrust.org.uk/places/steamyachtgondola;
   www.lakedistrictletsgo.co.uk/attractions/attractions_pages/gondola.html;
   www.visitcumbria.com/amb/gondola.htm

Builders: Jones Quiggin, Liverpool/Vickers Shipbuilding, Barrow-in-Furness

Engine builder: Locomotion Enterprises, Gateshead 1979

Owner: National Trust

Remarks: Coal-fired

1859: Built for the Coniston Railway Co. for use on Coniston Water. She was built with a distinctive appearance to attract tourists to the area, the railway branch to Coniston having been opened in this year.

1860: Entered service.

1862: Owners taken over by the Furness Railway Co.

1914-18: Laid-up during the First World War.

1923: Owners became part of the London, Midland and Scottish Railway.

1936: Withdrawn from service. Engine and boiler removed to power a local sawmill.

1946: Sold to Fred McCaddam, Barrow for use as a houseboat at Water Park, still on Lake Coniston. Flat-roofed cabin replaced funnel and engine room, and concrete was poured into the bilges to stop leaks in the rusty hull.

1963: Late: Driven ashore during a storm. A drop in the lake level caused her to be marooned on the shore, and she was about to be sold for scrap, when she was purchased by Arthur Hatton, who cut a channel, and returned her to the lake, where she was half-sunk.

1975-76: Interest started to be taken in her by local staff members of the National Trust.

1977: January: Holes plugged with cement and hull raised, and moved to Coniston Hall. Work continued on a survey, and Vickers Shipbuilding, Barrow, chosen to restore her.

1978: Sold to the National Trust.

March: Vickers carried out a hull survey and it was ascertained that the entire hull and frame had lost at least 30% of its original thickness. Moved by road to Vickers yard at Barrow in Furness for rebuilding.

1979: March: New hull almost complete, was fitted with a few parts from the original steamer.

3 September: Moved back to Coniston in four sections, which were welded there. New engine and boiler to the same design as the original made and fitted.

1980: 25 March: Re-launched.

24 June: Re-entered service.

2005: Four special 2-hour cruises to Lake Bank, her original destination, were carried out to celebrate the 25th anniversary of **Gondola**'s restoration.

2006: Saturday calls added at Monk Coniston, on the return leg from Brantwood, on all sailings.

Gondola is a joy to sail on with a magnificently fitted former first-class saloon with plush red upholstery. She would more accurately be described as a replica than as an 1859 steamer. In early years of preservation she sailed south to Park-a-Moor, but now she makes a southbound loop, before a call at Brantwood and a return to Coniston, calling at Monk Coniston, from where it is possible to walk to the renowned beauty spot of Tarn How, on the return leg. The sailing lasts 45 minutes, and she sails hourly from 11:00 to 16:00.

SL KITTIWAKE

Kittiwake on Windermere.
(Windermere Steamboat Museum)

Length: 12.2m
Propulsion: Single Screw   **Engine type**: Triple Expansion
Built: 1898   **Passenger capacity**: 12
Body of water: Lake Windermere   **Home port**: Bowness-on-Windermere
Frequency: Daily   **Period of operation**: Mid-March to First week November
Website address: www.steamboat.co.uk
Builder: T.W. Hayton, Bowness-on-Windermere
Engine builder: Sissons, Gloucester
Owner: Windermere Steamboat Museum
Remarks: Coal-fired, wooden hull

1898: Built as a Windermere steam launch for W.G. Groves, Windermere.

1929: Ownership transferred to H.L. Groves.

1947: Purchased by Arthur Fildes.

1952: Converted to a motor launch.

c.1984: Acquired by Windermere Steamboat Museum.

1984: Original steam engine found by owners, and re-fitted in her.

Late 1980s: Used for passenger trips from the museum.

2004: Started to be used regularly on the passenger trips from the museum after a major refit, and was a favourite for wedding charters.

2006: October: Museum closed for the season. A grant os almost £500,000 was obtained from the National Heritage Memorial Fund for the restoration and continued preservation of the exhibits in the museum, and it was expected to closed for at least two, and possibly five years, while this work was done.

Kittiwake operates along with **Swallow** and the motor launches **Water Viper** and **Penelope II**, on 45-minute lake trips from Windermere Steamboat Museum. These operate throughout the day and times are only advertised at the museum. **Kittiwake** is normally used as a relief for **Swallow**.

SL OSPREY

Osprey off Windermere Steamboat Museum, 1984.

Length: 14.85m
Propulsion: Single Screw   **Engine type**: Triple Expansion
Built: 1902   **Rebuilt** (most recent): 2006
Passenger capacity: 12
Body of water: Lake Windermere   **Home port**: Bowness-on-Windermere
Frequency: Return to service 2006
Period of operation: Mid-March to first week November
Website address: www.steamboat.co.uk
Builder: Neil Shepherd, Bowness   **Engine builder**: Sissons, Gloucester
Owner: Windermere Steamboat Museum
Remarks: Coal-fired, wooden hull

1902: Built as a private steam launch for service on Lake Windermere, later dieselised and used for passenger trips from Bowness by Bowness Bay Boating Co.
1981: Purchased by Windermere Steamboat Museum. Borrowed steam engine, which was probably first installed in **Water Viper**, fitted. Used for passenger trips from the museum.
2000: Out of service after engine returned to its owner.
2006: Was expected back in service after boiler repairs and the return of the engine, again on loan, although it is not certain if this happened.
October: Museum closed for the season. A grant of almost £500,000 was obtained from the National Heritage Memorial Fund for the restoration and continued preservation of the exhibits in the museum, and it was expected to closed for at least two, and possibly five years, while this work was done.

SL SWALLOW

Length: 13.90m
Propulsion: Single Screw   **Engine type**: Triple Expansion
Built: 1911   **Passenger capacity**: 12
Body of water: Lake Windermere   **Home port**: Bowness-on-Windermere
Frequency of operation: Daily
Website address: www.steamboat.co.uk
Builders: Shepherd, Bowness on Windermere
Engine builder: Sissons, Gloucester

Swallow at Windermere
Steamboat Museum, July 2003.

Owner: Windermere Steamboat Museum
Remarks: Coal-fired, wooden hull

1911: Built as a private steam launch for W. Warburton, Windermere, later sold to J. Parker, Kendal and Leslie Goldsmith, who completely restored her.

1984: Given on permanent loan to the Windermere Steamboat Museum by the widow of Leslie Goldsmith.

1990: New boiler fitted.

2000: Replaced sister *Osprey* on the steam launch trips from Windermere Steamboat Museum.

   Swallow operates along with *Kittiwake* and the motor launches *Water Viper* and *Penelope II*, on 45-minute lake trips from Windermere Steamboat Museum. These operate throughout the day and times are only advertised at the museum.

2006: October: Museum closed for the season. A grant of almost £500,000 was obtained from the National Heritage Memorial Fund for the restoration and continued preservation of the exhibits in the museum, and it was expected to closed for at least two, and possibly five years, while this work was done.

Windermere Steamboat Museum has a very interesting collection of old steam launches and other vessels. These include the cargo steamer *Raven* (1871), originally owned by the Furness Railway for use on the lake, and steam launches *Dolly* (c.1850), the oldest screw steamer in the world, *Esperance* (1869), now with the engine removed, which featured as Captain Flint's houseboat in Arthur Ransome's *Swallows and Amazons* books, *Bat* (1891), *Lady Elizabeth* (1895), *Branksome* (1896), *Otto* (1896), and a number of motor boats and dieselised steam launches such as *Water Viper* (1907). More details on these are, however, outside the scope of this volume

VARIOUS RIVERS

SL FIREBIRD

Length: 8.50m
Propulsion: Single Screw   **Engine type**: Compound
Built: 1904   **Passenger capacity**: 12
Body of water: River Stour   **Home port**: Sudbury
Frequency of operation: SuO
Website address: www.jbham.co.uk/stourpt2/sudbury.htm
Builders: Unknown, Hampton
Engine builder: A.G. Mumford Ltd, Colchester, c.1900
Owner: R. Baker
Former names: *Stromboli* 1973, *Cookham Dean* 1971, *Firebird* 1954
Remarks: Coal-fired, wooden-hulled

Firebird. (Brian Smith)

1904: Built for J.N. Hickey, Richmond, as a replica of an earlier launch named **Firebird**, from which the machinery was fitted.

1954: Hull rebuilt by Wooten's boatyard, Cookham, renamed **Cookham Dean**. New boiler fitted.

1971: Renamed **Stromboli**. New boiler fitted.

1973: Renamed **Firebird**. Sold to Hon. W.H. McAlpine, later to present owner.

1980: New boiler fitted.

1983: Aft saloon added.

2004: Fully restored for her centenary year.

Firebird has been reported as running passenger trips from Sudbury to Cornard on the River Stour, although no current details are available at the time of writing.

SL KING

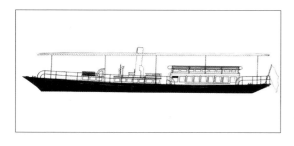

A profile of *King*.
(Steamboat King Preservation Trust)

Length: 21.80m

Propulsion: Single Screw   **Engine type**: Triple Expansion

Built: 1905   **Rebuilt** (most recent): 1998

Passenger capacity: 192 (originally)

Body of water: River Avon   **Home port**: Stratford-upon-Avon

Frequency of operation: Undergoing restoration

Website address: www.ybw.com/auto/newsdesk/20011121122734cbnews.html

Builders: C. Bathurst & Son, Tewkesbury

Engine builders: A. Savery & Co., Birmingham

Owner: Steamboat *King* Preservation Trust

Remarks: Teak hull

1905: Built as the steamer **King** for C. Bathurst & Son, Tewkesbury, and was the largest passenger steamer operating on the River Severn. Operated as a passenger steamer on the rivers Severn and Avon between Stourport and Evesham and Gloucester and Sharpness.

1959: Withdrawn from service. Sold for private use at Bristol. Steam engine replaced by a diesel. Later used as a houseboat.

1995: Found laid-up in a Bristol backwater in poor condition. Purchased by a group of Stratford-upon-Avon enthusiasts, who later formed the Steamboat *King* Preservation Society. Moved to Stratford. It was discovered that the original engine survived at the National Waterways Museum, Gloucester.

Fibreglass hull sheathing stripped off and various recent additions to the cabin removed. Restoration work commenced.

1996: October: Towed to George Judge's boatyard, Worcester, for restoration of her hull on land.

It is planned that when restoration is complete that *King* will be on display at Stratford as a museum exhibit, and will offer occasional short passenger trips. Major funding, e.g. from the National Lottery heritage Fund is required to complete the restoration.

PS MONARCH

Monarch at Grove Ferry, October 2005.

Length: 12.80m
Propulsion: Paddle Steamer   **Engine type**: Compound Diagonal
Built: 1984-2003   **Passenger capacity**: 12
Body of water: River Stour   **Home port**: Grove Ferry, Upstreet
Frequency of operation: MTX   **Period of operation**: May to end October
Website address: www.paddlers31.freeserve.co.uk/monarch/index.htm;
www.leisuresteam.co.uk
Builders: Stargate Marine, Rochester
Engine builder: Lee Howl, Watford, unknown date.
Owner: Leisure Steam   **Operator**: Sandwich River Bus

1984: Construction commenced at Stargate Marine, Hoo, near Rochester for Brian Waters. *Monarch* was planned as a small-sized traditionally-styled paddle steamer rather than a paddle launch. Moved to Chatham Historic Dockyard for fitting out when hull complete.

1994: Summer: Launched. Fitted with an engine, the cylinders of which were originally an air pump at Ness Tarworks, Caerphilly, and was converted for use as a marine engine by Stargate Marine. Berthed at Lemon's boatyard, Strood, while work was done on her.

2002: December: Completed. Ran trials on the River Medway.

2003: 11 December: Moved by road to Ramsgate, then, a few days later, sailed to Sandwich.

2004: Early in the year placed on land at Richborough where a bow thruster was fitted. Used at Sandwich for the Sandwich River bus service on the River Stour from Sandwich. Based at Sandwich in this season.

2005: Base moved from Sandwich to Grove Ferry, 9 miles upstream. Hull, originally, white, was painted black with a white upper strake.

Monarch offers 45-minute trips from Grove Ferry from Thursday to Sunday (daily during school holidays) from 12:00 to 19:00, from early May to late October. Charters are also operated.

2006 may be her last season under the present ownership as her captain and engineer are both in their seventies and find the work getting too strenuous for them. She is currently up for sale and will be replaced at Grove Ferry by a diesel sternwheeler in 2007.

SL SWAN OF AVON

Swan of Avon at Stratford. (Owners)

Length: 9.60m
Propulsion: Single Screw   **Engine type:** Compound
Built: 1898   **Rebuilt** (most recent): 1999
Passenger capacity: 24
Body of water: River Avon   **Home port:** Stratford upon Avon
Frequency of operation: Occasional public trips, charters
Website address: www.avon-boating.co.uk
Builders: Unknown
Engine builder: Simpson, Lawrence, Dartmouth, *c.*1896-1912, fitted 1998
Owner: Avon Boating Ltd

1898: Built as a steam launch for passenger trips on the River Avon at Stratford for the owners great-grandfather, at some time converted to motor.
1998: Steam engine fitted, which had been in the steam launch **Selina**. Operated for G.H. Rose & Sons.
2004: June: Owners became Avon Boating Ltd.

Swan of Avon operates as part of a fleet of six boats owned by Avon Boating Ltd, and is occasionally used on their river trips from Stratford, and also for charters, including a 'Steamboat Pimms Party'.

River Thames

SL ALASKA

Alaska near Henley, 2005. (A. Carvell)

Length: 18.30m   **Gross tonnage:** 16
Propulsion: Single Screw   **Engine type:** 2-cylinder simple expansion
Built: 1883   **Rebuilt** (most recent): 1987

Passenger capacity: 36
Body of water: River Thames   Home port: Marlow
Frequency of operation: Charters, Occasional public trips
Period of operation: April to October
Website address: www.thames-steamers.co.uk
Builders: J.S. & W.G. Horsham, Bourne End
Engine builder: Seeking, Gloucester
Owner: Suzanne and David Williams   Operator: Thames Steamers
Remarks: Coal-fired, wooden hull

1883: Built for W.H. Barbrook, Walton on Thames.

1886: Taken over by Salter Brothers, Oxford.

1887: Inaugurates their Oxford to Kingston service, which was weekly taking two days downstream with an overnight stop at Henley and three days upstream with overnight stops at Windsor and Reading.

1892: By this time more boats had been added to the fleet and the service was daily.

1914: New boiler fitted.

1935: New boiler fitted.

1939: Used as a guard boat on the Thames having latterly been used by Salters for private parties rather than being on the scheduled service.

Early 1940s: Sold, or possibly chartered, to Mears, Twickenham, moored at Eel Pie Island and used for trips from Richmond to Teddington Lock.

1943: Withdrawn from service, sold to Jackson Bros Ltd, Hammersmith, London and laid-up at Putney, later according to some sources used by Putney Sea Scouts.

*c.*1948: Sold to Dick Horton for use as a floating pontoon at Medley Boat Station, Oxford. He removed the steam engine and punted her up to Oxford with a punt pole. Once at Oxford her superstructure was removed and sold as firewood.

1974: 'Discovered' partially sunk after a new owner had taken over Medley Boat Station, purchased by Peter Freebody, Hurley for restoration. Restored fully at the Freebody yard at Hurley.

1975: Original steam engine found rusting on the riverbank, where it had been dumped after use as a sludge pump at Kingston Power Station, purchased and re-fitted.

1985: New boiler fitted as part of the restoration process.

1987: July: Returned to steam. Hull was at this time finished in white.

1999: Purchased by Suzanne and David Williams and leased to Thames Steamers Ltd. Hull painted yellow.

Alaska is normally only used for charters, but offers occasional public trips. In 2006 these are on 27 and 28 May and 15 and 16 July from Henley, and 29 May fropm Borune End, on each of which dates she offers 1-hour cruises. She also offers half-hourly public trips at the IWA rally at Beale Park during the August Bank Holiday weekend, 26-28 August.

SL ECLIPSE

Eclipse at Egham, 1987.

Length: 16.00m
Propulsion: Single Screw   **Engine type:** Compound, 70hp
Built: 1901
Passenger capacity: 12
Body of water: River Thames   **Home port:** Shepperton
Frequency of operation: Charters?
Builders: E.W. & W.E. Cawston, Reading
Engine builder: I. MacDougal & J. Ashton, Egham & Sheffield 1980
Owner: D. Dearden and J.M. Downes

1901: Built as a steam launch for Cawston's own hire fleet.
1931: Sold to H.G. Hastings, Kingston.
1937: Sold to Alfred Crouch, Kingston.
1943: Sold to A. Meikle, Richmond.
1949: Sold to L. Lightfoot.
1953: Sold to C. Whatford & Sons, Hampton Court.
1960: Sold to F. Parr, Kingston. by which time she was motor-powered and was used in the service from Kingston to Hampton Court.
1978: Purchased by Ian MacDougal and Mark Stanley, Egham. Restoration commenced.
1980: New steam engine built by MacDougal. New boiler fitted.
Mid-1980s: Re-entered service in the luxury charter trade.
1996: Sold to present owners and moved to Shepperton.

SS NUNEHAM

Nuneham passing under Maidenhead Bridge, 2006. (George Mair)

Length: 24.38m   **Gross tonnage:** 37
Propulsion: Single Screw   **Engine type:** Triple Expansion
Built: 1898   **Rebuilt** (most recent): 1990
Passenger capacity: 106
Body of water: River Thames   **Home port:** Windsor
Frequency of operation: Charters
Website address: http://www.boat-trips.co.uk/pc/pc4a.htm
Builders: Edwin Clarke & Co., Brimscombe
Engine builder: Sissons, Gloucester 1921, from *Oxford*
Owner: Thames Steam Packet Boat Co. Ltd, a subsidiary of French Brothers

1898: Built for Salter Brothers, Oxford. Used on the River Thames services between Oxford and Kingston.
1948: Converted to diesel.

1971: Sold to Jackson Brothers (River Services) Ltd, Westminster. Used from Westminster to Hampton Court.

1976: Sold to Harbourside Investments Ltd.

1983: Purchased by French Brothers, Runnymede, for restoration. The engine formerly in Salters' **Oxford** was acquired and fitted.

1990: New boiler fitted.

1997: Restoration completed. Operated on charters by the Thames Steam Packet Boat Co. Ltd, a subsidiary of French Brothers.

SS STREATLEY

Streatley berthed in central London on a charter, 1999.

Length: 26.06m   Gross tonnage: 39
Propulsion: Single Screw   Engine type: Compound, 160hp
Built: 1905   Rebuilt (most recent): 1995
Passenger capacity: 100
Body of water: River Thames   Home port: Windsor/London
Frequency of operation: Occasional public trips, charters
Website address: http://www.greatriverjourneys.com/;
www.boat-finder.com/2405/1644_ConnoisseurChartersRiverThames_11413_1.html
Builders: Salter Bros, Oxford   Engine builder: Sissons, Gloucester
Owner: Great River Journeys (Keith French)
Remarks: Coal-fired

1905: Built for Salter Brothers, Oxford. Used on their passenger services between Oxford and Kingston.

1914-18 and 1939-45: Regularly chartered by the Red Cross to take wounded ex-servicemen on river trips.

1958: Steam engine replaced by a diesel engine and passenger accommodation modernised, later white and red hull colours replaced the original black.

1994: Sold to Steamship Streatley Ltd. Completely restored and original steam engine re-fitted with a second-hand boiler built in 1950 and formerly in the **Colne Dredger**.

1995: Returned to service. Used for charters on the entire length of the Thames down as far as Greenwich. Operated by Steamship Streatley. Later converted from coal to oil firing.

2005: May: Sold to Great River Journeys (Keith French), Wallingford. Converted back to coal-firing. Continued to be used for charters.

1 June. Returned to steam for her new owner.

SL THAMES ESPERANZA

Length: 15.85m
Propulsion: Single Screw   Engine type: 2-cylinder simple expansion, 27hp
Built: 1898   Rebuilt (most recent): 1970

Thames Esperanza at an SBA rally at Caversham, 1995. (Anna Thomson)

Passenger capacity: 12
Body of water: River Thames   **Home port:** Henley
Frequency of operation: Charters
Builders: J. Bond, Maidenhead
Engine builder: W. Pope & Sons, Slough fitted 1970
Owner: D. Roberts & Dr R. Angold
Former names: *Esperanza*, 1970

1898: Built as the private electric launch *Esperanza*. Damaged by fire at some point. (A letter dated 1911 has been found which states that she was built in 1896 by S.E. Saunders, Goring on Thames.)
1910-13: Used by Lawrence Carr of the Ray Motor Co., Boulter's Lock.
1911: Owned by C. Fenner.
1913: Sold to Brooke Hitchins.
1920: Sold to Bond, Maidenhead, later converted from an electric to a petrol engine
1940: Sold to Golding Brothers, Windsor. Used for passenger trips from Windsor to Boveney Lock.
1968: Purchased by Lawrence Weaver. Restoration commenced.
1970: Steam engine replaced petrol engine. Renamed *Thames Esperanza*.
1992: Sold at auction to present owners.

Thames Esperanza is used for charters and may possibly offer passenger trips at the Thames Traditional Boat Rally, held at Henley on the third weekend of June each year.

SL WINDSOR BELLE

Windsor Belle at Peter Freebody's yard, Hurley, 1987.

Length: 18.10m   **Gross tonnage:** 23
Propulsion: Single Screw   **Engine type:** Compound
Built: 1901   **Rebuilt** (most recent): 1986
Passenger capacity: 40
Body of water: River Thames   **Home port:** Wargrave
Frequency of operation: Steam rallies, charters
Website address: http://www.tradboatrally.com
          www.riverthames.co.uk/boat/charter/upperthames/1501.htm
Builders: Edward Burgoine, Jacobs Yard, Windsor

Engine builder: McKie & Baxter, Paisley 1937, fitted 1986
Owner: Windsor Belle Ltd, Henley-on-Thames
Remarks: Coal-fired, wooden hull

1901: Built as a passenger steamer for Arthur Jacobs, Windsor. Used on the service from Windsor to Maidenhead.
1950: Diesel engine fitted.
1977: Withdrawn from service.
1986: Purchased for preservation. Restored at the yard of Peter Freebody, Hurley. Steam engine fitted, which had been in an Ouse Navigation Board Dredger from 1937 until 1965.
July: First steamed after preservation.
1997: New boiler fitted.

Windsor Belle is operated in the charter trade out of Wargrave or Henley on Thames, and passenger trips are scheduled to be operated at the Thames Traditional Boat Rally at Henley on the third weekend of July 2006.

SCOTLAND

East Coast

SS EXPLORER

Explorer in Leith Docks, January 2006.

Length: 61.80m   **Gross tonnage**: 831
Propulsion: Single Screw   **Engine type**: Triple Expansion, 1,000hp
Built: 1955   **Rebuilt** (most recent): ongoing
Body of water: Firth of Forth   **Home port**: Leith
Frequency of operation: Undergoing restoration
Website address: www.leithhistory.co.uk/ssexplorer/index.htm
Builders: Alexander Hall & Co., Aberdeen
Owner: SS *Explorer* Preservation Society

1955: Built for uses as a fisheries research vessel for the Department of Agriculture and Fisheries for Scotland. The triple expansion steam engine was the last such built at Aberdeen. Designed along the lines of a deep-sea steam trawler. Her hull was strengthened for use in Arctic waters off Iceland and Greenland, and in the Barents and White Seas off northern Russia.
21 June: Launched.
1984: Withdrawn from service and sold for breaking-up.
1986: Purchased by Aberdeen City Council for preservation.
1995: January: It was announced that *Explorer* would be scrapped and the engine placed on display at Aberdeen Maritime Museum. She was sold to Ishburn of Invergordon for breaking up.

1997: Acquired by SS *Explorer* Preservation Society, and moved to Leith where restoration has been slowly going ahead. Her berth at Leith has had an uncertain future over the years because of developments in the dock area.

The SS *Explorer* Preservation Society plan, when **Explorer** is restored, to run her along the lines of **Shieldhall**, with regular steaming and coastal passenger trips with a volunteer crew.

West Coast and Firth of Clyde

SS AULD REEKIE

Auld Reekie laid-up at Crinan, 1997.

Length: 20.40m   **Gross tonnage:** 96
Propulsion: Single Screw   **Engine type:** Compound, 130hp
Built: 1943   **Passenger capacity:** 12
Body of water: Firth of Clyde   **Home port:** Crinan
Frequency of operation: Charters
Website address: iancoombe.tripod.com/id23.html
Builders: Pimblott & Co. Ltd, Northwich   **Engine builder:** Crabtree, Gt Yarmouth
Former name: *VIC 27* 1979
Remarks: Aka *Vital Spark*, coal-fired

1943: Built as **VIC 27**, one of a class of 106 **V**ictualling **I**nshore **C**raft for the Ministry of War Transport, based on the design of Clyde puffers built by J. & J. Hay at Kirkintilloch on the Forth and Clyde Canal.
1947: Transferred to the Royal Navy.
1962: Withdrawn from service.
1966: Sold to Glenburn Shipping, Glasgow, who intended to covert her to a yacht. Laid-up at Ardrossan.
1968: Purchased by Sir James Miller and converted for passenger use, with sleeping accommodation in the cargo hold for up to twenty persons. Renamed **Auld Reekie** (a Scots vernacular term for Edinburgh, where Miller had been Lord Provost). Moved to Granton for conversion.
1969: Returned to steam after her conversion, sailed back to the Oban area, where she was operated by the Land, Sea and Air Trust, and chartered, mainly to youth groups, although private parties were also carried, including a couple of occasions when the Scottish Branch of the Paddle Steamer Preservation Society chartered her.
1978: Purchased by Bathgate Bros (Marine) Ltd. Still used for charter although not so much.
1994-95: Used in the BBC TV series *Para Handy*, starring Gregor Fisher and Rikki Futon, for which she bore the name **Vital Spark**, and was then laid-up at Crinan, in need of a new boiler. It is planned that this will be oil-fired. At the time of writing she is still at Crinan.

SY CAROLA

Carola at the Scottish Maritime Museum pontoon, Irvine, 1994.

Length: 21.50m   **Gross tonnage**: 40
Propulsion: Single Screw   **Engine type**: Compound, 80hp
Built: 1898   **Rebuilt** (most recent): 1970
Passenger capacity: 12
Body of water: Firth of Clyde   **Home port**: Irvine
Frequency of operation: Weekly cruises
Website address: http://www.nhsc.org.uk/index.cfm/event/getVessel/vref/9
Builders: Scott & Co., Bowling   **Engine builder**: Ross & Duncan, Govan
Owner: Scottish Maritime Museum, Irvine
Remarks: Coal-fired

1898: Built for the Scott family, who owned her builders' yard, for their personal use as a steam yacht. Designed to a standard steam drifter hull design. Used by them for cruises in the West Coast of Scotland, and to convey them to their holiday home at Colintraive each summer.

1914-18: Used as a tug during the war years.

1952: New boiler fitted.

*c.*1957: Ceased to be used by the Scott family, later sold to J. Manning. Lay at this time in the River Leven at Dumbarton, and became derelict.

1970: Purchased by Ken Gray who moved her to the Southampton area and restored her including a complete replating.

1983: Purchased by M.Varvill, at this time she was based at Buckler's Hard on the Beaulieu River.

1992: The access flap to her boiler failed, filling the engine room with steam and killing two crew members.

1994: Purchased by the Scottish Maritime Museum with help from the National Heritage Memorial Fund and the National Acquisition Fund, and steamed to Irvine.

1998: 9-11 August: Offered public cruises for the Loch Fyne Classics Weekend from Ardrishaig through the Crinan Canal to Crinan, back the following morning, and up to Inveraray that afternoon, with short cruises from Inveraray.

1999: September: Placed at the Clyde Built Museum, owned by the Scottish Maritime Museum at the then newly opened Braehead Shopping Centre, east of Renfrew on the River Clyde. In the first year or two there operated public trips from the pontoon on the River Clyde.

*c.*2001: Moved back to Irvine.

Carola is available for charter and may make occasional public trips for special events at the Scottish Maritime Museum. She is crewed on these occasions by members of the RNXS, the Royal Naval Auxiliary Service.

SS VIC 32

Length: 20.40m   **Gross tonnage:** 96
Propulsion: Single Screw   **Engine type:** Compound, 130hp
Built: 1943   **Rebuilt** (most recent): 1975
Passenger capacity: 12
Body of water: Firth of Clyde and West Highlands   **Home port:** Crinan
Frequency of operation: Expected back in service 2006
Period of operation: Summer
Website address: www.noots.org.uk/savethepuffer/
Builders: Dunston, Thorne   **Engine builder:** Crabtree, Gt Yarmouth
Owner: Puffer Preservation Trust (Nick & Rachel Walker), Lochgilphead
Operator: Puffer Steamboat Holidays Ltd
Remarks: Coal-fired
Former names: *C702* 1960s, *VIC 32* 1944

1943: November: Built as a **V**ictualling **I**nshore **C**raft for the Ministry of War Transport (see *Auld Reekie*). Used as a coastal cargo carrier. May also have been based at some time during the war at Corpach, moving ammunition from barges moored in Loch Eil to be loaded onto warships of the Atlantic Fleet, and also at Scapa Flow, delivering aviation spirit to the ships of the fleet.

1944: Transferred to the Admiralty, renamed *C702*, later worked as a day boat in Rosyth Naval Dockyard, latterly laid-up at Rosyth.

1963: December: Sold to Whites, Inverkeithing to be scrapped, then sold on to Keith Schellenburg and moved to Whitby for a proposed restoration. He may have intended using her for a supply boat for the island of Eigg, which he owned. Renamed *VIC 32*.

1975: October: Purchased by Nick Walker.

1976: May: Steamed to London, where she was restored in St Katherine's Dock and converted to take paying passengers. A two-level arrangement with sleeping accommodation below and a saloon above created in the hold area. Hatch boards raised by 23 inches and windows placed in sides to give clerestory effect. Used for trips down the Thames by her owner.

1977: Sailed on a cruise from London to Dieppe, Le Havre, Rouen and Chichester.

1978: Sailed from St Katherine's Yacht Haven, London, via Inverness and the Caledonian Canal, to Crinan.

1979: Offered seven-day cruises from Tarbert to Loch Fyne and the Firth of Clyde and, in September, on the Caledonian Canal which continued each year with a similar pattern of sailings. These were operated by Highland Steamboat Holidays Ltd, owned by Nick and Rachel Walker.

1994: Base moved to Crinan, pattern of sailings remained the same with the addition of sailings around the Argyll Coast to Tayvallich and across to Craighouse on Jura. The Caledonian Canal cruise changed about this time from going there and back in a week from Corpach to Inverness, to a single trip, heading on out the Moray Firth to Fort George.

2004: April: Boiler failed annual survey for insurance purposes. Ceased operating. Puffer Preservation Trust formed by Nick Walker to raise funds for a replacement boiler.

2005: March 14: National Heritage Lottery Funds agreed a grant for a replacement boiler.
    11 May: Towed from Crinan to Corpach where the old boiler was removed and the new boiler was installed. The hull plating below the boiler was also replaced at this time.

2006: Late April: New boiler delivered.
    September: Re-entered service with four one-way trips from Fort William to Inverness and vice versa. Puffer Steamboat Holidays Ltd took over the operation of *VIC 32* from Highland Steamboat Holidays Ltd.

2007: Full programme of cruises advertised from 6 May to 23 September , including two one-way cruises from Ardrishaig to Glasgow and back, and a visit to the Glasgow River Festival in mid-July.

PS WAVERLEY

Waverley approaching Largs.

Length: 73.13m **Gross tonnage:** 693
Propulsion: Paddle Steamer **Engine type:** Triple Expansion Diagonal, 2,100hp
Built: 1947 **Rebuilt** (most recent): 2000
Passenger capacity: 950
Body of water: Firth of Clyde, coastal **Home port:** Glasgow
Frequency of operation: Daily **Period of operation:** Easter to mid–October
Website address: www.pswaverley.org; www.waverleyexcursions.co.uk
Builders: A. & J. Inglis, Pointhouse, Glasgow
Engine builder: Rankin & Blackmore, Greenock
Owner: Waverley Steam Navigation Co. **Operator:** Waverley Excursions Ltd

1946: Ordered for the London & North Eastern Railway to replace *Waverley* of 1899 which had been sunk at Dunkirk in 1940.

1947: 2 October: Launched.

16 June: Entered service on the route from Craigendoran and Rothesay to Lochgoilhead and Arrochar, which was her regular route in her early years. From 1947 to 1953 she was also on the Craigendoran to Rothesay service from early May until the beginning of the summer season.

1948: 1 January: With the nationalisation of the railways, she was now owned by the British Transport Commission, although she operated as part of the Caledonian Steam Packet fleet. Funnels repainted buff with a black top before the beginning of the summer season.

1949: 18 February to 29 March: First spell in winter service, relieving *Talisman* for overhaul with sailings from Craigendoran to Gourock and an occasional trip to Rothesay.

1950: 13 January to 1 April: Operated on the winter service from Craigendoran to Rothesay.

1952: Now sailed to Arrochar on Tuesdays, Thursdays and Saturdays, and round Bute on Mondays, Wednesdays and Fridays.

December: Operated the Gourock to Dunoon winter service until 4 March 1953, which she also did from October 1953 to 4 January 1954, when she was replaced by the first car ferry on the Clyde, *Arran*.

1953: Ownership transferred to the Caledonian Steam Packet Co. Ltd. Deckhouses, which had been painted in scumbled (wood-effect) brown, repainted in white. Sailed to Arrochar on Tuesdays, Wednesdays and Thursdays, to Arran via the Kyles of Bute on Mondays, on a non-landing afternoon cruise to Brodick Bay on Fridays, and on railway connection work between Craigendoran, Gourock, Dunoon and Rothesay on Saturdays. A trip to Tighnabruaich was offered on Sundays.

1954: Now did relief sailings on Fridays.

1955: Round the Lochs cruise replaced the Arrochar sailings on Wednesdays.

1956–57: Winter: Converted from coal to oil firing.

1958: Upriver cruise from the Clyde resorts to Glasgow (Bridge Wharf) now offered on Fridays. Saturday sailings almost entirely between Wemyss Bay and Rothesay.

From now until 1962 replaced *Duchess of Hamilton* on the long-distance excursion to Inveraray and Campbeltown in September.

1959: Paddle boxes painted white.

1961: Alternated rosters week about with *Jeanie Deans*, so that in alternate weeks she had an afternoon cruise from Mondays to Fridays round Bute and a Saturday afternoon sailing to Tighnabruaich.

1963 and 1964: Replaced **Queen Mary II** on the Glasgow to Tighnabruaich cruise in September.

1965: Early: With the advent of British Rail's Corporate Image she was repainted, in common with the rest of the CSP fleet, with a Monastral Blue hull and red metal lions rampant added to the funnels.

Following the replacement of **Jeanie Deans** by **Caledonia**, did the mix of cruise sailings as before, but with a round Bute cruise on Mondays. Saturday sailings changed back to Craigendoran to Rothesay. She was used on a Sunday cruise to Skipness or round Bute on alternate Sundays. Lochgoilhead Pier closed in this year and the call there was substituted by a Loch Goil cruise.

1967: Replaced **Talisman** on the Sunday afternoon cruises from Millport and Largs to Rothesay and Tighnabruaich.

1969: The Caledonian Steam Packet became part of the Scottish Transport Group, and no longer under railway control.

1970: Hull became black again. With the withdrawal of **Caledonia** after the previous season she was now the sole steamer sailing from Craigendoran. Started a trip to Tarbert and Ardrishaig on Fridays. Following the withdrawal of **Caledonia** she was now the last sea-going paddle steamer in the world.

1971: Now based at Gourock as the Clyde excursion programme contracted. Still sailed on much the same trips, to Arran via the Kyles on Mondays, to Arrochar, on Tuesdays from Rothesay and on Thursdays from Largs, round the Lochs on Wednesdays, this now incorporating an afternoon cruise round Bute, to Tarbert and Ardrishaig on Fridays, and Round Bute on Sundays. For the latter part of the season she sailed with a stump foremast following a collision with Arrochar Pier on 15 July. Keppel Pier (Millport) closed after this season.

1972: Paddleboxes repainted in black. She now did a round Bute cruise on Mondays, and additional Round the Lochs sailing on Tuesdays, and no longer called at Ardrishaig on Fridays.

1973: The CSP became part of Caledonian MacBrayne Ltd. Funnels painted in their house colours, red with a yellow circle encompassing the lions, after a couple of days with an experimental livery of red with a yellow band and black top. Craigendoran and Arrochar piers closed, Thursday sailing was now Round Bute. Withdrawn from service after the end of the season.

1974: 8 August: Sold to the Paddle Steamer Preservation Society for preservation for a symbolic sum of £1.

1975: 22 May: Funnels repainted in the LNER red, white and black colours. Re-entered service, sailing at weekends from Glasgow (Anderston Quay) and in mid-week from Ayr. The Tuesday sailing from Ayr to Tarbert, Loch Fyne has endured in the timetable to the present day.

1977: May: First sailings away from the Clyde, when she offered a week's sailings out of Liverpool to Llandudno and other destinations.

15 July: Grounded on the Gantocks Rocks off Dunoon. Was off-service for six weeks for hull repairs.

1978: April to May: First sailings on the Solent and the Thames. These have been offered every season since, more recently in September. Glasgow berth moved from Anderston Quay to Stobcross Quay.

1979: Regular calls at Helensburgh instituted during the Clyde season. Made one-off calls at Kilmun and Ardyne on a PSPS charter. First sailings on the Bristol Channel.

1981: March: New boiler fitted.

April to June: Circumnavigated the British Isles for the first time, offering cruises on the Humber, Tyne and Forth. These were only offered in this and the following year.

1982: First sailings from Oban at the beginning of May, which are now a regular feature of her schedule. Offered a weekend's cruises from Dundee.

1985: 13 April: Sailed from Garlieston to Douglas, Isle of Man.

Made her first cruises from Dublin and other ports in the Republic of Ireland. These were also offered in 1986, but not again since.

1988: Trips from Kyle of Lochalsh and Portree added to the West Highland sailings.

1989: Sailings made from Tarbert, Harris, and Stornoway, which were also offered in 1990, but not since then.

1990: A sailing was offered from Castlebay, Barra and Lochboisdale, South Uist. These sailings from the Outer Hebrides were not repeated.

1992: September: Made a one-off call at Carradale.

1993: Easter: Made a one-off call at Otter Ferry.

1994: Called at the Admiralty Pier at the former torpedo testing station at Succoth, across Loch Long from Arrochar.

1995: Made a one-off call at Portencross.

1999: December to July 2000: Major £3 million rebuild at the yard of George Prior, Great Yarmouth, funded by the Heritage Lottery Fund. Her decks and deckhouses were removed and central and aft portions of the hull completely stripped and the engines dismantled and rebuilt. A new boiler was fitted and a new emergency exit from the dining salon to the aft deck constructed. The deckhouses were repainted in scumbled wood-effect finish, in a complete return to her LNER colours.

2000: 19 August: First sailing after her rebuild.

2002: 14 October to 2003: 11 June: Second stage of rebuild, where her forward accommodation was rebuilt and the forward deck shelter and foremast replaced

2003: 29 June: Lochranza Pier re-opened. This has become a regular call on her Sunday sailings.

2004: Glasgow berth moved to the Science Centre, on the south bank of the river, because of a new bridge being built at Finnieston and a lack of water at Anderston Quay at very low tides due to a lack of dredging in the upper river.

2005: 22 May: Blairmore Pier re-opened. This became a regular call on the Wednesday sailing to Loch Goil.

Waverley is a remarkable survivor, and is the last sea-going paddle steamer in the world. She normally, although not every year, starts her programme with a weekend on the Clyde at Easter, followed by the Bank Holiday weekend at the beginning of May sailing out of Oban, extended in some seasons with a visit to Skye during the next week, and the following weekend also sailing out of Oban. The remainder of May sees special sailings and charters on the Clyde. June sees her sailing on the Bristol Channel, July and August on the Clyde and in September she sails on the Solent for the first couple of weeks or so, then moving to the Thames until the second weekend in October, with, in some seasons, the season closing with a weekend of Bristol Channel sailings.

Her Clyde schedule is fairly constant:

Sundays: Glasgow at 10:00, Greenock and Largs to Lochranza and cruise to Skipness.

Mondays: Glasgow at 10:00, and Large to Ayr, Girvan and round Ailsa Craig, with passenger returning to Glasgow and Largs from Ayr by bus.

Tuesdays: Ayr at 10:00, Millport and Largs to Rothesay, Tighnabruaich and Tarbert and a cruise on Loch Fyne.

Wednesdays: Ayr at 10:00, Brodick and Largs to Dunoon, Blairmore, and a cruise on Loch Goil.

Thursdays: Greenock at 10:30 and Helensburgh to Millport, Brodick and a cruise round Holy Isle to Pladda.

Fridays: Glasgow at 10:00 and Kilcreggan to Dunoon and Rothesay, with an occasional evening cruise from Glasgow at 19:30.

Saturdays: Glasgow at 10:00, Greenock, and Helensburgh to Dunoon, Rothesay and Tighnabruaich.

Lochs

SL GERTRUDE MATILDA

Length: 11.00m	Gross tonnage: 8
Propulsion: Single Screw	Engine type: Compound, 15hp
Built: 1926	Rebuilt (most recent): 1986
	Passenger capacity: 12
Body of water: Loch Awe	Home port: Loch Awe Pier
Frequency of operation: Daily	Period of operation: Summer
Website address: www.loch-awe.com/history/boats.htm	
Builders: Breaker, Bownesss on Windermere	
Engine builder: Langley Engineering, Storrington 1986	

Gertrude Matilda off Loch Awe Pier, 1988.

Owner: Loch Awe Steam Packet Co. Ltd
Former Names: *Water Lily* 1984, *Lady Rowena* 2005
Remarks: Peat-fired

1926: Built as a motor launch for Lees, Bowness-on-Windermere.

1965: Sold to Borwick's for whom she operated until 1973.

1982: Noted as being at Nottingham.

1984: October: Acquired by Harry Watson, who moved her to Renfrew for rebuilding. A new steam engine to an old Sissons design was fitted in her. Renamed *Lady Rowena*.

1986: July: Restoration completed. Moved by road to Loch Awe, where she started passenger services on 9 August from a pier adjacent to the old Loch Awe station. In early years she made regular sailings to Portsonochan and Taychreggan as well as short non-landing trips from Loch Awe Pier.

1992: Harry Watson died, but the service was carried on by his widow Averil.

1996: Pier erected at Kilchurn Castle, and *Lady Rowena* mainly used on a ferry service from Loch Awe Pier to Kilchurn Castle.

1999: Sold to Loch Awe Steam Packet Co. Ltd, owned by the Ardanaseag Hotel.

2001: Sank at her mooring and was out of service.

2004: Returned to service.

2005: Renamed *Gertrude Matilda*.

2007: Now operating the ferry service to Kilchurn Castle again, with hourly sailings, after the withdrawal of the motor vessel *Flower of Scotland*.

PS MAID OF THE LOCH

Maid of the Loch at Balloch Pier, 2003.

Length: 58.20m   **Gross tonnage**: 555
Propulsion: Paddle Steamer   **Engine type**: Compound Diagonal
Built: 1953
Body of water: Loch Lomond   **Home port**: Balloch
Frequency of operation: Return to steam 200?
Website address: www.maidoftheloch.co.uk
Builders: A. & J. Inglis, Pointhouse, Glasgow
Owner: Loch Lomond Steamship Ltd

1952: Built for British Railways service on Loch Lomond, originally planned to be named *Princess Anne*. Built in sections at Inglis yard at Pointhouse on the Clyde and re-erected at Balloch. The buff funnel originally had a black top but by the time she entered service the funnel was buff all over.

1953: Entered service with one or two runs daily from Balloch to Balmaha, Rowardennan, Tarbet, Inversnaid, and Ardlui.

1957: January: Ownership transferred to the Caledonian Steam Packet Co. Ltd.

1963: Ardlui Pier closed at the end of the season, a cruise to the Head of the Loch was substituted from the following summer.

1969: 1 January: The Caledonian Steam packet became part of the Scottish Transport Group, ownership transferred to Walter Alexander & Sons (Midland) Ltd in the summer of this year, although all operation and marketing continued to be done by the Caledonian Steam Packet Co. Ltd.

1971: Balmaha Pier closed.

1973: Owners became Caledonian MacBrayne Ltd.

1975: Funnel painted briefly buff with a black top at the beginning of the season, then red with a black top from 4 June for the remainder of the summer, returning to all-over buff the following season. Tarbet Pier closed.

1978: Spring: Mainmast removed due to rot.

1980: 24 May: Luss Pier, which had closed in 1952 re-opened.

1981: Final day in service, following which she was laid-up at Balloch and used as a landing platform for the small motor vessel **Countess Fiona** until her withdrawal after the 1989 season.

1982: Purchased by Ind Coope Alloa Brewery.

1989: Purchased by Sea Management Corporation of Australia, which formed Maid of the Loch Ltd, to preserve her. They went into liquidation on 2 May 1990.

1990: Francis Hotel Group, Gateshead purchased her from the receivers.

1992: Early: Francis Hotel Group went into liquidation.

December: Purchased by Dumbarton District Council. Despite all the changes in ownership since withdrawal in 1981, no work had been done on her and she had steadily been getting more derelict. Paddle Steamer Preservation Society volunteers started to restore her about this time.

1995: Owners gifted her to the Loch Lomond Steamship Co. for preservation. Gradually the interior has been cleaned and restored. Her funnel was painted red with a black top, and her hull, previously white, was painted black.

1996: Boiler removed.

1997: New steel promenade deck laid. Former dining saloon and cafeteria opened as a café.

2000: Forward main deck area refurbished as a restaurant/café/bar.

2001: Forward deck saloon used as a small museum and shop, after deck saloon fully restored, and now named the Douglas Mickel Saloon.

2002: Paddle boxes repainted black.

2003: Lower tearoom refurbished.

2004: Awarded a 2-star Visitor Attraction award.

2005: £620,000 Heritage Lottery fund award announced for the restoration of the steam-powered slipway at Balloch. This will enable **Maid of the Loch** to be pulled out of the water for hull survey and painting.

2005-06: Winter: Slipway restored along with the steam slipway engine, for which a new boiler was built.

2006: 27 June: Pulled out of the water for a couple of hours, to test the work that had been done on the slipway.

Provided **Maid of the Loch**'s owners can obtain a grant or other funding for a new boiler, it looks likely that she will be back sailing on Loch Lomond before the end of the decade. Her engines have been overhauled as part of the restoration work of recent years, and can now be turned over by hand.

SS SIR WALTER SCOTT

Length: 33.70m   Gross tonnage: 115

Propulsion: Single Screw   Engine type: Triple Expansion, 140hp

Built: 1899   Passenger capacity: 320

Body of water: Loch Katrine   **Home port**: Trossachs Pier
Frequency of operation: Daily   **Period of operation**: Easter to late October
Website address: www.incallander.co.uk/steam.htm
Builders: Denny, Dumbarton   **Engine builder**: M. Paul, Dumbarton
Owner: Steamship Sir Walter Scott Trust
Remarks: Coal-fired

1899: Ordered by Loch Katrine Steamboat Co., owned by Eglinton Hotels Ltd, from Matthew Paul, Dumbarton, who sub-contracted the hull to the well-known shipyard of William Denny & Bros. The Hull was towed up Loch Lomond to Inversnaid, from where it was taken to Stronachlachar, pulled by steam traction engines, for fitting out and the installation of the engine.

1900: Entered service on Loch Katrine from Trossachs Pier to Stronachlachar. This had been a popular tourist area since it featured in Sir Walter Scott's poem *The Lady of the Lake* almost a century earlier. In her early years she made four return trips a day.

1902: The wheel, which had originally been on deck-level forward of the funnel, was raised to give the helmsman better visibility. A bridge was later added.

Late 1940s: Wheelhouse added.

1953: Sold to Glasgow Corporation Water Department. Loch Katrine has been a major part of the drinking water supply for Glasgow since 1856.

1956: New boiler fitted. Saloon windows replaced by portholes.

1969: Owners became the Lower Clyde Water Board. The funnel, which had previously been yellow, was painted white.

1975: Ownership transferred to Strathclyde Regional Council.

*c.*1982: Afternoon sailing to Stronachlachar replaced by two non-landing cruises after the Loch Lomond sailings by **Maid of the Loch** to Inversnaid, from which there was a bus connection, ceased.

1991: Reboilered.

1997: Ownership transferred to West of Scotland Water with local government re-organisation.

2000: Ben A'an Bar created in the aft saloon. Previous souvenir stall in the fore saloon removed.

2002: Scottish Water became owners.

2005: Steamship Sir Walter Scott Trust founded to operate and restore the steamer. Reverted from using smokeless coal to coal.

2006: Afternoon Stronachlachar trip reinstated in the main season on Wednesdays, Saturdays and Sundays. Winter-Spring: Bow thruster fitted, with a new bow, now with bulwarks up to rail level. Did not enter service until late May, sailing being taken by the biodiesel-powered motor launch **Ellen's Isle** until then.

Sir Walter Scott has a long operating season from Easter to the end of October. She offers a morning return at 11:00 to Stronachlachar, and 45-minute non-landing cruises at 13:15 and 17:00. From 1 July to the beginning of September, she offers an afternoon cruise to Stronachlachar at 14:30 on, Wednesdays, Saturdays and Sundays. Daily up to the end of June and from the beginning of September, and on Mondays, Tuesdays Thurdays and Fridays in the main season, she has two additional 45-minute trips at 14:30 and 15:45.

SS SPIRIT OF THE TAY

Length: 33.83m
Propulsion: Single Screw
Built: Under construction   **Passenger capacity**: 200
Body of water: Loch Tay   **Home port**: Kenmore
Frequency of operation: Under construction
Website address: www.lochtaysteamheritage.co.uk
Builders: Ferguson, Port Glasgow   **Engine builder**: Crabtree, Gt Yarmouth
Owner: Loch Tay Steam Packet Co. Ltd

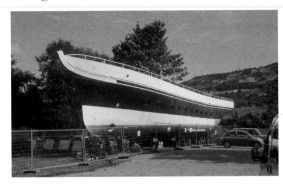

The hull of *Spirit of the Tay* at Dalerb,
August 2005.

2003: It was announced that a new steamer for Loch Tay, to be named **Spirit of the Tay**, and to be a replica of the 1855 **Rob Roy** on Loch Katrine, was to be built for the Loch Tay Steam Packet Co. Ltd.

2004: Hull sections, which had been built by Ferguson Bros of Port Glasgow, moved to Dalerb, a mile west of Kenmore, and welded together. Unfortunately X-rays of two of the welds found them to be faulty, and they were not passed by the MCA (Maritime and Coastguard Agency) who are in an ongoing dispute with Fergusons about this.

2005: 31 August: Funnel, propeller and deckhouse delivered to Dalerb. There is at the time of writing an impasse, the hull cannot be craned into the loch without an MCA certificate and the engine and other fitments cannot be fitted in the hull because the hull weights 60 tons and the maximum weight the crane can lift is 62 tons. A Crabtree steam engine has been obtained but at the time of writing is understood still to be in the south of England.

When this dispute is resolved and **Spirit of the Tay** is completed, she will offer short cruises from Kenmore with possibly occasional trips the length of the loch to Killin. A below-decks restaurant is part of the plans. Further plans are for a second similar steamer to be built to operate at the Killin end of the Lake in connection with a steam railway along the trackbed of the old Callander and Oban Railway branch line from Loch Tay Pier into Killin.

NORTHERN IRELAND

TSS NOMADIC

Length: 67.06m   **Gross tonnage:** 1273
Engine type: (was) 2 x Compound, 550hp
Built: 1911   **Rebuilt** (most recent): 2006+
Passenger capacity: was 1,000
Body of water: Belfast Lough   **Home port:** Belfast
Frequency: Undergoing restoration
Website address: savenomadic.com
Builder: Harland & Wolff, Belfast
Owner: Northern Ireland Office   **Operator:** *Nomadic* Preservation Society
Former names: *Iginieur Minard* 1968, **Nomadic** 1934

1911: 25 April: launched for the White Star Line. Used as a tender at Cherbourg, France, designed to be used to ferry first and second-class passengers and baggage to the **Olympic**-class vessels. Registered in the name of Geo Aug Laniece, so that she could be registered in France.

29 May: Attended the sea trials of **Olympic**, and her departure tow days later, then sailed for Southampton and on to Cherbourg.

3 June: Arrived at Cherbourg.

14 June: Tendered **Olympic** on her inaugural call at Cherbourg.

1912: 10 April: Tendered **Titanic** on her only call at Cherbourg.

Nomadic when a Japanese restaurant at Paris, 1989.

1917: 25 April: Requisitioned by the French Navy and moved to Brest, where she was used for ferrying US troops from their troopships to land.

1919: October: Returned to Cherbourg.

1927: Sold to Cie Cherbourgoise de Trasnbordeurs, Paris.

1934: Sold to Cie Cherbourgoise de Remorquage at de Sauvetage. Renamed **Inginieur Minard**. Funnel repainted black with a red band.

1940: June: Escaped to Portsmouth on the German invasion of France, where she was requisitioned by the Royal Navy. Some sources state that she was laid-up until 1942, and then used as an accommodation vessel, others that she was used as a troop transport from Southampton to the Isle of Wight.

1945: 27 June: Returned to service at Cherbourg.

1967-8: Withdrawn from service when Cunard's transatlantic service with **Queen Mary** and **Queen Elizabeth** was withdrawn.

1968: 4 November: Final day in service, tendering **Queen Elizabeth**.
Sold.

1969: 26 April: Towed to Le Havre, after her sale to Somairec for breaking-up there. Later sold to Roland Spinnewyn, who proposed to use her as a floating restaurant at Conflans Saint-Honorine. She was towed there and shortly after her engines and boiler were removed and sold for scrap. No further work was done and she was vandalised and became derelict and many items were stolen from her.

1974: Sold to Yvon Vincent, who converted her to a floating restaurant and renamed **Nomadic**. By this time her engine and boilers had been removed.

17 October: Moved to Paris when the Seine was at an exceptionally low level, where she was moored at the Quai Débilly, below the Eiffel Tower, where she was moored and converted for use as a restaurant ship and conference venue.

1977: 25 June: Opened for business following rebuilding.

1979: Upper deck extended fore and aft.

1986: Upper deck again altered and air-conditioning installed. Opened as the Japanese restaurant *Shogun*.

Early 1990s: Restaurant and disco *Le Colonial* opened in place of the above.

1998: Following the launch of the film *Titanic*, restaurant *Le Trasbordeur de Titanic* opened on board.

1999: March: Closed by the Pairs Port Authority and required to be dry-docked, but could not be moved under the bridges on the Seine, because of accommodation that had been added to her top deck. The nearest dry dock to Paris is at Rouen.

2000: Commercial licence cancelled, and ship closed.

2003: March: Belfast Industrial Heritage Ltd launched as 'Nomadic back to Belfast' appeal.

1 April: Moved to Le Havre using a pusher tug after her upper deck had been removed to get under the bridges, arriving on 4 April.

2004: June: Hull surveyed by Harland and Wolff at the instigation of Belfast City Council and the Northern Ireland Office.

2005: 10 November: Auctioned but the reserve price was not met.

2006: 26 January: Sold at auction to the Northern Ireland Office.

11 July: Towed on a barge to Belfast, where she arrived on 15 July. Restoration was expected to begin. This is expected to cost around £7m. If suitable steam engines and a boiler can be obtained, they will be re-installed on her, and she will be operable.

COAST

ST BJÖRN

Björn awaiting restoration.

Length: 26.20m   Gross tonnage: 135
Propulsion: Single Screw   Engine type: Triple Expansion, 450hp
Built: 1908   Passenger capacity: was 200
Home port: Randers
Frequency of operation: Undergoing restoration
Website address: www.dampskib.dk/index.php?id=7
Builders: Seebeck A G, Bremerhaven
Owner: Dansk Veteranskibsklub

1908: Built as a harbour tug for Randers Harbour Authorities for use at Randers. Used until the 1920s for towing sailing ships up as far as Skagen.

1909: 7 February: Entered service.

1928: Registered as a passenger ship, used for mainly charter cruises on the fjord for up to 200 passengers.

1942: 1 May to 1943: 12 January: Chartered to Svitzer.

1944: December: Chartered for one month to use at Rønne, Bornholm.

1945: 11 April: Taken by the German occupying force, attempting to escape from the advancing allied armies. Forced into Århus by allied aircraft.

Late 1940s: Chartered to A/S De Forenede Bugserselskaber for use at Copenhagen to tow lighters from Copenhagen to Kyndbyvaerket with goods unloaded from American Liberty Ships.

Early 1950s: Used with ammunition ships in Århus harbour.

1981: 6 February. After a short lay-up sold to the Dansk Veteranskibsklub for a symbolic 1 kroner. Moved to Kalundborg, later to Korsør.

1982: Sailed to Holmen in Copenhagen for restoration to begin.

1984: Drydocked at Orlogsværftem.

1993: Moved to Søminegraven.

1997: Moved to Lynettehavnen.

1999: 9 May: Moved to Helsingør for completion of restoration.

SS SKJELSKØR

Length: 20.57m   Gross tonnage: 49
Propulsion: Single Screw   Engine type: Compound, 75hp
Built: 1915

Skjelskør at Roskilde, 1985.

Passenger capacity: 80
Body of water: Roskilde Fjord   Home port: Frederikssund
Frequency of operation: SuO   Period of operation: Mid-June to mid-August
Website address: www.dampskib.dk
Builders: J. Ring-Anderson's Staalskibsværft, Frederiksøen, Svendborg
Engine builder: Steen & Kaufmann, Elmshorn, Germany
Owner: Dansk Veteranskibsklub
Remarks: Coal-fired

1915: Built as a passenger steamer for Dampskibsselskabet Skjelskør A/S for the ferry service from Skælskør to the small islands of Agersø and Omø in the Great Belt.

1962: 31 March: Withdrawn from service and sold to H.I. Hansen, Odense for scrap. By this time she was Denmark's last coal-fired coastal passenger steamer.

1963: 3 September: Sold to the newly founded Dansk Veteranskibsklub for preservation, in one of the first steamer preservation efforts worldwide.

6 October: Towed to Nyborg for restoration over the ensuing winter.

1964: 31 May: Entered summer service from Sakskøbing to Bandholm on the island of Lolland in connection with a preserved railway.

1967: Out of service at Nyborg for major repairs.

1968: June: Commenced trips out of Roskilde on the Roskilde Fjord, mainly on summer Sundays.

1969: Sailings from Roskilde ceased after the mole she moored at was damaged in a storm.

1972: Sailings from Roskilde recommenced.

1994: Moved to Frederikssund, further down the Roskilde Fjord.

2004: Was not in service due to boiler problems.

Over the years **Skjelskør** has visited a number of steam festivals, including those at Flensburg and at Vejle. She offers, in 2006, three 1-hour trips each Sunday in the operating period, at 13:00, 14:30 and 16:00.

INLAND LAKES

PS HJEJLEN

Length: 26.90m   Gross tonnage: 39
Propulsion: Paddle Steamer   Engine type: 2-cylinder Oscillating, 25hp
Built: 1861   Passenger capacity: 178
Body of water: Silkeborg Lakes   Home port: Silkeborg
Frequency of operation: Daily   Period of operation: Late June to early August
Website address: www.hjejlen.com
Builders: Baumgarten & Burmeister, Copenhagen
Owner: D/S Hjejlen ApS
Remarks: Coal-fired

1861: Built by Baumgarten & Burmeister (the predecessors of Burmeister & Wain), Copenhagen, for use on the Silkeborg Lakes at Silkeborg on the route from Silkeborg to the foot of the 147m-high

Himmelbjerget (Sky Mountain) and Ry. She replaced hand-propelled paddle boats.

11 June: Left Copenhagen for Silkeborg on her first and only sailing on the open sea.

15 June: Arrived Silkeborg after a difficult trip pulled by men and horses up the River Gudenaaen from Randers.

24 June: Inaugural voyage with King Frederik VII on board after several trial trips, also with the King on board.

Unknown date prior to 1896: Mast removed.

1900: New boiler fitted. Funnel moved forwards and shortened. Steering position changed from aft to amidships. Seating fitted on upper deck aft.

1906: Awnings erected over foredeck and upper aft deck.

1924: Hull painted white for one season only.

1932: Became an official mail boat between Silkeborg and Himmelbjerget.

1935: Wheelhouse fitted.

1947: New boiler fitted.

Hjeljen is the oldest steamer in the world in anything like original condition, the three that are older, **Skibladner**, **Tudor Vladimirescu** and **Rigi**, having been considerably altered over the years. She normally sails twice daily from Silkeborg to Himmelbjerget and Laven, a railway station across the lake from Himmelbjerget, at 10:00 and 13:45 with an evening non-stop sailing at 20:15 on Tuesdays, Wednesdays and Thursdays in high season.

3 Estonia

ST ADMIRAL

Admiral at Tallinn. (Owners)

Length: 29.87m	**Gross tonnage**: 264
Propulsion: Single Screw	**Engine type**: 500hp
Built: 1956	**Rebuilt** (most recent): 1996
	Passenger capacity: 60
Body of water: Baltic Sea	**Home port**: Muuga, Tallinn
	Frequency of operation: Charters
	Website address: www.aurulaev-admiral.ee/en_index.htm
	Builders: Unknown, Leningrad
	Owner: Restaurant 'Admiral'

1955: Built at St Petersburg as a steam tug for service in Soviet waters.

1989-90: Sold to an Estonian co-operative company.

1990: Visited Hamburg Harbour Birthday Celebrations. Used as a charter ship in the Baltic area.

1994-96: Converted to a saloon passenger steamer by Ju, Tallinn.

Admiral is normally moored as a restaurant ship at Tallinn, but may occasionally offer charters or special trips.

4 Finland

Surviving steamers in Finland can be mainly split between passenger steamers and tugs. The lakes that cover much of inland Finland have been home to passenger steamers for the past century and a half. Of the three main lake systems, Näsijärvi and Päijänne have one passenger steamer each with regular services, while on Lake Saimaa the steamer network has declined considerably since the late 1970s, when there was a network of nine steamers owned by Saimaan Laivamatkat, mainly running day-long routes out of Savonlinna to Lappeenranta, Mikkeli, Joensuu, and Kuopio, plus a couple of steamers running short trips each out of Savonlinna and Kuopio. Now the long distance steamers are all gone, and there are only three steamers left operating at Savonlinna and none at Kuopio.

There are a large number of privately preserved historic steam vessels in Finland, mainly tugs. Their owners are members of Suomen Höyrypursiseura (the Finnish Steam Yachting Association). These are listed below, and it is possible that public trips may be available on them at steam rallies, although some of these are private events for club members only. Rallies and normally held annually in the summer on each of the three main lake systems.

The Finnish language is notoriously difficult, the only languages related to it being Estonian and Hungarian. The endings of nouns change according to the preposition used.

Some useful Finnish words:
Höyry steam
Laiva ship
Vehne boat; actually vene, but vehne is the old spelling, used in a lot of operators' names historically
Oy Limited

COASTAL WATERS

ST ARMAS

Armas at Porvoo. (Bill Worden)

Length: 21.61m   **Gross tonnage:** 52.29
Propulsion: Single Screw   **Engine type:** Compound, 188hp
Built: 1908
Body of water: Finnish Coast   **Home port:** Porvoo
Frequency of operation: Rallies?
Website address: www.steamengine.cc/arkisto/koneet/ssarmas.html; www.mll-porvoo.com/armas-web/index.htm
Builders: Paul Wahl, Varkaus
Owner: Mannerheimin lastensuojeluliitto Porvoon yhdistys ry
Former name: *Toinen*
Remarks: Wood-fired

1908: Built for W. Gutzeit & Co., Savonlinna.

1927: Owners became Enso-Gutzeit Oy, Savonlinna.

1973: Sold to Arto Juva, Vääksy & Irma Saukonpää, Helsinki for preservation.

1983: Ownership passed to Ilkka & Nanna Juva.

1997: Sold to Mannerheimin lastensuojeluliitto Porvoon yhdistys ry, Porvoo. Moved to Porvoo.

SS HOVINSAARI

Steam tug *Hovinsaari*.
(Suomen Höyrypursiseura)

Length: 14.65m
Propulsion: Single Screw   Engine type: Compound, 50hp
Built: 1921
Body of water: Finnish Coast   Home port: Porvoo
Frequency of operation: Rallies?
Website address: www.steamengine.cc/arkisto/koneet/sshovinsaari.html
Builders: Laitaatsillan telakka, Savonlinna
Owner: Joakim Lybeck, Porvoo
Former name: *S 8*
Remarks: Wood-fired

1921: Built for Pohjois-Karjalan Uittoyhdistys for use as a tug on Lake Pielinen.

Unknown date: Purchased by Joakim Lybeck, Porvoo for preservation. Moved to Porvoo.

SS HYÖKY

Length: 40.20m   Gross tonnage: 275
Propulsion: Single Screw   Engine type: Triple Expansion
Built: 1912
Body of water: Finnish Coast   Home port: Hamina
Website address: www.hyoky.net;
www.feuerschiffseite.de/SCHIFFE/RUSSLAND/LIBAUS/hyoeky.htm
Builders: Putilov Gun and Engine Works, St Petersburg
Owner: Haminan Höyrylaiva Oy, Hamina : 0
Former names: *Helsinki* 1961, *Äransgrund* 193?, *Relandersgrund* 1921, *Libauskij* 1918

1912: Built as the steam lightship *Libauskij*.

1918: With the independence of Finland, repositioned to Relandersgrund, and renamed *Relandersgrund*.

1921: Relocated to Äransgrund, renamed *Äransgrund*.

1933: Relocated to Helsinki, renamed *Helsinki*.

1940: 29 February: Damaged in an air raid, funnel destroyed and remainder of ship damaged.

1941: September: Sunk after three German minelayers exploded close to her, damaging both sides of her hull. All fifteen crew were saved. Later raised.

1959: Taken out of service when replaced by a lighthouse.

1961: Used as a research ship of the hydrographical inspection service. Renamed **Hyöky**.

1983: Sold to Haminan Höyrylaiva Oy. Moved to Hamina and used as a restaurant.

Hyöky is normally based as Hamina as a restaurant ship, but occasionally visits other Finnish ports for special events. It is not know of she carries passengers on the positioning runs to such events.

SS NORRKULLA

Length: 25.20m   **Gross tonnage:** 81
Propulsion: Single Screw   **Engine type:** Compound, 120hp
Built: 1911   **Passenger capacity:** 80
Body of water: Baltic Coast   **Home port:** Helsinki
Frequency of operation: Occasional passenger trips
Website address: www.hoyrylaiva.fi
Builders: Lehtoniemi & Taipale, Joroinen   **Engine builder:** 1917
Owner: Helsingin Höyrylaivaosakeyhti, Helsinki
Operator: Travel Park Arabianranta, Helsinki
Former names: *Höyryjuho* 2006, *Figaro* 2005, *Saaristo* 1975, *Norrkulla* 1938, *Nagu* 1919

1911: Built as the passenger steamer **Nagu** for Ångbåta AB Nagulle for service out of Turku.

1919: Renamed **Norrkulla**. Lengthened by 3.84m at AB Vulkan, Turku. Now sailed out of Helsinki for Trafik AB Sibbo Skärgården.

1938: Sold to Kuopion Höyrymylly Oy Sampo for use as a tug at Kuopio on Lake Saimaa, renamed **Saaristo**.

1975: Sold to Kysönsalmen Höyryvenhe Oy for use on excursions at Savonlinna, renamed **Figaro**. By this time she was the last surviving steamer in operation year-round in Finnish waters.

2004: Sold to new owners, who planned to convert her to diesel.

2005: Sold to Lc Lesa Oy, Helsinki. Moved to Helsinki, after being out of service in Summer 2005. Renamed **Höyryjuho**.

2006: Spring: Helsingin Höyrylaivaosakeyhtiö (Helsinki Steamship Co.) formed to operate her. Renamed **Norrkulla**.

Norrkulla will be operating a handful of public passenger trips from Helsinki in Summer 2006.

ST TORNATOR II

Steam tug *Tornator II* awaiting restoration.
(Suomen Höyrypursiseura)

Length: 22.50m   **Gross tonnage:** 90
Propulsion: Single Screw   **Engine type:** Compound, 250hp
Built: 1905

Body of water: Finnish Coast   **Home port**: Helsinki
Frequency of operation: Undergoing restoration
Website address: www.opastin.com
Builders: Paul Wahl, Varkaus
Owner: Pekka Häkkinen, Espoo
Former names: *Amanda* 1996, *Mauri* 1968, *Tornator II* 1931

1905: Built as the tug *Tornator II* for Oy Tornator Ab.

1919: Sold to Ab W Gutzeit, Savonlinna.

1927: Owners became Enso-Gutzeit Oy, Savonlinna.

1931: Renamed *Mauri*.

1968: Sold to Juhani Uusmaa, Helsinki for preservation.

1973: Sold to Seppo Kivisaari, Marko Loikkanen, Eero Meurman, Mikko Rytsölä, Juha Saura and Juhani Uusmaa, renamed *Amanda*. Moved to Turku.

1986: Planed on land to prevent her sinking after engine failure. Boiler removed.

1996: Sold to Pekka Häkkinen, Juriperttu Wilska and Hannu Nikkinen, renamed *Tornator II*. Moved to Helsinki.

1999: Pekka Häkkinen became sole owner. Restoration work ongoing. Hull and engine repairs have taken place and a new boiler is to be fitted.

SS TURSO

Steam harbour icebreaker-cum-tug *Taifun*, now *Turso*, on her return voyage from Russia, 2005. (Suomen Höyrypursiseura)

Length: 36.03m   **Gross tonnage**: 411
Propulsion: Single Screw   **Engine type**: Triple Expansion, 750hp
Built: 1944
Body of water: Baltic Coast   **Home port**: to be decided
Website address: www.turso.fi
Builders: Wärtsilä, Helsinki
Owner: Satamajäänsärkijü S/S Turso yhdistys ry
Former names: *Taifun* 2004, *Turso* 1945

1942: July: Ordered as the harbour tug-cum-icebreaker *Turso* for the Port of Helsinki.

1944: 12 January: Launched.

 15 March: Delivered.

 December: Requisitioned by the Allies to clear the channel from Kronstadt to Leningrad.

1945: 8 February: Surrendered to the Soviet Union as war reparations. They were so happy with her that they ordered twenty identical tugs from Wärtsilä as war reparations. Renamed *Taifun*, used in Leningrad. Later ownership changed to the Baltic Shipping Co.

1962: Converted from coal to oil burning.

1995: Sold to ECO Phoenix Holding PLC, St Petersburg. Repaired and restored.

2004: 12 July: Purchased by Satamajäänsärkijü S/S Turso yhdistys ry (Harbour Icebreaker S/S Turso Association) for preservation.

6 August: Sailed through the Saimaa Canal to Lappennranta.

2 October: Renamed *Turso* at Savonlinna.

When *Turso* is fully restored, she will be based at a port on the Baltic Coast of Finland, and will make summer sailings in the Baltic Sea and possibly as far as the North Sea.

SS UKKOPEKKA

Ukkopekka at Naantali, 1995.

Length: 36.00m   **Gross tonnage:** 287
Propulsion: Single Screw   **Engine type:** Triple Expansion, 380hp
Built: 1938   **Rebuilt** (most recent): 1983
Passenger capacity: 199
Body of water: Turku Archipelago   **Home port:** Turku
Frequency of operation: Daily   **Period of operation:** May to early September
Website address: www.ukkopekka.com
Builders: Wärtsila, Helsinki
Owner: Höyrylaiva Oy SS Ukkopekka
Former names: *Hamina* 1986, *Turku* 1981

1938: Built as the light and buoy inspection steamer *Turku* for Merenkulkulaitos, the National Board of Navigation.

1939-40: Used by the Germans outside the island of Utö.

1941-45: Used as a convoy ship in the Åland Sea, also planting sonar equipment to detect enemy submarines.

1976: New oil-fired boiler fitted.

1979: Withdrawn from service.

1981: Sold and renamed *Hamina*. Upper deck extended aft.

1982: Used for occasional passenger trips out of Helsinki.

1986: Sold to Naantali Höyrylaiva Oy. Rebuilt as a passenger steamer with a new lounge, restaurant, and sun deck. Renamed *Ukkopekka*. Later sold to Höyrylaiva Oy SS Ukkopekka.

1988-89: Saloons and lounges extended and renovated.

Ukkopekka makes two daily return cruises from Turku to Naantali at 10:00 and 14:00 and also 4-hour evening cruises at 19:00 Mondays excepted.

ST VETÄJA V

Length: 21.50m   **Gross tonnage:** 29.94
Propulsion: Single Screw   **Engine type:** Compound, 143hp
Built: 1891   **Passenger capacity:** 12?

Vetäja V at Turku, 1995.

Body of water: Turku Archipelago   **Home port**: Turku
Frequency of operation: Occasional public trips, charters
Period of operation: Summer months
Website address: www.steamengine.cc/arkisto/koneet/ssvetajav.html;
www.forum-marinum.fi/english/laivoja.php?id=14
Builders: Lehtoniemi & Taipale, Joroinen
Owner: Vetäja V:n Kannatusyhdistys ry, Turku
Former names: *Wienti, Ilmari*

1891: Built as the passenger steamer **Ilmari** for Pielisjärven Höyryvenhe Oy, for use on Lakes Saimaa and
Pielinen, later converted to a cargo boat and to a tug.
1903: Sold to O. Lucanderille, Viipuri. Later renamed **Wienti** and operated at Porvoo and Turku.
1954: Purchased by Turku city, renamed **Vetäja V**. Used as a harbour tug.
1984: Withdrawn from commercial service, laid-up.
1986: Handed over to the Provincial Museum, moved to the Suomen Laivateoliisuus shipyard for
restoration, which started in 1993 after a support organisation had been formed.
1994: Returned to steam.

LAKE NÄSIJÄRVI

ST AURE

Aure at Tampere, 1994.

Length: 19.90m   Gross tonnage: 45
Propulsion: Single Screw   Engine type: Compound, 136hp
Built: 1926   Passenger capacity: 12
Body of water: Lake Näsijärvi   Home port: Tampere
Frequency of operation: Occasional public trips
Website address: kotisivu.mtv3.fi/nasijarven.rautalaivat/nasi.pdf (page 23)
Builders: A. Ahlström & Co., Varkaus
Owner: Höyrylaiva Oy Aure

1926: Built as a tug. Built in sections at Varkaus and assembled at Vilppula. Used for towing scows laden with firewood from Kuru, Ruovesi and Virrat to Tampere.

1942: Taken over by Kokemäenjoen Uittoyhdisty.

Early 1950s: Laid-up because Finnish Railways were no longer using firewoord to power steam locomotives.

1957: Sold to Ab J V Enqvist Oy, used to tow log rafts to a pulp mill at Tampere.

1958: Owners purchased by G.A. Serlachius Oy.

1969: Withdrawn from service.

1980: Autumn: Purchased by a group of local steam enthusiasts, who formed Höyrylaiva Oy Aure to operate her.

1981: Returned to steam, offering passenger charters and locally advertised public trips.

1983: Summer: Used for regular passenger traffic from Tampere to Kuru at weekends. These trips did not last for very long and since then she has mainly been engaged on charters.

SL HÄME

Häme on Lake Näsijärvi.
(Suomen Höyrypursiseura)

Length: 12.40m
Propulsion: Single Screw   Engine type: 39hp
Built: 1903
Body of water: Lake Näsijarvi   Home port: Tampere
Frequency of operation: Undergoing restoration
Website address: www.steamengine.cc/arkisto/koneet/H%c4ME.JPG;
     http://kotisivu.mtv3.fi/nasijarven.rautalaivat/nasi.pdf (page 24)
Builders: Sommers, af Hällström & Waldens, Tampere
Owner: L. Elo, Tampere
Former name: *Lauttakyla*
Remarks: Wood-fired

1903: Built for Lauttokylän Höyryvene Oy as the passenger and cargo steamer *Lauttakyla*.

1933: Sold to Hämeen Faneeritehtaale, Hämeenlinna, renamed *Häme*.

1958: Sold to Tyväntöön Lahdentaan sawmill.

1960s: Out of service.

1990: Sawmill closed.
1992: Purchased for preservation, moved to Tampere, where she was restored.

ST KOTVIO II

Kotvio II. (Suomen Höyrypursiseura)

Length: 33.03m
Propulsion: Single Screw   **Engine type**: Triple Expansion, 137hp
Built: 1884
Body of water: Lake Näsijarvi   **Home port**: Vilppula
Frequency of operation: Rallies, possibly
Website address: www.nic.fi/~vilven/kotvio2.htm;
www.nic.fi/~vilven/galleria/kotvio2/index.html;
http://kotisivu.mtv3.fi/nasijarven.rautalaivat/nasi.pdf (page 25)
Builders: Rosenlew & Co., Pori
Owner: Vilppulan Veneilijät ry, Vilppula
Former name: *Näsijärvi*

1884: Built as the tug *Näsijärvi* for her owners for service at Tampere.
1935: Purchased by the Kotvio sawmill and renamed *Kotvio II*.
1967: Sold to Olavi Kivimäki, later sold to Tampere Kaupunki (Town Council) for preservation.
1998: Sold to present owners.
2002: Returned to steam.

ST NÄSIJÄRVI II

Näsijärvi II at Tampere, 1995.

Length: 21.00m
Propulsion: Single Screw   **Engine type**: Compound, 160hp
Built: 1929   **Passenger capacity**: 40
Body of water: Lake Näsijarvi   **Home port**: Vilppula
Frequency of operation: Charters

Website address: info1.info.tampere.fi/a/tammela/koulu/opet/kaitsu/steam.html;
    kotisivu.mtv3.fi/nasijarven.rautalaivat/nasi.pdf (page 26)
Builders: A. Ahlström, Varkaus
Owner: Tampere Sailing Club
Former name: *Neptun II*
Remarks: Wood-fired

1929: Built for Neptun Oy, as the tug *Neptun II* for service towing barges from Längelmävesi to Vajanavesi and Pyhäjärvi.
1930: Moved to Lake Näsijärvi.
1930: Autumn: Owners bankrupt.
1931: *Neptun II* taken over by Rosenlew Oy, renamed *Näsijärvi II*. Used to tow log tows from Murole to Pispala.
1944: Taken over by Kokemäenjoki uittoyhdistys (Floating Association).
1967: Laid-up after timber began to be taken to the sawmills by lorry.
1970-71: Sold to private steam enthusiasts for preservation.
1976: Donated to the city of Tampere as a museum ship.
1980: Autumn. Rights of use and responsibility for her upkeep given to Tampereen Pursiseura (Tampere Sailing Club).
1981: Returned to steam.
1995: Started to be used as a passenger steamer, mainly for charters.

SS POHJOLA

Pohjola laid-up at Tampere, 1981.

Length: 29.50m   Gross tonnage: 147
Propulsion: Single Screw   Engine type: Triple Expansion
Built: 1905
Body of water: Lake Näsijarvi   Home port: Tampere
Frequency of operation: Awaiting restoration
Builders: Sommers, Tampere
Owner: Runoilijan Tie

1905: Built for Tampeeren-Virtain Höyrylaiva Oy for the service on Lake Näsijärvi from Tampere to Virrat.
1932: Lengthened, sold to Höyrylaiva Osuuskunta Tarjanne. Came under the same ownership as *Tarjanne* and ran in conjunction with her.
1941, 1943-44: Laid-up, a single steamer operating during the war years.
1967: Taken over by Runoilijan Tie Oy, owned by three local authorities (Tampere, Ruovesi and Virrat).
1975: Withdrawn from service and laid-up at Tampere.

Pohjola has been recently seen totally stripped down, without engine or boiler, on land at Jäminkipöhja, 50km north-east of Tampere. It is uncertain if she was being scrapped, restored, or the hull was being converted for some other use.

SL SATU

Satu at Tampere, 2006.

Length: 9.60m
Propulsion: Single Screw   Engine type: Compound, 10hp
Built: 1901   Passenger capacity: 12
Body of water: L Näsijärvi   Home port: Tampere
Frequency of operation: Rallies?
Website address: www.steamengine.cc/arkisto/koneet/sssatuv.html
Builders: Sommers, Tampere   Owner: J. Gummerus, Luopioinen
Former names: *Mary*, *Puritaan*

Satu is a small steam launch. At some stage recently she was moved north to Vanajavesi but is now back in Tampere.

SS TARJANNE

Tarjanne leaving Ruovesi, 1981.

Length: 29.50m   Gross tonnage: 133
Propulsion: Single Screw   Engine type: Triple Expansion, 300hp
Built: 1908   Passenger capacity: 133
Body of water: Lake Näsijarvi   Home port: Tampere to Virrat
Frequency of operation: Northbound TTSO, southbound WFSuO
Period of operation: beginning June to 20 August
Website address: www.finnishsilverline.com/poetsway/index.htm
Builders: Lehtoniemi & Taipale, Joroinen
Owner: Runoilijan Tie Oy

1908: Built for Tampereen-Virtain Höyrylaiva Oy, for the service from Tampere to Virrat.

1932: Sold to Höyrylaiva Osuuskunta Tarjanne. The service changed from a local passenger service to a tourist service, being known as Runoilijan Tie (The Poet's Way).

1940, 1942: Laid-up, a single steamer operating during the war years, most of the local traffic now going by bus.

1964: Converted to oil-firing.

1967: Taken over by Runoilijan Tie Oy, owned by three local authorities (Tampere, Ruovesi and Virrat).

1976: Operated the service alone after the withdrawal of **Pohjola**.

Tarjanne operates a long one-way service northbound from Tampere, leaving at 10:45 on Tuesday, Thursdays and Saturdays, arriving at Virrat at 18:30, and sailing back south the following day from Virrat at 10:45. There are bus connections available from Tampere to or from Virrat to enable the entire trip to be done, or bus connections to or from Ruovesi, about halfway. On some Fridays in July she also offers a 90-minute evening cruise from Virrat.

ST VISUVESI

Visuvesi at Tampere, 1995.

Length: 20.75m
Propulsion: Single Screw   **Engine type**: Compound, 60hp
Built: 1890
Body of water: Lake Näsijarvi   **Home port**: Tampere
Frequency of operation: Rallies?
Website sddress: www.steamengine.cc/arkisto/koneet/ssvisuvesi.html;
        http://kotisivu.mtv3.fi/nasijarven.rautalaivat/nasi.pdf (page 27)
Builders: Tampereen Pelleva ja Rautateollisuus Oy, Tampere
Owner: Seppo Häkli, Juha Järvinen, Rainer & Pasi Kokemäki, Sauli Korhonen, Lasse Suni, Mikko & Juhani Valanto, Tampere
Former names: *Aure* 1927, *Neptun* 1916, *Neptun II* 1912

1890: Built as the tug **Neptun II** for Oy Neptun.

1912: Renamed **Neptun**.

1916: Sold to Metsähallitus. Renamed **Aure**, moved to Kuru.

1927: Renamed **Visuvesi**. Sold to Visuvesi Oy, moved to Visuvesi.

1960: Withdrawn from service.

1978: Purchased for preservation, moved back to Tampere.

1998: Acquired by present owners.

SS WIRI

Length: 7.80m
Propulsion: Single Screw   **Engine type**: Single-cylinder, 10hp

Wiri on Lake Näsijärvi.
(Suomen Höyrypursiseura)

Built: 1910
Body of water: Lake Näsijarvi **Home port**: Tampere
Frequency of operation: Rallies?
Website address: kotisivu.mtv3.fi/nasijarven.rautalaivat/nasi.pdf (page 28)
Builders: Mäntylän konepaja, Varkaus **Engine builder**: 1916
Owner: M Valanto, Tampere
Former names: *Voima*, *Viri* 1951, *Tykkylänjoki*, 1940 *Saga* 1914
Remarks: Wood-fired

1910: Built as the small passenger launch *Saga* for Axel Lingern, Rantasalmi for use on Lake Saimaa.
1914: Sold to Johannes Ikonen, Sääminki, renamed *Tykkylänjoki*.
1940: Sold to Viktor Salo, Savonlinna, renamed *Viri*.
1941: Sold to Eino Konttinen, Savonlinna.
1943: Sold to Eino A Makkonen, Eninkoski.
1945: Sold to Toivo Kääpö, Punkasalmi.
1951: Sold to Savon Voima Oy, Kuopio, renamed *Voima*.
1954: Sold to Visuvesi Oy, moves to Lake Näsijärvi.
1985: Out of service.
1993: Purchased for preservation by Mikko Valamo.
1985: Out of service.
2000: Renamed *Wiri*. Returned to steam after restoration.

THE LAKE PÄIJÄNNE-KEITELE SYSTEM

Lakes Päijänne and Lake Keitele are connected by a canal opened in 1993.

ST HAAPANIEMI

Haapaniemi on Lake Keitele.
(Suomen Höyrypursiseura)

Length: 18.04m
Propulsion: Single Screw   Engine type: Compound, 85hp
Built: 1905
Body of water: Lake Keitele   Home port: Viitasaari
Frequency of operation: Rallies?
Website address: www.steamengine.cc/arkisto/koneet/sshaapaniemi.html
Builders: Veli Friisenin konepaja, Kokkola   Owner: H. Saraste, Viitasaari
Former name: *Riikko*   Remarks: Wood-fired

1905: Built as the tug *Riikko* for the Lauri Westerinen sawmill on Lake Kivijärvi.
1917: Taken over by SRS (Suomen Valtion Rautatiet) (Finnish State Railways) and moved to Lake Keitele based at Suolahti.
1940: Owners became Rauiatiehallituksen Polttoainettoimisto.
1945: Owners became Valtion Polttoainettoimisto (Vapu).
1954: Sold to Haapaniemi sawmill, renamed *Haapaniemi*.
1967: Withdrawn from service, sold to Erkki Saraste for preservation, later to Heikki Saraste.

SS ILONA

Restaurant steamer *Ilona* at Lahiti, 2004.
(Heikki Helen)

Length: 24.60m   Gross tonnage: 99
Propulsion: Single Screw   Engine type: Compound, 148hp
Built: 1927
Body of water: Lake Päijänne   Home port: Lahti
Frequency of operation: Restaurant ship
Website address: www.steamengine.cc/arkisto/koneet/ssriistavesi.html;
      www.hhlweb.biz/00-ilona.htm
Builders: Lehtoniemi & Taipale, Joroinen
Owner: Happy Consult Oy, Lahti
Former names: *Riistavesi* 2003, *Vehmersalmi* 1970, *Riistavesi* 1968

1927: Built as the passenger steamer *Riistavesi* for Riistaveden-Tuusniemen Höyryvenhe Oy for service on Lake Saimaa.
1945: Sold to Riistavesi Laiva Oy. Operated from Kuopio to Tuovilanlahti.
1956: Sold to Savo Oy. Used as a tug.
1968: Sold to Kauko Hiltunen, Iisalmi. Renamed *Vehmersalmi*.
1970: Used on a service from Kuopio to Iisalmi.
      Renamed *Riistavesi*.
1972: Sold to Kontekla Oy, Olavi Ebeling and Risto Lundén, Helsinki for preservation and use as a private yacht. After deckhouse on the upper-deck removed.
1991: Came under the sole ownership of Risto Lundén.
2000: Sold to Highball Oy, Lahti. Renamed *Ilona*, moved to Lahti, used as a static floating restaurant ship. Her new owner planned to convert her to diesel propulsion but was persuaded otherwise by the Finnish Steam Yachting Association.

ST JOH-PARVAINEN

Joh-Parvainen on Lake Päijänne.
(Suomen Höyrypursiseura)

Length: 21.38m   Gross tonnage: 53.76
Propulsion: Single Screw   Engine type: Compound, 173hp
Built: 1908
Body of water: Lake Päijänne   Home port: Vääksy
Frequency of operation: Rallies?
Website address: www.steamengine.cc/arkisto/koneet/ssjp.html
Builders: Borgå Mek Verstad, Porvoo
Owner: K Manninen Vääksy
Remarks: Wood-fired

1908: Built for Joh-Parvainen Oy, Säynätsalo.
1947: Sold to Enso-Gutzeit Oy, Säynätsalo.
1964: Withdrawn from service, later sold to AV-System Oy, Jyväskylä and Tauno Häkkinen, Vaajakoski for preservation.
1973: Sold to Jorma Manninen, Vääksy, later passed to Katariina Manninen, Vääksy.

SS KAIMA

Small passenger steamer *Kaima* at Haapiniemi, Lake Päijanne, July 2006. (Suomen Höyrypursiseura)

Length: 21.17m   Gross tonnage: 47
Propulsion: Single Screw   Engine type: Compound, 120hp
Built: 1898   Passenger capacity: 20
Body of water: L Päijänne   Home port: Haapiniemi
Frequency of operation: Charters
Website address: www.steamengine.cc/arkisto/kuvaarkistonkuvat/IMG0003.jpg;
www.steelyacht.com/UsedBoats/Kaima.html
Builders: Paul Wahl, Varkaus
Owner: Matti Nieminen: Operator: Jyväskylä-Päijänteen Laiva, Jyväskylä
Remarks: Wood-fired

1898: Built as a small passenger steamer for Jyväskylä-Päijänteen Laiva Oy, Jyväskylä. Operated from Jyväskylä to Korospohja.
1950: Sold to Heinolan Laiva (Kaaninen) for use out of Heinola.
1958: Sold to Olavi Ruutu for preservation.

1986, Sold to Timo Fredriksson.

1998: Sold to Erkki and Matti Nieminen.

2000: New boiler fitted as part of a major restoration.

2005: Up for sale.

Kaima is operated for charters by a company bearing the name of her original owners. She may make occasional public sailings.

SS KEITELE

Keitele at Keitele. (Suomen Höyrypursiseura)

Length: 21.00m
Propulsion: Single Screw   **Engine type:** Compound, 95hp
Built: 1877
Body of water: Lake Keitele
Frequency of operation: Private yacht
Website address: www.steamengine.cc/arkisto/koneet/KEITELE.JPG
Builders: Paul Wahl, Varkaus
Owner: Jouko Korpivaara's family
Former names: *Tiira* 197?, *Äänekoski 1* 1965, *Keitele* 1945
Remarks: Wood-fired

1877: Built as the passenger steamer **Keitele** for William Ruthin for use on Lake Keitele on the route from Äänekoski to Viitasaari.

*c.*1930: Began to be used as a tug. Sold to Äänekoski paper mill.

1941: Owners taken over by Wärtsilä.

1945: Renamed **Äänekoski 1**. Converted to a tug.

1953: Owners taken over by Metsäliiton Selluloosa Oy.

1965: Sold to a private individual for preservation, Renamed **Tiira**.

1970s: Sold to Jouko Korpivaara, Vantaa. Renamed **Keitele**. Now owned by his family.

SL KIRVESNIEMI

Steam launch *Kirvesniemi* on Lake Päijänne. (Suomen Höyrypursiseura)

Length: 8.30m
Propulsion: Single Screw   **Engine type:** ?, 5hp
Built: 1881
Body of water: L Päijänne

Frequency of operation: Rallies?
Website address: www.steamengine.cc/arkisto/koneet/sskirvesniemi.html
Owner: Esko Härö, Espoo

1886: Built
1996: Rebuilt at Lahti. Hull and engine fully restored.

Kirvesniemi can be carried on a trailer and has been used since restoration on all the major lakes in Finland, the Saimaa Canal and coastal waters.

SS LAITIALA

Laitiala as restaurant ship *Hopeasalmi* at Savonlinna, 1995.

Length: 26.80m   **Gross tonnage**: 168
Propulsion: Single Screw   **Engine type**: Compound, 138hp
Built: 1903   **Rebuilt** (most recent): 1998
Passenger capacity: 130
Body of water: Lake Päijänne   **Home port**: Lahti
Frequency of operation: Occasional public trips
Website address: www.lahdenjarvimatkailu.fi
Builders: Paul Wahl, Varkaus
Owner: Lahden Järvimatkailu Oy, Lahti : 0
Former names: *Hopeasalmi* 1998, *Mikkeli II* 1970, *Orivesi II* 1966, *Mikkeli* 1956, *Leppävirta* 1914

1903: Built as *Leppävirta* for Leppävirtan Höyrylaiva Oy for use on Lake Saimaa.
1914: Sold to Höyrylaiva Oy Kerttu, renamed *Mikkeli* for service from Mikkeli.
1951: Owners merged with Saimaan Höyrylaiva Oy.
1956: Renamed *Orivesi II*.
1966: Sold to Mikkelin Suur-Saimaan Laivat Oy. Renamed *Mikkeli II*. Used on the Savonlinna-Mikkeli-Lappenranta triangular route.
1970: Ran aground near Riistina en route from Lappeenranta to Mikkeli. After some years laid-up, sold for use as a static restaurant ship at Savonlinna, renamed *Hopeasalmi*. Fortunately her engines were retained in situ and were restored by her owner.
1980: Opened as a restaurant ship.
1998: Moved to Lahti on Lake Päijänne, renamed *Laitiala*. Completely restored and returned to steam. Used both as a restaurant ship moored at Lahti during the week and for lake cruises. There is a 4.5-hour trip to the Vääksy Canal at 18:30 from Wednesdays to Saturdays, and a 3-hour evening cruise at 19:00. Both are shared with her operator's two motor vessels *Aino* (1922) and *Vellamo*, a Mississippi type sternwheeler. *Laitiala* is mainly used at weekends.

ST METSÄ

Length: 18.67m   **Gross tonnage**: 32.16

Steam tug *Metsä* on Lake Päijänne. (Suomen Höyrypursiseura)

Propulsion: Single Screw   **Engine type**: Compound Diagonal, 104hp
Built: 1877
Body of water: Lake Päijänne   **Home port**: Soimasaari
Frequency of operation: Rallies?
Website address: www.steamengine.cc/arkisto/koneet/ssmetsa.html
Builders: Burgerhout & Kraak, Netherlands
Owner: Esko Härö & Taru Laatu-Härö, Espoo
Former names: *Ragnar*, *Metsä*   **Remarks**: Wood-fired

1898: Used in Holland under an unknown name.
    Sold to Swedish owners, named *Ragnar*.
1925: Purchased by Iisveden Metsä Oy, Iisvesi. Used on Lake Keitele. Renamed *Metsä*.
1927: New boiler fitted.
1956: Converted to oil firing.
1971: Sold to Kari Paussu, Jyväskylä for preservation.
1991: Sold on to Esko and Taru Härö.

SS SUOMI

Suomi at Jyväskylä, 1995.

Length: 31.00m   **Gross tonnage**: 239
Propulsion: Single Screw   **Engine type**: Compound, 200hp
Built: 1906   **Passenger capacity**: 199
Body of water: Lake Päijänne   **Home port**: Jyväskylä
Frequency of operation: Daily   **Period of operation**: Late June to late August
Website address: www.Paijanne-risteilythilden.fi
Builders: Lehtoniemi & Taipale, Joroinen
Owner: Päijänne Risteiliyt Hildén Oy, Haapiniemi

1906: Built for Päijäänteen Höyrylaiva Oy for the route from Lahti to Jyväskylä.
1964: Sold to Päijänneristeilyt Hildén Oy. At some stage her cabins were replaced by passenger saloons.
c.2001: Final year of the all-day Jyväskylä to Lahti sailings. Subsequently operated non-landing cruises out of Jyväskylä, the longer sailings being operated by two motor vessels.
2006: Hull reverted to all-white for her centenary year, having carried the PRH logo of her owners for the previous decade or so.

Suomi is the largest of the Finnish lake steamers and sails from Jyväskylä on 3-hour cruises at 12:00 on Thursdays, Fridays, Saturdays and Sundays only, at 15:00 Mondays excepted, with a 3.5-hour evening cruise at 19:00 Sundays and Mondays excepted.

ST TAPIO

Tapio on Lake Päijänne.
(Suomen Höyrypursiseura)

Length: 18.50m
Propulsion: Single Screw   **Engine type:** Compound, 87hp
Built: 1899
Body of water: Lake Päijänne   **Home port:** Iisvesi
Frequency of operation: Rallies?
Website address: www.steamengine.cc/arkisto/koneet/sstapio.html
Builders: Vulcan, Turku
Owner: Antero Aalto, Vantaa
Former names: *Akkas* 1925
Remarks: Wood-fired

1899: Built as the tug *Akkas* for Peilaveden Metsäosuuskunta for use on Lake Peilavesi.
1911: New boiler fitted.
1925: Renamed *Tapio*.
1986: Purchased for preservation by Antero Aalto.

SL TOIMI

Steam launch *Toimi* at Haapiniemi, July 2006.

Length: 15.55m   **Gross tonnage:** 26.54
Propulsion: Single Screw   **Engine type:** Compound, 57hp
Built: 1898
Body of water: Lake Päijänne   **Home port:** Haapiniemi
Frequency of operation: Rallies?
Website address: www.steamengine.cc/arkisto/koneet/sstoimi.html;
www.xonpuisto.com/index.php?mid=106
Builders: J.D. Stenberg & Söner, Helsinki
Owner: K Sorjonen, Jyväskylä
Remarks: Wood-fired

1898: Built as a saloon steam passenger launch-cum-tug for Julius Johnsson, Jyväskylä, used on a local
service from Jyväskylä to Haapakoski.
1917: Sold to Osuusliike Keskus, Jyväskylä, route now went to Vaajakoski.
1928: Sold to Samuel Peura, now ran from Jyväskylä to Säynätsalo.
1934: Sold to Oy Keskus.
1938: Sold to Laivuri Ville Hämäiänen, Äänekoski, used on Lake Keitele, possibly as a tug.
1940: Present engine installed. Commenced route Suolahti-Äänekoski-Sumainen, which lasted until 1946.

1959: Boiler replaced with a second-hand one, made in 1938.
1961: Now ran from Suolahti to Viitasaari.
1973: Sold to Jorma Manninen, Pertti Hammar and Eero Puranen, Vääksy for preservation.
1976: Eero Puranen now sole owner, later sold to Kauko Sorjonen, Jyväskylä.
1985: Moved to Mikkeli on Lake Saimaa.
2001: Moved back to Lake Päijanne.

ST UURASTAJA

Preserved tug *Uurastaja* at Haapiniemi, July 2006.

Length: 19.87m   **Gross tonnage:** 47.1
Propulsion: Single Screw   **Engine type:** Compound, 93hp
Built: 1908
Body of water: Lake Keitele   **Home port:** Haapiniemi
Frequency of operation: Rallies?
Website address: www.steamengine.cc/arkisto/koneet/ssuurastaja.html
Builders: Paul Wahl, Varkaus
Owner: Kaisa & Pertti Virtanen, & Markku Turunen, Tikkakoski
Former names: *Karl Boström* 1925
Remarks: Wood-fired

1908: Built as the harbour tug *Karl Boström* for Karl Boström, Hanko.
1914: Sold to Tukkukauppa and Laivaliike Hansa, Viipuri/Vyborg. Fitted with a diesel engine.
1925: Sold to sawmill Viipurin Saha Oy, renamed *Uurastaja*.
1930: Sold to Suolahden Tehtaat Oy, Suolahti.
1971: Sold to present owners for preservation.
1972: Present steam-engine fitted.

ST VAAJAKOSKI

Length: 16.60m   **Gross tonnage:** 21.7
Propulsion: Single Screw   **Engine type:** Compound, 88hp
Built: 1920
Body of water: Lake Päijänne   **Home port:** Jyväskylä
Frequency of operation: Rallies?
Website address: www.steamengine.cc/arkisto/koneet/ssvaajakoski.html
Builders: A. Ahlström Oy, Varkaus
Owner: M Nieminen, Jyväskylä
Former names: *Hellnäs*
Remarks: Wood-fired

1920: Built as the tug *Hellnäs* for the sawmill Hellnäs Såg AB, Vaasa.
1941: Sold to SOK, Vaajakoski.
1972: Sold to Pekka Salonen, partner Timo Fredriksson, Jyväskylä, later Pekka Salonen of Muurame
  became the sole owner.

ST VÄNNI

Tug *Vänni* on Lake Päijänne.
(Suomen Höyrypursiseura)

Length: 18.39m
Propulsion: Single Screw   **Engine type:** Compound, 83hp
Built: 1901
Body of water: Lake Päijänne   **Home port:** Vääksy
Frequency of operation: Rallies?
Website address: www.steamengine.cc/arkisto/koneet/ssvanni.html;
www.aj-consultants.com/fiajuva.html
Builders: Borgå Mek Verstad, Porvoo
Owner: Arto Juva, Vääksy
Former names: *Sven*
Remarks: Wood-fired

1901: Built as a tug for Henrik Mattson, Lahti.
1908: Sold to Oy Tornator, Lahti.
1932: Sold to Enso-Gutzeit Oy.
1970: Sold to Arto Juva, Vääksy for preservation.

ST YHTIÖ

Length: 15.30m   **Gross tonnage:** 21.66
Propulsion: Single Screw   **Engine type:** Compound, 41hp
Built: 1878
Body of water: Lake Päijänne   **Home port:** Haapiniemi
Frequency of operation: Rallies?
Website address: www.steamengine.cc/arkisto/koneet/ssyhtio.html
Builders: Paul Wahl, Varkaus
Owner: Juha Lahtinen, Jyväskylä
Remarks: Wood-fired

1878: Built as a tug for Kymin Uittoyhdistys.
1966: Withdrawn from service.
1976: Sold to Erkki Nieminen and Juha Kytölä, Jyväskylä, later sold to Juha Lahtinen, Vaajakoski.

LAKE SAIMAA

ST AHTI

Length: 21.03m   **Gross tonnage:** 45.76
Propulsion: Single Screw   **Engine type:** Compound, 97hp
Built: 1892
Body of water: Lake Saimaa   **Home port:** Savonlinna

Frequency of operation: Rallies?
Website address: www.steamengine.cc/arkisto/koneet/ssahti.html;
users.kymp.net/p404261a/
Builders: O Eklunder telakka & konepaja, Helsinki
Owner: s/s Ahti perinneyhdistys ry
Former names: *Liitto* 1971, *Saitta* 1958 *Ahti* 1955, *Fiskars I* 1945

1892: Built as the tug **Fiskars I** for Oy Fiskars Ab, Pohja for use at Tammisaari.
1945: Sold to Eino Löflund, Särkisalo, renamed **Ahti**.
1947: Sold to Osuuskunta Metsäliitto Oy. Moved to Lake Saimaa.
1955: Moved to Lake Päijänne, renamed **Saitta**, under the ownership of Metsänomistajain Metsäkeskus Oy.
1958 Returned to Lake Saimaa and the ownership of Osuuskunta Metsäliitto Oy: renamed **Ahti**, later **Liitto**. Based at Lappeenranta.
1971: Sold to Lauri Komulainen, Mikko Komulainen and partners for preservation, renamed **Ahti**.
2003: Sold to s/s **Ahti** perinneyhdistys ry.
2004: Slipped for work on hull.
2005: Work done on boiler tubes.

ST ANSIO

Length: 18.80m   Gross tonnage: 31.79
Propulsion: Single Screw   Engine type: Compound, 80hp
Built: 1889
Body of water: Lake Saimaa   Home port: Juotseno
Frequency of operation: Undergoing restoration
Website address: www.steamengine.cc/arkisto/koneet/ssansio.html
Builders: Tampereen Pelleva ja Rautateollisuus Oy, Tampere
Owner: V. & J. Tuominen, Lappeenranta
Remarks: Wood-fired
Former names: *Kotvio*, *Salmi* 1917, *Carolus*, *Ruija* 1889

1889: Built as the tug **Ruija** for E Feiring, Tampere.
  Sold to Nils Idman, Tampere. Renamed **Carolus**.
Unknown date between 1889 and 1917: Renamed **Salmi**.
1891: Sold to E Lehtinen, Tampere.
1904: Sold to Juho Mäntynen, Tampere.
1907: Sold to Jussi Virtanen.
1917: Sold to Kotvio Oy, Ruovesi, renamed **Kotvio**.
1944: Sold to Reino & Tauno Saarinen. Moved to Lake Päijänne.
1975: Sold to Pertti Hammar, Lahti for preservation. Renamed **Ansio**.
Unknown date: Sold to Johanna Tuominen, Lappeenranta, moved to Lake Saimaa.

ST ANTERO

Antero, with *Halla XVII* nearest the quay, Savonlinna, 1995.

Length: 18.41m   Gross tonnage: 37.47
Propulsion: Single Screw   Engine type: Compound, 125hp
Built: 1924
Body of water: Lake Saimaa   Home port: Puumala
Frequency of operation: Rallies?
Website address: www.steamengine.cc/arkisto/koneet/ssantero.html
Builders: Lehtoniemi & Taipale, Joroinen
Owner: A. & A. Juva, Espoo
Remarks: Wood-fired
Former name: *Hero*

1924: Built as the tug *Hero* for Valtion Rautitiot.
1945: Sold to VAPO.
1961: Sold to Löydön Saha (sawmill).
1973: Sold to Arja & Ari Juva for preservation. Renamed *Antero*.

ST HALLA IX

Halla IX in a winter scene on Lake Saimaa.
(Suomen Höyrypursiseura)

Length: 15.60m   Gross tonnage: 34.03
Propulsion: Single Screw   Engine type: Compound, 100hp
Built: 1896   Passenger capacity: 12
Body of water: Lake Saimaa   Home port: Savonlinna
Frequency of operation: Rallies?
Website address: www.steamengine.cc/arkisto/koneet/sshallaix.html
Builders: J.D. Stenberg & Söner, Helsinki
Owner: P. Hammar, Lahti
Remarks: Wood-fired

1896: Built as a tug or Halla AB, Kotka. Used on Lake Saimaa, mainly at Iisalmi and on Kallavesi.
1932: Sold to Kymin OY, Kotka and Mikkeli.
1968: Sold to Ilmari Lindberg.
1978: Sold to Pertti Hammar, Lahti for preservation.

ST HALLA XVII

Halla XVII on Lake Saimaa, 1995.

Length: 21.90m   **Gross tonnage**: 58.71
Propulsion: Single Screw   **Engine type**: Compound, 192hp
Built: 1908
Passenger capacity: 12
Body of water: Lake Saimaa   **Home port**: Savonlinna
Frequency of operation: Charters
Website address: www.steamengine.cc/arkisto/koneet/sshallaxvii.html;
     www.lakelandsteamship.com/
Builders: Kotkan Rauta Oy, Kotka
Owner: Saimaan Höyrymatkat
Remarks: Wood-fired

1908: Built for Halla AB, Kotka.
1932: Sold to Kymin Oy, Kotka and Mikkeli.
1971: Sold to Erkki Riimala, Helsinki, later to Reijo Valkonen, Espoo.
2005 (?): Sold to present owners.

Unlike the majority of the preserved tugs in Finland, **Halla XVII** is available for charter, and is advertised in the Savonlinna tourist brochure.

ST HEIKKI PEURANEN

Heikki Peuranaen at Lappeenranta, July 2006.
(Suomen Höyrypursiseura)

Length: 23.07m   **Gross tonnage**: 62.61
Propulsion: Single Screw   **Engine type**: Triple Expansion, 310hp
Built: 1897
Body of water: Lake Saimaa   **Home port**: Savonlinna
Frequency of operation: Rallies?
Website address: www.steamengine.cc/arkisto/koneet/ssheikkipeuranen.html
Builders: Gallenin konepaja, Viipuri (Vyborg)
Owner: A. Mökkönen, J. Larvanto, Mikkeli and K. Eerola, Vantaa
Former name: *P25*
Remarks: Wood-fired

1897: Built for the Russian Navy as the tug **P25**.
1917: Seized by Finland as war reparations, purchased by Enso-Gutzeit Oy.
1968: Sold to Mirja and Seppo Yläsaari, Espoo for preservation, later to A. Mökkinen, J. Larvanto, Mikkeli and K. Eerola, Vantaa.
2005: 25 June: Grounded and partly sank near Puumula. Later raised and repaired.

SS HEINÄVESI

Length: 26.90m   **Gross tonnage**: 145
Propulsion: Single Screw   **Engine type**: Compound, 150hp

Heinävesi off Savonlinna, 1995.

Built: 1906 **Passenger capacity**: 126
Body of water: Lake Saimaa **Home port**: Savonlinna
Frequency of operation: Daily **Period of operation**: Early June to mid-August
Website address: www.rarikilpi.com/slnlaivat
Builders: Paul Wahl, Varkaus
Owner: Savolinnan Laivat Oy
Former names: *Heinävesi I* 1976, *Heinävesi* 1907

1906: Built as ***Heinävesi*** for Heinävaden Höyrylaiva Oy the route from Kuopio via Heinävesi to Savonlinna.
1907: Renamed ***Heinävesi I***.
1965: Converted to oil firing.
1967: Owners became part of Saimaan Laivamatkat Oy.
1976: Renamed ***Heinävesi***.
1982: Spring: After Saimaan Laivamatkat Oy had become bankrupt, all steamers in the fleet were sold at auction. ***Heinävesi*** was sold to Savonlinnan Laivat Oy. Placed in service from Savonlinna to Punkaharju.

Heinävesi operates a daily return service to Punkaharju, leaving Savonlinna at 11:00, calling there at both the Retretti and Valtionhotelli jetties, with an afternoon non-landing cruise from Punkaharju. Prior to the main season from the beginning to the middle of June, short trips are offered at Savonlinna.

ST HURMA

Length: 23.60m
Propulsion: Single Screw **Engine type**: Compound, 216hp
Built: 1902
Body of water: Lake Saimaa **Home port**: Lappeenranta
Frequency of operation: Rallies?
Website address: www.steamengine.cc/arkisto/koneet/sshurma.html
Builders: Viipurin konepaja, Viipuri (Vyborg)
Owner: UPM-Kymmene Metsä, Lappeenranta

1902: Built as a tug for J.E. Salvesen.
1906: Owners now Kaukas Oy.
1969: Withdrawn from service.
1975: Sold to UPM-Kymmene Metsä, Lappeenranta.

ST JANNE

Length: 20.17m **Gross tonnage**: 52
Propulsion: Single Screw **Engine type**: Compound, 165hp
Built: 1907

Janne on Lake Saimaa. (Suomen Höyrypursiseura)

Body of water: Lake Saimaa   **Home port:** Savonlinna
Frequency of operation: Rallies?
Website address: www.steamengine.cc/arkisto/koneet/ssjanne.html
Builders: Savonlinnan konepaja/Paul Wahl, Varkaus
Owner: L. Korpivaara, Tammisaari
Remarks: Wood-fired
Former names: *Rannikko* 1913, *Nerkoo* 1912

1907: Built as the tug *Nerkoo* for an owner at Puruvesi, later sold to Nerkoon Höyryvenhe Oy.
1912: Sold to M Koistinen, Nurmes, renamed *Rannikko*.
1913: Sold to Nerkoon Saha, later to Enso-Gutzeit Oy, Savonlinna. Renamed *Janne*.
1966: Sold to Jouko Korpivaara, Vantaa for preservation.
1992: Boiler accident after fire tube fractured: Owner and boiler inspector killed, twelve-year-old son of
   owner escaped through the wood (fuel) hatch and survived.

ST JUNO

Juno on Lake Saimaa. (Suomen Höyrypursiseura)

Length: 17.80m   **Gross tonnage:** 31.83
Propulsion: Single Screw   **Engine type:** Compound, 77hp
Built: 1907
Body of water: Lake Saimaa   **Home port:** Ristiina
Frequency of operation: Rallies?
Website address: www.steamengine.cc/arkisto/koneet/ssjuno.html
Builders: Borgå Mekaniska Verkstad, Porvoo
Owner: S. & J. Puro, Helsinki
Former names: *Taunola 2*, *Juno*
Remarks: Wood-fired

1907: Built for Porin Tulitikkutehday Oy as the tug *Juno* for use at Pori. Also used as a passenger steamer.
1938: Sold to Nurmisen Saha Oy, Korpilahti, renamed *Taunola 2*.
1970: Sold to A S Härö for preservation, renamed *Juno*, later sold to Sohvi & Jaakki Puro, Helsinki.

SS KALLE TIHVERÄINEN

Kalle Tihveräinen on Lake Saimaa, 1995.

Length: 27.00m   **Gross tonnage:** 88.41
Propulsion: Single Screw   **Engine type:** Compound, 60hp
Built: 1916
Body of water: Lake Saimaa   **Home port:** Mähkö
Frequency of operation: Rallies?
Website address: www.steamengine.cc/arkisto/koneet/sskalletihverainen.html
Builders: Lehtoniemi & Taipale, Joroinen
Owner: T. Lehto, Savonlinna, & P. Roiton säätiö (foundation), Helsinki
Former names: *Puristaja IV* 1967, *Savo* 1957
Remarks: Wood-fired

1916: Built as the 'tar steamer' *Savo* for H. Saastamoinen & Pojat Oy, Kuopio.

1954: Sold to Emil Kauhanen, Leppävirta.

1956: Sunk after overloaded with a cargo of cement. Later raised.

1957: Sold to Enso-Gutzeit Oy, Savonlinna, rebuilt as a wood-bundling steamer.

1958: Renamed *Puristaja IV*.

1967: Sold to Tero Lehto, Savonlinna and Pentti Roitto, Helsinki for preservation.

Kalle Tihverainen is used as the lead and commodore ship for the Lake Saimaa regattas of the Finnish Steam Yacht Society.

SS KARJALANKOSKI

Karjalankoski at Suur Saimaa Pier, 1982.

Length: 24.30m   **Gross tonnage:** 107
Propulsion: Single Screw   **Engine type:** Compound, 134hp
Built: 1905
Body of water: Lake Saimaa   **Home port:** Riistina

Frequency of operation: Rallies?
Website address: www.steamengine.cc/arkisto/koneet/sskarjalankoski.html
Builders: Lehtoniemi & Taipale, Joroinen
Owner: O. Ebeling, Helsinki
Former name: *Apollo*, *Karjalankoski* 1967

1905: Built as the passenger steamer **Karjalankoski** for Kosken Höyryvenhe Oy for service from Kuopio to Karjalankoski.
1967: Became part of the fleet of Saimaan Laivamatkat Oy, renamed **Apollo**, later regaining the name **Karjalankoski**. At some stage the aft accommodation on her upper deck was removed.
1982: Following the bankruptcy of Saimaan Laivamatkat Oy, sold to Imatran Höyrylaiva Oy for use on excursions out of Imatra. She mainly operated short non-landing trips, but did a day cruise to the Suur Saimaa holiday camp each Thursday.
1990: Owners bankrupt.
1991: Sold to Olavi and Jussi Ebeling for private use as a steam yacht based at Riistina.

ST KEIHÄSLAHTI

Keihäslahti on Lake Saimaa.
(Suomen Höyrypursiseura)

Length: 15.20m
Propulsion: Single Screw   Engine type: Compound, 37hp
Built: 1900
Body of water: Lake Saimaa   Home port: Joensuu
Frequency of operation: Rallies?
Website address: www.steamengine.cc/arkisto/koneet/sskeihaslahti.html
Builders: Lehtoniemi & Taipale, Joroinen
Owner: Schauman Wood Oy, Kuopio
Remarks: Wood-fired
Former name: *Unnukka*

ST LAURI

Length: 19.90m   Gross tonnage: 47.33
Propulsion: Single Screw   Engine type: Compound, 130hp
Built: 1931
Body of water: Lake Saimaa   Home port: Savonlinna
Frequency of operation: Rallies?
Website address: www.steamengine.cc/arkisto/koneet/sslauri.html
Builders: A. Ahlström Oy, Varkaus
Owner: A. Lehto, Mexico City & E. Pakkanen, Valkeakoski
Remarks: Wood-fired

Lauri at Savonlinna, 1995.

1931: Built as a tug for Valtioin Rautatiet, Lappeenranta.

1945: Sold to Vapo, Lappeenranta.

1968: Withdrawn from service.

1971: Sold to Harri Lallukka, and Tero Lehto, Savonlinna and Pentti Roitto, Helsinki for preservation, later Esko Pakkanen purchased Pentti Roitto's share and Antti Lehto inherited Tero Lehto's share.

SS LEPPÄVIRTA

Leppävirta at Kuopio, 1995.

Length: 26.90m   Gross tonnage: 161
Propulsion: Single Screw   Engine type: Compound, 129hp
Built: 1904   Passenger capacity: 127
Body of water: Lake Saimaa   Home port: Leppävirta
Frequency of operation: 3x daily
Builders: Paul Wahl, Varkaus
Owner: Leppävirta Kunta
Former name: *Leppävirta II* 1976

1904: Built as *Leppävirta II* for Leppävirtan Höyrylaiva Oy for the Kuopio to Savonlinna service via Leppävirta and Varkaus.

1953: Started the 'week on Lake Saimaa cruises' which combined various regular routes in a week's cruise from Savonlinna to Lappeenranta and back and then from Savonlinna to Kuopio and back, one way via Varkaus and the other way via Heinävesi.

1955: Rebuilt to give her more cabin accommodation.

*c.*1965: Converted to oil-firing.

1967: Sold to Saimaan Laivamatkat Oy.

1976: Renamed *Leppävirta*.

1977: Moved to the Savonlinna-Mikkeli and Savonlinna-Lappenranta routes.

1982: Following the bankruptcy of Saimaan Laivamatkat, sold to Leppävirtan Kunta (local authority). Chartered to Roll Laivat, Kuopio. Operated the 'week on Lake Saimaa cruises' from Kuopio via Heinävesi to Savonlinna and on to Punkaharju, returning via Varkaus.

1990: Roll Laivat went bankrupt. New operator Roll Line took over.

1993: Roll Line now bankrupt, Roll Risteilyt took over.

1996: April: Kallaveden Höyrylaiva Oy, who were chartering her, went bankrupt. She was then run by her owners with only a handful of trips each year from Leppävirta.

1998: Chartered by Roll Risteilyt for short trips out of Kuopio.

2002: Autumn: Ran aground near Varkaus.

2002-03: Winter: Sank at Laitaatsilta shipyard. Raised and repaired.

2006: Was expected to be back in service out of Leppävirta, but was seen on land at a shipyard near Savonlinna.

SS LOKKI

Lokki arriving at Kuopio, 1995.

Length: 24.40m   **Gross tonnage**: 99.99
Propulsion: Single Screw   **Engine type**: Compound, 129hp
Built: 1913
Passenger capacity: 80
Body of water: Lake Saimaa   **Home port**: Savonlinna
Frequency of operation: Awaiting restoration
Website address: www.steamengine.cc/arkisto/koneet/sslokki.html
Builders: Paul Wahl, Varkaus
Owner: Kuopion Roll Risteilyt Oy, Kuopio

1913: Built as a passenger steamer for Kasurilan Höyryvenhe Oy for the route from Kuopio to Siilinjärvi and Pajukoski.

1916: Taken over by Kuopion Höyryvenhe Oy, later sold to Pohjois-Kallaveden Höyrylaiva Oy, Kuopio. Operated from Kuopio to Riistavesi.

1971: Service ceased. Taken over by Auto-Prima R W Stellberg Ky, Helsinki. Used as a private yacht.

1978: Transferred to Roll-Laivat, which was then owned by R W Stellberg, for excursions sailings out of Kuopio.

1981: Operated trips out of Iisalmi, returned to Kuopio the following season

1990: Roll Laivat went bankrupt. New operator Roll Line took over.

1993: Roll Line now bankrupt, Roll Risteilyt took over.

1997: Sank at Laitaatsilta shipyard, Savonlinna. Raised but not repaired.

Lokki faces an uncertain future as her owners have no money to restore her.

SS MIKKO

Length: 30.90m   **Gross tonnage**: 212
Propulsion: Single Screw   **Engine type**: Compound, 79hp
Built: 1914   **Rebuilt** (most recent): 1970
Body of water: Lake Saimaa   **Home port**: Savonlinna
Frequency of operation: Occasional public trips

Mikko at Savonlinna Museum harbour with statically preserved steamer *Salama* ahead of her, 1981.

Website address: www.savonlinna.fi/museo/museumships.htm
Builders: Savonlinna Konepaja Oy, Savonlinna
Owner: Savonlinna maakuntamuseo
Former name: *Ensi*
Remarks: Wood-fired

1914: Built as the 'tar steamer' **Ensi** for Frans Vilenius. (The Tar Steamer was the archetypical cargo steamer of Lake Saimaa, so named because the hull was wooden and covered in tar. They were of a standard length of 31m to as fit the locks of the Saimaa Canal, and were the Finnish equivalent of the Clyde puffer.) Based at Koivosto, sailing on Lake Ladoga, the River Svir and Lake Onega.
1920: Sold to Oy Faner Ab.
1925: Sold to Andreas Wagner & Söner.
1931: Sold to Toivo Kari.
1935: Sold to Maija Wager.
1937: 9 November. Purchased by Enso-Gutzeit Oy. Transferred to Lake Saimaa.
1938: Renamed **Mikko**.
1963: Laid-up.
1970: Acquired by Savonlinna Museum for preservation. Restored to operating condition.
1993: Made a special cruise from Savonlinna to Kotka.

Mikko is normally a static museum exhibit, but she is available for charter and makes occasional special cruises in connection with special events in the area.

ST OBERON III

Oberon III on Lake Saimaa, 1995.

Length: 26.18m   **Gross tonnage**: 77.09
Propulsion: Single Screw   **Engine type**: Compound, 203hp
Built: 1919
Body of water: Lake Saimaa   **Home port**: Savonlinna
Frequency of operation: Rallies?
Website address: www.steamengine.cc/arkisto/koneet/ssoberoniii.html;
www.aj-consultants.com/fiajuva.html
Builders: A. Ahlström Oy, Varkaus

Owner: M. Cederqvist, Lahti, I. Mäkinen, Pirkkala, M. Ruutu, Varkaus, A. Juva & A. Sipilä, Vääksy
Remarks: Wood-fired

1914: Built as a tug for her builders. Used on log tows from Joensuu to Varkaus.
1968: Sold to Tehdaspuu Oy.
1970: Sold to Harri Lallukka, Tero Lehto, Esko Pakkanen and Pentti Roitto for preservation, later sold to
   M Cederqvist, Lahti, I Mäkinen, Pirkkala, M Ruutu, Varkaus, A. Juva & A. Sipila, Vääksy.

ST OLLI

Olli at Mikkeli, July 2006. (Suomen Höyrypursiseura)

Length: 19.25m   Gross tonnage: 39.48
Propulsion: Single Screw   Engine type: Compound, 149hp
Built: 1920
Body of water: Lake Saimaa   Home port: Mikkeli
Frequency of operation: VIP cruises
Website address: www.steamengine.cc/arkisto/koneet/ssolli.html
Builders: Lehtoniemi & Taipale, Joroinen
Owner: Olavi Räsänen Oy, Mikkeli
Former Names: *Halla XV*, *Otso*

1920: Built as the tug *Otso* for Oy Lauttauskalusto, Värtsilä.
1939: Laid-up.
1947: Sold to Kymin Oy, Mikkeli, renamed *Halla XV*, returned to service.
1969: Sold to Olavi Räsänen Oy, Mikkeli, for preservation, renamed *Olli*. Rebuilt to carry passengers,
   makes VIP cruises for her owners, who own a sawmill and manufacture wooden products.

ST OTSO

Otso at Varkaus, 1995.

Length: 15.58m   Net tonnage: 30
Propulsion: Single Screw   Engine type: Compound, 74hp
Built: 1919
Body of water: Lake Saimaa   Home port: Varkaus

Frequency of operation: Rallies?
Website address: www.steamengine.cc/arkisto/koneet/ssotso.html
Builders: A. Ahlström Oy, Varkaus
Owner: J. Hulkkonen, Varkaus

1919: Built for Ahlström (Karhula Oy), Varkaus.

1964: Sold to Lars Colliander, Helsinki for preservation.

1971: Sold to Lauri Komulainaen, Helsinki.

1972: Sold to Tapani Virkili, Helsinki.

1974: Sold to Jarmo Ruutu, Varkaus.

1995: Sold to Jukka Hulkkonen, Varkaus after death of previous owner.

ST PALLAS

Length: 18.30m
Propulsion: Single Screw   **Engine type**: Compound, 124hp
Built: 1923
Body of water: Lake Saimaa   **Home port**: Leppävirta
Frequency of operation: Rallies?
Website address: www.student.oulu.fi/~mikar/pallas.html
Builders: A. Ahlström Oy, Varkaus
Owner: A. Holopainen & J. Ruusunen

1923: Built as a tug for Lohjan Kalkki Oy.

1967: Withdrawn from service.

1970: Purchased for preservation by Allan Holopainen and Jouko Ruusunen.

1971: Converted to oil-firing.

1970s: New passenger deck saloon added aft of funnel.

1989-90: Major overhaul.

1996: Individual cabins altered to form an 11-bed accommodation area.

IST PAPINNIEMI

Length: 19.80m   **Gross tonnage**: 46.29
Propulsion: Single Screw   **Engine type**: Compound, 80hp
Built: 1905   **Passenger capacity**: 12
Body of water: Lake Saimaa   **Home port**: Mikkeli
Frequency of operation: Charters
Website address: www.steamengine.cc/arkisto/koneet/PAPINNIEMI.JPG
Builders: Lehtoniemi & Taipale, Joroinen
Owner: A. & L. Reunanen, Lieto
Remarks: Wood-fired
Former name: *Karttula*

1905: Built as the passenger steamer *Karttula* for Oy H Saastamoinen Ltd, Kuopio.

1914: Converted to a tug and renamed *Papinniemi*.

1967: Withdrawn from service.

1969: Sold to Pentti Rantakoski and Esa Maimivaara, Kuopio for preservation.

1975: Sold to Pentti Julkunen and Juoko Kerte, Kuopio, later sold to Ari Reunanen, Mikkeli and Olli Kortman, Helsinki, then to Ari and Leena Reunanen, Lieto.

Papinniemi operates charters on occasion.

ST PARSIFAL

Parsifal at Savonlinna, 1982.

Length: 21.30m
Propulsion: Single Screw   **Engine type:** Compound, 173hp
Built: 1915
Body of water: Lake Saimaa   **Home port:** Sulkava
Frequency of operation: Rallies?
Website address: www.steamengine.cc/arkisto/koneet/ssparsifal.html
Builders: A. Ahlström Oy, Varkaus
Owner: S. Törnqvist, Helsinki
Remarks: Wood-fired

1915: Built as a tug for her builders.
1960s: Withdrawn from service and sold for preservation.

SS PAUL WAHL

Paul Wahl at Varkaus 1995.

Length: 27.00m   **Gross tonnage:** 125
Propulsion: Single Screw   **Engine type:** Compound, 150hp
Built: 1919   **Passenger capacity:** 99
Body of water: Lake Saimaa   **Home port:** Savonlinna
Frequency of operation: 5x daily   **Period of operation:** June to August
Website address: www.vipcruise.info
Builders: A. Ahlström, Varkaus
Owner: Oy VIP Cruise Ltd, Savonlinna
Former names: *Paasivesi*, *Joensuu* 1976, *Mikkeli* 1970, *Vehmersalmi* 1959, *Maaninka* 1939

1919: Built as the passenger steamer ***Maaninka*** for Maaningan-Pielaveden Höyryvenhe Oy for the route
   from Kuopio to Tuovilanlahti.

1939: Sold to Vehmersalmen Höyrywenhe Oy. Renamed *Vehmersalmi* for the service from Savonlinna to Vehmersalmi.

1959: Sold to Suur Saimaan Laivat Oy, renamed *Mikkeli* for the route from Mikkeli and Lappenranta to Savonlinna. Partially rebuilt for tourist traffic.

1967: Owners became part of Saimaan Laivamatkat Oy.

*c.*1970: Renamed *Joensuu*. Placed on the Savonlinna to Joensuu route.

1976: Renamed *Paasivesi*.

1982: At the auction following the bankruptcy of Saimaan Laivamatkat, sold to Varkaus town council. Renamed *Paul Wahl*, in honour of original owner of her builders yard, which was taken over by Ahlström in 1909/1910.

1986: Entered service for the enthusiast group Taipaleen Laivaosakeyhtiö.

2005: Her last season operating out of Varkaus. Because of economic difficulties Varkaus town council sold the ship after the 2005 summer season, and cancelled the operating contract with Taipaleen Laivaosakeyhtiö.

September: Sold to VIP Cruise Ltd, Savonlinna, and sailed to Savonlinna.

2006: 1 June to 30 August: Scheduled to operate short trips from Savonlinna every 2 hours from 12:00 to 20:00.

ST PEURA III

Length: 12.20m
Propulsion: Single Screw   Engine type: Compound, 43hp
Built: 1905
Body of water: Lake Saimaa   Home port: Kuopio
Frequency of operation: Private yacht
Builders: Lehtoniemi & Taipale, Joroinen
Owner: V. Karjalainen, Kuopio
Former names: *Wuotjärvi*
Remarks: Wood-fired

1905: Built as the tug *Wuotjärvi* for NSR.

1937: Sold to H Peura Oy, renamed *Peura III*.

1960s: Withdrawn and sold for preservation.

SS PUHOIS

Length: 23.70m
Propulsion: Single Screw   Engine type: Compound, 62hp
Built: 1925
Body of water: Lake Saimaa   Home port: Savonlinna
Frequency of operation: Rallies?
Website address: www.steamengine.cc/arkisto/koneet/sspuhois.html
Builders: Enso-Gutzeit Oy, Tainionkoski
Owner: N. Rantapuu, E. Ramirez & Rantapuu Oy, Nummela
Remarks: Wood-fired
Former names: *Puristaja I, Sampo*

1925: Built as the wood-bundling steamer *Sampo* for Enso-Gutzeit Oy, Savonlinna

1940s: Renamed *Puristaja I*.

1962: Final year in commercial service.

1968: Sold to Jorma J. Kontturi, Helsinki, for preservation, later sold to present owners and renamed *Puhois*.

SS PUNKAHARJU

Punkaharju at Savonlinna, 1982.

Length: 22.50m   **Gross tonnage:** 73
Propulsion: Single Screw   **Engine type:** Compound, 92hp
Built: 1905   **Passenger capacity:** 134
Body of water: Lake Saimaa   **Home port:** Savonlinna
Frequency of operation: Daily   **Period of operation:** 1 June to 31 August
Website address: www.savonlinnatravel.com/en/index_ie.php?sivu=kohteet
      www.vipcruise.info
Builders: Emil Kiiveri, Savonlinna
Owner: Oy VIP Cruise Ltd
Former names: *Taimi III* 1999, *Punkaharju* c.1988, *Kerttu* 1960, *Osuukunta I* 1949

1905: Built for Höyryvenhe Osuuskunta Yritklsaltä as the passenger steamer *Osuukunta I* for the route from Savonlinna to Vuoriniemi.

1913: Damaged by an engine room fire, later repaired.

1934: Sold to Höyryvenhe Oy Kerttu.

1949: Renamed *Kerttu*.

1951: Owners merged with Saimaan Höyrylaiva Oy, taking the latter company's name. Used on the route from Savonlinna to Punkaharju.

1960: Renamed *Punkaharju*.

1965: Taken over by Saimaan Linjat. Operated short excursions out of Savonlinna

1968: Owners became Saimaan Laivamatkat Oy.

1982: On the bankruptcy of Saimaan Laivamatkat sold at auction to Martti Sieranta, Helsinki, who formed Punkaharjun Laivat Oy to continue to operate her on trips from Savonlinna.

1987: Sold to Hotelli Joensuun Karelia Oy. Operated out of Joensuu, from the Jakokoski Canal Museum.

c.1988: Renamed *Taimi III*.

1990: Now owned by Karjalan Lomanmatkat.

1991: Out of service.

1993: Operated out of Lappeenranta for El Faro Lines and the Hotel Patria.

1999: Sold to current owners and moved back to Savonlinna, renamed *Punkaharju*.

Punkaharju operates non-landing cruises from Savonlinna every 2 hours from 11:00 to 19:00 during her operating season. Unlike most of the other surviving Finnish Lake steamers, she has no deckhouse aft on the upper deck and no cabin accommodation. She is a very tender vessel and passenger numbers may be limited on her upper deck.

ST RAUHA

Length: 25.95m   **Gross tonnage:** 73.93
Propulsion: Single Screw   **Engine type:** Compound, 180hp
Built: 1878

Rauha on Lake Saimaa.
(Suomen Höyrypursiseura)

Body of water: Lake Saimaa   **Home port**: Savonlinna
Frequency of operation: Rallies?
Website address: www.steamengine.cc/arkisto/koneet/ssrauha.html
Builders: Viipurin konepaja, Viipuri (Vyborg)
Owner: T. Kurhela, Nurmijärvi
Former names: *Humppa*, *Rauha*

1878: Built as the tug **Rauha** for Gustav Cederberg & Co.
1920: Sold to Kaukas Fabrik Ab.
1924: Used on tows from Joensuu to Kaukas.
1968: Sold to Tehdaspuu Oy.
1970: Sold to Harri H. Lallukka, Tero Lehto, Esko Pakkanen and Pentti Roitto for preservation.
1977: Sold to Paavo Airas, Helsinki, later to Taisto Kurhela, Nurmijärvi.

ST REPOLA 5

Repola 5 on Lake Saimaa, 1995.

Length: 21.37m
Propulsion: Single Screw   **Engine type**: Compound, 142hp
Built: 1904
Body of water: Lake Saimaa   **Home port**: Savonlinna
Frequency of operation: Rallies?
Website address: www.steamengine.cc/arkisto/koneet/ssrepola5.html
Builders: Lehtoniemi & Taipale, Joroinen
Owner: H. Poutianen, Lahti
Former names: *P Roitto*, *Repola 5*, *Matti* 1935, *Pielavesi* 1907
Remarks: Wood-fired

1904: Built as **Pielavesi** for use as a tug-cum-passenger steamer on Pielavesi.
1907: Sold to Kärkkäinen & Putkonen, Iisalmi, renamed **Matti**.
1935: Sold to Rauma-Repola Oy, renamed **Repola 5**.
1960s: Retained by her owners as a museum tug, later sold for private preservation.

SL RITO

Length: 8.20m
Propulsion: Single Screw   **Engine type**: Compound, 7-8hp
Built: 1906
Body of water: Lake Saimaa   **Home port**: Ristiina
Frequency of operation: Undergoing restoration
Website address: www.steamengine.cc/arkisto/koneet/ssrito.html
Owner: J Reunanen, Ristiina
Former name: *Nina*
Remarks: Wood-fired

1906: Built as a steam passenger launch for use on Lake Päijänne, later moved to Lake Saimaa.
c.1960: Sold to Heikki Kuosmanen, Nurmes.
1972: Sold to Pertti Hammar, Lahti for preservation.
1977: Sold to Jyrki I Reunanen, Mikkeli. *Rito* is the smallest steamer on Lake Saimaa.

SS SAIMAA

Length: 24.70m   **Gross tonnage**: 71.23
Propulsion: Single Screw   **Engine type**: Compound, 180hp
Built: 1893
Body of water: Lake Saimaa   **Home port**: Savonlinna
Frequency of operation: Special trips
Website address: www.steamengine.cc/arkisto/koneet/sssaimaa.html;
      www.fma.fi/vapaa_aikaan/kanavat/saimaa.php?page=saimaa_sssaimaa
Builders: Wm Crichton & Co., Turku
Owner: Merenkulkulaitos, Helsinki
Remarks: Wood-fired

1893: Built as a pilot steamer for the Saimaa and Kallavesi Pilotage District of Suomen Luotsi – ja Majakkalaitos for use on Lake Saimaa and on the Saimaa Canal, also operated on the Gulf of Finland. Based at Lappeenranta.
1894: Prince Mikhail Alexandrovich sailed on *Saimaa* during Tsar Alexander III's traditional cruise in the Gulf of Finland and south-western archipelago. *Saimaa* was one of a group of ten ships, mainly used to protect the Tsar.
1914: Used on a tour of Lake Ladoga by the governor-general of Finland.
1917: Owners now Suomen Merenkulkulaitos (the National Board of Navigation) after the independence of Finland.
1918: Home port changed to Savonlinna.
1919: From now on used as a light and buoy inspection steamer.
1925: New boiler fitted.
1939: Transferred to the Gulf of Finland. Used as a staff vessel.
1941-42: Based at Kotka, used by the Vyborg Pilotage District.
1941: 4 July: Damaged by air attacks whilst at Kotka.
1942: November: returned to Lake Saimaa.
1977: From now on regularly present at regattas of Suomen Höyrypursiseura (the Finnish Steam Yacht Club).
1980: Now used as PR steamer.
1984: Visited Helsinki.
1989-90: Major refit.
1990: Visited Kotka.
1993: Visited Turku.

Saimaa remains in service for the Finnish Maritime Administration which maintains the navigation aids on Lake Saimaa, although nowadays it is mainly used for PR purposes.

SL SATU

Satu at Lappeenranta, July 2006.

Length: 12.90m
Propulsion: Single Screw   **Engine type**: Compound, 40hp
Built: 1909,
Body of water: Lake Saimaa   **Home port**: Leppävirta
Frequency of operation: Rallies?
Website address: www.steamengine.cc/arkisto/koneet/sssatus.html
Builders: Lehtoniemi & Taipale, Joroinen
Owner: Pekka Buuri, Lappeenranta
Former names: *Ilmi*, *Hiekka*
Remarks: Wood-fired

1909: Built as a steam launch for Hiekan Höyryvenhe Oy, Viipuri, later sold to Annalan sawmill (Laatokanalue), and then to Karjalan Metsätoute Oy, Lappeenranta. At some stage in her career she was lengthened by 1.5m.

1957: Sold to Väinö Buuri, Lappeenranta for preservation, restored, later sold to Pekka Buuri, Lappeenranta.

SS SAVONLINNA

Savonlinna at Savonlinna
Museum harbour, 1995.

Length: 27.90m   **Gross tonnage**: 169
Propulsion: Single Screw   **Engine type**: Compound, 200hp
Built: 1903   **Passenger capacity**: 134
Body of water: Lake Saimaa   **Home port**: Savonlinna
Frequency of operation: Charters
Website address: www.savonlinna.fi/museo/museumships.htm

Builders: Paul Wahl, Varkaus
Owner: Savonlinna maakuntamuseo : o
Former names: *Suur Saimaa* 1982, *Savonlinna* 1976
Remarks: Wood-fired

1903: Built as the passenger steamer **Savonlinna** for Saimaan Höyrylaiva Oy for the route from Lappenranta to Savonlinna. She was the fastest steamer on the lake and was unofficially known as the **Saimaa Express**.

1904: 20 May: Entered service.

1920s: Transferred to the Savonlinna-Vuoksenniska-Lappenranta route.

1927: 20 April: Seriously damaged by fire. Rebuilt.

1951: Owners merged with Höyryvenhe Oy Kerttu.

1964: Converted to oil firing.

1965: Taken over by Saimaan Linjat, which has been formed the previous year by the towns of Savonlinna and Lappenranta.

1967: Owners became Saimaan Laivamatkat Oy.

1976: Renamed **Suur Saimaa**.

1982: Following the bankruptcy of Saimaan Laivamatkat Oy, the ship was sold at auction to the town of Savonlinna, to be converted to a museum ship. She was renamed **Savonlinna** and was originally intended to be restored as a static museum ship, but this idea was abandoned and she was restored to operating condition, and to wood-firing.

1987: Return to steam when she steamed to the new museum jetty at Rihisaari. Restoration work continued to return her to her 1927 condition.

SS SUUR SAIMAA

Suur Saimaa as *Kallavesi* at Kuopio, 1995.

Length: 26.60m   Gross tonnage: 148
Propulsion: Single Screw   Engine type: Compound, 135hp
Built: 1907   Rebuilt (most recent): 1978
Passenger capacity: 100
Body of water: Lake Saimaa   Home port: Savonlinna
Frequency of operation: Static use
Website address: hhlweb.biz/oo-suur-saimaa.htm
Builders: Paul Wahl, Varkaus
Owner: Kuopio Roll Risteilyt Oy
Former names: *Kallavesi* 1997, *Koli* 1994, *Puijo* 1991, *Imatra* 1979, *Sinikolmio* *c.*1970, *Punkaharju* 1960, *Orivesi II* 1956, *Liperi* 1912

1907: Built as the passenger steamer **Liperi** for Liperin Höyryvenhe Oy for the Joensuu to Savonlinna route.

1912: Sold to Höyryvenhe Oy Kerttu, renamed **Orivesi II**, remained on the same route

1951: Owners merged with Saimaan Höyrylaiva Oy, taking the latter company's name.

1956: Renamed **Punkaharju**. From about this time used on the Savonlinna-Mikkeli-Lappenranta triangle.

1960: Renamed **Sinikolmio**.

1964: Converted to oil-firing.

1965: Taken over by Saimaan Linjat.

1967: Owners became part of Saimaan Laivamatkat.

*c.*1970: Renamed **Imatra**.

1977: Ran aground en route from Savonlinna to Mikkeli. Raised and sold to Roll-Laivat Oy, Kuopio.

1979: Returned to service, named **Puijo**. Placed on the Kuopio to Savonlinna via Heinävesi service, later operated from Kuopio to Varkaus.

1989: Operated on non-landing cruises out of Savonlinna.

1991: Sold to Matti Turunen, Lieksa, renamed **Koli**. Operated on Lake Pielinen

1995: Returned to Lake Saimaa. Renamed **Kallavesi**. Operated from Savonlinna to Lappeenranta.

1997: In use as a static restaurant ship at Savonlinna, renamed **Suur Saimaa**. Placed in the same location as **Hopeasalmi**, after she had been moved to Lahti. As far as is known, **Suur Saimaa** retains her steam machinery and, with the precedent of **Hopeasalmi**, now **Laitiala** on lake Päijänne, it is not impossible that she may at some stage return to service.

SS SUVI SAIMAA

Suvi Saimaa at Suur Saimaa Pier, 1982.

Length: 26.7m   Gross tonnage: 149
Engine type: Compound, 150hp
Built: 1907
Body of water: Lappeenranta   Home port: Lake Saimma
Frequency: Restaurant ship
Website address: www.karelialines.fi/suvisaimaa/index.html
Builder: Paul Wahl, Varkaus
Owner: Karelia Lines Ltd
Former names: **Kallavesi** 1981, **Kuopio** 1976, **Heinävesi II** 19671907: Built as **Heinävesi II** for Heinävaden Höyrylaiva Oy for the route from Kuopio via Heinävesi to Savonlinna

1967: Owners became part of Saimaan Laivamatkat Oy.

*c.*1970: Renamed **Kuopio**.

1976: Renamed **Kallavesi**.

1982: Spring: Following the bankruptcy of Saimaan Laivamatkat Oy, sold at auction to Lappenrannan Laiva Oy, renamed **Suvi Saimaa** and placed on the Lappeenranta to Puumula route, also on the Saimaa Canal.

1993: Withdrawn from service and used as a static restaurant ship at Savonlinna.

I have included **Suvi Saimaa** here in view of the previous experience with **Hopeasalmi** being a restaurant ship for many years, and the return to steam as **Laitiala**.

ST TIPPA

Steam tug *Tippa* with a barge on Lake Saimaa.
(Suomen Höyrypursiseura)

Length: 17.10m   Gross tonnage: 26.27
Propulsion: Single Screw   Engine type: Compound, 70hp
Built: 1892
Body of water: Lake Saimaa   Home port: Kuopio
Frequency of operation: Rallies?
Website address: www.steamengine.cc/arkisto/koneet/sstippa.html
Builders: Umeå, Sweden
Owner: K Yläsaari, Kotka
Former names: *Repola 3*, *Stor-Klas*
Remarks: Wood-fired

1892: Built for unknown Swedish owners as the tug *Stor-Klas*.
1947: Purchased by Repola-Viipuri Oy, Savonlinna, renamed *Repola 3*.
1951: Owners became Rauma-Repola Oy, Savonlinna.
1973: Sold to Arja & Kauko Yläsaari, Kuopio for preservation, renamed *Tippa*; later sold to Kauko
    Yläsaari, Kotka.

ST TOIMI II

Length: 19.60m
Propulsion: Single Screw   Engine type: Compound, 97hp
Built: 1904   Passenger capacity: 12
Body of water: Lake Saimaa   Home port: Anttola
Frequency of operation: Charters
Website address: www.steamengine.cc/arkisto/koneet/sstoimiii.html
Builders: Lehtoniemi & Taipale, Joroinen
Owner: J Korpikallio, Anttola
Remarks: Used with barge *Loviisa*

Toimi II is a steam tug which offers passenger charters from Anttola along with the barge *Loviisa* which
carries passengers. She has an oil-fired steam generator inside her original boiler.

ST TOMMI

Length: 21.46m   Gross tonnage: 57.46
Propulsion: Single Screw   Engine type: Compound, 220hp
Built: 1943

Tommi on Lake Saimaa, towing
a barge alongside, 1995.

Body of water: Lake Saimaa   **Home port:** Savonlinna
Frequency of operation: Rallies?
Website address: www.steamengine.cc/arkisto/koneet/sstommi.html
Builders: R. Dunston, Hull, England
Owner: M. Kurppa, Helsinki, P. Alhainen, J. & P. Snellman, Vantaa
Former names: *B5*, *TID 35* 1946
Remarks: Wood-fired

1943: Built as the wartime standard tug *TID 35* for the Ministry of War Transport, Great Britain.
1946: Sold to Finnish Government, named *B5*.
1947: Sold to Savon Uittoyhdisystys, Kuopio.
1984: Sold to Jorma and Aila Kurppa for preservation, renamed *Tommi*.
1994: Sold to Miikka Kurppa, Helsinki, Peter and Jan Snellman, Vantaa, and Pasi Alhainen, Helsinki.

ST WARKAUS

Warkaus at an island on Lake Saimaa, 1995.

Length: 19.82m   **Gross tonnage:** 62
Propulsion: Single Screw   **Engine type:** Compound, 149hp
Built: 1910
Body of water: Lake Saimaa   **Home port:** Ristiina
Frequency of operation: Rallies?
Website address: www.steamengine.cc/arkisto/koneet/sswarkaus.html
Builders: A. Ahlström, Varkaus
Owner: P. Löppönen, Porvoo
Remarks: Wood-fired

1910: Built as a tug for A. Ahlström, Varkaus, her builders. Used as a harbour tug in Varkaus.

1955: Withdrawn from service, laid-up.

1968: Sold to Juhani Salovaara, Helsinki.

1972: Sold to Pauli and Jaakki Löppönen, Mikkeli, Kirkonummi, later owned solely by Pauli Löppönen, Porvoo.

ST WARKAUS VII

Warkaus VII at Varkaus, 1995.

Length: 21.30m   **Gross tonnage:** 53.5
Propulsion: Single Screw   **Engine type:** Compound, 180hp
Built: 1903
Body of water: Lake Saimaa   **Home port:** Varkaus
Frequency of operation: VIP trips
Website address: www.steamengine.cc/arkisto/koneet/sswarkausvii.html
Builders: A. Ahlström Oy, Varkaus
Owner: A. Ahlström Oy, Varkaus
Remarks: Wood-fired

1903: Built by A. Ahlström, Varkaus for their own use.

Warkaus VII remains in service for her builders, offering VIP trips for visitors to her owners and potential clients. Ahlström are now boiler makers and have been sold to the Foster-Wheeler group.

SS WENNO

Length: 30.80m   **Gross tonnage:** 167
Propulsion: Single Screw, **Engine type:** Compound, 96hp
Built: 1907   **Passenger capacity:** 99
Body of water: Lake Saimaa   **Home port:** Puumala
Frequency of operation: Occasional public trips
Website address: www.puumala.fi/wenno/wenno.htm
Builders: Unknown, Savonlinna
Owner: Puumala Veneseura ry, Puumala : 0
Former names: *Vetehinen*
Remarks: Wood-fired

'Tar steamer' *Wenno* at Puumula. (Owners)

1907: Built as the tar steamer **Vetehinen** for Miettula Sawmill, Puumala. Used to carry goods from sawmills there to St Petersburg and birch firewood to Stockholm, St Petersburg and Kotka. Also visited Lübeck and England.

1910: Sold.

1934: After a number of changes of ownership, purchased by Enso-Gutzeit Ltd, fitted with a second-hand boiler from a tug, and renamed **Wenno**.

1966: Withdrawn from service.

1972: Sold to Puumala municipality for preservation. Restored by the local enthusiast group Puumala Boat Society. Following preservation she has been used for occasional passenger trips.

ST WIPUNEN

Wipunen at Kuopio, 1995.

Length: 18.0m
Propulsion: Single Screw   Engine type: Compound, 93hp
Built: 1907
Body of water: Lake Saimaa   Home port: Kuopio
Frequency of operation: Rallies?
Builders: Paul Wahl, Varkaus
Owner: Oy Gust Ranin, Kuopio
Remarks: Wood-fired

1907: Built for Gust Ranin Oy, Kuopio.
Wipunen remains under their ownership.

Other lakes

SS KAJAANI I

Length: 23.50m
Propulsion: Single Screw   **Engine type:** Compound, 112hp
Built: 1911
Body of water: Oulujärvi   **Home port:** Kajaani
Frequency of operation: Rallies?
Website address: www.steamengine.cc/arkisto/koneet/sskajaanii.html;
    www.kajaaninkampus.oulu.fi/koky/kokl/lonnrot/rheikkin/Ouluj99/tietoja_oulujarven_
    vanhoista_laivoista.htm
Builders: Kajaanin Vanha telakka, Kajaani
Owner: J Ebeling, Kauniainen
Former names: *Salo II*

1911: Built as the passenger steamer *Salo II* for Kauppias Leinonen, Manamansalo for use on Lake
    Oulujärvi.
1936: Sold to Kajaani OY, renamed *Kajaani I*. Converted to a warping tug.
1959: Withdrawn from service.
1963: Sold to Jaakko Ebeling for preservation. Restored over the years.

SS KOUTA

Passenger steamer *Kouta* on Oulujärvi.
(Suomen Höyrypursiseura)

Length: 22.50m   **Gross tonnage:** 60
Propulsion: Single Screw   **Engine type:** Compound, 121hp
Built: 1921   **Passenger capacity:** 60
Body of water: Lake Oulujärvi   **Home port:** Kajaani
Frequency of operation: Occasional public trips
Website address: www.steamengine.cc/arkisto/koneet/KOUTA.JPG;
www.kajaaninkampus.oulu.fi/koky/kokl/lonnrot/rheikkin/Ouluj99/tietoja_oulujarven_vanhoista_
    laivoista.htm
Builders: A. Ahlström, Varkaus
Owner: M. Kuorikoski & A. Sointamo, Kajaani
Former names: *Vuokatti II*

1921: Built as the passenger steamer *Vuokatti II* for Sotkamon Höyrylaiva Oy for a service between
    Kajaani and Sotkamo on Lakes Rehja and Nuasjärvi.

1937: Sold to Oulujoen Uittoyhdistys. Used as a tug.

1967: Withdrawn from service. Sold to Matti Kuorikoski and Allan Sointamo of Kajaani for preservation. Renamed **Kouta**. Restored and used for charter trips with the occasional public sailing. **Kouta** is the most northerly publicly operating passenger steamer in Finland.

TST WELLAMO

Steam tug *Wellamo* on Vanajavesi.
(Suomen Höyrypursiseura)

Length: 21.18m
Propulsion: Twin Screw   **Engine type**: Compound, 190hp
Built: 1907   **Passenger capacity**: 25
Body of water: Vanajavesi   **Home port**: Valkeakoski
Frequency of operation: Charters
Website address: www.steamengine.cc/arkisto/koneet/sswellamo.html
Builders: Sommers, Tampere
Owner: Osmo Norvasto, Tampere

1907: Built for Ångbåts AB Mauritz Holmberg.
1960s: Purchased for preservation.

5 Norway

Norway, with its many miles of coastline, offers a rich variety of preserved steamers. Many are projects of local groups and sadly there are a number of preservation projects which have started and seem to have stalled.

COAST: WEST COAST AND FJORDS

SS HANSTEEN

Hansteen at Trondheim, 1999.

Length: 31.10m   Gross tonnage: 120
Propulsion: Single Screw   Engine type: Compound, 125hp
Built: 1866   Rebuilt (most recent): 1996
Passenger capacity: 50-100
Body of water: Trondheimsfjord   Home port: Trondheim
Frequency of operation: Awaiting hull repairs
Website address: home.online.no/~bjeren/hansteen.htm
Builders: Nyland Mek Verkstad, Oslo   Engine builder: Ålesund M V 1915
Owner: Stiftelsen DS Hansteen
Former names: *Ivar Elias* 1978, *Haarek* 1950, *Hansteen* 1899
Remarks: Coal-fired

1866: Built with a wrought iron hull as the hydrographic survey steamer **Hansteen** for Norges Geografiske Opmåling. Used only during the summer months for charting the Norwegian coast and for meteorological observations. Used both sail and steam.

1867: Delivered.

1876: New boiler fitted.

1879: New engine fitted.

1898: Sold to Inherred Forenede Dampskibsselskab, Steinkjer. Converted to a passenger-cargo vessel. Operated as a local passenger steamer in the inner Trondheimsfjord from Steinkjer to Trondheim.

1899: Rebuilt with passenger accommodation. Fitted with a well deck forward and a deck saloon aft. New boiler fitted.

1900: Sold to Det Helgelanske Dampskipsselskab, Sandnessjøen. Renamed **Haarek**. Used on services along the Helgeland coast but was not successful because she was too small, and was used as a reserve steamer.

1905: Laid-up.

1915-16: Superstructure rebuilt with an upper (storm) deck. Well deck removed. Placed on the route from Sandnessjøen to Træna.

1949: Withdrawn from service.

1950: Sold to Florø Pakkergruppe. Used as an accommodation ship for herring fishermen at Florø.

1957: Superstructure removed. Renamed **Ivar Elias**.

1962: Sold to Oslo Indremisjon, moved to Oslo and used as a hostel. A wooden structure, with a row of windows, was built over the entire deck and space provided for fifty-seven sleeping-places. All the accommodation below the main deck was retained and is still original.

1978: Taken over by a private individual who planned to sink her in deep water.
 Sold for preservation. Placed in dry dock at the Nylands Verksted yard in Oslo, where she was built. Restoration started to her 1872 condition. Renamed **Hansteen**.

1979: New (second-hand) engine and boiler fitted.

1985: Moved to Hansen & Arntzen, Stathelle, for further restoration.

1987: Restoration of hull completed. Towed to Trondheim.

1992: Ran engine trials.

1994: Restoration complete. Returned to steam. It was planned that she be operated as a charter yacht, sailing in the Norwegian Fjords in the summer months and the Caribbean in the winter months, but Olaf Engvig, the project leader, left Norway for a job in the USA and a lot of the impetus went out of the project.

1999: Summer. Hull severely damaged by sandblasting which her owners were advised against. This resulted in twenty hull plates being destroyed. Temporary repairs were made by doubling up the plates.
 Unfortunately, **Hansteen** has had a problem in getting a passenger certificate because her hull plates are too thin. Money for the repairs was promised by the Riksantikvarien (state restoration institution), but the offer was later withdrawn. She spent most, if not all, of her time, lying in Trondheim inner harbour.

2002: Further restoration began with a grant of 4 million Kroner from the Riksantikvarien.
 Autumn: Inner accommodation dismantled and taken to Norsk Fartøyvern in Hardanger. Towed to Bredalsholmen, Kristiansand where she arrived on 10 October and was dry-docked in December. Many hull plates and some frames were replaced during the dry-docking.

2003: Autumn: Left dry dock and sailed for Hardanger for re-installation of the interior and for work on the deck and rigging.

2005: Work on interior completed, returned to Trondheim.

Hansteen is an important ship, being the only survivor worldwide from the age of sail and steam in the mid-nineteenth century.

SS HESTMANDEN

Hestmanden in the Bredalsholmen
dry dock at Kristiansand, 1999.

Length: 59.40m   **Gross tonnage**: 755
Propulsion: Single Screw   **Engine type**: Triple Expansion, 550hp
Built: 1911
Body of water: Norwegian Coast   **Home port**: Kristiansand
Frequency of operation: Undergoing restoration
Website address: www.museumsnett.no/hestmanden
Builders: Laxevaag Maskin & Jernskibsbyggeri, Bergen
Owner: Stiftelsen Hetsmanden (Norsk Veteranskibsklub)
Former names: *Vegafjord* 1979, *Hestmanden* 1955

1911: Built as the engines aft cargo steamer **Hestmanden** for Vesteraalens D/S. Used along the Norwegian coast on a weekly cargo/passenger route from Bergen to Tromsø. Could carry 100 passengers.

1913: Made her first foreign voyage with a cargo run to Halmstad in Sweden.

1915: 4 January: Made the first of five trips over the next six months with timber from Trondheim to Hull, England.

August: Returned to the coastal service for a few sailings from Kristiania (now Oslo), then used on coal runs from England to Rouen, France.

1916: July: Returned to Norwegian coastal service.

1917: Was used on a convoy to Archangel with fish during which ten of the fifteen ships were lost.

8 November: Requisitioned by the British Government. Used as a cargo steamer as previously.

1919: February: Returned to her owners. Returned to coastal service, now sailing as far as Finnmark and Petsamo in what was then Finland.

1924: Started sailings from Oslo, still to Kirkenes.

1920s: Flying bridge added.

1930s: Cargo derricks altered so they could now lift 24 tons.

1939: About to be taken out of service, having been replaced by newer tonnage, when the war broke out.

1940: 9 April: In the Lofoten Islands when the Germans invaded. Requisitioned by the Norwegian Navy. Used for carrying soldiers to fight the advancing German army. Returned to her owners a month later and placed in service carrying coal from the mines in Svalbard (Spitzbergen) to northern Norway.

7 June: Sailed to Torshavn, Faeroe Islands after Germany invaded northern Norway.

24 June: Taken over by Notrtraship (The Norwegian Shipping and Trade mission, which oversaw all free Norwegian shipping during the Second World War) for the duration of the war.

4 July: Arrived on the Clyde, from Torshavn in the Faeroes. Later moved up to Glasgow for repairs, then lay off Gourock for a few months.

6 December: Acquired by British Sea Transport and managed by J. Hay & Sons, Glasgow.

1942: January: Started operating in British coastal waters. Mainly operated from Newcastle and Middlesbrough to London, but also operated along the English Channel, to South Wales, the west coast of England and Scotland, and to Belfast. Made one, and possibly two trips to Iceland.

1945: 5 July: Returned to Norway, returned to her owners in very poor condition and placed back in the coastal cargo service. Was the first ship sailing out of Oslo for Finnmark after the close of the war.

1946: Summer: Major rebuild at Akers Verft, Oslo. Converted from coal to oil-firing. Bridge enclosed and wheelhouse added. New crew accommodation and two passenger cabins added. Placed on international services to the Baltic and northern France in addition to her coastal sailings. Also made a couple of sailings from Egersund to London with cargoes of fish.

1955: 1 November: Sold to Høvding Skipsopphugging and renamed **Vegafjord**. Used to raise and clear wartime wrecks of German ships and submarines along the Norwegian Coast.

Mid-1960s: Laid-up.

1979: Sold to Norsk Veteranskibsklub for preservation after she was about to be scrapped. Regained the name **Hestmanden**.

1982: Autumn: Towed to Trondheim Mek. Verksted for restoration to begin. Restoration took place slowly.

1992: Towed to the Bredalsholmen yard at Kristiansand, where she was later dry-docked.

1995: Received a 5 million Kroner grant to mark the 50th anniversary of the end of the Second World War.

2002: 18 October: Taken out of dry dock. Work on hull completed. Work on superstructure and machinery ongoing. Returned to dry dock later that autumn.

2005: Autumn: By this time work on the deck was almost complete, but a lot of work still had to be done in the engine room and the interior.

It is planned that when restoration work on **Hestmanden** is completed that she will be used as a memorial to Norwegian seamen who lost their lives in wartime and to show the lives of Norwegian working seamen in the past century. It is possible that she will make occasional passenger trips at steam events or on positioning voyages.

SS OSTER

Oster. (Eilif Stene)

Length: 38.23m   **Gross tonnage**: 199
Propulsion: Single Screw   **Engine type**: Triple Expansion
Built: 1908   **Rebuilt** (most recent): 1999
Passenger capacity: 315
Body of water: Fjords   **Home port**: Lindås
Frequency of operation: Occasional public trips
Website address: www.oster.no
Builders: Christiansands Mek. Verkested, Kristiansand
Engine builder: Alexander Hall, Aberdeen, 1927, from *Clearway*
Owner: Nordhordland Veteranbåtlag
Former names: *Gamle Oster* 2000, *Vaka* 1964, *Oster* 1945, *Marder* 1940

1908: Built as the local passenger and cargo steamer *Oster* for Indre Norshordlands Dampskipselskap. November: Delivered. Was built for the route from Bergen to Modalen and was ice-strengthened to reach the community there in the winter months, which had previously been isolated.

1915: Rebuilt and lengthened by 3.8m. Passenger capacity increased from 265 to 312.

*c.*1920: Wooden saloon built on the promenade deck.

1923: Owners renamed Indre Nordhordland Dampbåtlag L/L.

1929-32: Rebuilt again.

1939: September: Requisitioned by the Norwegian Navy, equipped with armament and use as a guardship.

1940: 6 May: Abandoned at Televåg by her Norwegian crew, subsequently requisitioned by the invading Deutsche Kriegsmarine (German Navy), by whom she was renamed *Marder* with the pennant number *NB04* and used as a patrol steamer by Hafenschutz-Flotilla (the Harbour Protection Flotilla) in Bergen.

1943: June 5: Involved in a battle with two Norwegian MTBs.

1944: Spring: Modified to take two extra guns, Transferred to the 55 Vorposten-Flotille with the new pennant number of *V5504*, based at Florvåg.

1945: 9 February: Used as a flak ship during an allied aircraft attack on destroyer *Z33* at Førdefjord. Summer: Returned to her owners in poor condition and regained the name *Oster*.

1946: Major refit ay Stokmarknes Mek Verksted, modernised. Wheelhouse raised half a deck.

1950: Sides of after deck enclosed.

1960: From now on only used as a reserve vessel, spent the majority of the time laid-up.

1963: Christmas. Made her final passenger voyage. By this time she was Norway's last coal-fired local steamer. The boiler failed and a repair attempt was unsuccessful.

1964: April: Sold to Berge Sag & Trelastforretning, Ølensvik and rebuilt as an engines-aft diesel coaster at her new owners yard at Ølensvik after a failed preservation effort.

1966: Entered service as a coaster, renamed *Vaka*.

1974: Sold to Oddmund Tjoflot, Vikebyga. Used in the sand trade.

1980: Sold to P/R Kristoffersen & Gundersen, Flekkerøy. Based at Haugesund.

1983: Now based at Kristiansand.

1996: Purchased by Nordhordland Veteranbåtlag for restoration, renamed *Gamle Oster* (Old Oster). Laid-up at Bjørsvik in the Osterfjorden, where restoration and rebuilding commenced, to get the steamer back to her 1964 condition.

1998: December: The engine which had been in the dredger *Clearway*, operating at Whitehaven, Cumbria, England, and which had been built by Alexander Hall at Aberdeen in 1927, was fitted. This was almost identical to the original machinery. The boiler from *Clearway*, which had been built in France in 1957 and fitted in 1972, was also fitted and was converted from coal to oil firing, using the oil firing system from a former Royal Navy winch barge, built in 1957.

2000: 1 August: Renamed *Oster*. August: Was present and in steam for the steam event Nordsteam 2000 at Bergen. Work on the interior accommodation still had to be completed.

2001-02: Winter: Major work done on the passenger accommodation at Mastrevik Mek Verkstad.

2002: 19 April: Moved to the Fartøyvernsenteret at Norheimsund where more work was done, and then moved to Bjørsvik again.

2002: August: Commenced passenger trips for a few weeks.

2004: 2 October: Sailed to Norheimsund for work on her second-class saloon and completion of work on her crew accommodation and cabins.

2005: 11 June: Restoration completed.

Oster makes around thirty trips from Bergen each year, mainly charters. The few public trips are mainly in late June and early July. 2005 saw three sailings to Lygra and Sletta on Sundays 26 June, 3 and 10 July and sailings at the Nordsteam Steam Festival on the first weekend in August.

SS ROGALAND

Rogaland, then named *Gamle Rogaland*, leaving Stavanger, 1993.

Length: 57.43m   **Gross tonnage:** 851
Propulsion: Single Screw   **Engine type:** 4-cylinder compound, 900hp
Built: 1929
Body of water: Fjords   **Home port:** Stavanger
Frequency of operation: Charters, return to steam 200?
Website address: www.gamlerogaland.no
Builders: Stavangero Stiberi & Dok, Stavanger
Engine builder: Stocznia Gdanska, Poland 1959
Owner: Stiftelsen Veteranskipslaget Rogaland
Former names: *Gamle Rogaland* 2003, *Stauper* 1990, *Tungenes* 1965, *Rogaland* 1964
Remarks: Currently operated as diesel, to get engine from Russian trawler *Morozovsk*, 1959

1929: September: Built as the overnight passenger steamer **Rogaland** for Det Stavangerske D/S for the coastal route from Oslo to Stavanger and Sandnes. Originally fitted with a 144hp Lentz double-compound engine.

1940: 9 April. Was stopped south of Bergen with eight other steamers by Norwegian Patrol Boats following the German invasion. Landed her passengers in the Fanafjorden, and then sailed to Leirvik, Stord. Later used as a naval transport for a while.

   26 April: Laid-up at Lofthus, near Odda for a short while.

1941: 21 September: Heavily damaged by a mine in the inner Oslofjord, repaired at Nylands Verksted.

1944: 20 April: Seriously damaged and sank whilst lying at the quayside in Bergen when the Dutch ship **Voorbode**, loaded with ammunition, exploded. Over 150 people were killed in the explosion, including over fifty German soldiers. One waitress on **Rogaland** died, also one AB who was ashore at the time. Was taken over by the insurance company, but later re-purchased by Det Stavangerske D/S.

   Summer: Raised and towed to Ølesund, Ryfylke and laid-up awaiting repairs

1947: Rebuilding complete after 1944 explosion. Moved to the overnight cargo service from Sandnes and Stavanger to Bergen. Original steam engine replaced by a triple expansion engine.

1949: Steam engine replaced by a 1943-vintage US built Cleveland General V-16 engine.

1957: Rebuilt again. Moved back to the Stavanger to Oslo route.

1964: Withdrawn from service. Renamed **Tungenes**.

1965: Sold to Nika A/S, renamed **Stauper**. Rebuilt to a sandblasting vessel, with equipment placed in the former cargo hold. Based at Sandefjord and moved to various ship repair yards as necessary. Latterly moved to the Cityvarvet in Gothenburg, where she was used as an accommodation ship.

1989: July: Sold to Fritz Morland, Stavanger for preservation. Rebuilding of passenger accommodation started.

1990: February: Now owned by Stiftelsen Veteranskipslaget Rogaland.

10 May: Renamed **Gamle Rogaland**.

1992: Entered service on mainly charter trips from Stavanger to earn money for ongoing restoration work.

Late 1990s: Russian steam trawler **Morozovsk** purchased after she called at Stavanger en route for the scrapyard. Engine removed for eventual installation in **Gamle Rogaland**. Engine moved to Kristiansand for preservation, when this is complete it will be placed in the cargo hold until funds have been raised to install it

2002: December: Renamed **Rogaland**.

Rogaland continues to offer charter trips from Stavanger. There seems to be no hurry to re-install a steam engine, but it is a distinct possibility for some stage in the future.

SS SOUTHERN ACTOR

Southern Actor at Sandefjord, 1999.

Length: 38.00m   **Gross tonnage:** 428
Propulsion: Single Screw   **Engine type:** Triple Expansion, 1,800hp
Built: 1950   **Rebuilt** (most recent): 1989
Passenger capacity: 52
Body of water: Norwegian Coast   **Home port:** Sandefjord
Frequency of operation: Occasional public trips
Website address: http://www.mclaren.gs/s__actor.htm
www.sandefjord.kommune.no/Symfoni/guide.nsf/0/14C37FB6FDFFDC44C.1256BB100468350?openDocument (for charter details)
Builders: Smiths Dock, Middlesbrough
Owner: Christen Christiansons Hvalfangermuseum
Former names: *Itxas Uno* 1989, *Ibsa Dos*, *Polarbris 8* 1973, *Southern Actor* 1964

1950: Built as the whaling steamer **Southern Actor** for Sevilla Whaling Co. Ltd, a subsidiary of Christian Salvesen & Co., Leith, Scotland.

1951-52 to 1959-60: Used as a catcher for the factory ship **Southern Harvester**.

1960-61: Used out of Leith, South Georgia.

1961-62: Worked with the factory ship **Southern Venturer**, and was then laid-up.

1964: Sold to Elling Aarseth, Ålesund. Used at Skjelnan whaling station. Renamed **Polarbris 8**.

1971: Whaling finished at Skjelnan, laid-up.

1973: Sold for further whaling to Spanish owners at Vigo renamed **Ibsa Dos**, later **Itxas Uno**.

1985: Laid-up.

1989: Discovered by Norwegian whaling enthusiasts while she was waiting to be scrapped and purchased by the Whaling Club of Sandefjord for preservation.

25 October: Towed to Sandefjord for restoration. Renamed **Southern Actor**.

1995: 1 July: Donated to Sandefjord Museum, having been totally restored to operating condition. Opened as a museum.

Southern Actor is normally moored as a museum ship adjacent to Sandefjord whaling museum, but is available for charter and may offer occasional public trips.

SS STAVENES

Length: 34.00m   Gross tonnage: 187
Propulsion: Single Screw   Engine type: Triple Expansion, 350hp
Built: 1913   Rebuilt (most recent): ongoing
Body of water: Sognefjord   Home port: Kinsarvik
Frequency of operation: Undergoing restoration
Website address: www.sognafoto.no/bilder/Bilde.asp?key=5425;
   www.warsailors.com/homefleet/shipss2/html
Builders: Bergens M/V, Bergen   Engine builder: ?. Jönköping, 1893
Owner: Veteranskibslaget Stavenes, Sogn Folkemuseum

1904: Built as the local passenger and cargo steamer ***Stavenes*** for Nordre Bergenhus Amts Dampskibe, Bergen. Used at Dalsfjord and Førdesfjord in the Sunnfjord, also occasionally in the Nordfjord and around Florø. Until 1909 used in winter as a mail steamer from Gudvangen to Lærdal in the inner Sognefjord.
   September: Delivered.
1912: Summer: In service on the route Florø-Måløy-Nordfjordeid-Sandane.
1919: January 25: Owners became Fylkesbaatene I Sogn og Fjordane.
1934: Partially rebuilt to carry 7 or 8 cars on the foredeck. Wheelhouse and electricity added. Used as a car ferry each summer from Lærdal to Vadheim.
1945: After the war in service from Flåm to Balestrand and Fjærland in the summer months and from the Lustrafjorden to Årdal and from Flåm to Gudvangen in the winter.
1954: Spring: Rebuilt and dieselised with a second-hand (1942) diesel engine. Modern motorship-type funnel replaced original tall steamer-type funnel. After deck saloon widened to whole width of ship.
1956: New diesel engine fitted.
1959: Placed on the route from Bergen to Gule, Solund, and Hyllestad.
Late 1960s: Used as a reserve vessel by this time, later laid-up.
1969: Used in the film *Song of Norway*.
1973: March: Sold to J. Graham Kew, Rugby, England, for use as a yacht.
1972–75: Visited Western Norway with Jeffrey A. Hoffman as skipper, who was later to become a NASA astronaut. Later laid-up at Grimsby for three years after the death of her owner.
Late 1970s: Taken over by Monks Ferry Training Trust, Birkenhead. Moved to Port Penrhyn, North Wales, where she was placed in a dry dock and it was intended she be restored using unemployed workers and in connection with the Duke of Edinburgh Awards scheme.
1982: 27 March: Moved to Birkenhead. Some restoration was done, but not a lot.
1991: May: Purchased for preservation by Veteranskibslaget Stavenes. Towed from Birkenhead to Solund by the British tug ***Ardneil***. New deck installed and diesel engine removed. Moved to Kaupanger.
1994: Sank at her moorings because of the weight of snow on her. Raised and a temporary cover fitted over her entire length. Later moved to a remote spot called Kinsedal on the Lustrafjord.
1998: Steam engine from a scrapped Swedish tug purchased along with a boiler from Måløy Sildoljefabriuk (herring oil factory).
2005: August: Towed to Bergen for the Nordsteam 2005 Steam Festival, the moved to Dåfjorden, to the yard where much of the work on ***Oster*** had been done, for completion of restoration, although little work had been done there at the time of writing.
2008: Proposed completion of restoration to 1934 condition for FSF's 150th anniversary. Proposed stave church cruises on the Sognefjord, with calls at Vik, Balestrand, Kaupanger, Undredal, Lærdal and Luster.

SS STORD I

Stord at Nordsteam, Bergen, 2005. (Eilif Stene)

Length: 47.30m   **Gross tonnage:** 469
Propulsion: Single Screw   **Engine type:** Triple Expansion, 500hp
Built: 1913   **Rebuilt** (most recent): 2005
Body of water: Western Fjords   **Home port:** Bergen
Frequency of operation: Undergoing restoratioin
Website address: www.fjordabaaten.no
Builders: Laxevaag Maskin & Jernskibsbyggeri, Laxevaag
Engine builder: W.J. Yarwood, Northwich, 1942
Owner: Veteranskipslaget Fjordabåten, Bergen
Former names: *O T Moe* 1981, *Stord* 1969

1913: Built for Hardanger Søndhordlandske Dampskibsselskap, Bergen.

21 April: Ran trials and was delivered.

1914: October: placed on the Sandnes-Stavanger-Bergen day service, jointly run with Stavangerske D/S and Sandnes Aktie-Dampskibsselskab.

1915: Taken off the Stavanger service.

1930: October: Company name changed to Hardanger Sunnhordland Dampskibsselskap.

1931: Major rebuild and modernisation. Lengthened by 3.3m. Placed in the express service from Bergen to Sunnhordland.

1944: 20 April: Was at Bergen when the explosion occurred (see **Rogaland**) but escaped major damage when her mate sailed her into the fjord before the spreading fire reached her.

1947-49: July: Rebuilt as a motorship. Squat funnel fitted.

1949: 13 July: Re-entered service after rebuild. Placed on the service from Bergen to Odda.

1959: Became reserve boat for her owners.

1969: 27 August: Sold to the Oslo branch of the Blå Kors (Blue Cross). Renamed *O T Moe* and used as a floating welfare facility for alcoholics.

1980: Sold to Norsk Veteranskibsklubb for preservation.

1981: Ownership transferred to Föreningen Fjordabåten (Stord) which became Veteranskipslaget Fjordabåten. Renamed **Stord 1**.

1981-87: Restored to 1931 condition using the steam engine from the British naval water tanker *C 609(F)* built in 1942 by W.J. Yarwood, Northwich. (Note that some Norwegian sources erroneously state that the builders were Cammel Laird.)

1987: May: Ran technical trials.

19 May: Almost totally destroyed by fire after a boiler blow-back en route from Sunnhordland and Stord to Bergen. Towed to Høydalsbygd to await repairs. Restoration was slow because of a lack of funding but got under way in earnest around 2002. This was funded partly by local authorities and heritage bodies and partly by profits from cruises on the preserved motor vessel **Granvin**, also owned by Veteranskipslaget Fjordabåten.

2005: 3 August: Returned to steam at Nordsteam 2005 after second restoration, although her interiors still had to be rebuilt.

Work is ongoing on the completion of restoration work on **Stord**, and it is hoped that this will be complete in the not too distant future and that she will offer passenger trips from Bergen.

SL THOROLF

Thorolf on the Norwegian coast. (Owners)

Length: 18.50m   **Gross tonnage**: 27
Propulsion: Single Screw   **Engine type**: Compound, 75hp
Built: 1911   **Passenger capacity**: 35
Body of water: Norwegian Coast   **Home port**: Ålesund
Frequency of operation: Charters
Website address: www.thorolf.net
Builders: Andreas Svoldal, Hardanger
Engine builder: Brunholmen Mek. Verksted, Ålesund
Owner: Oystein Ramalsi, Thorolfs Venner
Remarks: Wooden hull

1910-11: Built for O.A. Devold, a knitwear and hosiery firm, for use as in delivering their goods and bringing raw materials to their factory at Langevåg, south of Ålesund.
1912: Entered service.
Early 1960s: Laid-up after latterly being used more as a private yacht than for deliveries, etc.
1988: D/S Thorolf's Venner (SS *Thorolf*'s fan club) founded.
  21 May: Taken over by D/S Thorolf's Venner. Taken back to Langevåg where restoration commenced.
1999: Slipped at the Mellemverftet at Kristiansund as part of ongoing restoration work. Boiler replaced.

Thorolf is moored at Langevåg and used for charters.

COAST: OSLOFJORD

SS BØRØYSUND

Børøysund at Nordsteam 2005, Bergen.
(Helge Sunde)

Length: 33.10m   **Gross tonnage:** 179
Propulsion: Single Screw   **Engine type:** Triple Expansion, 256hp
Built: 1908   **Rebuilt** (most recent): 1935
Passenger capacity: 100
Body of water: Oslofjord   **Home port:** Oslo
Frequency of operation: Charters
Website address: home.online.no/%7ebjeren/brsund.htm: www.nvsk.no
Builders: Trondhejms Mek Verkstad
Owner: Norsk Veteranskibsklub
Former names: *Hyma* 1969, *Børøysund* 1960, *Skjergar* 1925, *Odin* 1923
Remarks: Coal-fired

1908: Built as the combined passenger steamer and tug *Odin* for Trondhjems Lagtercompagni.

19 June: Launched.

11 August: Entered service. Chartered to various local shipping companies in the area between Kristiansund, Trondheim and Rørvik.

1911: September/October: Chartered to Wilhelm von Koppy for use as a steam yacht for a trip from Trondheim to Kongsmoen, 86km north-east of Trondheim.

1914-18: Requisitioned by the Royal Norwegian Navy and used as a guardship.

1923: February: Sold to Hjelme & Herlø Dampskibsselskab. Renamed *Skjergar*. Used on the routes from Bergen to the islands of Øygarden.

1925: Autumn: Sold to Vesteraalens Dampskibsselskab.

November: Renamed *Børøysund*.

12 December. First sailing from her new home port of Stokmarknes, from where she was used on local services to Sortland, Svolvær, Skutvik and Hanøy. Post office added in the officers' mess forwards.

1935: Rebuilt at Tromsø Skibsverft with new midships deckhouse, now extended to the edge of the hull, and a new post office in the forward part of this. A new aft deckhouse, containing two new passenger cabins and a smoking saloon, were added.

1940: 15 April: Requisitioned by Norwegian forces. Lay at Stokmarknes until 3 June, when she sailed for Finnmark, returning to Stokmarknes on 15 June after the Norwegian capitulation. Returned to local services in August.

1945: March: Laid-up because of coal shortage.

13 July: First post-war sailing.

1948: New enclosed wheelhouse added.

1955: 22 July: Laid-up.

October: Chartered to Finnmark Fylkesrederi og Ruteselskap (FFR) for seven weeks for use on local routes in Finnmark then returned to Stokmarknes to lay-up.

1956-60: Spent much of the time laid-up, but occasionally relieved on various routes for her owners.

1961: 21 February: Sold to Hadsel Yrkesskole (Technical College), Melbu. Renamed *Hyma*. Used as a training ship for engineers. Hull painted grey.

1969: May: Purchased by Norsk Veteranskibsklub (Norwegian Veteran Ship Club), and sailed to Oslo for preservation. Renamed *Børøysund*. Hull painted black again.

1972: Started to be used for charters out of Oslo after some restoration work was done on her.

1981: Spring: Slipped at Donsö Varv, Gothenburg for six months for hull repairs then sailed to the Vesterålen islands to celebrate VDS's Centenary.

1995 and 1999: Sailed to Flensburg for the Dampf-Rundum steam event.

2005: 3-7 August: Participated in Nordsteam 2005 at Bergen.

2006: July: Proposed visit to Vejle Steam Festival in Denmark.

Børøysund normally operates charters out of Oslo from late May to the end of June. These are mainly corporate charters. In July she normally undertakes a long trip of a week or more for club members, often to the western fjords.

SS FORLANDET

Forlandet. (Norsk Fartøyvern)

Length: 34.45m   **Gross tonnage:** 199
Propulsion: Single Screw   **Engine type:** Triple Expansion, 650hp
Built: 1921   **Passenger capacity:** 100
Body of water: Oslofjord   **Home port:** Oslo
Frequency of operation: Occasional public trips
Website address: home.online.no/~bjeren/forland.htm
Builders: Bokerøens Skibsbyggeri, Svelvik   **Engine builder:** Bergens M V
Owner: Föreningen Norsk Fartøyvern
Former names: *Femern* 1931, *Foca* 1929

1921: Built as the whaling steamer *Foca* for Compania Argentina de Pesca, Buenos Aires.
  September: Launched and towed to Bergen Mek.Verksted for the installation of the engine and boiler, then towed back to Svelvik for fitting out.
  November: Delivered and based at South Georgia.
1927: Converted from coal to oil firing.
1929: Sold to Hvalfangerselskabet Atlas, Larvik. Came under the Norwegian flag. Renamed *Femern*.
1929-30 and 1930-31: Used in conjunction with the factory ship *Solglimt*.
1931: Returned to Sandefjord. Taken over by A/S Framnæs Mek Verksted, then sold to A/S Ishavet, Sandefjord, and renamed *Forlandet*. Used in Arctic waters. Later sold to A/S Fangstskibene, Sandefjord.
1934: Purchased again by A/S Framnæs Mek Verksted.
1935: Rebuilt as a tug, and used by the shipyard as a tug and icebreaker.
1983: Sold to a private individual for preservation. Later came under the ownership of Stiftelsen Norsk Fartøyvern, who are slowly restoring her with the help of the group Foreningen D/S Forlandet's Venner. The organisation which owns *Forlandet* is very small and work on restoring her and returning her to steam has gone very slowly.
1997: Work on the restoration of *Forlandet* ceased after the group Forlandet's Venner ceased to exist.

Norsk Fartøyvern also own the small steam launch *Pelle*, built in 1882 at Motala Verkstad as the steam yacht *Pippi*. She has been stored on land under cover in a garden in Oslo for many years and there seems no realistic prospect of her returning to steam.

SS KYSTEN I

Length: 45.12m   **Gross tonnage:** 377
Propulsion: Single Screw   **Engine type:** Triple Expansion, 383hp
Built: 1909   **Rebuilt** (most recent): 1950
Passenger capacity: 150

Kysten I at Tønsberg, 1985.

Body of water: Oslofjord   **Home port**: Tønsberg
Frequency of operation: Daily   **Period of operation**: May to September
Website address: www.evensens.net/kysten/kysten.html;
home.online.no/~bjeren/kysten.htm
Builders: Trondhejms Mek Verkstad
Owner: AS Jubilemsskipet Tønsberg
Former names: *Askaas* 1970, *Kysten* 1964

1909: Built as the coastal passenger and cargo steamer *Kysten* for Namsos Dampskipsselkap for the route from Trondheim to Namsos. This had forty-five stops and she left Trondheim on a Saturday morning at 08:00 and arrived at Namsos on a Monday at 01:00.

15 November: Delivered.

1940: 20 April Lay in the shipyard at Trondheim and was taken over by the invading Germans.
September: Returned to her route.

1944: Autumn: Used for evacuating the population from Troms and Finnmark for two months when the retreating German army laid waste to northern Norway.

1945: Laid-up because of a coal shortage. Later converted to oil firing at Fosen Mek. Verksted. Lengthened by 14ft to accommodate the oil bunkers. Thirty-two passenger berths added.

1964: Sold to A/S Audun, Tvedestrand for use as a seamen's training ship. Renamed *Askaas*.

1968: Used as an accommodation ship.

1970: Sold to A/S Jubilemsskipet, Tønsberg for preservation as part of the celebrations of the 1,100[th] anniversary of the town. Renamed *Kysten I*. Started making 3.5-hour round trips from Tønsberg in the summer months.

1985: Made a cruise of several days from Oslo to Mandal, with each sector available as a day trip with return to the starting point by bus.

2003: December: Moved to Bredalsholmen yard at Kristiansand for replacement of a number of hull plates and other work.

2009: Expected back in service.

Kysten I normally makes a circular island cruise from Tønsberg at 12:00 daily in the summer months. This trip only takes place if there are twenty or more passengers. The trip can be highly recommended.

SS OSCARSBORG I

Length: 29.90m
Propulsion: Single Screw   **Engine type**: Compound, hp
Built: 1904   **Rebuilt** (most recent): 200?
Body of water: Oslofjord   **Home port**: Drammen
Frequency of operation: Undergoing restoration
Website address: www.ta.no/nyheter/article787324.ece
Builders: Södra Varvet, Stockholm (W Lindberg)

Oscarsborg I as *Reigun* at Oslo, 1981.
(Author's collection)

Engine builder: Bergsund, Stockholm, 1906 from *Östanå I*
Owner: Carl Fr Thorsager
Former names: *Reigun* 2004, *Oscarsborg I* 1953?, *Styrsö I* 1911

1904: Built as the passenger steamer *Styrsö I* for Styrsö Nya Badhus AB for service in the northern archipelago of Gothenburg.

1911: Sold to Nesodden Dampskibsselkap and renamed *Oscaraborg I*. Used on the service from Drøbak to Kristiania (now Oslo), with two return runs daily.

1918: Rebuilt for year round service, with new large saloon aft and new cargo hold. Placed on the route from Kristiania to Son via Oscarsborg, Drøbak and Hvitsten. Part of the costs of the rebuild were met by Fred Olsen, on the condition the route was extended to Hvitsten, where the Olsen family had properties.

1920: Sold to A/S Borgå (Fred Olsen & Co.), Oslo, but still managed by Nesodden Dampskibsselkap although she now had a Fred Olsen funnel. Continued on the previous route.

1941: February: Managing company became A/S Nesodden-Bundefjord Dampskipselskap.

1953: Withdrawn from service, her traffic having been taken over by buses and cars.
June: Sold to John and Nils Nilssen, Fredrikstad.

1954: Sold to Reidar K Olsen, Svelvik. Rebuilt on the slipway at Nærsnes as an engines-aft diesel coaster. Renamed *Reigun*. Mainly used in the Oslofjord, partly in the sand trade.

1981: Sold to Petter Olsen, who planned to return her to her earlier condition as a passenger ship. Lay at Aker Brygge, Oslo, for a while.

1990s: Moved to Drammen where she was beached.

2002: Sold to Firmament AS (Petter Olsen).

2004: A feasibility study for her restoration was undertaken. The engine formerly in the Stockholm steamer *Östanå I* has been purchased to be fitted in her.

2005: February to March: Cut up at Drammen after which the sections of the hull were stored at Petter Olsen's farm. Restoration plans now call for a new hull using parts of the old ship.

SL STJERNEN

Stjernen at her base at the
Norwegian Naval Museum at Horten.

Length: 18.00m
Propulsion: Single Screw   **Engine type**: Single-cylinder, 55hp
Built: 1899   **Rebuilt** (most recent): 2001
Passenger capacity: 12
Body of water: Oslofjord   **Home port**: Horten
Frequency of operation: WO   **Period of operation**: May to September
Website address: www.kongesjaluppenstjernen.no/index.html
Builders: Akers M/V Oslo
Owner: Marinemuseet, Horten
Remarks: Ex Royal Yacht launch

1899: Built as the steam launch ***Stjernen*** for King Oscar II of Sweden.

1905: With Norwegian independence, used by King Haakon VIII, later by his son King Olav.

1940: Seized by the occupying German forces. Funnel and other fittings stripped.

1945: Sold by the Direktoratet for Fieldtlig Eiendom to Brede Gulliksen and Kåre Ivar Karlstad, Minnesund, for use on Lake Mjøsa. Fitted with a diesel engine and used as a cargo boat.

1955: Sold to Erling Bjerkek, Kapp. Used as a sand lighter from Brøttum to Kapp to serve his cement factory there, then laid-up for many years.

1969: Sold to Johs. Lindstad's transport firm, Breiskallen. Rebuilt for use as a pleasure boat and fitted with an engine and steering wheel from a truck.

1995: Sold to Marinemuseet (Naval Museum), Horten for restoration to her original condition. Her original steam engine, having been preserved at the museum, was re-fitted in her, along with a new boiler.

2001: 23 May: Restoration complete. Returned to steam.

Stjernen makes passenger trips from Horten on Wednesdays at 12:00, 13:30 and 15:00 in the summer months.

ST STYRBJÖRN

Styrbjörn at Nordsteam, Bergen, 2005.
(Eilif Stene)

Length: 28.56m   **Gross tonnage**: 166
Propulsion: Single Screw   **Engine type**: Compound, 550hp
Built: 1910   **Rebuilt** (most recent): 1994
Body of water: Oslofjord   **Home port**: Oslo
Frequency of operation: Charters
Website address: www.norsteam.com; www.nvsk.no
Builders: Göteborgs Mek Verkstad, Göteborg
Owner: Norsk Veteranskibsklub
Former names: *Atlet* 1979, *Styrbjörn* 1963
Remarks: Coal-fired

1910: Built as the steam tug ***Styrbjörn*** for Trafikaktiebolaget Grängesberg-Oxelösund, Stockholm. At the time she was Scandinavia's largest and most powerful tug. Stationed at Narvik, and chartered to LKAB, the owners of the railway from the iron ore mines at Kiruna and 90% owned by the shipowner, to assist iron ore ships in the harbour there. Also used as a salvage tug.

1910: 30 July: Delivered.

1940: April: Sunk by German air raid on Narvik harbour.

 July: Raised and returned to service for the Germans.

1945: Returned to her Swedish owners after the war.

1950: Rebuilt and modernised at Götaverken, Gothenburg.

1951: August: Returned to service at Narvik.

1963: 28 October: Withdrawn from service and sold to Høvding Skipsopphugging, Sandnessjøen. Renamed *Atlet*.

1972: Laid-up awaiting scrapping.

1979: 15 April: Purchased for preservation by Norsk Veteranskibsklub, Oslo. Taken to Oslo where restoration progressed slowly. Renamed ***Styrbjörn***.

1998: 22 December: Towed to Drammen for dry-docking for the renewal of some hull plates.

2002: December: Returned to Oslo. Work on the cabins started. Hull painted grey, as it was when she was in service.

2005: February: Main engine started for first time since she was laid-up in 1963.

 June to August: Long trip along the Norwegian coast to celebrate the centenary of Norwegian independence. This included a visit to the Nordsteam 2005 Festival at Bergen.

LAKES

TSS AMMONIA

Ammonia at Mæl, 1999.

Length: 73.50m   **Gross tonnage:** 932
Propulsion: Twin Screw   **Engine type:** 2 Triple Expansion, 800hp
Built: 1929   **Passenger capacity:** 150
Body of water: Tinnsjø   **Home port:** Mæl, near Rjukan
Frequency of operation: Return to steam planned
Website address: www.norsk-fartoyvern.no/fartoyhistorikk_a_j.htm
Builders: Moss Værft, Moss
Owner: Stiftelsen Rjukanban

1929: Built for Norsk Hydro as a train ferry for service on the Tinnsjø from Tinnoset to Mæl in connection with the railway from Rjukan to Mæl, carrying rail wagons from the fertiliser and ammonia factory at Rjukan. She could carry sixteen rail wagons and was fitted with plush passenger accommodation. Built in sections and assembled at Tinnoset, at the southern end of the lake. Originally she had taller funnels than now, and the sides of her upperworks were clad in teak.

 18 June: Launched.

1944: 20 February: Heavy Water to make an atom bomb was being produced at Rjukan. Sister ship **Hydro** (1914) sabotaged and sunk by saboteurs of the Norwegian resistance.

1951: Boiler converted from coal to oil firing.

1965: Used to represent sister ship **Hydro** in the film 'Heroes of Telemark', starring Kirk Douglas.

Late 1970s: A proposal by Framnæs Mek. Verksted to convert her to diesel propulsion was never carried out.

1985: Passengers ceased to be carried on the Tinnsjø train ferries.

1991: Works at Rjukan closed, laid-up after a number of years when she was used as a reserve ferry.

1997: Taken over by the Stiftelsen Rjukanban for preservation.

Ammonia is open to the public and it is hoped at some stage to return her to steam.

SS BJOREN

Length: 21.03m   **Gross tonnage**: 26.9
Propulsion: Single Screw   **Engine type**: Compound, 42hp
Built: 1867   **Rebuilt** (most recent): 1994
Passenger capacity: 55
Body of water: Byglandsfjord   **Home port**: Byglandsfjord
Frequency of operation: FSSuO   **Period of operation**: July
Website address: www.setesdal.com/index.php?m=produkt&m_action=vis_prod&id=12&parent=29&spraakSet=no
Builders: Kristiansands M V   **Engine builder**: Kristiansands M V 1914
Owner: Byglands Kommun
Remarks: Wood-fired

1867: Built for Det Oplandske Dampskibsselskab as a passenger steamer for service on the Kilefjorden, south of the Byglandsfjord, from Kile to Nikkelværket. Owners later became Dampskibssaktieselskabet Bjoren og Dølen.

1896: Narrow gauge Setesdalbanen Railway (now preserved) opened to the Byglandsfjord.

1897: **Bjoren** transferred to the Byglandsfjord and lengthened by 1.83m.

1914: Lengthened by a further 3.05m and fitted with a new engine and boiler by Kristiansands Mek. Verksted.

1920: Buses took over the main transport service to the communities along the lake.

1950s: By this time she only served a few isolated settlements along the west side of the Byglandsfjord. A road was built there at this time and the reason for her sailings stopped.

1957: 27 December: Service ceased. Laid-up at Ose and became derelict.

1991: Her rusty remains taken to Drammen for restoration. As no 1914 plans survived, a lot of this was done relying on old photographs. Original engine restored and new wood-fired boiler fitted.

1994: June: Restored by Drammen Skipsreparasjonen and returned to steam on the Byglandsfjord.

In 1999, which is the most recent information I have for her, **Bjoren** ran short non-landing trips from Byglandsfjord on Fridays and Saturdays at 16:00 and 17:45 and a return sailing at 13:00 from Bygland through the lock at Storstrøm to Ose on Sundays, returning down the lake to Byglandsfjord in the evening.

SL PRØVEN

Length: 8.40m
Propulsion: Single Screw
Built: 1998   **Passenger capacity**: 12
Body of water: Kornsjø   **Home port**: Kornsjø

Frequency of operation: SSuO
Period of operation: Midsummer to mid–August (charters May to October)
Website address: www.kornsjoedamp.no
Builders: Unknown, Sweden   Engine builders: Bredings
Owner: Kornsjø Dampskipsselkap
Former names: *Vikens Drottning* 1999

1998: Built as the steam launch *Vikens Drottning* for private use on the Göta Canal and Lake Viken, west
   of Lake Vättern in Sweden.
1999: 9 October: Sold to present owners and moved to the Kornsjø. Renamed *Prøven*.
2000: May: Entered service on the Kornsjø.

Prøven offered, in Summer 2006, 1-hour trips from the pier at Kornsjø, near the border with Sweden
on Saturdays and Sundays at 13:00. Sailings have also in past years been offered from Bokerød, and from
Bästorp.

PS SKIBLADNER

Skibladner on Lake Mjøsa, 1993.

Length: 50.13m   Gross tonnage: 206
Propulsion: Paddle Steamer   Engine type: Triple Expansion Diagonal, 606hp
Built: 1856   Rebuilt (most recent): 1888
Passenger capacity: 230
Body of water: Lake Mjøsa   Home port: Gjovik
Frequency of operation: MX
Period of operation: Midsummer to mid–August
Website address: www.skibladner.no
Builders: Motala Mek Verkstad, Motala   Engine builder: Akers M V 1888
Owner: AS Oplandske DS, Hamar

1856: Built in sections at Motala, and shipped to Oslo by sea, then to Eidsvoll by rail where she was
   assembled. Built for Oplandske Dampskibsselkap as a two-funnelled paddle steamer for service on Lake
   Mjøsa. Originally had a green hull with pink superstructure and a deck saloon aft, and two small holds
   for cargo, one fore and one aft of the funnel, each with its own crane.
   2 August: Entered service. Originally made a single trip from Lillehammer to Eidsvoll in one day,
   returning the next day.
1888: Rebuilt in present condition with a single funnel, lengthened by 6.1m, and new engine fitted.
   Foremast with jib fitted to handle cargo. Aft saloon extended. Hull now light grey and superstructure
   white.
1891: Commenced daily service along the whole of Lake Mjøsa.
1917-18: Laid-up because of the First World War.
1920: Boiler converted from coal to oil firing.

1926: Upper deck extended aft to the stern and forward to the mast.

1937: 5 March: Sank at her moorings, and soon raised. Inner accommodation refurbished and modernised.

1940-44: Laid-up due to the Second World War.

1967: 6 February: Sank at her moorings, and soon raised.

1968: Designated Norway's first historic ship and an attempt was made to return her to her 1888 appearance.

1983: Upper deck replaced, but suffered from major damage due to rot after a couple of years.

1984: New boilers fitted. Not in service for summer season while this work was done

1991: Base moved from Eidsvoll to Gjøvik, and the long daily return trip from Eidsvoll to Lillehammer replaced by trips on alternate days from Gjøvik to Eidsvoll and to Lillehammer.

1992-95: Major restoration work undertaken by Hardanger Fartøyvernsenter. Returned to her external appearance of 1888.

1992-93: Wooden decking renewed.

2006: Celebrated her 150th birthday. Ladies saloon below deck aft restored to original 1888 condition. New pier built at Lillehammer, at Vingnes, on the west side of the river.

Skibladner is the oldest regularly operating steamer in the world. She sails from Gjøvik at 09:30 Mondays excepted; on Sundays, Wednesdays and Fridays she sails south to Hamar and Eidsvoll, and on Tuesdays, Thursdays and Saturdays to Hamar, back to Gjøvik, and north to Lillehammer, returning via the same calls.

SS STADSHAUPTMAND SCHWARZ

Stadshauptmand Schwarz on the slip, 1999.

Length: 18.50m   **Gross tonnage**: 46
Propulsion: Single Screw   **Engine type**: Compound
Built: 1903
Body of water: Lake Eikern   **Home port**: Eidsfoss
Frequency of operation: Return to steam 200?
Website address: www.museumsnett.no/jarlsbergmuseum/snk_schw.htm; www.eikerbygda.no/
bildesider/eikerenbilder-stadshauptmannschwartz.shtml
Builders: Drammens Jernstøberi & Mek Verksted, Drammen
Owner: Stiftelsen Ekerns Dampskibsselkap
Remarks: Scuttled 1931, raised 1995

1903: Built for Ekerns Dampskibsselkap for service as a passenger steamer on Lake Eikern.

21 June: Entered service from Eidsfoss, where there was a rail connection from Tønsberg, to Vestfossen.

1926: Withdrawn from service. Latterly, due to bus competition, she had mainly been used for carrying goods, and as a timber-towing tug. Machinery and fittings removed.

1931: February: Sank at her mooring at Eidsfoss Pier.

1995: 28 October: Raised and taken to Eidsfoss, where she was placed on land for restoration. She has more recently been placed in a specially constructed dry dock at Eidsfoss. At the moment it is planned that she will remain on land as a static exhibit.

HALDEN CANAL

ST ARA

Ara at Ørje, 1999.

Length: 13.78m
Propulsion: Single Screw   **Engine type:** Compound
Built: 1910
Body of water: Halden Canal   **Home port:** Ørje
Frequency of operation: Charters
Website address: www.kanalmuseet.no/asp/dampbatene.asp
Builders: C.J. Wennbergs Mek Verstad, Karlstad
Owner: Asbjorn O Braarud, Øymark Damp & Supply, Ørje
Former names: *Ragnvald Bødtker, Alster*
Remarks: Coal-fired

1910: Built as the tug *Alster* for Alster Bruk och Valsekvarn, Karlstad, Sweden.

1941: Sold to Henry Mossberg, Dals Ed. Machine and boiler removed but at some stage were re-installed.

1954: Sold to Haldenvassdraget Fløttningsföreningen, Halden and renamed *Ragnvald Bodtker*.

1964: Sold to Sheriff Gulbrand Melby, Aremark, renamed *Ara*.

1992: Sold to Asbjorn Otto Braarud (Øymark Damp & Supply), Ørje. Used as a supply boat for communities along the canal.

Ara is normally in private use but is quite possibly available for charter and may run passenger trips for special events in the Halden Canal area.

SL ENGEBRET SOOT

Length: 24.00m   **Gross tonnage:** 32
Propulsion: Single Screw   **Engine type:** Compound, 60hp
Built: 1862   **Rebuilt** (most recent): 1995
Passenger capacity: 18
Body of water: Halden Canal   **Home port:** Ørje

Engebret Soot at Ørje, 1999.

Frequency of operation: Occasional public trips
Website address: www.dsengebretsoot.no
Builders: Nyland Mek Verkstad, Kristiania, now Oslo
Engine builder: Akers M V 1901
Owner: Stiftelsen DS Engebret Soot
Remarks: Wood-fired

1862: Built for Saugbrugsforeningen (sawmill association) Fredrikshald for service as a timber-towing tug and passenger launch on the Halden Canal, as Yard No. 1 of Nylands Mek. Verksted.

1863: Purchased by Gudbrand Eng, Øymark.

*c.*1877: Rebuilt as a passenger launch. Used on the route from Skulerud to Tistedalen until 1887.

1887: Passenger service ceased. Purchased by Fredrikshaldvassdragets Flöttningsföreningen and used as a tug again.

1901: New engine and boiler fitted by Akers Mek. Verksted.

1904: New wheelhouse fitted.

1913: New deckhouse over the engine fitted.

1926: Laid-up.

1934: Purchased by Gunerius Soot, grandson of the canal builder whom the steamer was named after, and used as a yacht.

1939: Sold to Einar Haneborg.

1940-42: Hull heightened by 61cm. Aft cabin removed. Boiler replaced with one built in 1908 by Glommens Mek. Verksted from *Vister*.

1941: Purchased by Haldenvassdragets Fellesfløttning. (The waterways (canals and lakes) above Halden are known as the Halden Vassdraget.)

1942: Started to be used as a tug again.

1966: Out of service.

1969: Donated to the Aker Group, which had taken over the Nyland yard.

1972-74: Cosmetically restored.

1974: 24 October: Towed to Oslo and placed on display on the quayside at the site of the former Nylands yard.

1987: Returned to Ørje by road.

   14 March: Stiftelsen D/S Engebret Soot founded to take over and restore the steamer.

1989: Acquired by Stiftelsen D/S Engebret Soot. Restoration commenced.

1991: Restoration work continued by a co-operation between Indre Østfold Arbeidskontor, the Stiftelsen, and Marker Kommun. Some work was done by unemployed youths.

1995: 7 June: Was returned to the water, having been returned to her 1942 condition.

1996: Returned to service with occasional public passenger trips from Ørje.

Engebret Soot's sailings are almost entirely charters, with occasional public trips for special events.

SS LELÅNG

Lelång en route back to Ørje, 2003.

Length: 15.20m   **Gross tonnage**: 20
Propulsion: Single Screw
Built: 1872   **Rebuilt** (most recent): 2004
Passenger capacity: 54
Body of water: Halden Canal   **Home port**: Ørje
Frequency of operation: Undergoing restoration
Website address: web.telia.com/~u30207616/lelang.htm
Builders: Akers Mek Verksted, Kristiania (now Oslo)
Owner: Kanalmuseet Ørje

1872: Built as a timber-towing tug for Saugbrugsforeningen, Fredrikshald for use on Lake Stora Lee, over the Swedish border, and based at Strands bruk, Nössemark. Also carried passengers on occasion.
1915: Purchased by AB Lee Bruk, Dals Ed.
1943: Purchased by AB Strands Sågverk.
1955: 28 July: Sold to the Sinclair brothers, Lee Bruk, who had purchased Strands sawmill from the Föreningen. Chartered to Västsvenskas Virkesföreningen, Bengstsfors.
1957: Laid-up at Nössemark.
1959: Returned to Strands Bruk.
1978: Sold to Stig Holm, Gothenburg. Moved to Gothenburg.
1986: Laid-up on land near Lilla Edet, Västergotland, where she became derelict.
2003: 1 July: Returned to Ørje by land for restoration, having been purchased by the Kanalmuseet at Ørje.

SL PASOP

Pasop undergoing restoration at Ørje, 1999.

Length: 13.11m

Propulsion: Single Screw   Engine type: Compound

Built: 1908

Body of water: Halden Canal   Home port: Ørje

Frequency of operation: Undergoing restoration

Website address: www.kanalmuseet.no/asp/dampbatene.asp

Builders: Glommens Mek Verkstad, Fredrikstad

Owner: Stiftelsen DS Engebret Soot

Remarks: Coal-fired

1908: Built as a timber-towing tug for Haldenvassdragets Fløttningsforening for use on the Halden Canal and connecting waterways.

1928: Lengthened by 2.4m.

1959: Withdrawn from service, Sold to Mr Natvig, used as a private steam launch.

1973: Sold to steamboat enthusiast Pål Ulsteen and moved to the Oslofjord.

1982: Placed on land at Gressholmen, Oslo, for projected restoration.

1996: Donated to Stiftelsen Engebret Soot, moved to Ørje where she lies in a shed awaiting restoration.

SS TURISTEN

Length: 25.05m   Gross tonnage: 76.41

Propulsion: Single Screw   Engine type: Triple Expansion, 100hp

Built: 1887   Rebuilt (most recent): 2000

Passenger capacity: 135

Body of water: Halden Canal   Home port: Tistedal

Frequency of operation: Return to steam 200?

Website address: www.kanalmuseet.no/asp/dampbatene.asp

Builders: Nyland Verksted, Kristiania (now Oslo)

Owner: Hof Kommune (?)

Remarks: Sunk 1967, raised 1997

1887: Built as a passenger steamer for Interessentskapet Turisten, a joint venture of the families Skollenborg, Haneborg, and Nordby, for service on the Halden Canal to replace *Engebret Soot* on the route from Tistedal to Skulerud.

15 July: Entered service.

1906: Owners became A/S Dampskipet Turisten.

1921: Owners became Interessentskapet Turisten again.

1925: Sold to A/S Turisten, backed by NSB (Norwegian railways), and Fredrikshald Kanalselskap. Now used only in the summer months on tourist trips. Former cargo room converted to cabins. Three round trips per week now undertaken.

1939-45: Laid-up during the war years.

1963: Withdrawn from service.

1967: Engine and superstructure removed and hull scuttled in the Femsjøen.

1997: Found, raised and taken to Tistedal, where restoration commenced on land. This has been progressing very slowly.

It is the intention of those restoring her that *Turisten* will be returned to her 1909 condition and have her steam engine re-fitted.

6 Sweden

Sweden is a country rich in preserved steamers. Of particular note are the 'white boats', the passenger steamers of the Stockholm archipelago, and the large number of steam warping tugs that survive on Lakes Siljan and Runn in Dalarna. Small passenger launches, known as *ångslups*, have survived in good numbers throughout the country, and new restoration projects keep turning up all the time.

Some useful Swedish words:

Ång	steam
Slup	launch
Båt	boat
Fartyg	ship
AB (aktiebolaget)	Limited Company
Varv	shipyard
Rederi	shipping company
Föreningen	Foundation
Stiftelsen	Society

STOCKHOLM

The white steamers of the Stockholm archipelago are very much part of the tourist image of the city. In addition to those mentioned below, there are a good number of former steamers, now motorised, operating in Stockholm waters.

Two of the steamers, **Storskär** and **Norrskär**, are still operated by Waxholmsbolaget, which operates a wide network of lifeline services to the islands of the archipelago. They still serve many small piers and jetties on their routes, serving local passengers, those that live on the islands year-round and those that have summer cottages there, as well as tourists.

The typical Stockholm passenger steamer has two decks, with an open foredeck formerly used for cargo, a tween deck (main deck) aft of this with the toilets, galley, purser's office, etc., sometimes a small café forward on the deck below, and a restaurant on the upper deck with open deck seating around the outside of the upper deck accommodation, and the bridge forward on the upper deck, apart from **Norrskär**, which has the bridge on top of the upper deck. Reservations in the restaurants, where the speciality is *ångbåtsbiff* (steamer steak, grilled steak with potatoes and onions), are advised to be made as soon as you board to ensure a table. Access to the engine room is often available once the engineer knows that you are a steam enthusiast.

Archipelago – Saltsjön

SS BLIDÖSUND

Blidösund approaching her berth at King Gustav's statue, Stockholm, 1999.

Length: 35.29m   Gross tonnage: 214
Propulsion: Single Screw   Engine type: Compound, 320hp
Built: 1911   Passenger capacity: 250
Body of water: Stockholm Archipelago   Home port: Stockholm
Frequency of operation: Daily   Period of operation: Early May to late October
Website address: www.blidosundsbolaget.se
www.faktaomfartyg.com/blidosund_1911.htm
Builders: Eriksbergs M V, Göteborg
Owner: Ångfartyget Blidösund KB
Former names: *Express II* 1968, *Blidösund* 1965
Remarks: Coal-fired

1910: November: Launched.

1911: 3 March: Final trial before delivery.

7 March. Arrived Stockholm on her delivery voyage from Gothenburg.

10 March: Entered service from Stockholm to Norrsund on the island of Blidö, on the Blidösund.

1949: 6 November: Ran aground and sank by the stern near Leirviksudde. Raised and repaired eight days later.

1961: Service withdrawn. Laid-up.

1965: Sold to Stockholms Ångslups AB, renamed *Express II*. (This name was not registered and was only painted on.)

1968: Sold to Roslagens Skeppslag, run by enthusiast Eric Jägeborg, and renamed *Blidösund*

1969: 19 July: After renovation, placed in weekend service from Stockholm to the Blidösund and Furusund. Also relieved *Mariefred* one day per week on the Stockholm to Mariefred route until 1985.

1973: Evening music cruises started.

1977: Purchased by a group led by Thure Moberg, following the death of Eric Jägeborg. They formed Ångfartyget Blidösund KB.

1982: New boiler fitted.

1988: Yellow portion of funnel painter black, gradually returning to yellow as funds were raised for major replacement of hull plates.

8 December. Advent cruises started.

Blidösund offer evening cruises from Monday to Thursday at 18:30 from Stockholm and a Friday evening single trip at 16:45 to Norrtälje via the Blidösund, with a motor vessel connection back to Stockholm from Norrsund, or a bus back from Norrtälje enabling a round trip to be enjoyed. On Saturdays she offers day excursions from Norrtälje or Furusund to various destinations in the archipelago, and on Sundays a trip from the Blidösund piers to Svartlöga, with an 09:00 connection from Stockholm , by motor vessel, steaming back to Stockholm in the evening. She offers special *Julbord* advent cruises in December, including trips to Christmas markets at Blidö and Nynäshamn, and a Christmas eve trip to the Blidösund.

She is the only surviving coal-burning steamer operating in the Stockholm archipelago. She sails from Gustav III's statue at the northern end of Skeppsbron, outside the Royal Palace.

SS NORRSKÄR

Length: 34.84m   Gross tonnage: 227
Propulsion: Single Screw   Engine type: Compound, 298hp
Built: 1910   Rebuilt (most recent): 1965
Passenger capacity: 265
Body of water: Stockholm Archipelago   Home port: Stockholm
Frequency of operation: Daily
Period of operation: Early May to late September
Website address: www.waxholmsbolaget.se/index2.html
http://www.faktaomfartyg.com/sandhamn_express_1910.htm

Norrskär in the Stockholm archipelago, 1995.

Builders: Eriksbergs M V, Göteborg
Owner: Waxholms Ångfartygs AB
Former names: *Sandhamn Express* 1949
Remarks: New boiler 1999–2000

1910: Built as **Sandhamn Express** for the wholesaler B.O. Seippel for the service from Stockholm to Sandhamn.
1915: Taken over by Stockholms-Sandhamns Rederi AB.
1947: Taken over by Waxholms Nya Ångfartygs AB, Vaxholm.
1949: Renamed **Norrskär**.
  Placed on the route from Stockholm to Furusund and Björkö.
1952: Moved to the route from Stockholm to Vasbystrand on Ljusterö. From now until 1960 used for winter traffic on various routes.
1953: Converted to oil-firing.
1956: Placed on the routes from Stockholm to Sandö and from Stockholm to Ingmarsö and Brottö.
1957: Placed on the route from Stockholm to Finnhamn and Husarö.
1964: Owners became Waxholms Ångfartygs AB.
1965: Major refurbishment.
1970: New boiler fitted. Moved back to the Stockholm to Sandhamn route.
1999: Sandhamn sailings restricted to weekends only.
2000: New boiler fitter at Oskarhamns Varv.

On Mondays to Fridays **Norrskär** offers a return sailing to Grinda at 11:00 with an evening trip at 18:30 to Vaxholm and Ramsö, while on Saturdays and Sundays she offers a day return to Sandhamn at 10:30. These sailings operate from Midsummer to late August. Like the remainder of the Waxholmsbolaget fleet, she wails from Strömkajen, outside the Grand Hotel.

Being part of the local authority-owned fleet of vessels serving the islands of the Stockholm archipelago, she has many intermediate stops on each sailing and the passengers are more likely to be the inhabitants of the islands, or those with a summer house there, than international tourists.

ST ÖSTA

Length: 17.42m
Propulsion: Single Screw   **Engine type:** Compound, 55hp
Built: 1898   **Passenger capacity:** 12
Body of water: Stockholm Archipelago   **Home port:** Waxholm
Frequency of operation: Charters
Website address: www.osta.nu
Builders: Gefle Verkstader, Gävle
Owners: Östa Rederi AB, Åkersberga
Remarks: Coal-fired

Östa at a steam event in Karlstad, 1985.

1898: Built as a warping tug for Stora Kopparbergs Bergslags AB as a sister of **Laxen** (p.150) and **Bäsingen** (p.149).
1930: Sold to Nedre Dalälvens Flottledsförvattning.
*c.*1960: Converted to oil firing.
1970: Sold to U. Fredler for use as a yacht.
1972: Moved to Stockholm.
1975: Sold to Alf Kvist. Converted back to wood firing.
Mid-1980s: Around this time was a regular visitor to steam events, e.g. at Karlstad in 1985. Was fitted with a steam calliope.
1997: Owners became Östa Rederi AB, Åkersberga.
2000: Started to be used for charters from Vaxholm.

Östa offers charter trips in the northern part of the Stockholm archipelago from Vaxholm. She is a regular visitor to steam events throughout Sweden.

SS SALTSJÖN

Saltsjön at her berth in Stockholm, 1999.

Length: 37.5m   Gross tonnage: 250
Propulsion: Single Screw,   Engine type: Compound, 450hp
Built: 1925   Passenger capacity: 290
Body of water: Stockholm Archipelago   Home port: Stockholm
Frequency of operation: MX
Period of operation: Late May to mid-September
Website address: www.saltsjon.nu;
www.faktaomfartyg.com/saltsjon_1925.htm;
www.swecox.se
Builders: Eriksbergs M V, Göteborg
Owner: Swecox International, Västerås
Operator: Skärgårdsångaren Saltsjön AB
Former names: *Björkfjärden* 1993, *Saltsjön* 1970

1925: 11 April: Launched.

11 June: Delivered to owners.

20 June: Entered service as the passenger steamer **Saltsjön** for Waxholms Nya Ångfartygs AB, Vaxholm. Operated from Stockholm and Dalarö to Ornö and Utö and in the winter months from Stockholm to Vaxholm and neighbouring islands. Continued on these services until 1948.

1934: 30 March: Ran aground near Betsö jetty in the Saxarfjärden. Towed to the Hammarby yard for repairs.

1939: Used during the war as **Hjälpkanonbåt 20**, an auxiliary gunboat.

1951: 3 September: Suffered a fire on board while moored at Nybroviken, Stockholm. Repairs took over two years at the Hammarby yard.

1953: During the summer months, sailed with a dummy side wheels as **New Orleans** from Stockholm to Vaxholm.

1954: Used for charters in the summer.

1957: 8 May: Rammed by **Svan** in the Nybroviken in Stockholm.

1959: Used as a reserve steamer.

1963: Used on the service from Nynäshamn to Nåttarö and Rånö.

1964: Returned to traffic in the central archipelago after an accident meant **Saxaren** was out of service.

1 October: Taken over by Rederi AB Svea.

1965: 12 March: Sold to Nya Rederi AB Saltsjön.

Used in the summer from Stockholm to Utö, and in the winter months as a floating nightclub.

1966: Converted to oil firing.

1967: Owners went into liquidation.

1968: Chartered by the liquidators to Ångfartygs AB Stockholm-Sandhamn. Used in the summer from Stockholm to Sandhamn.

1 December. Made an advent cruise from Strängnäs to Stockholm with only three passengers on board. On return to Strängnäs, caught by the wind and hit the railway bridge there

1970: 5 May: Sold to Nya Ångfartygs AB Strömma Kanal, Stockholm, towed to Djurgårdsvarvet for restoration, renamed **Björkfjärden**.

1971: 13 June: Entered service on Lake Mälar from Stockholm to Bjorkö, Adelsö and Strängnäs.

1975: Laid-up after boiler problems.

1977: Sold to Ångfartygs AB Saltsjön-Mälaren, Stockholm.

1977-78: Renovated and boiler repaired.

1978: Returned to service chartered to Nya Ångfartygs AB Strömma Kanal from Stockholm to Bjorkö, continued on this route until 1983.

1984: Moved to the Stockholm to Vaxholm service.

1994: 15 April: Renamed **Saltsjön**.

Placed into service at the weekends in the summer months on her original route from Stockholm to Dalarö and Utö with occasional trips to the outer archipelago, e.g. to Svenska Högarna, Söderarm and Norrpada.

1998: Charter to Strömma Kanalbolaget finished, now run in connection with Waxholms Ångfartygs AB.

1999: Sold to Swecox International, Västerås. Continued on same services.

2000: 1 July: Ran aground off Gruvbryggan, Utö. Later docked at Beckholmen and resumed service without repairs.

2001: 15 September: Sailed for Algots Yard, Mariehamn, where several hull plates were replaced.

2006: For sale. Only one public sailing was scheduled to operate in Summer 2006, on Skärgårdsbåten Day on 7 June. It is hoped to resume public sailings in 2007.

Saltsjön normally offers the long day trip to Utö on Saturdays and Sundays departing at 09:30 from Strömkajen, and evening jazz cruises at 19:30 from Gustav III's statue during the week. The trip to Utö can he highly recommended, sailing through a number of narrow channels between the islands. Like a number of the other Stockholm steamers she offers advent *Julbord* cruises.

In 2006 she was lying laid-up at her normal berth at Gustav's statue near the Royal Palace in Stockholm.

SS STOCKHOLM

Stockholm. (B. Worden)

Length: 48.72m   **Gross tonnage**: 649
Propulsion: Single Screw   **Engine type**: Triple Expansion, 725hp
Built: 1931   **Rebuilt** (most recent): 1999
Passenger capacity: 385
Body of water: Baltic Coast   **Home port**: Stockholm
Frequency of operation: Daily
Period of operation: February to December (steam only in December)
Website address: www.strommakanalbolaget.com
www.faktaomfartyg.com/oland_1931.htm
Builders: Oskarshamns Mek Verkstad
Owner: Strömma Turism & Sjöfart AB
Former names: *Korsholm af Wästerås* 2000, *Korsholm* 1996, *Öland* 1989 *Korsholm III* 1986,
Korsholm 1967, *Öland* 1968

1931: 2 July: Launched as the passenger steamer ***Öland***.

28 September: Trails. Delivered to Kungliga Generalpoststyrelsen (Royal Post Office).

1 November: Entered service from Kalmar to Färjestad and Kalmar to Borgholm carrying the post to the island of Öland. She was normally in service from 1 November to the end of April each year.

1946: Converted to oil firing.

1952: Sold to Ångbåts AB Kalmarsund, Kalmar. Used from Kalmar to Färjestaden in winter and from Kalmar to Borgholm in summer.

6 February. Ran aground on the Enstensgrundet. The seven passengers on board were rescued by pilot boats from Kalmar. Refloated the following day.

1954: 11 July. Ran aground outside Borgholm. Sprang a leak in the engine room. Temporary repairs were made by a diver and she sailed to Kalmar for permanent repairs.

1955: From now only used in the summer months.

1956: Laid-up at Kalmar after the summer season.

1958: 1 June: Sold to Rederi AB Vaasa-Umeå, Vaasa, Finland.

August to December: Rebuilt at FV Holming Oy, Vaasa. Lengthened and converted to a car ferry with side doors. Renamed ***Korsholm III***.

15 December: Entered service from Vaasa to Umeå.

1959: 23 May: Started regular summer service from Vaasa to Umeå after the ice had cleared. Ran each year from April or May to November or December.

1965: Only ran from 22 June to 31 August.

1966: Ran from Vaasa to Örnsköldsvik from 27 May to 30 August.

1967: Sold to the Finnish Navy. Renamed ***Korsholm***. Converted to a base ship.

1975: Used as a mother ship for sailors.

1985: November: Taken out of service and laid-up at Turku.

Sold to Oy Kanora AB, Naantali, remained at Turku.

1986: 1 July: Sold to Marin & Maskin I Stockholm AB (Tommie Avelin), Stockholm. Towed to Stockholm on 14 July. Renamed **Öland**. Interiors stripped when at Stockholm. A planned purchase by Kalmar Museum for preservation was never fulfilled.

12 September: Sold to Café Casablanca Aps, Aarhus, Denmark. Much of the interior and the destroyed bridge interior was removed. Towed to Aarhus, where the intention was to rebuilt her as a restaurant ship, but work never commenced on the conversion.

October: Sold to Funktionaernes Fagforeningen. Planned to be used as a floating office in Copenhagen.

1987: 24 June: Towed from Stockholm to Nakskov, laid-up there.

1989: February: Sold to Json Shipping, Mariehamn, Finland.

7 July: Towed to Thomsen and Thomsen repair yard, Marstal, Denmark.

November: Sold back to Marin & Maskin, Stockholm. Was to have been towed to Stockholm, was sold whilst under tow and was instead taken to Turku Renamed **Korsholm**.

12 December: Sold to Höyrylaiva OY Ukko-Pekka, Naantali. Planed to be used as a consort to **Ukkopekka** on trips out of Turku.

1991: 3 September: Taken over by Naantalin Höyrylaiva Oy, Naantali.

1992: 2 May: Owners name changed to Marcato Oy, Turku. Remained laid-up at Turku in poor condition.

1996: 12 June: Sold to Swecox International, Stockholm. Registered as **Korsholm af Wästerås**. Towed to Beckholmen, Stockholm, later moved to Saltsjökvarn quay.

1998: January: Sold to Strömma Kanalbolaget, Stockholm.

12 October: Towed to Rönnängs Varv, Tjörn, for a total rebuild. At this time a diesel engine was installed in addition to the steam engine.

2000: April: Delivered back to Stockholm. Renamed **Stockholm**.

Summer: Operated coastal cruises south from Stockholm to Västervik, these lasted four days each way with overnight stops at Nyköping, Söderköping/Mem, and Valdemarsvik. These were offered four times in 2000 and three times in 2001.

2002: Used on Brunch cruises from February to November from Stockholm to Vaxholm, and also on *Julbord* cruises in December.

Stockholm offers 3-hour trips from Stockholm to Vaxholm and back at 12:00 and 15:00, also at 19:00 in the summer months. The only time she is advertised to utilise her steam machinery is during her *Julbord* cruises.

SS STORSKÄR

Storskär at Vasbystand on the island of Ljustero.

Length: 38.95m   Gross tonnage: 256
Propulsion: Single Screw   Engine type: Triple Expansion, 659hp
Built: 1908   Passenger capacity: 320
Body of water: Stockholm Archipelago   Home port: Stockholm
Frequency of operation: Daily

Period of operation: Early May to late September
Website address: www.waxholmsbolaget.se
www.faktaomfartyg.com/strangnas_express_1908.htm
Builders: Lindholmens Varv, Göteborg
Owner: Waxholms Ångfartygs AB
Former names: *Strängnäs Express* 1940

1904: April: Launched.

1908: 11 July: Arrived at Strängnäs on her delivery voyage.

July: Entered service as **Strängnäs Express** on the route from Strängnäs to Stockholm for Strengnäs Nya Rederi AB, Strängnäs. She was the fastest and most elegant steamer in the Lake Mälar trade.

1918: Owners sold to Ångfartygs AB Drottiningholm-Fittja, Stockholm.

1923: 6 June: King Gustav V travelled on board from Stallarholmen to Strängnäs.

1925: Owners changed name to **Trafikaktiebolaget Mälaran-Hjelmaren**.

1935: Sold to Rederi AB Mälartrafik.

1939: 26 April. Towed from Strängnäs to Stockholm for lay up.

5 December: Sold to Vaxholms Nya Ångfartygs AB, Vaxholm.

1940: 30 May: Renamed **Storskär**.

Placed in service from Stockholm to Furusund and Backa and from Stockholm to Furusund and Norrtälje.

1943: Moved to the Stockholm to Arholma service.

1963: Now only served Arholma once a week, serving as a relief boat to **Norrskär** on the Husarö run the remainder of the week.

1964: Owners became Waxholms Ångfartygs AB, Waxholm.

1964-65: winter: Major refit.

1969: 'Quarter-to-five' evening sailing to Ljusterö started. At that time she sailed on a Friday to Husarö, later the Friday sailing went to Möja, and then on the same Ljusterö sailings as on Monday to Thursday.

1976: New oil-fired boiler fitted at Mälarvarvet, Stockholm.

1998-99: New boiler fitted at Oskarshamn Varv.

Storskär sails on Mondays to Fridays on a 12:00 lunch sailing round Rindö, and on a 16:45 evening sailing to Vasbystrand on Ljusterö, returning at 22:15. On Saturdays she sails from midsummer to late August at 11:00 to Ljusterö and at 18:30 to Ramsöberg. Sundays see an 11:30 departure for Finnhamn and Husarö from midsummer to late August. From mid-May to midsummer and late August to mid-September, she sails to Grinda on Saturday and Sundays at 11:00.

Being part of the local authority-owned fleet of vessels serving the islands of the Stockholm archipelago, she has many intermediate stops on each sailing and the passengers are more likely to be the inhabitants of the islands, or those with a summer house there, than international tourists.

Stockholm harbour

SS DJURGÅRDEN 3

Length: 20.87m
Propulsion: Single Screw   Engine type: Compound, 55hp
Built: 1897   Rebuilt (most recent): 1983
Passenger capacity: 97
Body of water: Stockholm harbour   Home port: Stockholm
Frequency of operation: Occasional public trips
Period of operation: Early June and early December
Website address: hem.passagen.se/djurgarden3; www.skargardsbaten.se
Builders: O A Brodins Varv, Gävle
Owner: Stockholms Ångslups AB

Djurgården 3 at her berth in Stockholm, 1995.

Former names: *Nybron 1* 1901, *Stadsgården 1* 1898
Remarks: One screw each end, coal-fired

1893: Built as the double-ended harbour ferry *Stadsgården 1* for Ångfärje AB for the route in Stockholm
  harbour from Stadsgården to Alkärret on Djurgården.
1898: Moved to the route from Nybroviken to Alkärret, renamed *Nybron I*.
1900: 16 August: Sold, along with the owning company, to Stockholms Ångslups AB. Renamed
  Djurgården 3, placed on the service from Slussen to Allmänna Gränd on Djurgården.
1969: By this time she was in reserve and occasionally used on the routes from and to Skeppsholmen.
1970: 20 August: Owners sold to Waxholmsbolaget.
1973: By this time *Djurgården 3* was the last steam ferry in Stockholm harbour.
  Laid-up.
  March: Sold for a symbolic 1 Krona to Stiftelsen Skärgårdsbåten (Archipelago Boat Association) for
  preservation.
1975: 12 August: Restoration started on land at the Svartvik yard, Traneberg.
1980: 14 April: Returned to the water.
1983: Ångslups AB Djurgården formed to operate *Djurgården 3*.
1984: 21 September: new boiler fitted.
1985: 21 May: Returned to steam.
1993: Owners changed name to Stockholms Ångslups AB.
1995: Operated a summer route from Gustav III's statue to Prins Eugen Waldemarsudde on Djurgården.

Djurgården 3 mainly operates for special events in Stockholm harbour. These include Spårvagnens
Dag (tramway day) on the first Sunday in June when she operates to the tramway museum at Alkärret,
Skärgårdsbåtens Dag (archipelago boat day), the first Wednesday in June and on the first Saturday of December
when she runs from Gamla Stan to the town hall for a Christmas market. She also operates occasional
enthusiast excursions, organised by Stiftelsen Skärgårdsbåten for their members, and is available for charter.

SL FRITHIOF

Frithiof in Stockholm harbour.
(Peter Flemström)

Length: 19.88m
Propulsion: Single Screw   Engine type: Compound, 55hp
Built: 1897   Rebuilt (most recent): 2002
Passenger capacity: 62
Body of water: Stockholm harbour   Home port: Stockholm
Frequency of operation: Occasional public trips
Website address: www.magasin1.net/mariefred; www.steamship.se; www.mariefred.info
Builders: W. Lindberg, Stockholm (Södra Varvet)
Engine builder: G.F. Flodman 1897, fitted 2002
Owner: Ångslups AB Stockholm Omgifningar

1897: Built as the passenger launch *Frithiof* for Stockholms Ångslups AB, Stockholm. Used initially to serve a major art and industrial exhibition on Djurgården, then on various local services in the Stockholm area.
1900: Rebuilt by Bergsunds Mek Verksted. Afterdeck enclosed to make a saloon.
1903: Rebuilt at Ekensburgs Varv with an icebreaking bow.
1953: Withdrawn from service, sold to Ulf Anderson for preservation. Laid-up for many years.
Early 1970s: Seriously damaged by fire whilst in dock, later sold to an owner in Västerås, then to Stiftelsen Skärgårdsbåten, who removed the boiler and engine and installed them in *Tärnan*.
1999: Major restoration effort started, second-hand engine and new boiler fitted.
2002: Retuned to steam at the time of Stockholm's 750th anniversary.

Frithiof is mainly used for charter traffic, with occasional public trips on special occasions in connection with special events, e.g. tramway day in early June.

SS MÄLAREN 3

Mälaren 3 on ferry service, 1934.
(Stiftelsen Skärgårdsbåten)

Length: 15.55m   Gross tonnage: 46
Propulsion: Single Screw   Engine type: Compound, 40hp
Built: 1903
Body of water: Stockholm harbour   Home port: Stockholm
Frequency of operation: Return to steam ?
Website address: www.faktaomfartyg.com/sexan_1903.htm
Builders: Södra Varvet, Stockholm (W Lindberg)
Owner: Stockholms Ångslups AB
Former name: *Sexan* 1913
Remarks: On land or laid-up since 1957

1880: Built as the ferry *Sexan* for Nya Ängslups AB Smedsudden, for the route on Lake Mälar from Mariahissen to Klara Strand.
1913: Sold to Stockholms Ångslups AB, renamed *Mälaren 3*.
1950: Withdrawn from service. Laid-up for many years at the Djurgårdsvarvet.
1968: Sold to a private individual at Norrhammar.

1973: 13 June: Purchased for preservation by three members of Stiftelsen Skärgårdsbåten.
  4 October: Towed to Kummelnäs Varv for hull work.
  Loaned to Ångfartygs AB Strömma Kanal for use as a booking office at Klara Mälarstrand.
1982: 15 July: Towed to Riddarholmen, where the steam engine was removed. Then towed back to Klara Mälarstrand.
1984: 4 July: Placed on land at the Lumakajen, Hammarbyhamnen.
  Donated to Stiftelsen Skärgårdsbåten subsidiary Ångslups AB Djurgården for preservation.
1987: 28 September: Moved to Beckholmen for eventual restoration.
1988: Ultrasound survey of hull, which was found to have strong rust damage.
1991: 2 October: Placed on land at Beckholmen.
1993: Owners changed name to Stockholms Ångslups AB.

Mälaren 3 has often had to take second place as far as restoration is concerned, with steamers such as **Djurgården 3** and **Tärnan** taking precedence.

SL NOCTURNE

Nocturne in her early years as *Trafik*.
(From the book *Alla våra Ångsluper*)

Length: 18.30m
Propulsion: Single Screw, **Engine type**: , 80hp
Built: 1884   **Passenger capacity**: *c.*30
Body of water: Stockholm   **Home port**: Stockholm
Frequency of operation: Charters
Website address: www.steamship.se/html_N/index_n.htm
Builders: OA Brodins Varv, Gävle
Engine builder: R Runeberg, Borgå, Finland, 1899, from **Tunadal**
Owner: Ångslups AB Stockholm Omgifningar
Former names: **Gustav** *c.*1965, **Nocturne** 1954, **Trafik 1**

1884: Built as the steam launch **Trafik I** for Nylands Trafik AB, also known as Ångslupsbolaget Nyland, for service on the Ångermanälven river.
1911: Sold to Ångslupsbolaget Ragnhild.
1932: Sold to owners at Lörvik, later to Frånö and yet again to Barstu.
1934: Converted to a tug.
1936: Rebuilt as a cargo boat with a petrol engine.
1939: Laid-up because of a fuel shortage due to the war.
1942: Sold to new owners at Noraström.
1945: Sold to I Wallén, Nordingrå.
1951: Sold to Svanö AB, renamed **Sven**, converted to a barge.

1966: Taken over by NCB.

1978: Sold to Stockholm owners.

1982: Renamed **Nocturne**.

Early 2000s: Purchased by Ångslups AB Stockholm Omgifningar. Restored at Beckholmen. 1947-vintage engine and boiler fitted which were in **Tunadal**, and which were originally built in 1899 in Finland.

Nocturne is expected back in steam in Summer 2006, and will offer charters in the Stockholm area.

SS ORION

Orion at her berth in Stockholm.

Length: 32m
Engine type: Compound, 180hp
Built: 1929
Home port: Stockholm
Frequency: Undergoing restoration
Website address: www.ss-orion.se
Builder: Helsingborgs Varv och Svetsningsbolag
Owner: Museiföreningen S/S Orion's Vänner
Remarks: Coal-fired
Former names: **Orion af Stockholm**, **Orion af Göteborg** 1987, **Orion** 1977, **Kalmar** 1961

1929: Built for Kungliga Lotsverket (The Royal Swedish Pilot Service) as the pilot steamer **Kalmar**. Used in the Eastern Pilotage District, which covered an area from Karlskrona in the south to Trosa in the North, including Lake Vättern. Her duties also included work as a lighthouse and buoy tender.

1956: Placed in reserve.

1961: Rebuilt: Open bridge roofed over. Lengthened by 3m. Now used as a lighthouse construction vessel for Sjöfartsverket (Swedish National Administration of Shipping and Navigation). Renamed **Orion**.

1979: Withdrawn from active service. Sold to a private individual in Gothenburg who planned to use her for cruises along the Norwegian Coast. Renamed **Orion af Göteborg**. She was laid-up and became derelict.

1987: Sold to Museiföreningen S/S Orions Vänner and moved to Stockholm for restoration. Renamed **Orion af Stockholm**. Moored at the back of Skeppholmen. Restoration work started and has been continuing.

SS SANKT ERIK

Length: 61m   Gross tonnage: 1,441
Propulsion: Twin Screw   Engine type: 2 Triple Expansion, 4,000hp
Built: 1915   Passenger capacity: 200
Body of water: Swedish Coast   Home port: Stockholm
Frequency of operation: Occasional public trips

Sankt Erik at Nynäshamn, 1995.

Website address: www.sbf.org.se/sjobefal/1997/MB397/angbat.html (note this refers to 1997 sailings
to Kalmar and Flensburg);
www.vasamuseet.se/Vasamuseet/Om/Museifartygen/Sankt%20Erik.aspx?lang=en
Builders: Finnboda Varvet, Stockholm
Owner: Statens Sjöhistoriska Museum, Stockholm
Former names: *Isbrytaren II* 1958
Remarks: Icebreaker, 1 screw each end

1915: Built as the harbour icebreaker *Isbrytaren II* for Stockholms Hamnstyerlse (harbour authority).
18 March: Delivered.
1958: Modernised. Renamed *Sankt Erik*.
1977: Taken out of service.
1980: Donated to Statens Sjöhistoriska Museum for preservation. Moored as part of the Vasamuseet.
Initially she was only a static exhibit, not open to the public.
1988-90: Boat deck, which was rotten, replaced by a steel deck covered by pine planks, main engine and
boiler overhauled.
1990-95: Fore engine overhauled, captain's saloon and galley restored to the condition they would have
been *c*.1915. The Captain's saloon is now used for events at the Vasamuseet.
1991: In steam without passengers for the first Stockholm Water Festival.
1994: Carried passenger for the second Stockholm Water Festival.
1995: Sailed to Luleå, back round the coast to Oslo and back to Stockholm under charter to a Swedish
company celebrating its centenary.
1996: After deck re-laid in steel covered by pine planks.
1997: Visited a maritime festival at Kalmar and the Dampf-Rundum at Flensburg.
1999: Did not sail because boiler tubes had to be replaced.
2007: Proposed sailings under stame in connection the the visit of the Tall Ships Race to Stockholm.

Sankt Erik has not made any advertised passenger trips in recent years. She is normally open as a museum
ship near the *Vasa*.

SL TÄRNAN AF WAXHOLM

Length: 19.89m
Propulsion: Single Screw   **Engine type:** Compound, 47hp
Built: 1901   **Rebuilt** (most recent): 1996
Passenger capacity: 83

Tärnan at a steam festival in 1998. (Bill Worden)

Body of water: Stockholm Archipelago   **Home port**: Stockholm
Frequency of operation: Occasional public trips
Website address: http://www.faktaomfartyg.com/tarnan_1901.htm;
www.skargardsbaten.se
Builders: Södra Varvet, Stockholm (W Lindberg)
Engine builder Södra Varvet Stockholm 1897, from *Frithiof*, fitted 1990
Owner: Ångslups AB Union (Stiftelsen Skärgårdsbåten)
Former names: *Brynhilda* 1985, *Amaranth* c.1980, *Tärnan* 1952
Remarks: Coal-fired

1901: Built for Waxholms Nya Ångfartygs AB as the ångslup (steam launch) *Tärnan* for the service from Vaxholm to Tynningö, connecting with the larger steamers which had come out from Stockholm.

*c.*1905: Rebuilt. After section enclosed to make a saloon.

1951: Sold to Hilding Alexandersson, Norrköping. He replaced the steam engine with a diesel and renamed her *Amaranth*.

1952: Operated to Esterön on Bråviken.

*c.*1978: Withdrawn from service.

Early 1980s: Returned to Stockholm, name *Brynhilda* painted on for the TV series *Öbergs på Lillöga*.

1985: Purchased by Stiftelsen Skärgårdsbåten for preservation. Renamed *Tärnan af Vaxholm*. Completely restored to her 1905 condition. Steam engine and boiler formerly in *Frithiof* installed. Ångslups AB Union formed to operate her.

1993: Ownership passed to Stockholms Ångslups AB.

Tärnan sees passenger service at special events in Stockholm harbour and is available for charters.

SY TIFFANY

Tiffany fitting out at Beckholmen.
(Peter Flemström)

Length: 17m
Engine type: Compound, 18hp
Built: 2006   **Passenger capacity**: 12

Body of water: Stockholm harbour   **Home port**: Stockholm
Frequency: Charters
Builder: Beckholmen, Stockholm
Engine builder: Swedish Navy, Karlskronavarvet, 1890s
Owner: Ångslups AB Stockholm Omgifningar

Tiffany is a newly built steam yacht, which is expected to enter service in the charter trade at Stockholm in Summer 2006. She is fitted with a compound engine built at Karlskrona for the Swedish Navy in the 1890s and originally used in small steam launches of about 8–10m in length.

LAKE MÄLAR AND NEIGHBOURING WATERWAYS

SS BORE

Bore at Västerås, 1988.

Length: 39.81m   **Gross tonnage**: 374
Propulsion: Single Screw   **Engine type**: Compound, 605hp
Built: 1894   **Rebuilt** (most recent): 1984
Passenger capacity: 60
Body of water: Lake Mälar   **Home port**: Västerås
Frequency of operation: Demonstration steamer
Website address: www.djurgardsvarvet.se/tugs/bore/bore.htm
Builders: Kockums M V, Malmö
Owner: Swecox International AB/Knut Borg
Remarks: Icebreaker; fore and aft screws; coal-fired

1894: Built as a harbour icebreaker for Malmö Hamnförvalting (Harbour Board). At the time she was
    Sweden's largest icebreaker.
    17 November: Entered service. Used to keep the Öresund open, also used as a passenger steamer
    between Malmö and Copenhagen when the Öresund was icebound.
1914–18: Used by the Swedish Navy as armed gunboat number 21.
1963: Last winter in service. Laid-up. Later used in a film about the Swedish Polar explorer Andrée, then
    laid-up again.
1968: Laid-up totally, over the years got more derelict.
1984: Purchased by Swecox International AB, and moved to Västerås. Restored over the years and
    returned to steam for her owners, who are boiler manufacturers. Used as a private yacht and on special
    sailings for invited VIP guests and customers.
2005: For sale.

SS DROTTNINGHOLM

Drottningholm on Lake Malar
en route to Drottningholm Castle.

Length: 22.75m **Gross tonnage:** 109
Propulsion: Single Screw **Engine type:** Triple Expansion, 85hp
Built: 1909 **Rebuilt** (most recent): 1982
Passenger capacity: 150
Body of water: Lake Mälaren **Home port:** Stockholm
Frequency of operation: Daily **Period of operation:** 1 May to early September
Website address: www.strommakanalbolaget.com
Builders: Motala Mek Verkstad, Motala
Owner: Mälarörnas Ångfartygs AB **Operator:** Ångfartygs AB Strömma Kanal
Former names: *Nya Strömma Kanal* 1969, *Valkyrian* 1968

1909: Delivered as the small passenger steamer (ångslup) **Valkyrian** for Stockholms Ångslups AB, Stockholm. Was one of a trio of sister ships, others being **Angantyr**, still in service for Strömma Kanal AB, albeit with a diesel engine, and **Fylgia**, which was sold for use in the Finnboda shipyard in 1919. Placed in service from Stockholm to south Lidingö.

1911: Moved to the service from Stora Essingen to Stockholm. Rebuilt with an upper deck.

1918: 22 June: Sold to Waxholms Nya Ångfartygs AB, Vaxholm.

1944: Deck saloon with wooden seats fitted on the upper deck aft.

1945: Entered service as a *passbåt* (a term used for a boat which connected with the main service boat running to smaller islands) running from Saltsjöbaden to Ingarö.

Late 1940s: New boiler fitted.

1952: Placed in service from Tegelön to Östra Tynningö, also with a few sailings from Vaxholm to Stockholm.

1956: Used as a reserve boat.

1960: Used in the winter service from Stockholm to Vaxholm and Ramsö.

1962: Used on the summer as a *passbåt* from Vaxholm to the Lindalsund.

1963-67: Chartered on occasion to Olle Hellborn, for use in a film. Given the name **Saltkråkan I** in the TV series 'Vi på Saltkråkan'.

1964: 30 April: Sold to Stockholms Ångslups AB, Stockholm.

May: Placed in traffic to Möja.

1968: Winter: Laid-up in the Djurgårdsvarvet. Damaged by vandalism.

Sold to Strömma Kanalrederiet, Stockholm. Renamed **Nya Strömma Kanal**.

September: Made one trip from Stockholm to Sandhamn via the Strömma Kanal, but hit the bottom of the canal at Kolström because her draught was too great, and returned to Stockholm.

Autumn: Rebuilt with a restaurant in the upper deck saloon.

Later in the autumn: Made a trip to Möja and Sandhamn. Ran out of coal on the return journey and parts of her interior fittings were used to fire her until she got back to the Djurgårdsvarvet, where the coal bunkers were filled to get her back to the city.

1969: Sold to K/B Drottningholms Ångfartygs AB, although still operated and marketed by Strömma Kanalrederiet. Renamed **Drottningholm**.

1969: 3 May: Entered service on the route from Stockholm to Drottningholm for Strömma Kanalbolaget.

1969-70: Winter Converted to oil firing.

1974: July: Out of service for the remainder of the season after cracks were found in the engine bed. A conversion to diesel was proposed but rejected because 15% of the passengers to Drottningholm would only sail if they were on an actual steamer.

1980: Owners became Mälarörnas Ångfartygs AB, Stockholm. Sailings still operates by Strömma Kanal AB. 7 May: Gutted by fire which broke out on board while lying at Klara Mälarstrand berth, Stockholm. *Mariefred*, which was lying next to her, was also damaged.

1982: 14 May: Returned to service after rebuilding. The saloons had been completely rebuilt and the canopy on the upper deck aft removed.

1999: Winter: New boiler fitted.

Drottningholm offers a return trip from Klara Mälarstrand, near Stockholm Town Hall, to Drottningholm Palace every 2 hours from 10:00 until 16:00.

SS EJDERN

Ejdern at Södertälje, 1985.

Length: 22.39m   Gross tonnage: 59
Propulsion: Single Screw   Engine type: Compound, 65hp
Built: 1880   Rebuilt (most recent): 1974
Passenger capacity: 90
Body of water: Lake Mälaren   Home port: Södertalje
Frequency of operation: FSSuO
Period of operation: Early May to mid-September
Website address: www.ejdern.org
Builders: Göteborgs Mek Verkstad, Göteborg
Owner: Museiföreningen Ångfartyget Ejdern
Remarks: Coal-fired

1880: Built for Göteborgs Nya Ångslups AB for service in Gothenburg's northern archipelago from Björkö to Gothenburg, giving two return services daily.

1893: Rebuilt to enclose the tween deck and improve passenger accommodation there. Wheelhouse added.

1898: March: Sold to Roxens Ångbåts AB, Linköping. Moved to Linköping for use on Lake Roxen from Grensholmen to Linköping. Also used for towing in this period.

1899: 11 October to 19 December: chartered to Ångfartygs AB Gripsholms to run from Stockholm to Mariefred.

1901: March: Sold to new owners, remained on the same route from Linköping.

1904: May: Refitted at Stockholm, corrugated iron canopy added over upper deck.

1906: May: Sold to Södertälje Ångslups AB, moved to Södertälje, used on the service from there to piers on the island of Mörkö and on to Trosa. Also used on market trips from Mörkö to Södertalje, leaving about 03:00 on Market day (Saturday) with goods for the market at Södertälje. Also made occasional freight trips to Stockholm.

1910-13: Also operated from Södertälje to Mariefred on Mondays.

1924: April: Transferred to Södertälje Nya Ångslups AB after previous owners went into liquidation.

1925: January: Sold to her crew (Rikard Fredmark (captain), Ulriksson (engineer) and Jakobsson (helmsman).

1956: Final season. Captain Fredmark retired at the age of seventy-six. Laid-up at Södetjälje.

1958: 27 February: Sold to Södertälje Stad (town council). Remained laid-up.

1959 and 1960: Used as a café.

1964: 16 May: After a proposal to scuttle her in deep water, donated to Föreningen för bevarande av gamla ångbåter (association to save old steamers). Towed to Norr Mälarstrand in Stockholm, so that restoration could begin.

1965: Diesel engine fitted.

1966: Spring: Steam engine and boiler from the steam tug **Wikingen** fitted in place of the diesel, which was sold.

1968: Skrufångfartget Ejdern AB founded to operate her.

1970 to 1972: Operated on charter to Mälartrafik AB from Sigtuna to Skokloster and Skarholmen.

1972: Association re-formed as Museiföreningen Ångfartyget Ejdern.

1974: September: to 1975: May: Original steam engine re-installed.

1975: Summer: made a special trip to Sjötorp with 20 members onboard to see the restoration work in *Trafik*.

September: Made a special trip to Gothenburg.

1976: Started summer operation out of Södertälje.

1984: Converted back to coal-firing.

2005: 13 June to early July: Made a trip beck to Gothenburg for her 125th anniversary.

Ejdern operates, from two quays in Södertälje, Borgmästarudden, on the southern (Baltic) side of the locks which is her home base and Mälarhamnen on the northern (Lake Mälar) side of the lock. She makes a regular Saturday trip to Birka and Adelsö, a Friday trip in July to Drottningholm and Stockholm, both of these departing from Borgmästarudden at 08:45 and Mälarhamnen half an hour later. Once a year she makes a Sunday trip to Mariefred on the third Sunday of July, and one south to Oaxen on the third Sunday of August. Evening cruises to dance on the pier of a Lake Mälar island were provided in the mid-eighties, but are no longer in the advertised schedule.

SL GERDA

Gerda, wrapped up to protect her from the rain, on the Näshultasjön, 1999.

Length: 13.50m
Propulsion: Single Screw **Engine type**: single-cylinder, 10hp
Built: 1865 **Rebuilt** (most recent): 1996
Passenger capacity: 40
Body of water: Näshultasjön or Lake Mälaren
Home port: Eskilstuna, Torshälla
Frequency of operation: FSSuO **Period of operation**: Early May to late August
Website address: www.gerda.nu
Builders: Lindholmens Varv, Göteborg
Engine builder: Finland 1900, fitted 1995

Owner: Faktorimuseet, Eskilstuna Operator: Föreningen Ångslupen *Gerda*
Former name: *Haneberg* 1996, *Gerda* 1894
Remarks: Wood-fired

1865: Built as the passenger launch *Gerda* for Stockholms Ångslups AB.

1894: Sold to Haneberg in Södermanland for use on the Näshultasjön. Transported by rail to Bälgviken station. Renamed *Haneberg*.

1915-20: Steam engine replaced by a hot bulb semi-diesel during this period.

1932: Laid-up under a tarpaulin on land.

1976: Purchased by Eskilstuna Museum, who planned to restore her to run to the factory museum there, but her condition was so poor that little work was done.

1993: Work started on her restoration, during which a 1900 vintage ex-Finnish steam engine was fitted.

1996: Returned to steam, renamed *Gerda*, sometimes known as *Gerda af Haneberg*.

Gerda shares her time between Eskilstuna, where she operates to Torshälla and on Lake Mälar, and the Näshultasjön.

SS MARIEFRED

Mariefred at her Klara
Mälarstrand berth, Stockholm, 1995.

Length: 32.84m Gross tonnage: 178
Propulsion: Single Screw Engine type: Compound, 295hp
Built: 1903 Rebuilt (most recent): 1994
Passenger capacity: 230
Body of water: Lake Mälaren Home port: Stockholm
Frequency of operation: MX
Period of operation: Mid-May to early September
Website address: home.online.no/~roommun/emariefredhistory.htm; www.mariefred.info/
Builders: Södra Varvet, Stockholm (W Lindberg)
Owner: Gripsholms-Mariefreds Ångfartygs AB, Mariefred (Stiftelsen Skärgårdsbåten)
Remarks: Coal-fired

1903: Built for Mariefreds Ångfartygs AB, Mariefred for the route from Mariefred to Stockholm. Ran to Stockholm each day bringing the country people to the city with goods for market, etc.
  14 April: First sailing.

1905: Sold to Gripsholms-Mariefreds Ångfartygs AB, Mariefred, previously a competitor.

1907: Electric light installed.

1936: Company purchased by her captain, Arvid Andersson.

1938: By now all traffic was tourist traffic and she started from Stockholm each day, the local passenger and cargo traffic being taken by buses and lorries.

1942: Open afterdeck enclosed with glass.

1966: Owners taken over by enthusiast group Stiftelsen Skärgårdsbåten.

1980: 7 May: Seriously damaged by fire which broke out on *Drottningholm*, berthed next to her at Klara

Mälarstrand, Stockholm. Repaired and returned to service for the summer season.

1982–83: New boiler fitted.

1994: 8 May: Damaged again by fire whilst lying at Stockholm. Back in service after eight weeks.

Mariefred offers a return service on Lake Mälar from Stockholm to Mariefred, leaving at 10:00 daily except Mondays from mid-June to mid-August. On Saturdays and Sundays she offers an afternoon trip from Mariefred at 13:50 to Taxinge Näsby during her layover time at Mariefred.

Members of Stiftelsen Skärgårdsbåten get a return trip on *Mariefred* for the price of a single ticket as part of their membership. The membership is well worth it for the quarterly magazine *Skärgårdsbåten*, which is excellently produced and has news and historical articles on steamers in the Stockholm area and throughout Sweden.

ST REX

Length: 14.80m   Gross tonnage: 37
Propulsion: Single Screw   Engine type: Compound, *c.*80hp
Built: 1902
Body of water: Strömsholms Canal   Home port: Halstahammar
Frequency of operation: Charters
Website address: www.steamboatassociation.se/bilder12.html; www.sfmf.nu/rex2.htm; www.steamboatassociation.se/thorskog/rex.html
Builders: Torskogs Mekaniska Verkstad, Torskog
Owner: Hallstahammars Kommun   Operator: Strömsholms Kanalhistorik Förening
Remarks: Wood-fired, tows barges *Albert* and *Skantzö*

1902: Built for A. & L. Beijer & Co., Stockholm, for use as a harbour tug, later sold to AB Kasper Höglund, Stockholm. May have been used at Gothenburg.

1918: 2 May: Sold to A Klinkowström, Stockholm.

10 June: Sold to ASEA, Västerås, moved to the Strömsholms Canal, used to tow barges carrying coal, sandstone and other supplies to Sörstafors paper mill and Surahammars Bruk (iron works).

1920: ASEA's fleet of tugs sold to Surahammars Bruk.

1948: Withdrawn from service, replaced by road and rail transport.

1950: Sold to Svenska AB Christian & Nielsen, Stockholm to help in the building of the Hjulstabro bridge.

1954: Returned to Surahammar.

1966: In derelict condition, lying on the canal bottom. Sold to three youths from Halstahammar. Restoration started, replacement boiler fitted, which was originally used by the Swedish Navy.

1972: Restoration completed, returned to steam.

1988: 1 May: Taken over by Hallstahammars Kommun. Four-year restoration process began. Replacment boiler fitted, originally in sister ship *Inga*. New wheelhouse and accommodation areas fore and aft fitted.

1992: Restoration complete.

2002: On the occasion of her centenary, made a four-week return trip to her place of building at Torskog.

Rex normally operates towing the barges *Albert* and *Skantzö*. She offers occasional locally advertised public trips and charters.

SOUTHERN SWEDEN (SOUTH OF THE GÖTA CANAL)

SL BLENDA

Length: 6.0m   Engine type: Single cylinder, 3hp, built 1980
Built: 1986   Passenger capacity: 6

Body of water: River Lagaån Home port: Ljungby
Frequency of operation: Occasional public trips Period of operation: Summer
Website address: www.gasagarden.se
Builder: Shettlands snipa Owner: Rolf & Hilhe Persson
Former name: *Lulnåset* 2007

SS BOXHOLM II

Boxholm II at Malexander, 1985.

Length: 20.61m Gross tonnage: 37
Propulsion: Single Screw Engine type: Compound, 85hp
Built: 1904 Rebuilt (most recent): 1966
Passenger capacity: 116
Body of water: Lake Sommen Home port: Tranås
Frequency of operation: MTX Period of operation: 30 May to end August
Website address: www.boxholm2.com;
  www.tranas.se/vanstermeny/turism/english/welcometotranas/steamshipssboxholmii.4.5c2fee10170
c9cb8d80001805.html
Builders: Ljunggrens Mek Verkstad, Kristiansstad
Owner: Rederiaktiebolaget S/S Boxholm II
Remarks: Wood-fired

1904: Built for use on Lake Sommen. Supplied in sections and re-erected on the shore of the lake. Built
 as a tug to tow barges and timber for Boxholms AB.
 July: Maiden voyage.
1922: Aft area rebuilt and seats fitted for use as a passenger steamer. These are round the engine and give
 a good view of the fireman loading wood into the boiler.
1966: From now on used solely as a passenger steamer.
1982: Sold to Rune Hektor and Sven-Olof Sjöberg, her captain and engineer.
1999: Taken over by Rederi AB S/S Boxholm II.
2005: Ownership transferred to Rederiaktiebolaget S/S Boxholm II.

Boxholm II offers a variety of cruises during her brief season. On Wedsendays she makes a 3.5-hour
trip at 10:30 and on Saturdays a similar trip at 14:00. Those in July go to Torpön and in August to the
Hotel Lugnalandet, both with time for swimming. Wednesdays in July see a guided nature tour of the
lake at 10:30 from Torpön whilst on Thursdays there are 2-hour trips from Hätteboden at 10:30 and from
Malexander at 15:00. Fridays see the highlight of the week, the market trip to Tranås. This leaves Idebo at
07:30 and calls at another seven jetties before arriving at Tranås at 10:30. The return trip is at 14:00 and
returns direct from Malexander to Tranås, giving an interesting afternoon excursion covering the entire
lake. There are 3.5-hour Sunday music trips at 13:00 from Tranås.

SS CARL JOHAN

Length: 25.90m Gross tonnage: 89
Engine type: Compound, 52 IHP

Carl Johan, c.1910. (Lennart Holm collection)

Built: 1874   **Passenger capacity**: Was 202
Body of water: Lake Sommen   **Home port**: Torpön
Frequency: Undergoing restoration
Builder: Motala Mek Verkstad   **Owner**: Lennart Holm

1874: Built in sections at Motala and assembled at Stalbergs Gård. Built with a wooden hull on iron frames. Owned by R L Rääf, who formed Ångbåts AB Carl Johan to operate her. Owners later renamed Sommens Ångbåtsbolag. She was the largest steamer to operate on the lake.
30 June: Launched.
29 August: Entered service.
1880: Rebuilt with a raised poop deck and larger after saloon, with a cover over the quarter deck.
1890: Hull, originally black repainted white.
1900: Wheelhouse extended to provide a captain's cabin and a smoking lounge. Fixed cover added to central upper deck.
1931: Taken out of service and laid-up at Torpön.
1937: Moved to Skoboviken Tranås.
1970: Opened as a café.
1987: Purchased by present owner.
1989: Restoration started.

At some stage the steam engine and boiler were removed and the engine placed on display in the Tekniska Museet in Stockholm. The present owner is slowly restoring the wreck of **Carl Johan** and hopes to re-install a steam engine and boiler and return her to steam.

SS HERBERT

Herbert at her base at Alingsås, 1999.

Length: 15.25m   **Gross tonnage**: 30
Propulsion: Single Screw   **Engine type**: Compound, 45hp
Built: 1905   **Rebuilt** (most recent): 1992
Passenger capacity: 25
Body of water: Lake Mjörn   **Home port**: Alingsås
Frequency of operation: SuO   **Period of operation**: End June to mid-August
Website address: www.bxn.se/herbert2.htm

Builders: Eriksbergs M V, Göteborg   **Engine builder:** Ljungrens Mek Verkstad
Owner: Mjörns Ångbåtsföreningen
Remarks: Wood-fired

1905: Built as a tug for Strands Ångsåg (steam sawmill) on the Dalsland Canal. Used for towing barges from Strand to Gothenburg.
27 February: Launched.
5 May: Delivered.
1907: Sold to Lennartsfors Trämassafabrik (bulk wood factory), on the Dalsland Canal. Later towed barges to Ed, from where the contents were taken by rail to Halden in Norway.
1940: Runs to Ed ceased after Germany invaded Norway.
1946: Sold to Valdemar Ek and Elof Johanesson. Still used mainly for towing barges full of timber or paper. Also used occasionally as a passenger steamer.
1965: 3 December: Out of service. Laid-up at Lennartsfors.
1985: Purchased by Mjörns Ångbåtsföreningen, later moved to Lake Mjörn.
1992: Returned to service after a major restoration and rebuild, offering passenger trips now rather than being used as a tug.
2005: Celebrated her centenary with a trip to Gothenburg, where she was built, the Dalsland Canal, Lennartsfors and Strand.

Herbert normally operates Sunday trips in July at 11:00 and also 13:00 on certain dates, with a few Wednesday evening trips at the beginning and end of the season.

SL LAGAHOLM

Lagaholm. (Lagaholms Ångbåt Förening)

Length: 9.40m   **Gross tonnage:** 6
Propulsion: Single Screw   **Engine type:** 1-cylinder, 15hp
Built: 1888   **Rebuilt** (most recent): 2004
Passenger capacity: 12
Body of water: River Lagan   **Home port:** Laholm
Frequency of operation: SuX   **Period of operation:** Midsummer to 24 August
Website address: www.lommarp.se/sslagaholm/index.htm;
        www.buyit.se/bokahalmstad/lista.asp?subKategori=95;
        www.laholm.se/l_templates/L_PageFull.aspx?id=1350
Builders: Mekaniska Verkstad Vulcan, Norrköping
Owner: Laholms Ångbåtsföreningen
Former names: *Sofiero* 2002, *Anna* 1985, *Carl* 1957, *Bore* 1907
Remarks: Wood-fired
1888: Built as the steam launch *Bore*, used for timber towing on Lake Boren.
1907: Sold to Carl Nilsson, Höstbäck, a sawmill owner. Renamed *Carl*. Used on lakes Hövern and Lången in Östergötland.
1916: Laid-up on land after trucks took over the transportation of timber.
1957: Purchased by Lars Lundberg, Linköping. Renamed *Anna* and restored over a number of years.

1985: Purchased by Sofiero Brewery, Laholm, renamed **Sofiero**. Used in connection with the brewery (and boat)'s centenary in 1988.

1994: Started passenger trips on the River Lagan, chartered by Laholms Tourist Office.

1998: New boiler required, which the brewery were unable to fund. Fund started locally to purchase this. Purchased by Laholms Kommun after brewery went into liquidation.

1999: 10 November: Laholms Ångbåtsföreningen founded to preserve and operate steamer.

2001: River trips recommenced.

2002: 9 May: Renamed **Lagaholm**.

2003: 24 May: Visited Borås, where she carried passengers at a steam rally.

2003-04: winter: Restored at Gilleleje Båtbyggeri, Denmark.

2004: Visited Græsted, Denmark, for a steam rally.

Lagaholm offers afternoon cruises from Laholm at 14:00 and 16:00 from Mondays to Fridays. The first trip is a short trip, lasting 90 minutes, while the second is also a short trip on Mondays, Wednesdays and Fridays, and a long 3-hour trip on Tuesdays and Thursdays. On Saturdays there is only the 14:00 sailing and Sundays are given over to charters.

ST NALLE

Length: 21.6m   Gross tonnage: 69
Engine type: Compound, 250hp
Built: 1923   Rebuilt (most recent): 2000-06
Passenger capacity: 12
Body of water: Oskarshamn harbour   Home port: Oskarshamn
Frequency of operation: Occasional public trips   Period of operation: n/a
Website address: www.sjofartsforeningen.se/nalle/index.htm
Builders: Oskarshamn Mekaniska Verkstad
Owner: Föreningen SS Nalle
Former names: *Nalle Puh* 2000, *Nalle* 1963

1923: Built for use as a harbour tug and icebreaker at Oskarshamn for Oskarshamn Hamn.
 April: Entered service.

1963: Withdrawn from service, sold to K.V. Lundeberg, Goethenburg, renamed **Nalle Puh**.

1984: Sold to P. Kugler, Copenhagen, later to Hans Heger, Copenhagen, where she was used as a houseboat.

2000: Sold to Föreningen SS Nalle for restoration, regained the name **Nalle**. Restoration work commenced.

2004: 14 October: returned to steam in Oskarshamn harbour.

2006: 21-22 July: Offered trips on Oskarshamn Harbour Festival days, mainly for members of her preservation society, but non-members were carried on payment of a higher fare.

SL NOSSAN AF STALLAHOLM

Nossan af Stallaholm.

Length: 7.00m   Gross tonnage: 2
Propulsion: Single Screw   Engine type: Compound, 5hp

Built: 1933   Rebuilt (most recent): 1983
Passenger capacity: 12
Body of water: River Nossan   Home port: Nossebro
Frequency of operation: Daily   Period of operation: Mid-July to 10 August
Website address: www.hembygd.se/index.asp?DocID=7333; www.ssnossan.se
Builders: Unknown, Dalarna
Owner: Ångbåtsföreningen Nossan
Remarks: Wood-fired

1933: Built as a timber bundling boat with a hot bulb semi-diesel engine for service on the Dalälven River in Dalarna.

1981: Converted to steam, with an engine built by her then owner.

1994: Bought by her present owner, moved to the present location and restored, Passenger trips started.

Nossan operates in the summer months from Norrebrö to Bredöl. Scheduled sailings take place from mid-July to early August daily at 17:00 and 18:00. She is available for charters from late May to early September.

SL SCHEBO

Schebo at Malmö. (Malmö Museums)

Length: 12.80m   Gross tonnage: 17
Propulsion: Single Screw   Engine type: 1-cylinder, 24hp
Built: 1874   Rebuilt (most recent): 1993
Passenger capacity: 20
Body of water: Malmö harbour   Home port: Malmö
Frequency of operation: Occasional public trips
Website address: axelnelson.com/skepp/angfyr.htm
Builders: Kockums M V, Malmö   Engine builder: Kockums 1991
Owner: Karlsson Sjöfartsmuseet Malmö
Former names: *Fritiof* 1993, *Gullan* 1954, *Schebo* 1916
Remarks: Coal-fired

1874: Built by Kockums as Yard Number 3, the steam launch *Schebo* for Schebo Bruk ironworks for use on Lake Närdingen in Uppland.

24 April: Sailed under her own steam to Hallstavik.

11 May: Arrived at Hallstavik, and was then transferred by rail to Lake Närdingen, where she was used to tow timber.

1916: Sold to Gustav E. Reuter, a Gothenburg coal merchant, renamed *Gullan*.

1918: Dieselised, over the next seventy years changed owners and home port several times, the engine was also changed and she was rebuilt.

1943: Sank after an explosion on Lake Värmeln. Raised and lay on land for a number of years.

1956: Returned to service and was renamed *Fritiof*, owned by Uddeholms AB.

Late 1960s: Sold to AB Sjunkbärgningar, Skoghall (Varberg).

1987: Sold to Sandinge Bogsering & Sjötransport, Lysekil.

1991: November: Purchased by Malmö Sjöfartsmuseet (Maritime Museum). Moved back from Nynäshamn, where she then was, to Kockums yard at Malmö, where she was rebuilt to her original condition and a new steam engine and boiler fitted. Renamed *Schebo*.

1993: Restoration complete. Renamed **Schebo**.

In the first few years after restoration, **Schebo** offered passenger trips in Malmö harbour, but latterly she has been mainly a museum exhibit and is currently awaiting overhaul.

SL THOR

Thor at Växjö, 1985.

Length: 15.40m   **Gross tonnage**: 12
Propulsion: Single Screw   **Engine type**: 1-cylinder, 35hp
Built: 1887   **Rebuilt** (most recent): 1971
Passenger capacity: 70
Body of water: Helgasjön   **Home port**: Växjö
Frequency of operation: WSSuO   **Period of operation**: Mid-June to late August
Website address: kanaler.arnholm.nu/kronobergs.html;
www.steamesteem.com/index.html?steamboats/thor;
www.smalandsmuseum.se/angaren%20Thor/thor_start.htm
Builders: Bergsund's Mek. Verkstad, Stockholm
Owner: Smålands Museum, Växjö
Remarks: Coal-fired

1887: Built as the steam passenger launch **Thor**, open forward with a saloon aft, for Reppe–Asa Kanal AB. Used on the route from Reppe to Asa with cargo and passengers, often towing up to three barges behind her.
1930s: Traffic now going by road, scheduled trips were stopped and she was used on tourist trips.
1957: Donated to Smålands Museum.
1970-71: Complete restoration. New boiler fitted. Placed in summer tourist service.

Thor operates a day-long trip from Växjö to Asa on five or six Sundays each summer, departing at 10:00, with the return by a London bus, and 2-hour trips through a lock at 15:00 on Wednesdays, with a second trip at 18:00 in the peak weeks in July, and on Saturdays and the Sundays when she is not on the Asa trip at 13:00 and 16:00.

The funnel is removed by hand to pass through low bridges and facilities are rather basic, with the toilet being a bucket in a cupboard and no catering on board.

Gothenburg

SS BOHUSLÄN

Length: 43.13m   **Gross tonnage**: 304
Propulsion: Single Screw   **Engine type**: Triple Expansion, 700hp
Built: 1913   **Passenger capacity**: 280
Body of water: Bohuslän coast   **Home port**: Gothenburg
Frequency of operation: WSuO   **Period of operation**: June to August
Website address: www.steamboat.o.se/start.shtml

Bohuslän at the Flensburg Dampf-Rundum, 1995.

Builders: Eriksbergs M V, Göteborg
Owner: Sällskapet Ångbåten

1913: 15 December: Launched.
1914: 14 May: Trials, and delivered to Marstrands Nya Ångfartyg AB, Marstrand.
  19 May: Placed in passenger service from Gothenburg to Marstrand, Lysekil, Smögen and Gravarne.
1951: Owners sold to a consortium based at Skärhamn, with the name of Marstrands Rederi AB.
1953: Rebuilt. Aft deck area enclosed to form a cafeteria. Duty-free kiosks added in the tween decks.
  Autumn: Placed in service from Landskrona to Copenhagen.
1954: 1 April: Placed in service from Helsingborg to Copenhagen.
1957: 17 May to 1958: Chartered to Nya Köpenhamnslinjen, later to Centrumlinjen for the route from Malmö to Copenhagen.
1958: Final summer on the Gothenburg-Gravarne service.
1961: Summer: Sailed from Strömstad to Sandefjord.
1962: Sold to Rederi AB Sundfart Malmö, continued in service from Strömstad to Sandefjord.
1963: Autumn: Withdrawn from service, laid-up at Marstrand.
1965: Sold to Skrot och Avfallsprodukter, Gothenburg (a scrapyard).
  February: Towed from Marstrand to Ringön.
  2 April: Sällskapet Ångbåten founded to save *Bohuslän*.
  Later: Towed from Ringön to Packhuskajen Gothenburg.
1966: January: Purchased by Sällskapet Ångbåten. Restoration commenced.
  27 June: Started operating on excursions from Gothenburg with a volunteer crew.
1975: Summer: Visited a steam event at Tønsberg, Norway.
1978: Summer: Visited a steam event at Copenhagen.
1980: Summer: Visited a steam event at Oslo.
1988: July: Made a visit to Stockholm for a steam event.
2005: Was a participant in Nordsteam 2005 at Bergen.

Bohuslän continues on these excursions from Gothenburg after almost forty years in preservation. She regularly makes a 3-hour Wednesday evening cruise from Gothenburg departing at 18:30 in June, July and August, Sunday return trips to Marstrand, with en extension from there, e.g. round Tjörn on occasion, on most Sundays in July and August, normally departing at 10:00, and a one-day single trip to Kungshamn once per season towards the end of July. This continues up to Strömstad or an intermediate point, on a second day.

SS FÄRJAN 4

Length: 20.55m   **Gross tonnage**: 48
Propulsion: Single Screw   **Engine type**: Compound, 70hp
Built: 1920   **Passenger capacity**: 100
Body of water: Göteborg harbour   **Home port**: Göteborg
Frequency of operation: SO   **Period of operation**: September and October
Website address: www.steamboat.o.se/farjan/index.shtml
Builders: Motala Verkstad, Göteborg

Färjan 4 at Gothenburg, 1988.

Owner: Sjöfartsmuseet Göteborg   **Operator**: Sällskapet Ångbåten

Remarks: Double-ended; coal-fired

1920: Built as the harbour ferry *Färjan 4* for Göteborgs Hamnstyerlse, Gothenburg. Operated on route 5 from Residensbron to Götaverken.

1954: Replaced by a diesel ferry. From now on used as reserve ferry.

1968-70: Placed back on her old route for long periods.

1970: 31 July: Route 5 closed. Laid-up.

1972: 29 June: Donated to Sjöfartsmuseet Göteborg for preservation. She was by now the last steam ferry in Gothenburg.

1973: 5 February: Placed under the care of Sällskapet Ångbåten.

Färjan 4 operates 2.5-hour harbour cruises at Gothenburg at 14:00 on Saturdays in September and October.

Göta Canal and connecting waterways

SL ANN I

Ann I at the Stockholm steamer meeting in 1998.

Length: 8.25m

Propulsion: Single Screw   **Engine type**: Compound, 6hp

Built: 1995   **Passenger capacity**: 12

Body of water: Kinda Canal   **Home port**: Linköping

Frequency of operation: Charters

Website address: www.steamboatassociation.se/bilder18.html

Builders: Alfred Steamship, Åtvidaberg

Owner: Henric Nilsson

Remarks: Wood-fired

Ann I is a small modern steam launch with a deck cabin aft in Edwardian style which operates public trips on the Kinda Canal from Linköping.

SL FORSVIK

Forsvik at Forsvik, 1999.

Length: 9.50m
Propulsion: Single Screw   **Engine type:** 1-cylinder
Built: 1867   **Rebuilt** (most recent): 1998
Passenger capacity: 12
Body of water: Göta Canal   **Home port:** Forsvik
Frequency of operation: SSuO (4 trips each day)
Period of operation: June to August
Website address: www.nordevall.com (click on 'Förening')
Builders: Lindahl & Runer, Gävle
Owner: Föreningen Forsviks Varv
Former Names: *Tämnaren* 1997, *David* 1874
Remarks: Wood-fired

1867: Built as the steam launch *David* for passenger service at Gävle.
1874: Sold to Strömbergs Bruk, an ironworks in Uppland on Lake Tämnaren. Used for carrying freight and iron ore from Lake Tämnaren to Tierp. Renamed *Tämnaren*. Also towed timber.
1930: Laid-up in a boathouse on the shore of the lake.
1972: Purchased for preservation by two men from Dalarna, Moved to Leksand, Lake Siljan.
1974: Purchased by Göran Ekblad. After a year's restoration work started trips on Lake Sävelången.
1979: Moved to Beateberg, Lake Viken.
1997: Donated to Forsviks Bruk by the Ekblad family. Over the winter restored and name changed to *Forsvik*.
1998: Summer: Started trips on the Göta Canal and Lake Viken from Forsviks Bruk.

Forsvik operates locally advertised trips from Forsviks Bruk Industrial Museum. She is the oldest ångslup (steam launch) in Sweden with her original engine.

The steam launch *Maryonette*, which operated from Linköping until 2004, was sold to Stockholm owners Rederiet Ångfartygs AB Stockholms Omgifningar in 2005, and was dieselised over the 2005-06 winter.

The small steam launch *Vikens Drottning III*, which operated charters on Lake Viken and the Göta Canal from Tåtorp until 2004, is now in private use on Lake Sommen.

Lake Vänern

SS POLSTJÄRNAN

Length: 30.20m   **Gross tonnage:** 115
Propulsion: Single Screw   **Engine type:** Compound, 190hp
Built: 1929   **Rebuilt** (most recent): 1960
Passenger capacity: 80
Body of water: Lake Vänern   **Home port:** Karlstad

Polstjärnan at Karlstad, 1985.

Frequency of operation: Occasional passenger trips
Period of operation: End May to late August
Website address: www.polstjarnan.nu
Builders: Lindholmens Varv, Göteborg
Engine builder: Motala Verkstad, Motala
Owner: Ångbåtssällskapet Polstjärnan
Former names: *Polstjärnan af Vänern*, *Polstjärnan* 1985
Remarks: Coal-fired

1929: Built as a buoy and lighthouse steamer for Vänerns Seglationsstytrelse. Built at Gothenburg, then towed to Motala for the installation of the engine.
12 October: Trials.
1960: Lengthened by 2.9m at Karlstads Varv.
1966: Converted to oil firing.
1983: Withdrawn from service. Sold to a Stockholm owner, moved there but not used.
1984: Purchased by Ångbåtssällskapet Polstjärnan for preservation, returned to Karlstad. Used for passenger trips about fifteen times per year. Many of these were evening cruises to a new pier at Sätterholmarna for 'dancing on the pier', a traditional Swedish summer activity.
1985: Hosted a steam event celebrating 150 years of Karlstad harbour. Visiting steamers included *Ejdern*, *Bohuslän* and *Östa*.
1989-90: Converted back to coal firing. Original steam lighting generator re-fitted.
1998: Visited Stockholm for a steam event.

Polstjärnan operates 3-hour archipelago cruises from Karlstad on selected dates in July. In 2006 these were at 14:00 on 15 and 22 July, with evening dance-on-the-pier trips the previous day at 18:00, returning at 23:00.

Dalsland Canal

SL HAMFRI

Length: 7.00m
Propulsion: Single Screw   **Engine type**: Compound, 8hp
Built: 1983   **Passenger capacity**: 12
Body of water: Dalsland Canal   **Home port**: Håverud
Frequency of operation: Daily   **Period of operation**: Mid-June to end August
Website address: www.hantverkshuset.com/hamfri.shtml
Builders: Unknown, Askersund   **Engine builder**: Unknown, Moholm
Owner: Per Axel Johansson, Dals Rostok
Remarks: Wood-fired

Hamfri at a steam event in Karlstad, 1985.

Hamfri is a small modern steam launch which operates on the Dalsland Canal from Upperud to Håverud with trips every hour. She is named after Humphrey Bogart and modelled on the *African Queen*.

Lake Vättern

PS ERIK NORDEVALL II

Erik Nordevall in the building shed, 2006.
(Reinhardt Grosch from a postcard)

Length: 28.62m   **Displacement tonnage**: 150
Propulsion: Paddle Steamer   **Engine type**: 2 Side Lever, 34hp
Built: Under construction   **Passenger capacity**: *c.*80
Body of water: Göta Canal   **Home port**: Forsvik
Frequency of operation: to be completed 200?
Website address: www.nordevall.com
Builders: Forsvik Bruk
Owner: Föreningen Forsviks Varv

1995: Work began on a project to build a replica of the paddle steamer **Erik Nordevall** of 1836. She was built by Hammersten of Norrköping as what was known as a 'fiddle-steamer' with the paddle wheels placed inboard to fit the locks of the Göta Canal. She sank two days after running aground in Lake Vättern in 1856 and is remarkably well preserved. Much data for building the replica has come from the wreck.

The replica is being built at Forsviks Industrial Museum, and the engine at Motala Verkstad. When the hull is complete it will be towed across Lake Vättern to Motala where the engine will be fitted. Originally planned to be launched in 2000, work has been progressing more slowly than expected.
2007: 5 August: Planned launching by Crown Princess Victoria.

When completed **Erik Nordevall II** will be the only operating steamer in the northern hemisphere with side lever engines.

SS MOTALA EXPRESS

Motala Express at Askersund, 1999.

Length: 35.66m   **Gross tonnage**: 249
Propulsion: Single Screw   **Engine type**: Triple Expansion, 360hp
Built: 1895   **Passenger capacity**: 150
Body of water: Lake Vättern   **Home port**: Askersund
Frequency of operation: MTWX   **Season**: June to September
Website address: user.tninet.se/~xes687v/motalaexpress.htm
Builders: Jönköpings Mek Werkstad
Owner: Rederiet Ångfartygs AB Stockholms Omgifningar
Remarks: Coal-fired

1895: Built as **Motala Express** for AB Motala Expressångare, Motala for service on Lake Vättern. Known as the 'Prisoner of Vättern' because she was too long to the Göta Canal locks.
24 July: Launched.
21 August: Delivered: Maiden voyage Jönköping to Motala. Used year round on the route from Motala to Jönköping.
1899: 19 May: Sold to AB Jönköpings Expressångare, Jönköping after previous owners became bankrupt.
1903: February to May: Replaced **Trafik** on the Hjo to Hastholmen service whilst the latter was being repaired after running aground.
1915: May: Sold to Ångbåta AB Vista, Jönköping. Operated from Jönköping to Visingsö and Gränna.
1929: June: Owners in liquidation, Laid-up in November.
1931: Sold to AB Vättertrafik, Jönköping. Returned to summer tourist service on her old route with two return sailings daily.
1960: Final year operating out of Jönköping.
1962: Ran from Jönköping to Visingsö after a year laid-up.
8 November: Sold to John Bergman & Son (Rederi AB Kind, Motala). Moved to Motala for the winter.
1963: Summer: Operated from Jönköping to Visingsö.
1964: Moved to Askersund to operate short cruises from there to the north of Lake Vättern and occasional cruises to Motala or Vadstena.
1980: Returned to coal-firing after the owner purchased a large supply of coal from the Swedish Railways' strategic reserve.
1985: Owners became Bergmans Ångfartygs AB, Motala (Bertil Bergman).
1988: Owners became Motala Expressångare AB, Motala.
1990: Ownership reverted to Rederi AB Kind.
2005: It was rumoured that the Bergman family were planning to dieselise **Motala Express**.
8 March: Sold to Rederiet Ångfartygs AB Stockholms Omgifningar. There was a plan to remove 3.5m from her bow and take her to Stockholm for restoration and then return her to Askersund, but instead she is being restored at Motala.
December: Chartered back to Rederi AB Kind for advent cruises out of Jönköping, then returned to Motala.
2007: Operating mainly out of Motala with afternoon cruises, generally on Sundays at 13:00, evening cruises at 19:00, mainly ThFO and day trips to Forsvik, Askersind, Karlsborg or Vadstena SO, one per season to each place, with a single trip to Visingsö and Jönköping SO in mid-August, returning the following day.

SS TRAFIK

Trafik at Hjo, 1999.

Length: 31.66m   **Gross tonnage:** 162
Propulsion: Single Screw   **Engine type:** Compound, 176.5hp
Built: 1892   **Rebuilt** (most recent): 1978
Passenger capacity: 180
Body of water: Lake Vättern   **Home port:** Hjo
Frequency of operation: SuO   **Period of operation:** Mid-June to mid-August
Website address: www.trafik.just.nu
Builders: Bergsunds Mek Verkstad, Stockholm
Owner: SS Trafik Ekonomisk Föreningen
Remarks: Coal-fired

1892: Built for Ångfartygs AB Hjo-Hästholmen, for a year-round passenger service across Lake Vättern from Hjo to Hästholmen. This connected with narrow gauge railways at either end to form part of a minor route across Sweden.
    30 June: Launched.
    20 October: Trials.
    1 November: Entered service.
1903: 5 February: Ran aground north and sank off Visingsö whilst on an extra overnight emergency sailing from Hästholmen to Jönköping. Not raised until May, then repaired and refurbished at Motala.
1931: 1 October: Service ceased because of owners' financial difficulties.
1933: Owners went into liquidation, taken over by Hjo Rederi AB. Service recommenced.
1958: Laid-up at Hjo after the summer season. Over the years became more derelict and lay half-sunk at the quay in Hjo.
1972: 23 September: SS Trafik Ekonomisk Föreningen founded by enthusiasts to preserve and operate *Trafik*. *Trafik* had been towed to the Sjötorp yard on the Göta Canal for restoration two days previously.
1977: 21 July: Returned to Hjo after restoration. Entered service supported by the enthusiast group S/S Trafiks Vänner (steamship *Trafik*'s fans).

Trafik offers Sunday day trips at 10:00 from Hjo to Visingsö on most Sundays from mid-June until mid-August, also occasional non-landing trips and evening cruises from Hjo, with a once a year foray on her old route to Hästholmen.

CENTRAL SWEDEN (BETWEEN THE GÖTA CANAL AND DALARNA)

SS FREJA AF FRYKEN

Length: 20.26m
Propulsion: Single Screw   **Engine type:** 1-cylinder, 30hp

Built: 1868   Rebuilt (most recent): 1997

Passenger capacity: 55

Body of water: Lake Fryken   Home port: Sunne, Torsby, Fryksta

Frequency of operation: MX   Period of operation: Mid-May to late August

Website address: www.varmland.nu/freja

Builders: Motala Mek. Verkstad, Motala

Owner: Ångbåtsföreningen Freja

Former names: *Freja*, *Kalmarsund No 3* 1888

Remarks: Sank 23/7/1896, raised 2/7/1994; engine was at Paris Exhibition 1867; wood-fired

1867: The engine, fitted in steam launch **Mathilda**, was exhibited at the World Exhibition in Paris, and won a gold medal. The launch was sold in France, but the engine returned to Sweden where it was fitted in **Kalmarsund No 3**.

1868: Hull built as **Kalmarsund No 3** for Ångfartygs-Bolaget Kalmar Sund for the service from Kalmar to Färjestaden and other harbours on the island of Öland.

1887-1888: winter: Sold to Nils Persson, Råby for service on Lake Fryken. Renamed **Freja**.

1889: Ownership transferred to Ångbåts AB Freja.

1896: 23 July: Sank in a storm whilst en route from Fryksta to Torsby. Six persons were saved but eleven drowned.

1976: 15 August: Wreck located by members of Karlstads Diving Club.

1994: 23 July: Raised after ninety-eight years underwater. Taken to Fryksta and moved to the Brårudsvarvet in Sunne where restoration commenced.

1996: 2 July: Seriously damaged by fire when restoration almost complete. The original plan to have **Freja** in service for the centenary of her sinking had to be cancelled.

1997: 20 July: Returned to service from Fryksta.

Freja offers a true 1890s steamer experience unrivalled anywhere. Souvenirs and snacks are dispensed from a basket brought round the deck by a stewardess, whilst meals in the tiny dining saloon are served in the original crockery, which was recovered with the wreck when it was raised.

Sailings vary daily, most being non-landing trips out of Sunne with some out of Fryksta or Torsby and occasional one-way trips between these places.

SL HÅFRESTRÖM VI

Length: 13.00m

Propulsion: Single Screw   Engine type: Compound, 12hp

Built: 1872   Rebuilt (most recent): 2003

Passenger capacity: 12

Body of water: Lake Anten   Home port: Kvarnabo

Website address: www.ttela.se/artikelmall.asp?version=61639;

www.omnibus.just.nu

Builders: Lindholmen, Gothenburg

Owner: Antens Kommunicationsmuseum

Former names: *Nestor* 2000, *Järnsjön*, *Årjäng*, *Gustavsfors*, *Billingsfors*

Remarks: Wood-fired

1875: Built as the tug **Billingsfors** for Billingsfors Bruk (Some sources quote 1867 as the building date), later sold to Gustavsfors bruk, then to Årjäng bruk and renamed accordingly, then moved to the Järnsjön, east of Årjäng, and renamed **Järnsjön** about the beginning of the twentieth century. At some point the steam engine was replaced by a petrol engine.

Mid-1960s: Used as a tug at Gothenburg under the name **Nestor**.

1970s: Came under private ownership. Steam engine re-fitted.

1998: Came under the ownership of Skålleruds Hembygdsföreningen.

2000 Returned to steam after restoration, renamed **Håfreström VI**.

2003: 4 July: Purchased by BernSten Sailing AB. Started making cruises from Håverud on the Dalsland Canal.

2005: Sold to a private owner at Åmal, and sold on to Antens Kommunikationsmusuem, Gräfsnäs, for use on Lake Anten, between Askersund and Örebro. There was a complaint made because an EC grant of 109,000 Kroner was used in the restoration, a condition of which was that she remain on the Dalsland Canal for fifty years. She may be used in connection with the preserved railway Anten-Gräfsnäs Järnväg.

2007: Expected to re-enter service after restoration.

SS KRISTINA

Kristina on Lake Skuten. (Ingvar Arvidsson)

Length: 10.50m   **Gross tonnage**: 6.5
Propulsion: Single Screw   **Engine type**: Compound, 5hp
Built: 1973   **Rebuilt** (most recent): 1982
Body of water: Lake Skuten   **Home port**: Finspong
Frequency of operation: Charters
Website address: home.online.no/~bjeren/kristina.htm;
     www.steamboatassociation.se/batar/kristina/bat.html
Builders: Vedberg, Andersson & Olssen, Borlånge
Engine builder: Haganas Nafvekwarf 1912, fitted 1985
Owner: ABB Stal Slottsklubb

1973: Built at Borlänge. (Other sources say she was built in 1873.)
Owned prior to 1982 by Infrasonic.
1982: Owners bought by Stal-Laval, moved to Finspong.
1984: Made her first trip on Lake Skuten after a major overhaul.
   Autumn: Present engine altered to compound and fitted, replacing the previous single-cylinder engine.

Kristina is operated by a club for the employees of ABB Stal, and their guests, and makes regular trips each summer on Lake Skuten, Dovern and Glan.

Dalarna

The two major lakes in the region of Dalarna, Runn and Siljan, are home to a remarkable collection of steam warping tugs. These were used to warp long tows of timber down the lake bank and along rivers from the forests to the sawmills. A large winch or wheel amidships, normally housed in a deckhouse, carried up to 2km or cable for this purpose. Most of these winches have been removed.

Lake Runn and the lower Dalälven River

SS BÄSINGEN

Bäsingen at Torsång cafe, 2006.

Length: 17.40m
Propulsion: Single Screw   **Engine type:** Compound, 75hp
Built: 1905   **Passenger capacity:** 12
Body of water: Lake Runn and Dalälven River   **Home port:** Torsång
Frequency of operation: MTWX
Period of operation: Midsummer to early August
Website address: www.falukuriren.se/artikel.asp?id=902831
Builders: AB Gefle Verkstäder, Gävle
Owner: Lars Lindström, Torsångs Café AB
Remarks: Wood-fired

1905: Built as the warping tug **Bäsingen** for Nedre Dalelfvens Flottningföreningen.
1970: Withdrawn from service when timber towing stopped.
1972: Sold for use as a private yacht on Lake Runn.
1996: Runns Ångbåts Föreningen founded to support the surviving steam vessels on Lake Runn, and to organise a steam day on the second Saturday in August each year.

Bäsingen operates from Torsångs Café, with 2-hour sailings at 18:00 on Thursday and Friday evenings, and 14:00 on Saturday and Sunday afternoons from midsummer to early August, and offers charters for the remainder of the summer season.

SS DOMNARFVET

Length: 18.45m
Propulsion: Single Screw   **Engine type:** Compound
Built: 1863   **Passenger capacity:** 12
Body of water: Lake Runn   **Home port:** Torsång
Frequency of operation: Charters
Period of operation: Mid-May to mid-September
Website address: web.telia.com/~u24330631/index.htm
Builders: Södra Varvet, Stockholm (W Lindberg)
Engine builder: Härnosands Mek. Verkstad 1903
Owner: O. Arvidsson, Borlänge
Former names: *Korsnäs*, *Domnarfvet*
Remarks: Wood-fired

1862: July Built for Stora Kopparbergs Bergslag as a steam launch to carry timber between Domnarfvet and Korsnäs on Lake Runn, from where the timber was taken to Gävle by rail.

Domnarfvet on Lake Runn. (Micheal Forslund)

1863: February: Delivered.

1886: Moved to the Nedre Dalälven and the Hedesundsfjärden, warping wheel fitted and used to tow timber floats along with **Östa**, **Bäsingen** and **Laxen**.

1890: Owned by Nedre Dalelfvens Flottningsföreningen.

1970: Withdrawn from service after the timber tows were stopped.

1972: Purchased by Nils Nyström, Sater, moved back to Lake Runn. Warping wheel removed.

1986: Purchased by Ove Arvidsson.

Domnarfvet normally operates charters, but offers public passenger trips at midsummer and at the steam day in August.

SS ENGELBREKT

Length: 16.50m

Propulsion: Single Screw   **Engine type**: Compound, 120hp

Built: 1903

Body of water: Lake Runn   **Home port**: Staberg

Frequency of operation: Ångbåtsdagar (mid-August)

Website address: hemsidor.torget.se/users/a/arneld/sbatar.html

Builders: R. Sjöströms Mek. Verkstad, Gävle

Owner: E. Wimmer, Falun

Former names: *Sveden II*, *Engelbrekt* 1928, *Mackmyra Sulfit*, *?* 1905

Remarks: Wood-fired

1903: Built as a timber towing tug for an unknown owner with an unknown name.

1905: Sold to Mackmyra Sulfit AB, used for warping timber for the sulphate factory at Hammarby. Renamed **Mackmyra Sulfit**. Renamed **Engelbrekt** a few years after.

1928: Sold to Sven-Anders Andersson, Svedgården, unofficially renamed **Sveden II** but soon regained the name **Engelbrekt**.

1965: Withdrawn from service.

1970s: Purchased for preservation.

Like the other steamboats on Lake Runn, it is possible to sail on **Engelbrekt** at midsummer and on the steam day in August.

SS LAXEN

Length: 17.39m

Propulsion: Single Screw   **Engine type**: Compound, 65hp

Built: 1899   **Rebuilt** (most recent): 2002

Passenger capacity: 12

Body of water: Dalälven   **Home port**: Gysinge

Laxen on land at Gysinge
timber-floating museum, 2006.

Frequency of operation: Occasional public trips
Website address: www.sandviken.se/4.195dd5bf9174c73697fff1906.html;
www.steamboatassociation.se/laxen/laxen.html
Builders: AB Gefle Verkstäder, Gävle
Owner: Dälalvarnes Flottnings Museum, Gysinge
Remarks: Wood-fired

1899: Built for Nedre Dalelfvens Flottningsförening as an open-decked warping tug for service on the Hedesundsfjärden, towing timber.

1940s: Deckhouse and wheelhouse added. Converted to oil-firing.

1970: Withdrawn from service.

1974: Moved to Lake Siljan.

1978: Flottningsmuseum opened at Gysinge, with **Laxen**, which has been moved back there from Siljan, as one of the main attractions.

Early 1980s: Made short passenger trips. Funnel made collapsible to pass under a road bridge.

1999: Boiler condemned. Laid-up.

2002: 14 July: Returned to steam following a major restoration including the restoration of the warping wheel and the rebuilding of the engine and boiler, the latter being converted back to wood-firing.

Laxen is normally an exhibit on land at Dälalvarnes Flottnings Museum in Gysinge, and is available for charter. A steamboat day is held once a year on the second Sunday in July, when **Laxen** is in steam, and offers passenger trips.

SL MARIA

Length: 9.00m
Propulsion: Single Screw   Engine type: 1-cylinder
Built: 1952   Rebuilt (most recent): 1988
Body of water: Dalälven   Home port: Torsång
Frequency of operation: Ångbåtsdagar (mid-August)
Period of operation: August
Website address: hemsidor.torget.se/users/a/arneld/sbatar.html
Builders: Övermo Varv
Owner: Kenny Mårtensson, Falun
Former names: *Kalle* 1988

1952: Built as the open timber-towing boat **Kalle** with a diesel engine for Dalelfvarns Flottnings Föreningen.

1988: Steam engine fitted. Renamed **Maria**.

Like the other steamboats on Lake Runn, it is possible to sail on **Maria** at midsummer and on the steam day in August.

SS SVEDEN

Length: 13.20m
Propulsion: Single Screw   Engine type: Compound
Built: 1942   Passenger capacity: 12
Body of water: Dalälven   Home port: Torsång
Frequency of operation: Ångbåtsdagar (mid-August)
Period of operation: August
Website address: hemsidor.torget.se/users/a/arneld/sbatar.html
Builders: Lidwalls Mek, Verkstad, Övermo
Engine builder: Sven Anders Andersson, Torsång 1890
Owner: Björn Gustavsson, Borlänge
Remarks: Wood-fired

1942: Built as the warping tug **Sveden** for Sven-Anders Andersson, Svedgården. Engine and boiler
transferred from a wooden-hulled boat built in 1890. Used on Lake Runn.
1965: Withdrawn from service, later purchased for preservation and restored.

Like the other steamboats on Lake Runn, it is possible to sail on **Sveden** at midsummer and on the steam
day in August.

SL SMÅNGAN

Length: 10.00m
Propulsion: Single Screw
Built: 1946   Rebuilt (most recent): 1990
Body of water: Dalälven   Home port: Torsång
Frequency of operation: Ångbåtsdagar (mid-August)
Period of operation: August
Website address: hemsidor.torget.se/users/a/arneld/sbatar.html
Builders: Lidwalls Mek, Verkstad, Övermo
Owner: Rev Börje Andersson

1946: Built as an diesel-powered open timber towing boat for Ljusnans Flottningföreningen.
1990: Rebuilt to a steamboat. Amidships deck saloon added.

Like the other steamboats on Lake Runn, it is possible to sail on **Smångan** at midsummer and on the
steam day in August.

SL TORSÅNGAREN

Torsångaren at a steam rally, with passenger aboard.
(From the book *På Sjö och Älv I Dalarna*)

Length: 8.50m
Propulsion: Single Screw

Built: Unknown   Rebuilt (most recent): 1973
Body of water: Dalälven   Home port: Torsång
Frequency of operation: Ångbåtsdagar (mid-August)
Period of operation: August
Builders: Övermo Varv
Owner: Kjell Eriksson
Former name: *Holmsån*

Unknown date: Built as the diesel-powered warping boat **Holmsån** for Dalelfvarns Flottnings Föreningen.
1973: Sold to Erik Norman, Falun, who installed a steam engine and boiler, later sold to Kjell Eriksson
and renamed **Torsångaren**.

Like the other steamboats on Lake Runn, it is possible to sail on **Torsångaren** at midsummer and on the
steam day in August.

Lake Siljan and surrounding waters

SL AGNES

Agnes on Lake Ljugaren, 1999.

Length: 10.60m
Propulsion: Single Screw   Engine type: Compound, 12hp
Built: *c.*1890   Rebuilt (most recent): 1981
Passenger capacity: 12
Body of water: Lake Ljugaren   Home port: Born
Frequency of operation: MThO   Period of operation: June to August
Builders: Unknown, probably at Umeå
Engine builder: Södra Varvet, Stockholm 1899
Owner: Gösta Karlberg
Former names: *Vanan* 1955, *Fyrisan* 1920
Remarks: Wood-fired; also occasionally sails on other lakes

*c.*1890: Built as **Fyrisan** for service on the River Fyrisan at Uppsala.
1920: Moved to Vansbro, used at the sawmill there, renamed **Vanan**.
1955: Moved to Orsa as a diesel pleasure boat. Renamed **Agnes**.
1968: Laid-up on land.
1989: Purchased by Gösta Karlberg. Hull restored, 1899-built steam engine and new boiler fitted.
   Normally used on Lake Ljugaren at Born, a few miles from Rättvik, but she can be towed and has
   visited special events at a number of locations in Dalarna.

Agnes operates Monday and Thursday evening trips from June to August on Ljugaren, departing Born at
18:00. There is a stop at an islet in the lake where passengers climb to the Vasa Stone, reputedly connected
with King Gustav Wasa, and there is a second stop where passengers walk through the forest to a small
farmstead, where coffee is served.

SS ELFDALEN

Elfdalen dressed overall for midsummer.

Length: 21.37m
Propulsion: Single Screw   **Engine type:** Compound
Built: 1888   **Passenger capacity:** 12
Body of water: Lake Siljan   **Home port:** Leksand
Frequency of operation: Ångbåtsdagar (end of August)
Period of operation: August
Website address: biphome.spray.se/per.hilding/Steam/Elfdalen.html
Builders: Ljusne Mek.Verksted
Owner: Jan-Erik Gullback, Leksand
Remarks: Wood-fired

1888: Built as a warping tug for timber towing on Lake Siljan for Dalelfvarnes Flottningsföreningen. Also had a passenger certificate.
  July: Entered service.
1926: New boiler fitted.
1965: Withdrawn from service.
1966: Sold to Sören Svenn for preservation.
1969: Sold to Per Hilding.
1978: Siljans Fartygs Föreningen established to assist with the preservation of the surviving warping tugs and other vessels on Lake Siljan.
1980: Sold to Olle Nordesjö.
  End of August: Ångbåtsdag established. **Elfdalen**, **Flottisten**, **Insjön I** and **Siljan**, the four surviving steam tugs on Lake Siljan are granted a temporary one-day passenger certificate annually for this event.
1996: Out of service. Major restoration undertaken.
1999: End of August: Returned to steam on ångbåtsdag (steamer day) at Leksand.
2005: Sold to Jan-Erik Gullback, remained at Leksand.

Elfdalen normally lies with the other preserved steamers on the south side of the river at Leksand. She may offer charters, but otherwise the only day she is in operation for the public is on *ångbåtsdag* at the end of August.

SS ENGELBREKT

Engelbrekt heading upriver from Norsbro, July 2006, with her funnel removed to get under a bridge. (Rune Lindenor)

Length: 24.10m   **Gross tonnage:** 77
Propulsion: Single Screw   **Engine type:** Compound, 80hp

Built: 1866   Rebuilt (most recent): 1997
Passenger capacity: 66
Body of water: Lake Siljan and Nedre Dalälven River   Home port: Leksand
Frequency of operation: MFSuO   Period of operation: Mid-May to mid-August
Website address: www.steamship.nu
Builders: Motala Verkstad, Lindholmen, Göteborg
Engine builder: Robert Sjöströms MV Gävle 1904, fitted 1996
Owner: Ångfartygs AB Engelbrekt, Leksand
Former name: *Mora* 1903
Remarks: Wood-fired

1866: Built as the passenger steamer **Mora** for use on Lake Siljan for Mora Ångbåtsbolag, Mora. Built at Gothenburg in sections and erected at Lövholmen, Mora Operated daily from Insjön to Mora and on one day per week towed a barge laden with supplies.

1875: Owners became Österdalarnes Ångbåts AB, Mora. Now operated on the Dalälven River from Gråda, now Gagnef, to Orsa.

1902-03: Major rebuild, new compound engine fitted. Owners became Österdalarnes Ångbåtsbolag, renamed **Engelbrekt**. Now operated from Insjön to Mora year-round, being ice-strengthened.

1914: Southern terminal altered to Leksand, as a railway bridge had been erected there.

1950: Sank at the quay in Leksand during her winter lay-up, but was raised.

1952: Withdrawn from service after the summer season, sold and used as a floating summer cottage on the south side of the river at Leksand.

1971: Sold to Olle Nordesjö, Leksand. Used as a diesel pleasure craft.

1994-95: Sold to Stiftelsen S/S Engelbrekt, Leksand. Towed under the railway bridge to the site of a new slipway on the site of the old shipyard at Övermo. Major restoration and rebuild. Fitted with an engine built in 1904, and a boiler built in 1916.

1996: Return to service.

Engelbrekt offer trips on Fridays, Saturdays and Sundays from June to August from Leksand to Marielund and Insjön, and evening dance cruises from Mora, with occasional sailings from Rättvik and Tällberg. There are also occasional one way trips between these places, some marketed as Nostalgia trips, and a handful of Wednesday evening cruises and church trips from Tällberg on Thursday evenings.

SS FLOTTISTEN

Flottisten at Rättvik, 1999.

Length: 18.55m   Gross tonnage: 38
Propulsion: Single Screw   Engine type: Compound, 110hp
Built: 1889   Rebuilt (most recent): 1910
Passenger capacity: 12
Body of water: Lake Siljan   Home port: Rättvik
Frequency of operation: Ångbåtsdagar (end of August)
Website address: w1.248.telia.com/~u24802227
Builders: Härnosands Mek Verkstad

Owner: Karl-Erik Olsson & Helèn Karlsson, Rättvik
Remarks: Wood-fired

1890: Built as an inspection and pleasure steamer for the chief of Dalelfvarnes Flottningsföreningen.
  Steamed from her builders to Gävle, then transported to Insjön by rail.
1910s: Converted to a warping tug. Winch fitted amidships.
1964: Sank, but later raised.
1966: Sold to Olle Lindberg, Borlånge for preservation.
1982: Laid-up, later sank at her moorings.
1993: Raised and sold to Karl-Erik Olsson & Helèn Karlsson, Rättvik. Sailed to her new home port of
  Rättvik on 5 June.

Flottisten may offer charters, but otherwise the only day she is in operation for the public is on *ångbåtsdag*
at the end of August. A steamboat day is held annually at Rättvik on the first Thursday in August.

SL GRÖNLAND

Grönland on Lake Siljan.

Length: 7.30m
Propulsion: Single Screw   Engine type: 2-cylinder
Built: 1925   Rebuilt (most recent): 1994
Passenger capacity: 12
Body of water: Lake Siljan   Home port: Västanvik
Frequency of operation: Ångbåtsdagar (end of August)
Website address: web.telia.com/~u86703503/b%E5tbildlista/Gr%F6nland.jpg
Builders: Unknown   Engine builder: Stuart
Owner: Arne Risander

1925: Built as an open diesel warping boat for Dalelfvarnes Flottningsföreningen.
1994: Stuart steam engine fitted.

SS INSJÖN I

Length: 16.50m
Propulsion: Single Screw   Engine type: Compound
Built: 1873   Rebuilt (most recent): 1947
Passenger capacity: 12
Body of water: Lake Siljan   Home port: Norsbro
Frequency of operation: Ångbåtsdagar (end of August)
Period of operation: August
Builders: Eriksbergs Mek. Verkstad, Göteborg
Engine builder: Bobergs Mek, Verkstad, Umeå
Owner: Åke. Danielsson & L Jan-Olof, Leksand

Insjön I at Leksand, 1999.

Former name: *Totte* 1913
Remarks: Wood-fired

1873: Built as the tug **Totte**.

1913: Purchased by Insjöns Sågverk (sawmill). Moved from Gävle to Insjön by rail. Renamed **Insjön I**.

1918: Lengthened from 11m to 17.5m, also rebuilt to carry passengers.

1947: Laid-up, later used for dredging.

1960: Sold to an owner at Nusnäs. Lay there for many years stripped to a bare hull with the engine and warping wheel removed.

1977-78: Restored. Fitted with the engine of **Erik** and a new boiler. Steel deck, wheelhouse and deck saloon added.

Insjön I may offer charters, but otherwise the only day she is in operation for the public is on *ångbåtsdag* at the end of August.

SS SILJAN

Siljan when in service on Lake Siljan.

Length: 20.80m
Propulsion: Single Screw   **Engine type:** Compound, 110hp
Built: 1868   **Passenger capacity:** 12
Body of water: Lake Siljan   **Home port:** Insjön
Frequency of operation: Ångbåtsdagar (end of August)
Period of operation: August
Website address: web.telia.com/~u25003635/siljan/siljan.htm
Builders: Södra Varvet, Stockholm (W Lindberg)
Engine builder: Robert Sjöströms Mek. Verkstad. Gävle 1904
Owner: Bengt and Bjorn Bergkvist, Insjön
Former names: *Siljan II*, *Siljan*
Remarks: Wood-fired

1868: Built as the warping tug **Siljan** for service on Lake Siljan for Stora Kopparbergs Bergslags AB, used in connection with Korsnäsbolag. The hull was probably taken to Smedjebacken by the Strömsholms

Canal, and then dragged by horse to Tunsta, where she was completed. She was fitted with a steam warping wheel from the beginning.

1904: New compound engine replaced the old single-cylinder engine. The original engine survived and is now in the Flottningsmuseum at Gysinge.

1966: Laid-up when timber floating finished.

1969: Spring: Sold to Axel Bergkvist AB, Insjön. Used for timber towing from Leksand to Insjön for a few years.

1972: 19 August: Final day towing timber, which was now taken to the sawmill by road. Now used as a VIP boat for the company and used by the owners' family.

Siljan is still owned by the same family and her warping wheel is still in operation. She may offer charters, but otherwise the only day she is in operation for the public is on *ångbåtsdag* at the end of August.

SS TOMTEN

Tomten at her new home at Venjan, July 2006.

Length: 16.50m
Propulsion: Single Screw   **Engine type:** Compound, 55hp
Built: 1862   **Rebuilt** (most recent): 1970
Passenger capacity: 12
Body of water: Venjansjön   **Home port:** Venjan
Frequency of operation: occasional public trips   **Period of operation:** summer
Website address: www.mora.se/ArticlePages/200508/03/20050803073956_UK099/20050803073956_UK099.dbp.html
Builders: Södra Varvet, Stockholm (W Lindberg)
Engine builders: Hernosands Mek. Verksted 1903
Owner: Å/F Tomtens vänner, c/o Göran Solén, Venjan
Remarks: Wood-fired

1862: Built as Ore Elfs Timmerdrifningsbolag as the first steam warping tug for Lake Siljan and the first screw steamer on the lake. Used for moving large tows of timber down the lake to the sawmills.

1865: Sold to Grönwallska Gråda Bolag.

1871: Sold to Ångbåtsbolaget på Siljan.

1878: The newly formed Dalelfvarnes Flottningsföreningen took over the steamboats on Siljan. Pulled by hand to the Venjansjön.

1888: Original horizontal warping wheel, driven by the propeller shaft, replaced by another horizontal wheel, mainly below deck.

1903: Compound engine replace original single-cylinder engine.

1966: Timber towing finished on the Venjansjön, sold to two private individuals, moved to Lake Runn and used as a steam yacht.

1982: Returned to Lake Siljan. Rebuilt with a traditional wheelhouse.

2005: 1 July: Sold to present owners and moved back to the Venjansjön by road.

Tomten is berthed at a new jetty at Venjan, and will be offering passenger trips on a steam day (ångbåtsdag) at least once a year.

Lake Norra Barken – Smedjebacken

Lake Norra Barken at Smedjebacken is connected to Lake Mälar by the Strömsholms Canal.

SL EWA

Ewa at Smedjebacken, 1999.

Length: 9.50m
Propulsion: Single Screw   **Engine type**: Compound, 6hp
Built: 1931,   **Rebuilt** (most recent): 1978
Passenger capacity: 10
Body of water: Norra Barken   **Home port**: Smedjebacken
Frequency of operation: Charters
Website address: hem.bredband.net/b235962/;
Builders: Övermo Slip, Leksand (probably)
Engine builder: Erik W Andersson, Borlänge 1930
Owner: Hans Eriksson, Barkens Ångslupen AB, Smedjebacken
Former name: *Horrmund* 1975
Remarks: Wood-fired

1931: Built as the motor timber-towing tug **Horrmund** for Dalarnas Flottnings Föreningen for use on Lake Horrmund in north Dalarna.

Early 1960s: Timber towing ceased. Sold to Evert W. Anderson and moved to Lake Runn. Renamed **Ewa** after the initials of her owner.

1975-78: Major rebuild. Original engine replaced with a stem engine and a wood-fired boiler. Cabin added.

1985: Moved to Ludvika on Lake Väsman, sold to Slup Wäsman.

1998: Sold to Barkens Ångslupen AB, Smedjebacken and moved to Smedjebacken from where she offers charters and locally advertised trips, including trips on Smedjebacken steam day on the second weekend in August.

ST HARGE

Length: 16.30m   **Gross tonnage**: 19
Propulsion: Single Screw   **Engine type**: Compound, 45hp
Built: 1907   **Rebuilt** (most recent): 1996

Harge at Smedjebacken, 1999.

Body of water: Lake Barken   **Home port:** Smedjebacken
Frequency of operation: Charters and steam day
Builders: Wennbergs M V, Karlstad
Owner: Olle Ridelius, Sven-Olof Könberg and Jan-Åke Ekholm
Former names: *Rannick*, *Blidö*, *Kind* 1960, *Wulf* 1959, *Harge* 1940s, *Harge II*
Remarks: Wood-fired

1907: Built as the tug *Harge II* for Harge AB, later renamed *Harge* and then *Wulf*.
1959: Sold and rebuilt as a passenger boat, renamed *Kind*. Used on the Kinda Canal.
1960: Sold to Ångfartygs AB Stockholm-Blidösund, renamed *Blidö*. Used on a service from Solö to Furusund and Rödlöga, connecting with *Blidösund* from Stockholm.
  Laid-up following an engine failure.
1961: Sold, later renamed *Rannick*.
Late 1980s: Sold. Restoration commenced. Renamed *Harge*.
*c.*1996: Returned to steam and moved to Smedjebacken.
2006: Placed up for sale.

Harge offers public passenger trips once a year on the Smedjebacken Steam Day on the second weekend in August.

SS RUNN

Runn undergoing restoration at Smedjebacken.

Length: 17.5m
Built: 1907   **Rebuilt** (most recent): 2005
Body of water: Norra Barken   **Home port:** Smedjebacken
Website address: www.ss-runn-smedjebacken.nu
Builder: C.J. Wennbegr, Karlstad
Owner: Vänföreningen S/S Runn

1907: Built as a passenger launch for Runns Ångbåtstrafik AB, Vika. Delivered to Korsnäs by rail. Used on the route from Falun to Hagudden. Later taken over by AB Wika Ångsåg.

1932: Sold to Runns Nya Ångbåtstrafik.

1937: Sold to Anders Andersson, Torsång, taken over by his son Bror after his death.

1965: May: Withdrawn from service, used as a private yacht. Now owned by Gunnar Holme, Djursholm (a suburb of Stockholm). Moved to the Stockholm archipelago.

1979: Sold to Peter Suwe, Djursholm.

1980: By this time the hull was in poor condition. Sank in 18m off Kummelsnäs yard. Sold to Sockerbagaren Östen Brolin, Brolin. Raised after two weeks on the bottom. Some restoration done on her.

2002: Sold to enthusiast organisation Vänföreningen Å/F Runn, Smedjebacken, who placed her on land there and commenced a major restoration.

2004: 20 October: craned into the water.

2005: Restoration completed.

NORTHERN SWEDEN: NORTH OF DALARNA

SS ALMA AF STAFRE

Alma af Stafre, 1999. (Owners)

Length: 17.27m   Gross tonnage: 32
Propulsion: Single Screw   Engine type: Compound, 80hp
Built: 1873   Rebuilt (most recent): 1993
Passenger capacity: 30
Body of water: Revsundssjön   Home port: Stavre
Frequency of operation: WSSuO   Period of operation: 29 June to end August
Website address: www.ss-alma.nu
Builders: Lindbergs Södra Varvet, Stockholm
Engine builder: Hernösands M V 1908
Owner: Ångbåtsföreningen 'Alma af Stavre', Gällö
Remarks: Wood-fired. Also fitted with a diesel

1873: Built as a passenger steamer for Sjönviks AB, Stavre. Shipped to Stavre in parts and erected there for service on the Revsundssjön.

1879: Sold to Gimåns Flottningsbolag, later Flottningföreningen. Used both as a timber towing tug and as a passenger steamer. Used as a church boat on Sundays and for carrying corpses to the cemetery at Revsund church.

1909: (1903 according to some sources.) Original 15hp engine replaced by the present one of 85hp.

1914: New boiler fitted.

1957: Laid-up on the slipway.

1959: Sold to Bengt Röslund, Stavre.

1963: Sold to Revsunds Kommun. Remained laid-up, planned to be restored but no work was done because of a lack of money.

1966: Sold to Nils Granlund, Djursholm. Used as a steam yacht in the Stockholm archipelago.

1971: Sold to Magnus Östlund and others, Gothenburg. Moved to Gothenburg. Used at sea, even sailing as far as Poland on one occasion.

1985: Sold to Interesseföreningen Alma, Bräcke. Returned to the Revsundssjön. Was now in very poor condition.

1990: Sold to Stavre Bygdegårdsföreningen. Restoration started. New smaller boiler fitted to make way for a restaurant below decks.

1993: Sold to Ångbåtsföreningen 'Alma af Stavre'. Returned to service after restoration.

Alma offers evening cruises at 18:00 on Wednesdays, fishing trips at 18:00 on Saturdays and lunch cruises on Sundays at 12:00, each cruise lasting 2 hours. These sailings operate in July, and she continues with the Sunday cruises throughout August. She uses both her diesel and steam machinery on these trips.

ST FORTUNA

Length: 16.20m
Propulsion: Single Screw   **Engine type**: Compound
Built: 1858   **Rebuilt** (most recent): 1999
Body of water: Dellen Lakes   **Home port**: Moviken
Website address: www.bruksminnen.com/fortuna_1.htm
Builders: Unknown, GB   **Engine builder**: C.J. Wennbergs Mek Verkstad 1915
Owner: Stiftelsen Hudiksvalls Bruksminnen, E. Holm

1857: Built in sections in England as the tug *Fortuna* and shipped to Hudiksvall. Built for the English-owned Hudiksvall Steam Sawing Mill Co. Ltd. Used for towing on the Dellen lakes and to Forsa sawmill.

27 June and 17 July: The schooners *Götha* and *Maren Catharina* respectively arrived at Hudiksvall from London with the machinery. These and the hull sections were moved to Forsa on the Dellen Lakes by rail, on what was then the world's most northerly railway. Hull re-erected at Forsa.

1858: 23 May: Delivered.

1864: Owners taken over by Vestra Helsingland Trävaru AB.

1868: Sold to Hudiksvalls Trävaru AB.

1878: Moved to Hudiksvall by rail.

1880: Ran aground and sank in the Vintergatsfjärden. Was raised soon after.

1884: Major rebuild. Shortened by 14ft. New engine fitted.

1915: Second new engine fitted.

1918: Owners taken over by AB Iggesunds Bruk.

1961: Withdrawn from commercial service when road transport took over.

Early 1970s: Sold to Lasse Hamrin and Rune Strömbom for preservation.

1972: Sold back to AB Iggesunds Bruk. New oil-fired boiler fitted.

1988: Laid-up.

1989: Sold to Kommanditbolaget Hästaholmen.

1999: Purchased by Hudiksvalls Bruksminnen.

16 June: Moved to Moviken by land for restoration.

Fortuna is in operation, although no details are available.

SL HEBE

Length: 15.60m
Propulsion: Single Screw   Engine type: Compound, 80hp
Built: 1889   Rebuilt (most recent): 1996
Body of water: Landösjön   Home port: Rönnöfors
Frequency of operation: Occasional public trips
Website address: www.offerdal.com/8.htm
Builders: Wilhelmsbergs M V, Göteborg   Engine builder: 1909
Owner: Kulturföreningen SS Hebe, Offerdal
Remarks: Wood-fired

1889: Built as a passenger launch for unknown owners.

1904: Moved to the Landösjön. Operated as a passenger steamer-cum-tug. Originally owned by Hallman, Östersund and Axel Friedenfalds, Dvärsätt, later sold to Indalsälven Flottningsföreningen.

Mid-1930s: Rebuilt to be used purely as a tug. Engine and boiler replaced with those formerly in **Kaparen** on Gesunden.

1969: Timber towing ceased. Laid-up.

1971: Sold to a private owner. Moved to the Störsjön as a private yacht.

1985: Sold to another owner and moved to Vaxholm.

Late 1990s: Moved back to the Landösjön for restoration.

ST NORDKUST 4

Nordkust 4 on the slip.

Length: 24.00m
Propulsion: Single Screw
Built: 1885
Body of water: Ådalen River   Home port: Skellefteå
Frequency of operation: Undergoing restoration
Website address: www.skellefteamuseum.se/2002/stackgr/nordkust.html
Builders: Gävle   Owner: Museiföreningen s/s Nordkust 4
Former names: *Nordkust 1, Munksund 4, Ytterfors 4, Ophelia*

1885: Built as the tug **Ophelia** for Galtström ironworks.

1904: Moved to the Gulf of Bothnia, known as '**Fyran**' (Four). Later renamed **Ytterfors 4**, then **Munksund 4**, **Nordkust 1** and finally **Nordkust 4**. Used as a timber towing tug.

1961: Home port now Luleå. Not in service.

1982: Donated to Stiftelsen Skellefteå Museum.

1991: Moved to Stackgrönnans Båtmuseum as a static exhibit on land.

2005: June: Ownership transferred to Museiföreningen s/s Nordkust 4 for restoration.

The hull and frames of **Nordkust 4** are in poor condition and, if restoration is not started soon, she may be scrapped.

SS ÖSTERSUND

Östersund on the Störsjön, 1999.

Length: 25.16m   **Gross tonnage**: 88
Propulsion: Single Screw   **Engine type**: Compound, 120hp
Built: 1874   **Rebuilt** (most recent): 1989
Passenger capacity: 100
Body of water: Lake Storsjön   **Home port**: Arvesund
Frequency of operation: Occasional public trips   **Period of operation**: July and August
Website address: www.angarenostersund.com
Builders: Oskarshamn M V   **Engine builder**: Härnösands M V, Härnösand 1903
Owner: Föreningen Bevara Ångaren Östersund
Former names: *Las Vegas* 1982, *Östersund* 1960
Remarks: Wood-fired

1874: Built as a passenger steamer for Östersunds Ångbåtsbolag. Built in sections and transported by sea to Sundsvall and then by road to Östersund.
1875: Summer: Entered service from Östersund to Berg.
1886: Lengthened by 3m. Mast and winch fitted.
1902-03: winter: New engine fitted.
1904: Hull painted white.
1931: 20 May: Purchased by Captain P.O. Ek and others.
1952: Sold to Leander Olsson for the route from Östersund to Sandviken and tourist trips round Fröson.
1959: Purchased by Tage Lindgren, Fröson.
1963: Withdrawn from service.
1965: Renamed *Las Vegas*. Used as a club at Östersund.
1970: Out of service.
1971: Sold to a scrap merchant, later owned for a short time by Fröso boat club, by the late seventies lay on the beach at Arvesund.
1982: Purchased by the preservation group Föreningen Bevara Ångaren Östersund (Foundation to save the steamer Östersund). Moved to Arvesund where a new pier and slipway was built.
1986: 11 August. Returned to steam after major restoration.

Östersund makes about half-a-dozen trips in July each year, including one steam day, normally on the second Thursday in July when she sails with *Thomeé* to one of the islands on the lake.

ST PRIMUS

Primus arriving at Sundsvall, 1999.

Length: 19.19m
Propulsion: Single Screw   Engine type: Compound, 65hp
Built: 1875   Rebuilt (most recent): 1994
Passenger capacity: 50
Body of water: Sundvallsfjärden   Home port: Sundsvall
Frequency of operation: MSSuX   Period of operation: July
Website address: www.primussundsvall.nu
Builders: Södra Varvet, Stockholm (W. Lindberg)
Engine builder: Sunds Verkstäder, Sundsvall 1902
Owner: Medelpads Sjöhistoriska Föreningen
Remarks: Coal-fired

1875: Built as a tug for Skönviks AB, stationed at Skönviks sawmill.

1887: Sold to Karlviks Trävan AB, stationed at Karlsviks sawmill.

1903-04: New 120hp engine from Hernösands Verkstad fitted, deck heightened to house the new engine. Wheelhouse and awning probably fitted at this time. The boiler was too small for the engine.

1905: Lengthened by three metres. New boiler fitted. New iron deck installed.

1915: Moved to Mons sawmill, managed by A. Wikström.

1919: Returned to Karlsviks sawmill.

1933: Purchased by J.A. Enhörning, founder of Sundsvallsbolaget which became SCA.

1938: Moved to Skönviks sawmill.

1954: Used at Tunedals sawmill, but overnight mooring remained at Skönvik.

1960: Sold to Rune Högström for scrapping. Engine and boiler removed.

1967: Sold back to SCA. Diesel engine fitted. Rebuilt as a chain boat, to unlock the chained sections of timber tows, later used as a tug again.

1984: Withdrawn from service.

1985: April: Donated to Medelpads Sjöhistoriska Föreningen.

20 November: Placed on land by a crane at Johannedals Industriområde for rebuilding to 1920s condition, 1902-built steam engine acquired which was previously in **Gustav** ex **Nocturne** (p.124-125), and installed in **Primus**. 1974-built boiler purchased and installed.

1991: 18 June: Craned into water again.

1993: 26 November: Returned to steam.

1994: Passenger services commenced.

Primus has offered trips from Sundsvall to the island of Tjuvholmen thrice daily except Mondays in July, however in 2006 she was merely on charter trips.

SL STJÄRN

Length: 7.3m   Engine type: Unknown, 4hp
Built: 1955   Passenger capacity: 10
Body of water: Vågsfjorden   Home port: Nordingrä
Frequency of operation: Daily   Period of operation: Summer
Website address: www.angbat.se
Builder: Lidwall & Söner
Owner: Nordingrå Ångåtsföreningen
Remarks: Wood-fired

1955 (or 1954 according to another source): Built as a major warpng boat for the River Klarälven.

c.1980: Sold for private use and converted to a steam launch; deck saloon added at unknown date.

2007: Sold to present owners and moved on land to Nordingrå.

It is planned that **Stjärn** will be in regular service between six jetties on the Vågsfjorden.

SS THOMÉE

Length: 26.93m   Gross tonnage: 106
Propulsion: Single Screw   Engine type: Compound, 150hp
Built: 1875   Rebuilt (most recent): 1975
Passenger capacity: 130
Body of water: Lake Storsjön   Home port: Östersund
Frequency of operation: MX   Period of operation: Early June to early September
Website address: turist.adeprimo.se/app/projects/turistbyranny/images/Thomee_2006.pdf?PHPSES
   SID=4e8f640f32017c5adc764b7bc87f8450
Builders: Motala Mek Verkstad, Motala
Engine builder: Bergsund, Stockholm 1919 from *Bravo*, fitted 1933
Owner: Tekn Verks Östersunds Kommun

1875: Built for Refsunds Ångbåts AB for use on the Revsundssjön. Originally she was an open-decked
   steamboat with no superstructure.
1879: Laid-up for this year only.
1880: Spring: Moved to the Storsjön by rail.
1885: Laid-up for this year only.
1908-09: Lengthened by 3.6m, new boiler fitted.
1918: Sold to Indals Älfs Flottningföreningen for use as a timber towing tug.
1926-30: Laid-up.
1931: Sold to L. Larsson, M. Linden, E. Hansson and Captain P.O. Ek. Renovated on Minnesgårds slipway.
   New engine and boiler fitted. Icebreaking bow fitted and used as an icebreaker.
   Sold to Norderöns Rederi AB. Used as a passenger steamer on the route from Östersund to Norderön
   and Arvesund.
1933: After an engine failure the previous May, which had been repaired temporarily, a 'new' engine was
   fitted. This was actually second-hand and had been built in 1919 for the steam tug *Bravo* of Sundsvall.
1937: February: New boiler fitted.
1955: 21 August. Final scheduled service from Östersund.
   Sold to Östersunds Gotdemplares Bygnads AB. Used on the route from Östersund to Sandviken.
1962: Sold to Manne Eriksson.
1968: November: Sold to Lennart Boman, then to Storsjötrafik KB.
1972: 28 June: Sold to Östersunds Kommun.
1973: 22 September. First sailing after restoration.
1974-75: Major rebuild.
1991: New oil-fired boiler fitted.

Thomée offers a variety of trips from Östersund. 2006 sailings were:

Tuesdays: 13:30 (2-hour non-landing trip), 16:00, 18:00 and 19:30 (1-hour non-landing trips).
Wednesdays and Sundays: 12:00: trip to Verkön with 2.5 hours ashore.
Thursdays: 11:00: 2-hour Non-landing trip, 13:30, trip to Andersön with 2 hours ashore.
Fridays and Saturdays: 11:00 and 13:30: 2-hour non-landing trips.
There are also occasional evening music cruises.

SS WARPEN

Length: 20.55m   Gross tonnage: 80
Propulsion: Single Screw   Engine type: Compound, 75hp
Built: 1873   Rebuilt (most recent): 1993
Passenger capacity: 57
Body of water: Lake Varpen   Home port: Bollnäs

Frequency of operation: Thursdays only
Period of operation: Early May to late September
Website address: www.tuppz.se/warpen/; www.warpen.se
Builders: Södra Varvet, Stockholm (W Lindberg)
Engine builder: Jönköpings M V 1900, fitted 1913
Owner: Bollnäs Ångbåtssällskap
Former names: *Norsbro* 1994, *Korsnäs* 1900

1873: Built as the warping tug *Korsnäs* for Korsnäs Sågverk AB for use on Lake Runn.

1904: Sold to Norsbro Sägverks AB, Leksand, renamed *Norsbro*. Moved to Lake Siljan. Converted to oil-firing at some stage.

1959: Sold to Bergkvist Sägverks AB, Insjön.

1969: Sold to Hans Daniels and Lennart Eriksson, Leksand, for preservation and restoration.

1994: Sold to Ångbåtsrederiet Warpen AB, Bollnäs, rebuilt as a passenger steamer to operate excursions on Lake Varpen from Bollnäs. Renamed *Warpen*.

2000: Owners became bankrupt, operation taken over by Tuppzbolaget.

2005: Re-purchased by Ångbåtsrederiet Warpen AB.

2006: March: Fitted with a diesel engine, although the steam engine remains, but will only be used on special occasions. Passenger capacity reduced from fifty-three to forty-five.

Warpen currently operates 3-hour evening cruises from Bollnäs at 19:00 from Tuesday to Saturday in the peak season. In earlier years at Bollnäs, at least until 1999, she also offered afternoon cruises.

7 Austria

LAKES

PS GISELA

Gisela at Gmunden, 1998.

Length: 48.80m   **Gross tonnage:** 187
Propulsion: Paddle Steamer   **Engine type:** Compound Oscillating, 120hp
Built: 1871   **Rebuilt** (most recent): 1986
Passenger capacity: 300
Body of water: Traunsee   **Home port:** Gmunden
Frequency of operation: SSuO   **Period of operation:** Mid-July to early August
Builders: Ruston, Wien-Floridsdorf   **Engine builder:** Prager Maschinenfabrik 1870
Owner: Gesellschaft der Freunde der Stadt Gmunden
Operator: Traunseeschiffahrt Karlheinz Eder GmbH
Remarks: Coal-fired

1871: Built for Josef Ruston for service on the Traunsee from Gmunden.

24 September: Maiden voyage on the lake.

Spring: Entered regular service.

1895: 2 March: Josef Ruston died at the age of eighty-six, ships and services taken over by his son John Ruston.

1907: New boiler fitted.

1916: Ruston, who was English, discussed selling the steamers to Rudolf Ippisch, who at that time operated a small fleet of motor boats on the lake.

1918: 1 January: Sold to Ippisch. Now owned by Traunsee Schiffahrts-Gesellschaft.

1939: New boiler fitted.

1953: 2 March: Rudolf Ippisch died; the lake steamers and motorships were inherited by his son of the same name.

1975: New boiler fitted after **Gisela** was threatened with scrapping.

1976: 25 April: Rudolf Ippisch Jr died, ships taken over by Karl Eder.

Late 1970s: By this time **Gisela** was seeing very little service, with only a handful of trips each year, and spent most of her time laid-up at Ebensee-Rindbach.

1980: Withdrawn from service. Laid-up at Ebensee-Rindbach.

1981-86: Rebuilt on land at Ebensee with support from the 'Freunde der Stadt Gmunden'.

1986: 5 July: Returned to service.

Gisela is normally in service only in fine weather in the peak season of July and August. She mainly operates twice daily on Sundays at 11:30 and 14:00 on the route the full length of the lake from Gmunden to Ebensee, at the foot of the lake, and also on Saturdays and public holidays when traffic is high.

PS HOHENTWIEL

Hohentwiel off Meersburg, 1990.

Length: 56.90m   **Gross tonnage:** 295
Propulsion: Paddle Steamer   **Engine type:** Compound Diagonal, 950hp
Built: 1913   **Rebuilt** (most recent): 1990
Passenger capacity: 700
Body of water: Bodensee   **Home port:** Hard
Frequency of operation: 2-3x weekly
Period of operation: May to early October
Website address: www.dampfschiff-hohentwiel.de
Builders: Escher Wyss, Zürich
Owner: Internationales Bodensee-Schiffahrtsmuseum

1913:1 May: Entered service for the Königlich Würtembergische Dampfschiffahrt, (part of the Würtemberg State Railway) on the Bodensee (Lake Constance). Operated out of Friedrichshafen and used on sailings to Konstanz and Bregenz.

1920: 1 April: Owners became part of Deutsches Reichsbahn.

1932-33: Rebuilt: New first-class saloon forward, with sun deck above fitted, new smoking saloon on the promenade deck fitted, bridge and wheelhouse raised above this.

1934-35: Winter: Rebuild continued: New wheelhouse and bridge built, stability blisters added to hull to improve stability, mainmast added, paddle boxes shortened by 1.5m forwards.

1945: After the war, owners became Generaldirektion der Südwestdeutschen Eisenbahn as part of the French-controlled zone of Germany.

1950: Solid bulwarks replaced the previous railings on the foredeck.

1952: Owners became Deutsche Bundesbahn.

1957: February: Used for three weeks for training helmsmen between Friedrichshafen, Meersburg and Konstanz. This was her last scheduled winter service.

1960: 13 September: Moved to operate out of Konstanz.

1961: On short trips in the Überlinger See, the northern part of the Bodensee.

1962: Her final season in service, replacing temporarily the new motor vessel *München*, whose entry into service had been delayed.

3 September: Laid-up after an engine failure.

1 November: Officially withdrawn from service.

1963: Sold to Bregenzer Segelklub (Bregenz Sailing Club) and towed to Bregenz harbour on 23 April.

1964: 25 May: Moved to the sailing club after repainting. Used as a clubhouse.

1979: The prospect of using her as a Bodensee Shipping museum was mooted.

1984: 30 October: Taken over by Internationales Bodensee-Schiffahrtsmuseum e.V. Towed to Fussach for the beginning of restoration.

1986-90: Totally rebuilt partly at Fussach and partly at Hard. Stripped to the hull frames and rebuilt upwards. New boiler fitted.

1989: 3 November. Moved for the first time since 1963 under her own power.

1990: 17 May: Returned to service.

The operators of **Hohentwiel** have not been able to come to any arrangement with the three (German, Swiss, and Austrian) operators of scheduled service on the Bodensee, and she offers a variety of shorter cruises from various towns on the lake, mainly in the Austrian and German sections, with a few sailings from Swiss ports.

SS THALIA

Thalia leaving Maria Worth, 1990

Length: 38.50m   **Gross tonnage:** 132
Propulsion: Single Screw   **Engine type:** Compound, 150hp
Built: 1909   **Rebuilt** (most recent): 1989
Passenger capacity: 300
Body of water: Wörthersee   **Home port:** Klagenfurt/See
Frequency of operation: ThSuO   **Period of operation:** Late June to late August
Website address: www.stw.at/inhalt/schifffahrt.htm
Builders: Dresdner Maschinenfabrik & Schiffswerf Ubigau, Dresden
Owner: Stadtwerke Klagenfurt
Former names: *Klagenfurt* 1939, *Thalia* 1925

1909: Built as **Thalia** for Wörther-See-Dampfschiffahrt von Kapitän Julius Czyzek und Druckerei-Direktor Pietz.

20 June: Maiden voyage.

1910: Steam steering machine fitted, manufactured by her builders.

1913: Operators taken over by the town of Klagenfurt, and became Wörther-See-Dampfschiffahrtsgesell-chaft der Stadtgemeinde Klagenfurt GmbH.

1915-18: Very rarely in service due to coal shortage.

1919-43: In regular year-round passenger service.

1927: Operators renamed Wörther-See-Schiffahrt der Stadtgemeinde Klagenfurt.

1928: Renamed **Klagenfurt**.

1932: Renamed **Thalia**.

1941: Operators became Wörthersee-Schiffahrt der Gauhauptsadt Klagenfurt.

1944-45: Laid-up because of coal shortage.

1945: Owners became Stadtwerke Klagenfurt: Abteilung Wörthersee-Schiffahrt.

1946: Diesel engine ordered but never installed.

1959: Owners became Stadtwerke Klagenfurt, Verkerhrsbetriebe Schiffahrt.

1965: New oil-fired boiler fitted.

1966: Major refit. New wheelhouse fitted, engine room enlarged, saloons renovated.

1970: Steam steering gear replace by electro-hydraulic steering gear.

1974: 24 July: Withdrawn from service. Laid-up at Klagenfurt-See.

1986-88: Rebuilt and restored.

1988: 2 July: Returned to service.

2005: Withdrawn from daily scheduled service.

2006: Day trips reinstated.

Thalia is the only surviving screw steamer of any size in the Alpine area. In the peak summer season, in the scheduled service from Klagenfurt-See to Velden, she offers two express return sailings daily at 11:15 and 15:45 calling only at Maria Wörth and Pörtschach in both directions.

In 2005 she offered an evening moonlight cruise on Thursdays leaving Klagenfurt at 20:00 for Velden and return direct, and a Sunday morning *Frühschoppen* trip from Klagenfurt at 09:30 to Velden and return via the various intermediate piers.

RIVER DANUBE

ST FREDERIC MISTRAL

Frederic Mistral under steam on the Danube after restoration.

Length: 26.35m   **Tonnage:** 145
Propulsion: Single Screw   **Engine type:** Compound, 250hp
Built: 1912   **Rebuilt** (most recent): 2000
Body of water: River Danube   **Home port:** Vienna
Frequency of operation: Undergoing restoration
Website address: www.fhs-austria.com
Builders: Gertruidenburg Shipyard, Netherlands
Owner: Kapitän Scheriau
Former name: *Columbia*

1912: Built as the tug **Columbia** by N.V. Maschinfabriek v/h Schipper & Van Dongen, Geertruidenberg, Netherlands, for Ungarische Fluss- und Seeschiffahrts AD. Operated by DDSG. It is claimed that at one point Kaiser Franz Josef I sailed incognito on the steamer.

1914-18: Used by K.u.K Kriegsmarine (Austrian Navy) on the Danube and the Black Sea.

1918: taken over as war reparations by France.

1920: Ownership transferred to French Danube operator SFND, continued to be used on the Danube.

1930: Renamed **Frederic Mistral**.

*c.*1940: Used in a planned blockade of the Iron Gates by the Allies. Captured by German troops. Later converted to a minesweeper.

1943: Used by DDSG in the Black Sea and along the Greek Coast. Later reportedly fell into Russian hands. Transferred to Yugoslavian ownership and was used as a command ship for General Tito.

1945: Returned to SFND, used in the Romanian section of the Danube, based at Braila.

1997: Withdrawn from service and laid-up.

1999: Found in Romania and purchased by present owner. Towed back to Vienna-Friedenau for restoration.

2002: 8 June: Return to steam.

ST PASCAL

Pascal awaiting restoration at Vienna.

Length: 21.80m   **Tonnage:** 78
Propulsion: Single Screw   **Engine type:** Compound, 170hp
Built: 1907   **Rebuilt** (most recent): 2000
Body of water: River Danube   **Home port:** Vienna
Frequency of operation: Undergoing restoration
Website address: http://www.fhs-austria.com
Builders: Wiemann, Brandenburg
Owner: Kapitän Scheriau
Former names: *Leine* 1918, *Berta-Anna* 1916, *West-Havelland*

1907: Built as the tug **West-Havelland** for G. Gladow, Plaue, Germany.

Unknown date: Renamed **Berta-Anna**.

1916: Moved to the Danube by Zentral-Einkaufs-GmbH, a wartime controller of inland shipping, renamed **Leine**. Used by DDSG and the Imperial (K.u.K.) Navy on the Danube and Black Sea.

1918: Taken over as war reparations by France, renamed **Pascal**.

1920: Ownership transferred to French operator SFND.

*c.*1940: Used in a planned blockade of the Iron Gates by the Allies. Captured by German troops. Later converted to a minesweeper and fell into Russian hands. Transferred to Yugoslavian ownership and used as a command ship for General Tito.

1943: Used by DDSG.

1945: Returned to SFND, used in the Romanian section of the Danube.

1967: Sold to Romanian operator NAVROM.

1992: Laid-up.

1999: Found in Rumanian waters and purchased by present owner, towed to Vienna-Friedenau for restoration.

PS SCHÖNBRUNN

Schönbrunn arriving at Vienna, 2003. (B. Worden)

Length: 74.60m   **Gross tonnage:** 556
Propulsion: Paddle Steamer   **Engine type:** Compound Diagonal, 710hp
Built: 1912   **Rebuilt** (most recent): 1999
Passenger capacity: 960-day passengers, thirty-eight bunks
Body of water: River Danube   **Home port:** Linz
Frequency of operation: Occasional public trips
Website address: www.oegeg.at/oegeg/deutsch/frameset_4.htm
Builders: Werft Altofen, Budapest
Owner: Österreichische Gesellschaft für Eisenbahngeschichte (OeGEG)

1912: Built as a passenger paddle steamer for Danube operator DDSG. Built as a sister to *Wien* and *Budapest*.

1913: February: Entered service, used on the route from Vienna to Budapest.

1914-18: Used as a troop transport during the First World War.

1921: First sailing to the lower Danube, sailing occasionally to Belgrade, Moldova, Turnu Severin and Russe.

1936: Following the loss of *Wien*, which sank after hitting a pier of the Reichsbrücke in Vienna, used on the Linz to Vienna service.

1940-43: Used as a hospital ship and troop transport on the Balkan and Eastern fronts on the Danube in Bulgaria and Romania.

1944: Used, still as a hospital ship and troop transport, purely on the Austrian section of the Danube

1945: Spring: Fell into the hands of the advancing American troops.

1952: 12 July: DDSG services recommenced after the war. Operated from Linz to Vienna.

1954: Major rebuild, wooden upper works replaced by new ones of steel and aluminium. Steam steering engine fitted. Engine completely dismantled and rebuilt, new oil-fired boiler fitted. Placed on the Passau-Linz-Vienna mail service.

1980: Major refit, fitted out in 'Nostalgic' style.

1985: Final year operating on the Vienna to Passau service.

1986: Used on twice-weekly two-day cruises from Vienna to Budapest, and Sunday cruises to Dürnstein. These were operated as 'Nostalgic Danube Steamer Cruises' by Mondial Travel.

1987: Operated Vienna to Passau, with sailings to Budapest only operated if there was a demand. Riverboat Shuffles from Vienna operated.

1988: Withdrawn from service.

1989: Used in Budapest as a static casino ship.

1994: Used statically at the Oberösterreich Landesaustellung (Upper Austrian Provincial Exhibition) at Engelhartszell.

1995: 19 October: Sold to the Österreichische Gesellschaft für Eisenbahngeschichte (Austrian Organisation for railway history) for a symbolic 1 Schilling for preservation.

2002: 20 May: Returned to steam after major restoration.

Schönbrunn offers cruises on the Austrian section of the Danube only about half a dozen times a year, often in connection with special steam-hauled trains organised by her owners.

The paddle steamer ***Johann Strauss*** is in static use as a waltz-café on the Donau-Kanal in Vienna. She was constructed in 1945 from the hull of the steamer ***Grein*** (1853) and the machinery of ***Johann Strauss*** (1913).

8 Czech Republic

PS VLTAVA

Vltava, with *Vysehrad (IV)* outside her, at Prague, 1994.

Length: 53.10m   Gross tonnage: 1676n
Propulsion: Paddle Steamer   Engine type: Compound Diagonal, 150hp
Built: 1940   Rebuilt (most recent): 1991
Passenger capacity: 200
Body of water: Vltava River   Home port: Prague
Frequency of operation: Daily in fine weather   Period of operation: All year?
Website address: www.plavba.cz/cz/forum/prispevek.asp?ID=200005161;
www.paroplavba.cz/index_en.php
Builders: Ustecki Lodi, Usti   Engine builder (if different from builder): CKD Prague
Owner: PPS, Prague
Former names: *Moldau* 1945, *Vltava* 1941

1939-40: Built as *Vltava* at Weft Aussig, Aussig (now Usti), on the Czech section of the Elbe for PPS, Prague, for operation at Prague. Was to have been the first of a class of six, only one of which (*Labe*, now *Wappen von Minden*) was built due to the war.

1940: 16 October: Entered service.

1942: Renamed *Moldau* during the German occupation.

1945: Regained the name *Vltava*. Owners became the nationalised CPSLO.

1960: Deck saloon and upper deck added.

1961: Upper deck removed because of stability problems. Owners now OP Praha.

1979: Converted to oil-firing.

1991: Owners became PPS again with the ending of communism. Major refit. New boiler fitted.
September: Return to service.

Vltava and *Vysehrad* (IV) offer trips mainly in the city of Prague, with sailings downstream to Melnik, at the junction of the Vltava and the Labe (Elbe) on three days a year.

The trips at Prague are mainly evening dinner cruises, with occasional daylight sightseeing trips. These are not advertised as such in the timetable, and those advertised as paddle steamer cruises are often not operated by a paddle steamer but by one of the smaller motor vessels if there are not a lot of passengers.

PS VYSEHRAD (III)

Length: 62.00m
Propulsion: Paddle Steamer   Engine type: Compound Diagonal
Built: 1938   Rebuilt (most recent): 1991
Body of water: Vltava River   Home port: Prague
Frequency of operation: Awaiting restoration
Website address: www.schaufelraddampfer.de/links/epps.htm
Builders: Ustecki Lodi, Usti

Vysehrad (III) in a derelict state at Prague, with *Labe* to the left and *Vltava* or *Vysehrad (IV)* forward of her. (S. Ellerman)

Owner: PPS, Prague
Former names: *Dr Edvard Benes*, 1952, *Wischerad* 1945, *Labe* 1942, *Dr Edvard Benes* 1939

1938: Built as *Dr Edvard Benes* for PPS, Prague, for service on the Vltava at Prague.
1939: Renamed *Labe*.
1942: Renamed *Wischerad* under German occupation.
1945: Regained the named *Dr Edvard Benes*. Owners nationalised, became CSPLO.
1952: Renamed *Vysehrad*.
1959: Major rebuild. Deck saloon added, hydraulic lowering of funnel replaced manual lowering.
1980: Converted to oil-firing.
1991: Owners became PPS. Withdrawn, rebuild began.
  10 October. Work ceased on her rebuild when money ran out.

Vysehrad has lain since then at the yard in Prague with her superstructure removed awaiting restoration since then. At one time it was reported that when rebuilt she would take the name *Hradcany*.

PS VYSEHRAD (IV)

Vysehrad (IV) at Prague, 1994.

Length: 62.00m
Propulsion: Paddle Steamer   Engine type: Compound Diagonal, 220hp
Built: 1938   Rebuilt (most recent): 1992
Passenger capacity: 300
Body of water: Vltava River   Home port: Prague
Frequency of operation: Daily in fine weather   Period of operation: All year?
Website address: www.plavba.cz/cz/forum/prispevek.asp?ID=200005161;
      www.paroplavba.cz/index_en.php
Builders: Ustecki Lodi, Usti   Engine builder (if different from builder): CKD Prague
Owner: PPS, Prague
Former names: *Devin* 1992, *T G Masaryk* 1952, *Karlstein* 1945, *Antonin Svehla* 1942

1938: Built for PPS, Prague as **Antonin Svelha** as a sister of **Dr Edvard Benes** (above).

1 May: Entered service.

1942: Renamed **Karlstein** under German occupation.

1944-45: Used as a floating kitchen for bombed-out Dresden.

1945: Renamed **T G Masaryk**. Owners nationalised and became CSPLO.

1952: Renamed **Devin**.

1961: Major rebuild. Deck saloons added and funnel converted from manual to hydraulic lowering.

1979: Converted from coal to oil firing.

1991: Owners became PPS again. Major refit following fall of communism. Planned to be renamed **Bohemia**. New boiler fitted.

1992: 26 July: Returned to service as **Vysehrad** (IV) after the decision was taken not to complete the rebuild of **Vysehrad** (III).

9 France

France is a country that has little interst in preserving powered craft, steam or diesel, with the little maritime preservation effort there is being devoted to sailing ships.

SWS MARK TWAIN

Mark Twain at Euro Disney, 1990.

Length: 37.00m
Propulsion: Sternwheeler
Engine type: 2-cylinder simple expansion horizontal
Built: 1992   **Passenger capacity**: 380
Body of water: Disneyland Paris   **Home port**: Marne La Vallée
Frequency of operation: Daily   **Period of operation**: Year-round
Website address: www.disneylandparis.com/uk/disneyland_park/frontierland/attractions.htm
Builders: Disney Workshop, Marne La Valleé
Owner: Disneyland Paris

1992: Built for Euro Disney theme park at Marne la Vallée, east of Paris. **Mark Twain** is similar to **Mark Twain** in Disneyland, California, and **Liberty Belle** at Disney World, Florida. Like them, she does not have normal steering, but runs on a guide rail. She runs alongside **Molly Brown**, which is a replica of a walking-beam side wheel steamer, but is diesel-powered. Although all the parts of the replica walking beam engine move, it is not steam-powered.

10 Germany

Germany has a large number of surviving steamers. The highlight must be the nine-strong Dresden paddle steamer fleet. The Rhine has a sole survivor of a once strong paddle steamer fleet, whilst in Berlin, there is a long tradition of tugs being used for passenger service, which is carried on by a handful of survivors. Other steamers are dotted here and there around the country, with Hamburg being the only other place with a concentration of operating survivors, although there are a number of non-operational ones at the Westphalian Industrial Museum at the Heinrichenburg ship-lift near Dortmund. The website www.dampfschiff.de has pages on many preserved German steamers.

Some useful German words:

Dampf	steam
Schiff	ship
Schiffahrt or Schifffahrt	shipping
Gmbh	limited

BALTIC COAST

SS ALEXANDRA

Alexandra departing Vejle Steam Festival, 2004.

Length: 36.96m   **Gross tonnage:** 140
Propulsion: Single Screw   **Engine type:** Compound, 420hp
Built: 1908   **Rebuilt** (most recent): 1990
Passenger capacity: 120
Body of water: Flensburg Förde   **Home port:** Flensburg
Frequency of operation: SuO
Period of operation: end May to end September
Website address: www.dampfer-alexandra.de

Builders: Janssen & Schmilinsky/Schiffswerft & Maschinenfabrik
Owner: Förderverein Salondampfer Alexandra e.V
Remarks: Coal-fired

1908: June: Entered service as flagship of the fleet of Vereiniget Flensburg-Ekensunder und Sonderburger Dampfschiffs-Gesellschaft sailing on local services out of Flensburg. Named by Princess Alexandra of Schleswig-Holstein-Glücksburg.

1914-18: Requisitioned by Kaiserliche Marine.

1919: Range of services curtailed because the Danish border had moved south so that the north bank of the Flensburger Förde was now Danish.

1923: Vereiniget Flensburg-Ekensunder und Sonderburger Dampfschiffs-Gesellschaft renamed Flensburg-Ekensunder Dampfschiffs AG. *Alexandra* was on the Flensburg-Glückstadt-Langballigau service at this time.

1935: Flensburg-Ekensunder Dampfschiffs AG bankrupt. Taken over by Förde-Reederei.

1936: Used as escort steamer at Yachting Olympics in Kiel.

1939-45: Used as torpedo recovery ship for the Kriegsmarine (German Navy) in the Baltic and Danzig Bight.

1945: February: Used to carry thousands of refugees from the encroaching Russian army in the Eastern territories.

1969: With the withdrawal of **Albatros** (now a museum on land at the holiday resort Damp 2000), **Alexandra** became the last steamer in service at Flensburg.

1972 Used as escort steamer at Yachting Olympics at Kiel. Painted with vari-coloured diagonal stripes on funnel and part of hull.

1975: 31 August: Final scheduled service from Flensburg to Glücksburg. Thence laid-up at Flensburg.

1979: Enthusiast organisation founded to preserve **Alexandra**. Steamer painted and externally restored.

1986: 1 October. Steamer gifted by Förde-Reederei to present owners.

1988: 17 December: Returned to steam.

1993: Host steamer at first *Flensburger Dampf-Rundum*, a weekend steam event which attracts a number of steamers and other steam machines including traction engines. This has been celebrated every two years since then.

Alexandra normally operates short trips from Flensburg on Sundays in July, August and September, with some sailings in June and additional trips for special events in the Flensburg area.

SS BUSSARD

Length: 40.60m   **Gross tonnage**: 247
Engine type: Triple Expansion, 540hp
Built: 1950   **Rebuilt** (most recent): 2006
Passenger capacity: Unknown
Body of water: Kiel Harbour   **Home port**: Kiel
Frequency of operation: Possible future trips
Website address: www.kiel.de/kultur/museen/bussard.php
Builders: J.L. Meyer, Pepenburg
Owner: Keiler Stadt-und Schiffahrrtsmuseum
Remarks: Coal-fired

1905-06: Built as a buoy tender for Koningreich Preussen Regieringsbezirk Schleswig, Wasserbauinspektion Flensburg (Kingdom of Prussia Governmaent area Schleswig, waterway inspection Flensburg). Operated to Hadersleben via the Alsensund, on the Flensburger Forde, to the island of Fehmarn, and as far as Darss near Rugen. based at Flensburg.

1919: Following the transfer of the Sonderburg area to Denmark, base moved to Kiel. Operated on the Kieler Forde and Flensburger Forde, and occasionally also in the North Sea until 1965.

Mid-1960s: used as the official start ship for Kieler Woche yachting regatta.

1979: 23 June: Withdrawn from service.

1981: Opened as a museum ship in static display at Kiel Maritime Museum.

2002: Boiler steamed again.

2006: 21 February: Steamed for the first time since preservation.

  5 November: Second trial trip.

It is uncertain if **Bussard** will be operating regular passenger trips, but it is hoped she will be present at events such as the Flensburg Danmpf-Rundum and the Hamburg Harbour birthday celebrations.

PS FREYA

Length: 51.60m
Propulsion: Paddle Steamer   **Engine type**: Compound Chain Drive, 140hp
Built: 1905   **Rebuilt** (most recent): 1990

Freya at Sehestedt on the Kiel Canal, 2004

Passenger capacity: 300
Body of water: Kiel Canal and Kieler Förde   **Home port:** Kiel
Frequency of operation: Daily   **Period of operation:** May to December
Website address: www.adler-schiffe.de; www.raddampfer-freya.de/
Builders: J. & K. Smit, Kinderdijk   **Engine builder:** Netherlands 1923 from dredger
Owner: Adler-Schiffe
Former names: *De Nederlander* 1988, *De Zwaan* 1990, *Westerschelde* 1935
Remarks: Also has diesel

1906: 2 January: Entered service for Provinciale Stoomboot Dienst, Vlissingen. Operated from Vlissingen up the Schelde to Terneuzen, Hansweert and Walsoorden.
1907: 13-14 September: Used as Royal yacht.
1933: November: Sold to F. de Klerk, Terneuzen (shipyard).
1935: Sold to P.J. Zwaarns, Oosterhut, for use as a bunker ship. Renamed *De Zwaan*.
1944: Stormed by SS troops looking for Jews.
1965: Sold to Gebr. Spes.
1988: Sold to F. Key, Rotterdam. Rebuilt and returned to service with a small steam engine from a dredger, powering the paddles by belt drive, also a diesel engine powering a Schottel unit aft. Renamed *De Nederlander*.
1990: 16 May: Entered service on party cruises and charters from Rotterdam.
1999: December: Sold to S. Paulsen (Adler-Schiffe), List (Sylt). Renamed *Freya*. Used for trips from List.
2001: Moved to Kiel.

Freya offers a variety of trips from Kiel, many to the Kiel Canal, as far as Rendsburg, or a one-way trip to Brunsbüttel, and on to Hamburg on a second day, returning by bus. Her steam engine sees little use on these trips. Brunch cruises are offered on certain days out of Kiel. She also visits various yachting events on the German Baltic Coast, e.g. at Travemünde and Rostock. Sailings are offered on a daily basis with no regular weekly schedule.

Mecklenburg Lakes

SS EUROPA

Length: 36m   **Engine type:** 2-cylinder, 120hp
Built: 2005   **Passenger capacity:** 217
Body of water: Müritz   **Home port:** Röbel
Frequency: TX   **Period of operation:** summer months
Website address: www.mueritzschiffahrt.de
Builder: Stocznia Odra, Szczecin   **Engine builder:** Klawitter & Steimig, Danzig, 1925
Owner: Weisse Flotte-Müritz.de
Remarks: Also has diesel-electric drive

2005: 20 October: Ran trials at Szczecin.

30 November: Sailed from Sczeczin to Schiffswerft Malz on the first stage of her delivery voyage.

Europa is a new steamer built for use on the Müritz, a lake north of Berlin, built to the design of the 1910 steamer **Theodor Fontane**. She also has a diesel-electric propulsion system.

She entered service in Summer 2006. She is the first passenger steamer to have been built for use in Germany for many years. Her engine can be observed in operation by her passengers behind a glass partition.

She sails from the Stadthafen at Waren daily except Tuesdays, with sailings at 10:30, 13:00 and 15:00. Most of these are 2-hour three-lake trips, covering the Müritz, Eldenburger See and Kölpinsee, with some 90-minute Müritz round trips to Klink. An evening cruise is offered at 20:00 on Saturdays.

BERLIN AND SURROUNDINGS

ST ANDREAS

Andreas at Berlin's Binnenschiffahrtmuseum, 2002.

Length: 35.18m	Gross tonnage: 228
Propulsion: Single Screw	Engine type: Triple Expansion, 275hp
Built: 1944-50	Passenger capacity: 66
Body of water: River Spree	Home port: Berlin

Frequency of operation: Occasional public trips

Website address: www.historischer-hafen-berlin.de/ad.htm

Builders: Wiemann, Brandenburg   Engine builder: Wiemann, Brandenburg, 1925

Owner: Berlin-Brandenburgische Schiffahrtsgesellschaft e.V

Remarks: Coal-fired

1944: Laid down as a tug for Bittkow & Geiseler, Dorotheenhof, planned to be diesel-powered. Because all the available diesel engines were earmarked for the Kriegsmarine (German Navy) she was fitted with a triple expansion engine which had previously been in the tug *Saaleck*, built in 1925 and dieselised in 1937.

1945: April: Hull completed, engine still to be fitted. The hull was sunk in an air raid and broken in two. The two parts were raised after the end of the war and rebuilt with a new midships portion.

1950: Finally entered service.

1950s and 1960s: Saw service as a tug, mainly on the Elbe between Niegripp and Magdeburg.

1970: Moored on the east bank of the Rummelsberger See, Berlin during winter months for use as a steam heating plant for Electro-Apparate-Werkes Treptow. Every three or four years sailed to the yard at Plaue for overhaul. This journey had to be made by a roundabout route to avoid sailing through the waters of West Berlin.

1989: Spring: Final trip to Plaue.

1991: Sold to preservation organisation Berlin-Brandenburgische Schiffahrtsgesellschaft e.V.

Andreas is normally moored at Berlin Historic Harbour, at the Mühlendamm lock, where she is the flagship of the fleet of vessel preserved there. She makes occasional day trips from there with passengers, and occasional longer trips, e.g. to Hamburg or Duisburg, towing a barge with an exhibition about the history of shipping on the Spree and Havel on board the barge.

TST GEHEIMRAT GARBE

Geheimrat Garbe laid-up at Potsdam, 1991.

Length: 21.85m   Gross tonnage: 107
Propulsion: Twin Screw   Engine type: 2 Compound, 150hp
Built: 1892   Rebuilt (most recent): 200?
Body of water: River Havel   Home port: Potsdam
Frequency of operation: Undergoing restoration
Website address: www.dampfschiffe.de/frameset.htm
Builders: J.H.N. Wichhorst, Hamburg
Owner: C. Lebek, Postdam
Former names: *Forelle* 1980s, *Eintracht* 1928, *Schönebeck* 1910
Remarks: Coal-fired

1892: Built as the inland waterways tug *Schönebeck*. Her early history is unclear and certain sources state
    she was built in 1902.
1910: New boiler fitted. Owner at this point was B. Stein, Malz.
    Sold to O. Gerhardt, Fürstenberg renamed *Eintracht*.
1921: Owned by G. Ulbrich and A. Mayer, Mainz.
1928: Sold to A. & A. Lemke, Ketzin. Renamed *Forelle*.
1971: Out of service. Sold to a private individual at Brandenburg, to be used in a houseboat in a side arm
    of the River Havel.
1975: Sold to Lothar Bischoff.
1983: Sold to C. Lebek, Plaue.
1985: Slipped at Plaue. Hull found to be in good condition.
198?: Renamed *Geheimrat Garbe*.
1989: Moved to Potsdam for restoration work to be done on her.
1990 onwards: Gradually totally restored and rebuilt. Moved to Plaue. Her owner is now in his eighties,
    and the work is proceeding very slowly.

It is not known what the plans are for *Geheimrat Garbe* are once she is back in steam, but it is hoped
that these will include passenger service somewhere.

ST GUSTAV

Length: 31.98m
Propulsion: Single Screw   Engine type: Triple Expansion, 250hp
Built: 1908   Rebuilt (most recent): 2000
Body of water: River Havel & Spree   Home port: Potsdam
Frequency of operation: MTWX   Period of operation: Easter to mid-October

Gustav at Potsdam, 2002.

Website address: www.schiffahrt-in-potsdam.de/pages/flotte/flotte.htm
Builders: Wiemann, Brandenburg
Owner: Haveldampfschiffahrt GmbH
Former names: *Auguste* 1929
Remarks: Coal-fired

1908: Delivered as tug **Auguste** to Hamburg owners Schmeil & Friedrich. Used on the Elbe and tributaries, mainly between Hamburg and Berlin.

1929: October: Sold to G. Thiele, Lehnin (southeast of Brandenburg). Renamed **Gustav**.

1950: Transferred to G. & A. Thiele.

*c.*1976: Lengthened by 5m. New coal bunker added in new area to give a wider operating range.

1987: Still in service as the last active non-passenger steamer in the DDR.

1989: Placed on land for a slow piece-by-piece restoration.

2001: Purchased by present owners. Restored at Schiffswerft Bolle, Neu Derben. New coal-fired boiler fitted. Converted to passenger steamer by the addition of an awning aft and a small kiosk amidships. Easter. Entered excursion service at Potsdam.

Gustav operates three daily 90-minute 'Castle Cruises' from Thursdays to Sundays. These sail from Potsdam on the lakes eastward in the direction of Berlin, departing at 11:00, 13:00 and 15:00.

TSS KAISER FRIEDRICH

Kaiser Friedrich approaching Haus der Kulturen der Welt landing place, 2002.

Length: 31.22m
Propulsion: Twin Screw   **Engine type**: 2 Compound Oscillating, 92hp
Built: 1886   **Rebuilt** (most recent): 1993
Passenger capacity: 150
Body of water: River Spree   **Home port**: Berlin
Frequency of operation: Several times daily
Period of operation: Mid-April to early October
Website address: www.sternundkreis.de/Uebersicht/Innenstadt/Stadtrundfahrten/stadtrundfahrten.html
Builders: Möller & Holberg, Stettin
Engine builder: Unknown, Netherlands *c.*1930; from dredger
Owner: Deutsches Technikmuseum **Operator**: Stern -und Kreisschiffahrt
Former names: *Siegfried* 1994, **Kaiser Friedrich III** 1929

1886: Built as the passenger steamer **Kaiser Friedrich III**.

1918: Renamed **Siegfried** following the end of the monarchy.

1923: Sold to Paul David for service on the Oder.

1925: Sold to J. Schmiede, Breslau (now Wroclaw in Poland).

1929: Sold to F. & E. Griese. Returned to Berlin waters. Used in the summer months as a passenger steamer and in the winter months as a tug.

1934: Boiler replaced with a second-hand one.

1936: Upper deck cover fitted, removed when used as a tug.

1949: Used by BVG as ferry from Wannsee to Stössensee. Fixed upper deck fitted around this time.

1965: Chartered to Stern -und Kreisschiffahrt for the service from Tegel via Spandau to the Gleinicker Brücke. By this time she was the last passenger steamer in service in West Berlin.

1967: Laid-up at end of season.

1968: Towed to Wannsee for 80th anniversary of Stern -und Kreisschiffahrt. Later sold to a private individual for use as a houseboat, firstly at Spandau, later at Plötzensee.

1972: Engines and boiler removed and scrapped.

1986: Purchased by Museum für Verkehr und Technik, now Deutsches Technikmuseum. Restoration commenced.

1987: Two engines formerly in a Dutch dredger obtained in exchange for icebreaker **Elbe** (p.186).

1991: March to 1993: June. Restored at Laubegast yard, Dresden.

1993: June to October: Restoration completed at Werft Stralau.

1994: 27 April: Re-entered service as **Kaiser Friedrich**. Operated on charter to Stern -und Kreisschiffahrt.

Kaiser Friedrich operates on 1-hour return trips several time daily cruises in the historic centre of Berlin from the Nikolaiviertel to Haus der Kulturen der Welt.

ST NORDSTERN

Nordstern with funnel lowered, approaching a bridge in Brandenburg.

Length: 26.37m   **Gross tonnage:** 121
Propulsion: Single Screw   **Engine type:** Triple Expansion, 303hp
Built: 1902   **Rebuilt** (most recent): 1991
Passenger capacity: 50
Body of water: River Spree   **Home port:** Berlin
Frequency of operation: 4x daily   **Period of operation:** Summer
Website address: www.nordstern-reederei.de
Builders: Gebr. Wiemann, Brandenburg
Owner: Nordstern-Reederei, Brandenburg, Havel
Remarks: Coal-fired

1902: Built as a tug for Golsch & Kahle, Brandenburg. Unusually painted with a white hull. Used as a passenger steamer in the summer months and as a tug in the remainder of the year.

1910: Purchased by Otto Sutor. Worked on weekdays towing barges filled with stones from Beetzsee to Charlottenburg, and at weekends on passenger trips on the Wannsee with seating on deck and an awning fitted over the aft deck. She then had a passenger capacity of 264.

1932: Fitted with one of the first Kort Nozzles to be installed on a tug.

1938: 30 October. Sailed in the official parade at the opening of Rothensee ship-lift, connecting the Mittelland Canal to the Elbe.

December: Taken over by the son of Otto Sutor.

1939: New boiler and wheelhouse installed. Now regularly sailed, as a tug, to Hamburg.

1942: Superstructure and funnel destroyed by an aerial mine at Spandau. Repaired by Wiemann, Brandenburg.

1965–66: Adapted for pusher tug use.

1979: Purchased by Lothar Bischoff, Brandenburg.

1979–84: Much restoration work done by owner.

1990: April. Used for the last time as a pusher tug. Chartered to Stern und Kreisschiffahrt for passenger trips from Wannsee.

1992: 8 May and 8-10 May 1994: Visited Hamburg for 803rd and 805th Harbour Birthday Celebrations.

1990s: Operated as a passenger steamer on charters and occasional public trips from Brandenburg, where she was normally moored at the foot of her owner's garden.

2001: Commenced summer service on a tourist route in the centre of Berlin.

2006: Suffered bunker room fire, repaired at Havelberg. Missed main summer season of operations. Both passenger saloons had to be refurbished because of the damage caused.

ST SEIMA

Seima. (Author's collection)

Length: 19.92m   Gross tonnage: 120
Propulsion: Single Screw   Engine type: Compound, 110hp
Built: 1908   Passenger capacity: 20
Body of water: River Spree   Home port: Berlin
Frequency of operation: Occasional public trips
Builders: Wiemann, Brandenburg
Owner: Deutsche Binnenreederi AG
Operator: Berlin-Brandenburgische Schiffahrtsgesellschaft e.V
Former names: *Sejma* 1949, *Eintracht* 1945
Remarks: Coal-fired

1908: Built as tug **Eintracht** for F. Lietzmann, Lehnin.

1914: Sold to D. Wernstedt, Parey.

1914-18: Requisitioned for Militär-Kanal-Direction, Brussels.

1945: By this time in use on the Oder. Taken over by the Red Army with a Russian crew and renamed **Sejma**. Later operated by Sowjetische Staatliche Oderschiffahrts AG (SOAG).

1949: Came back into German ownership under Deutsche Oderschiffahrt. Renamed **Seima**.

1953: Ownership changed to DSU.

1957: Ownership now VEB Deutsche Binnenschiffahrt, Berlin.

1972: Rebuilt as a pusher tug. Also used as icebreaker and for steam heating. Used mainly in the Berlin and Brandenburg areas.

1981: Autumn: Major overhaul at Laubegast.

1990: Owners became Deutsche Binnenschiffahrt AG. Following German reunification, commercial towing work dried up for **Seima**. She was used for charters and as an official tradition-ship in the Berlin area.

2000: Laid-up. Offered for sale.

2001: Agreement reached with Berlin-Brandenburgische Schiffahrtsgesellschaft e.V., owners of *Andreas* to operate her, moved to Berlin Historic Harbour since then.

Bodensee

SL FELICITAS

The steam launch *Felicitas* at Wasserburg on the Bodensee. (Owners)

Length: 10.75m   **Gross tonnage:** 4.8
Propulsion: Single Screw   **Engine type:** 1-cylinder, 13.5hp
Built: 1991   **Passenger capacity:** 14
Body of water: Bodensee   **Home port:** Wasserburg
Frequency of operation: ThO   **Period of operation:** Late May to end September
Website address: www.dampfboot.de/boote/boot_felicitas.html
Builders: Bootsbau H. Biatel   **Engine builder:** Emil Stark, Götzis, Austria
Owner: Felizitas Schmid, Wasserburg

Felicitas is a modern steam launch offering public passenger trips on Thursdays in the summer months from Wasserburg.

PS HOHENTWIEL
See Austria

Cruise ship

TSS MAXIM GORKIY   Bahamas Flag

Length: 194.72m   **Gross tonnage:** 24,220
Propulsion: Twin Screw   **Engine type:** 2 turbines, 22,660hp
Built: 1969   **Rebuilt** (most recent): 1987
Passenger capacity: 650
Body of water: Worldwide   **Home port:** Bremerhaven
Frequency of operation: Cruises   **Period of operation:** All year
Website address: www.skip-siden.com/Maxim%20Gorkiy/Maxim%20Gorkiy.htm;
www.phoenix-reisen,.com;   www.simplonpc.co.uk/HamburgMaximGorky.html
Builders: HDW, Kiel   **Engine builder:** AEG
Owner: Belata Shipping, Russia (Sovcomflot)   **Operator:** Phoenix Reisen
Former names: *Maksim Gorkiy* 1991, *Hanseatic* 1974, *Hamburg* 1973

1968: 21 July: Launched as *Hamburg*.
1969: 20 March: Delivered to Deutsche Atlantik-Linie, Hamburg.

28 March: Maiden Voyage Cuxhaven to South America, then operated cruises.

1973: 25 September: Renamed **Hanseatic**.

1 December: Laid-up at Hamburg.

1974: 25 January. Purchased by Black Sea Shipping Co., Odessa. Renamed **Maksim Gorkiy**. Chartered to Neckermann Travel for cruises for the German market.

1975: November: Hull damaged below the waterline en route from San Juan to New York by two bombs, which had been planted during repairs at San Juan, Puerto Rico. Repaired at Bethlehem Steel, Hoboken.

1988: September: Chartered to Phoenix Reisen, Bonn.

1989: 19 June. Damaged in pack ice near Spitzbergen. Passengers evacuated. Ship towed to Spitzbergen. Repaired at Lloyd Werft, Bremerhaven.

17 August: Return to service.

2–3 December: Presidents George Bush and Mikhail Gorbachev held summit on board.

1991: December Registered in Bahamas. Name changed to **Maxim Gorky**.

1992: 16 December: Sold to Belata Shipping, Limassol, Cyprus.

1996: Sold to Maxim Gorkiy Shipping Co., Nassau, Bahamas.

Maxim Gorky continues to be operated by Phoenix Reisen, with cruises that taker her to many ports around the world.

HAMBURG

ST CLAUS D

Claus D at the Oevelgönne Museum harbour, Hamburg, 2004.

Length: 17.76m   Gross tonnage: 46
Propulsion: Single Screw   Engine type: Compound, 220hp
Built: 1913   Rebuilt (most recent): 1984
Passenger capacity: 30
Body of water: Hamburg harbour   Home port: Hamburg
Frequency of operation: Occasional public trips
Website address: www.jia-hh.de/pro_clausd.html; www.claus-d.de
Builders: Janssen & Schmilinsky/Schiffswerft & Maschinenfabrik, Hamburg
Owner: Museumshafen Oevelgonne, Hamburg
Former names: *Moorfleth* 1956, *Schulau* 1933

1913: Entered service as the Hamburg harbour **Schulau** tug for J.H.N. Heymann.

1933: Sold to J.F.T. Lütgens, renamed **Moorfleth**. Used to tow barges carrying iron ore and gravel from Güster, near Lauenburg, to Hamburg harbour.

1956: Sold to C.R. Eckelmann. Renamed **Claus D**.

1957: New oil-fired boiler fitted.

1970s: Used in Hamburg harbour as a mobile steam source for e.g. tank cleaning.

1983: Laid-up. By this time, she was the last active working steamer in Hamburg harbour.

1984: 28 August: Donated to Museumshafen Oevelgönne.

1984: September: Restoration started.

1995–98: Rebuilt by Jugend im Arbeit Hamburg e.V.

1999: Returned to service.

Claus D is normally moored at the museum harbour at Oevelgönne, and is mainly used on charters with only very occasional public sailings, e.g. for special events.

SS ELBE

Length: 30.80m

Propulsion: Single Screw   **Engine type**: Compound, 280hp

Built: 1911   **Rebuilt** (most recent): 200?

Body of water: River Elbe   **Home port**: Hamburg

Frequency of operation: Undergoing restoration

Website address: www.dampfschiffe.de/schiffsregister/elbe.html

Builders: Wiemann, Brandenburg

Owner: Matthias Kruse, Hamburg

Remarks: Coal-fired

1911: Entered service on the River Elbe for the Königliche Elbstrom-Bauverwaltung (Royal Elbe River Management), Magdeburg. Based at Lauenburg.

1974: Withdrawn from service. Kept in reserve.

1976: Last day in service, offering passenger trips on Elbschiffahrtstag (Elbe Shipping Day) in conjunction with **Kaiser Wilhelm**.

1980: June: Laid-up at Geesthacht. Sold to a private individual.

1982: Taken over by Museum für Verkehr & Technik, Berlin (now Deutsches Technikmuseum), West Berlin. Lay in Berlin-Spandau harbour.

1987: 24 July: Towed to Enkhuizen, Holland. She had been swapped for two steam engines for **Kaiser Friedrich** (q.v.). Her Dutch owner did little with her. Later moved to Medmblik.

1995: Purchased by M. Kruse, Hamburg.

1997: 6–9 September. Towed to Hamburg via the North Sea. Work on restoration started. Boiler replaced with one from **Vampyr**. Superstructure, which had rotted, replaced.

2006: 27 May: Ran trials.

   24 July: Made a 3-hour Elbe trip.

It is hoped that restoration of **Elbe** will be completed soon and that she will be utilised for passenger sailings in Hamburg harbour.

TSY NAHLIN

Nahlin awaiting restoration at Liverpool. (Edward Brian-Davis)

Length: 89.3m   **Gross tonnage**: 1,392

Engine type: 2 turbines, 4,000hp

Built: 1930   **Rebuilt** (most recent): 2005

Passenger capacity: 351

Home port: Hamburg
Frequency: Undergoing restoration
Website address: www.merseyshipping.co.uk/photofeatures/historicships/nahlin0803/nahlin.htm
Builder: John Brown & Co., Clydebank   Engine builder: Brown-Curtis
Owner: ?, Hamburg
Former names: *Libertatea* 2001, *Luceafarul* 1948, *Nahlin* 1937

1930: Built as the steam yacht **Nahlin** for Lady Annie Henrietta Yule, a jute heiress. Designed by G.L. Watson. Initially used worldwide by Lady Yule, including one world cruise, then later chartered out by her. Covered over 200,000 miles during her years as a privately owned yacht.

August: First sailing to Cowes Week.

1936: Chartered for a cruise down the Adriatic and on to Istanbul by the Duke of Lancaster, an alias used by King Edward VIII, to entertain Mrs Wallis Simpson, this was one of the catalysts that brought about his abdication at the end of the year.

1937: Purchased by King Carol II of Romania. Renamed **Luceafarul**. The King's mistress, Helen Lupescu, insisted on the purchase of the yacht because of her romantic associations with Edward VIII and Mrs Simpson. She made only one cruise on her to the Aegean, before world events intervened.

1939: The invading Nazis overthrew King Carol and **Luceafarul** was laid-up in the Danube Delta throughout the war years.

1948: Renamed **Libertatea**. Used as a passenger steamer on domestic coastal service.

1960s: Used as a floating restaurant at Galati.

*c.*1989: Following the end of communism, sold to a private company. By this time, she was probably no longer in use as a restaurant.

1999: Purchased by William Collier and Nicholas Edmiston. Moved to the UK on the heavy lift ship **Swift**. Initially taken to Devonport.

2000: 3 May: Moved to the Cammell Laird yard, Liverpool, for restoration. Placed in the Clarence Dry Dock. The intention was that she be placed in the luxury yacht charter trade when restoration was complete.

October: G.L. Watson & Co., her designers, appointed special consultants to the project, which was being undertaken by Yachtworks Ltd. It was intended that she be dieselised, but although the boiler was removed, the steam turbines remained in situ. Renamed **Nahlin** and registered in Glasgow.

2001: 23 July: Moved to a berth elsewhere in the Liverpool docks system. Asbestos and other debris was removed.

2005: 27 July: Sold to a so far unidentified German owner, and moved to Hamburg on the heavy lift ship, then moved to the Nobiskrug yard at Rendsburg, on the Kiel Canal, for restoration at a cost of €60 million.

2007: Expected date for completion of restoration.

SL OTTO LAUFFER

Otto Lauffer at Hamburg. (Heinz Trost)

Length: 17.00m   Gross tonnage: 34
Propulsion: Single Screw   Engine type: Compound, 147hp
Built: 1928   Rebuilt (most recent): 1984
Passenger capacity: 30

Body of water: Hamburg harbour   Home port: Hamburg
Frequency of operation: Charters
Website address: www.dampfbarkasse.de; www.dampfschiffe.de/frameset.htm
Builders: H.C. Stülcken & Söhn, Hamburg
Owner: Museum für Hamburg Geschichte
Former names: *Wasserschutzpolizie 6* 1969, *Hafenpolizei VI* 1937
Remarks: Coal-fired

1928: 13 July: Trials. Entered service as police launch *Hafenpolizei VI*.
1937: Renamed *Wasserschutzpolizie 6*. At this time, she was one of eighteen launches in the fleet of the Wasserschutz-Polizei-Gruppe Hamburg.
1968: Withdrawn from service.
1969: 3 October. Purchased by Museum für Hamburger Geschichte (Museum for Hamburg's History) to replace the preserved steam launch *Geheimrat Just* which had sunk and was not repairable. Renamed *Otto Lauffer*.
1978-84: Restored at Blohm + Voss yard.
1984: 5 May. Re-entered service.

Otto Lauffer offers occasional passenger trips in the Hamburg area in the summer months and has also visited Glückstadt, Lübeck and the Flensburg Dampf-Rundum.

TSS SCHAARHÖRN

Schaarhörn leaving Hamburg, 2002.

Length: 41.66m   Gross tonnage: 225
Propulsion: Twin Screw   Engine type: 2 Triple Expansion, 824hp
Built: 1908   Rebuilt (most recent): 1995
Passenger capacity: 85
Body of water: River Elbe   Home port: Hamburg
Frequency of operation: Occasional public trips
Period of operation: Late May to ?
Website address: www.schaarhoern.de
Builders: Janssen & Schmilinsky/Schiffswerft & Maschinenfabrik
Owner: Stiftung Hamburg Maritim
Former names: *Scharhörn* 1995, *Schaarhörn* 1948
Remarks: Coal-fired

1908: 9 October: Delivered as Peildampfer (soundings steamer) *Schaarhörn* to the Hamburger Senat for use from Hamburg to the mouth of the Elbe Estuary, taking depth measurements and thus keeping the charts correct in this area of constantly changing sandbanks. Also used as the official State Yacht for Hamburg. In this capacity, the Kaiser is believed to have made an annual trip on her and she was later, erroneously, known as 'The Kaiser's Yacht'.
1914-18: Used by the Kaiserliche Marine (German Navy) as an auxiliary minesweeper stationed at Cuxhaven.

1919-25: Laid-up at Hamburg.

1921: Ownership transferred to the Reich.

1925: Re-activated.

1927: Steam steering installed.

1933: Rebuilt. Wooden masts replaced with steel ones. Engine room ventilators replaced. Echo-finder installed.

1936: Used at yachting Olympics at Kiel as escort steamer.

1938: Wheelhouse extended aft.

1945: Used to bring refugees back from Danzig and Stolpemünde in the face of the advancing Red Army. Laid-up at the end of the war.

1948: Renamed **Scharhörn**. Returned to service, now for the government-owned Wasser- und Schiffahrtamt.

1965: Converted from coal to oil-firing.

1972: 15 January: Officially withdrawn from service. She had been laid-up during the previous year and had seen little service since the mid-1960s.
Sold to H. Ropeter for preservation. Little work was done on her.

1973: 30 August. Sailed from Cuxhaven to Whitby. Sold to Keith Schellenberg.

1974: December. Moved to Buckie.

1979: August. Sold to the Treloar Brothers, towed to Maryport. She was to be the centrepiece of a proposed maritime museum there. Little work was done on her there.

1989: Owners became bankrupt. Purchased by Hamburg group, 'Jugend in Arbeit Hamburg e.V.'.

1990: May. Brought back to Hamburg on a heavy lift ship in time for the Harbour Birthday Celebrations. Restoration commenced.

1995: 25 May: Returned to service, beautifully restored. Renamed **Schaarhörn**.

Schaarhörn is a regular visitor to the Flensburg Dampf-Rundum and other special events in northern Germany, often offering all or part of the positioning voyages to such events as a public cruise. She has a regular programme of cruises from Hamburg beginning at the Harbour Birthday Celebrations in early May and continuing through the summer. These include Kiel Canal trips. Her Hamburg berth is on the other side of the river from the Landungsbrücke.

SS ST GEORG

St Georg on the Alster Lake, 2002.

Length: 20.80m   Gross tonnage: 36
Propulsion: Single Screw   Engine type: Compound, 75hp
Built: 1876   Rebuilt (most recent): 1994
Passenger capacity: 84
Body of water: Alster Lake   Home port: Hamburg
Frequency of operation: SSuO   Period of operation: April to October
Website address: www.alsterdampfer.de
Builders: Reihersteg, Hamburg
Engine builder: Werft Laubegast, Dresden 1928, fitted 1993/4
Owner: Verein Alsterdampfschiffahrt e.V
Former names: *Planet* 1994, *Deutschland* 1968, *St Georg* 1950, *Galatea* 1936, *Falke* 1911

1876: Built with half-saloons fore and aft as **Falke** for H.E. Justus for service on the Alster, the lake in the centre of Hamburg.

1888: Justus sold his fleet of Alster steamers to Otto Wichmann.

1910: Lengthened, rebuilt to flush-decked steamer.

1911: January: Renamed **Galatea**.

1920: Taken over by Hamburger Hochbahn AG.

1936: Renamed **St Georg**.

1939: Withdrawn from service.

1948: November: Sold to R.K. Krenz. Planned to be used on service from Hamburg to Lüneburg. Laid-up at Hamburg.

1950: November: Sold to B. Frost, West Berlin, renamed **Deutschland**. Operated by Stern- und Kreisschiffahrt. Occasionally used on the ferry route from Wannsee to Kladow.

1952: Steam engine removed. Converted to diesel.

1963: Rebuilt: Lengthened by 4m.

1968: Sold to Teltowkanal-AG, West Berlin (Stern -und Kreisschiffahrt). Renamed **Planet**.

1972: Re-engined.

1978: Used as a supply ship, fitted with refrigerated accommodation carrying catering supplies for the other vessels in the Stern -und Kreisschiffahrt fleet. Normally moored at Wannsee. Windows boarded up. Nicknamed the 'Purolator'.

1984: Withdrawn from service.

1988: Donated by Stern- und Kreisschiffahrt to Hamburg Senate. Moved to Hamburg Oevelgönne Museum harbour.

1989: Taken over by Verein Alsterdampfschiffahrt.

1992: Moved to Dresden on a barge, towed by steam tug **Sachsenwald**.

1992-94: Rebuilt at Laubegast to her 1920s condition. Steam engine and new boiler fitted.

1994: June: Sailed to Hamburg under her own power.

12 July: Re-entered service on the Alster.

St Georg normally runs from the Jungfernstieg landing stage to Barmbek, near the Museum fur Arbeit, with sailings each operating day at 10:45, 12:45, 14:45 and 16:45, the single journey taking 50 minutes. She operates from the end of March until late October on Saturdays, Sundays, and public holidays.

SS STETTIN

Stettin at the Flensburg Dampf-Rundum, 1995.

Length: 51.75m   **Gross tonnage:** 836
Propulsion: Single Screw   **Engine type:** Triple Expansion, 2200hp
Built: 1933   **Rebuilt** (most recent): 1982
Passenger capacity: 300
Body of water: North & Baltic Seas   **Home port:** Hamburg/Travemünde
Frequency of operation: Occasional public trips
Website address: www.dampf-eisbrecher-stettin.de

Builders: Stettiner Oderwerke, Stettin
Owner: Fördeverein Eisbrecher Stettin e.V., Lübeck
Remarks: Coal-fired

1933: November: Entered service as icebreaker for Stettiner IHK-Eisbrecherverwaltung der Seeschiffahrt. Operated clearing sea routes out of Stettin and Swinemünde, now Szczecin and Swinoujscie in Poland.

1939-45: Used by the Kriegsmarine right along the German Baltic Coast. Later in the war had anti-aircraft guns installed.

1945: March: Used to carry refugees from Stettin to Stralsund and Copenhagen. Transferred to Hamburg. Used during icy winters to keep the waterway clear from Hamburg to Cuxhaven and in the North Sea, Kiel Canal and the Kieler Förde. Ship was owned by the Deutsche Industrie- und Handelskammer, as successor to the Stettin owners, Stettin by this time being in Poland, and was chartered to the Wasser- und Schiffahrtsamt.

1978-79: Last winter in service as an icebreaker.

1981: August: Taken over by Fördeverein Eisbrecher Stettin e.V. September: Overhauled at Blohm + Voss, Hamburg. Rebuilt as museum ship.

1982: 14 June: Maiden voyage under preservation. Now based at Lübeck, Travemünde.

2001: Base moved to Hamburg.

Stettin is a regular visitor to steam events in northern Germany, e.g. Kiel week and the biennial Dampf-Rundum at Flensburg. She often makes public sailings to and from these events, as well as other occasional passenger trips in German waters.

ST TIGER

Tiger at Oevelgönne Museum harbour, Hamburg, 2004.

Length: 15.98m   **Gross tonnage**: 38
Propulsion: Single Screw   **Engine type**: Compound, 240hp
Built: 1910   **Rebuilt** (most recent): 2001
Passenger capacity: 75
Body of water: Hamburg harbour   **Home port**: Hamburg
Frequency of operation: Occasional public trips
Website address: www.jia-hh.de/pro_tiger.html
Builders: Schiffswerft & Maschinenfabrik (Janssen & Schmilinsky) AG, Hamburg
Owner: Museumshafen Oevelgonne e.V., Hamburg
Remarks: Coal-fired

1910: Entered service as a harbour tug at Hamburg for J.H. Steffen. Used for towing barges and lighters in the harbour area and down the Elbe as far as Brunsbüttel. Also offered passenger trips on summer Sundays with a capacity of 101. For this she was fitted with deck seating and an awning covering her entire deck.

1966: Withdrawn from service and laid-up.

1978: 9 January. Purchased by Museumshafen Oevelgonne e.V for preservation. Restoration work started.

1979: May Returned to steam for the Harbour Birthday Celebrations.

1997-2001: Rebuilt at Hamburg-Harburg by Jugend in Arbeit e.V. New boiler fitted.
2001: 9 November: Returned to service.

Tiger is based at Oevelgönne and makes occasional passenger sailings in the Hamburg harbour area.

ST VAMPYR

Vampyr at Hamburg.

Length: 22.10m   **Gross tonnage**: 52
Propulsion: Single Screw   **Engine type**: Compound, 227hp
Built: 1911   **Rebuilt** (most recent): 1949
Body of water: Hamburg harbour   **Home port**: Hamburg
Frequency of operation: Undergoing restoration
Website address: www.dampfschiffe.de/schiffsregister/vampyr.html
Builders: Johann van Bergh, Delfzijl, Netherlands
Engine builder: Oelkers Werft, Christiansen & Meyer, Hamburg-Harburg 1947
Owner: Freunde des Schleppdampfers Vampyr e.V
Former names: *Vampyr II*, *Vampyr* 1961, *Waltersdorf* 1958, *Expert* 1949, *Hugo Stinnes V* 1927, *Collet* 1916
Remarks: Coal-fired

1911: Entered service for A.E. Peters, Hamburg as the harbour tug **Collet**.
1916: Sold to Hugo Stinnes, renamed **Hugo Stinnes V**.
1926: Hugo Stinnes taken over by HAPAG.
1927: Transferred to HAPAG subsidiary Lütgens & Reimers, Renamed **Expert**.
1939: September: Requisitioned by Kreisgmarinebauaufsicht for use at the Neptun-Werft, Rostock.
1944: 10 February: Sunk at Rostock by a flying bomb. Raised.
1945: 8 April. Sunk at Hamburg during an air raid.
  December. Taken to J. Oelkers shipyard for repair. Lengthened by 4m.
1949: 2 August: Returned to service for Lütgens & Reimers. Renamed **Waltershof**.
1957: Sold to H. Bonertz. Converted for use as a tank cleaning and oil-removal ship. Towing gear removed and two large vacuum tanks mounted on deck. Operated in the harbours of both Hamburg and Bremen.
1958: Renamed **Vampyr**.
1961: Renamed **Vampyr II**.
1965: Boiler replaced by one built in 1931 by Christiansen & Meyer.
Mid-1970s: Converted to an unpowered vessel. Engine retained as ballast, but screw, rudder and auxiliary machinery removed. Now stationed at Hamburg Travehafen.
1993: June: Withdrawn from service.
1995: Purchased by Verein Alsterdampfschiffahrt e.V., owners of **St Georg**.
2000: Taken over by newly founded Freunde des Schleppdampfers Vampyr e.V.
2002: Boiler removed for use in **Elbe**.

Vampyr is a long-term restoration project. She will probably be restored as **Waltershof**.

Right: 1 *VIC 32* in winter lay up at Crinan, 1994. (See page 34.)

Below: 2 *Sir Walter Scott* approaching Stronachlachar on her centenary cruise, 2000. (See pages 39-40.)

3 *Hjejlen* at Silkeborg. (See page 44.)

4 *Norrkujla* as *Figaro* off Savonlinna, 1981. (See page 48.)

5 *Bjoren* leaving Byglandsfjord, 1999. (See page 107.)

6 *Freja af Fryken* at Sillegården Pier, 1999. (See page 147.)

7 *Thomée* on the Störsjön, 1999. (See page 165–166.)

8 *Maxim Gorky* in the Geirangerfjord, 1993. (See page 184.)

9 *Pillnitz* arriving at Pillnitz, 2002. (See page 201–202.)

10 *Succes* leaving Dordrecht up river at *Dordt in Stoom*, 2004. (See page 212.)

11 *Pieter Boele* at *Dordt in Stoom*, 2004. (See page 225.)

12 *Lötschberg* at Brienz, 2002. (See page 229.)

13 *Schiller* departing Treib, 1979. (See page 239-240.)

14 *American Queen* at Louisville, 1996. (See page 344.)

15 A bow view of *American Queen* showing the wedding cake-style decorative features. (See page 344.)

16 *Waverley* on her first call at Canna, 2002.

17 Decorative scrollwork on the bow of *Lötschberg*.

18 *Kurort Rathen* in Saxon Switzerland, 2002. (See page 199.)

19 *Saimaa* on Lake Saimaa (from a booklet cover). (See page 82.)

20 *Dockyard V* at Rotterdam, 1989.

21 *Oceanic* anchored at Villefranche, 2005. (Bruce Peter) (See page 267-268.)

22 *Minnehaha* at Minneapolis, 2005. (B. Worden) (See page 352.)

23 *Blidösund*, seen here at Svartlöga in 1982, carrying excursion passengers for a day out to sunbathe.

24 A glimpse of the glowing coals.

25 An engine room telegraph from *Stettin*.

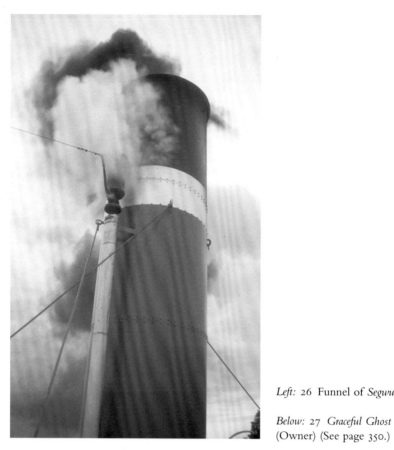

Left: 26 Funnel of *Segwun* with whistle blowing.

Below: 27 *Graceful Ghost* on the Caddo Lakes. (Owner) (See page 350.)

Right: 28 *Liberty Belle* leaving LaConner. (Lou Keller) (See page 358-359.)

Below: 29 Paddle launch *Liberty Belle* on Lake Lucerne, 2004. (Beat Bolzern) (See page 237-238.)

30 *Above:* The ornamental cannon on *Skibladner.*

31 *Left:* The paddle boxes of *La Suisse.*

SS WINTERHUDE

Winterhude in early condition at
Jungfernsteig on the Alster, Hamburg.
(From the book *Geschichte der Alsterschiffahrt*)

Length: 20.00m   Gross tonnage: 38
Propulsion: Single Screw   Engine type: Compound, 50hp
Built: 1879   Rebuilt (most recent): 2001
Body of water: Alster Lake   Home port: Hamburg
Frequency of operation: Return to steam 200?
Builders: Reiherstegwerft, Hamburg
Owner: Verein Alsterdampfschiffahrt e.V
Former names: *Möwe*, *Bottrop* 1973, *Mulheim a.d Ruhr* 1956, *Herrenwyk* 1951, *Hohenfelde* 1941,
Neptun 1936, *Winterhude* 1904

1878: Entered service on the Alster Lake as half-saloon steamer *Winterhude* for Otto Wichmann.

1904: November: Fitted with new engine and boiler. Promenade deck added. Renamed *Neptun*.

1914, or before: Rebuilt as flush-decker.

1920: Taken over by Hamburger Hochbahn AG.

1936: March: Renamed *Hohenfelde*.

1941: Sold to Städtische Werke, Lübeck. Renamed *Herrenwyk*.

1945: Sold to Trave-Transport-Gesellschaft Ahrens & Co., Lübeck. Operated from Lübeck to Travemünde/ Priwall.

1947: Steam engine replaced by a Deutz diesel.

1951: Rebuilt with open deck forwards. Sold to Betriebe der Stadt Mühlheim a.d.Ruhr. Renamed *Mühlheim A. D. Ruhr*. Operated from Wasserbahnhof Mühlheim to Baldeneywehn, on special trips from Mühlheim to Kupferdreh, and on harbour trips at Duisburg-Rurhort.

1956: August: Renamed *Bottrop*.

1973: Sold to Mühlheimer Rudergesellschaft and renamed *Möwe*. Moored at Mühlheimer Nordhafen as a floating clubhouse for Yachtclub Mühlheim a.d.Ruhr.

1998: Purchased for preservation and a return to the Alster, with the fitting of a steam engine, and a return to service on the Alster as a half-saloon-proposed steamer.

ST WOLTMAN

Length: 20.00m   Gross tonnage: 38
Propulsion: Single Screw   Engine type: Compound, 268hp
Built: 1904   Rebuilt (most recent): 2003
Passenger capacity: 50
Body of water: Hamburg harbour   Home port: Hamburg
Frequency of operation: Charters
Website address: www.jia-hh.de/pro_woltman.html
Builders: Sachsenberg, Rosslau/Elbe
Owner: Förderverein Schleppdampfer Woltman e.V
Remarks: Coal-fired

Woltman at Vejle Steam Festival, 2004.

1904: Built for Hamburger Staat as a sea-going tug with collapsible wheelhouse and funnel. Used on the Lower Elbe from Hamburg to Cuxhaven. Based at Ritzebüttel near Cuxhaven.

1927: Steam steering gear installed.

1940-45: Stationed at Dunkirk.

1966: Replaced by a new diesel tug. Kept in reserve.

1977: Sold to Dutch owners for preservation.

1984: Purchased for a new museum harbour at Kappeln. Steamed back from Holland to Cuxhaven, and then to Husum. Used in the film *The Riddle of the Sands*. Boiler damaged during the filming because it was fired up with no water in. Boiler repaired at Flensburg.

1992: Towed to Hamburg for further repairs at the Buschmann-Werft.

1994: 28 January: Returned to steam. Taken over by Förderverein Schleppdampfer Woltman e.V.

1997-2003: Major rebuild by Jugend in Arbeit Hamburg e.V. at Hamburg-Harburg.

NORTH SEA COAST

TSS KAPITÄN MEYER

Kapitän Meyer, with *Wal*, at Flensburg Dampf-Rundum, 1995.

Length: 52.10m   Gross tonnage: 555
Propulsion: Twin Screw   Engine type: 2 Triple Expansion, 1,000hp
Built: 1950   Passenger capacity: 70
Body of water: North Sea   Home port: Wilhelmshaven
Frequency of operation: Occasional public trips
Website address: www.dampfschiffe.de/schiffsregister/kapitaen_meyer.html
Builders: A.G. Weser Seebeck, Bremerhaven   Engine builder: 1944
Owner: Seglerkameradschaft 'Klaus Störtebeker' e.V

1950: 1 May: Delivered to the Bundesverkehrsministeium as a buoy tender. Fitted with two war-built triple expansion engines and boilers. Fitted with an icebreaker bow. Initially used throughout the German North Sea Coast area, later between the mouth of the Elbe and List (Sylt), including Helgoland.

1952: Funnel lengthened. Used as a supply and transport ship to Helgoland during the rebuilding of the island following its return to Germany.

1965: August, to January 1966: Boilers replaced at Flensburg Schiffsbau-Gesellschaft by new oil-fired boilers.

1967: Masts and funnel shortened to pass through a temporary bridge during the building of the Eidersperrwerk.

1980: Aft accommodation rebuilt after a fire.

1983: 17 October: Withdrawn from service because her eighteen-man crew made her uneconomic to operate. Laid-up at Rendsburg.

1984: 15 May: Taken over by Seglerkameradschaft 'Klaus Störtebeker' Wilhelmshaven e.V. Used as a restaurant and museum ship in Wilhelmshaven.

Kapitän Meyer is a regular visitor to steam events such as the Dampf-Rundum at Flensburg but is infrequently in steam, and is normally a static exhibit at such events rather than offering passenger trips.

TSS PRINZ HEINRICH

Length: 37.0m   Gross tonnage: 212
Engine type: To be sourced, originally Twin Compound
Built: 1909   Rebuilt (most recent): Ongoing
Passenger capacity: n/a, was 350
Body of water: North Swa   Home port: Emden
Frequency of operation: Rebuilding
Website address: www.prinz-heinrich-1909.de
Builders: J.L. Meyer, Pepenburg
Owner: Traditionsschiff Prinz Heinrich e.V.
Former names: *Mississippi* 2003, *Hessen* 1969, *Prinz Heinrich* 1952

1909: Built for Borkumer Kleinbahn und Dampfschiffahrt AG as the passenger steamer **Prinz Heinrich** for the service from Emden to Borkum.

1914: 2 November to 4 September 1915: In service for the Kaiserliche Marine (Imperial German Navy).

1939: 25 August to 1945: In service for the Kriegsmarine (German Navy).

1952: Renamed **Hessen**.

1958: Diesel engines fitted at the yard of C. Cassens, Emden.
Ownership changed to A.G. 'Ems', continued in the same service.

1969: 14 February: Withdrawn from service. Sold to M. & A. Castens, :Lubeck, renamed Mississippi and used for static use as an ethnographical exhibition of objects collected by the owner when he was a ship's captain travelling the world, including ethnic masks from the South Seas and bizarre items as an elephant's penis.

2002: Exhibition sold to owners at Warnemunde. Vessel laid-up in Rostock Harbour.

2003: Summer: Preservation group Traditionssschiff Prinz Heinrich e.V. purchased vessel and moved her to Leer for restoration.

2005: August: Pulled up on land at the site of the former Janssen Werft yard for hull restoration.

The preservation group hope to source and install two steam engines, and when restoration is complete, moor **Prinz Heinrich** at Leer, and occasionally use her for passenger trips in her old teade to Borkum and the Dutch port of Delfzijl.

SS WAL

Length: 50.00m   Gross tonnage: 639
Propulsion: Single Screw   Engine type: Triple Expansion, 1,200hp
Built: 1938   Rebuilt (most recent): 1995
Passenger capacity: 100
Body of water: North Sea   Home port: Bremerhaven
Frequency of operation: Occasional public trips
Website address: www.janmaat.de/wal.htm; www.schiffahrts-conpagnie.de

Wal at Vejle Steam Festival, 2004.

Builders: Stettiner Oderwerke, Stettin
Owner: Schiffahrts-Compagnie Bremerhaven e.V

1938: 20 July: Delivered to the Wasserstrassen-Maschinenamt Rendsburg for use as an icebreaker on the Kiel Canal (Nord-Ostsee Kanal).
1939-45: Used by the Kriegsmarine both in the Canal and right along the German Coast.
1942: 26 April. Whilst at Rostock hit by a bomb and sunk. Raised and repaired at Lübeck.
1945: Returned to service in the Kiel Canal. Based at Rendsburg.
1952: May: Used in the rebuilding of Helgoland to carry drinking water to the island in her large ballast tanks.
1963-65: Boilers replaced by new oil-fired boilers.
1989: Withdrawn from service.
1990: 1 June: Taken over by Deutsche Schiffahrtsmuseum, Bremerhaven. Sailed to Bremerhaven under her own power. Overhauled at Bremerhaven and rebuilt as museum ship.
2004: Operation taken over by Schiffahrts-Compagnie Bremerhaven e.V.

Wal is a frequent visitor to steam events in Northern Europe, often making passenger-carrying cruises of several days length en route to these. Eight trips are schedules for Summer 2006, including visits to Hamburg Dordt im Stoom at Dordrecht, Delfzijl, Helgoland (twice from Bremerhaven and once from Wyk auf Föhr) and a long Baltic trip from Kiel with calls at Rønne (Bornholm), Kaliningrad, Copenhagen and Warnemünde.

RIVER ELBE: DRESDEN AREA

Dresden Steamers: ownership. The paddle steamer fleet at Dresden was owned until the late forties by the Sächsische-Böhmische-Dampfschiffahrts AG, from 1945 by the nationalised organisation Elbreschiffahrt-Sachsen, from 1950 to 1956 by DSU (Deutsche Schifffahrts- und Umschlagzentrale) and from 1956 until the fall of the wall in 1989, by VEB Fahrgastschiffahrt - Weisse Flotte Dresden. In 1991 Sächsische DS GmbH was formed, owned by Conti Shipping, a Hamburg container ship operator.

The survival of so many nineteenth-century veterans at Dresden is partly because some six paddle steamers dating from 1902 to 1925 were taken by the Soviets as war reparations in 1945.

There were another two paddle steamers out of service at the Laubegast yard at Dresden until 2002. *Schmilka* and *Junger Pionier*, both dating from 1898, were scrapped in that year after their hulls had rotted after years on land. The machinery of both was saved and it was stated that this could possibly be used in the future in newly built hulls. *Schmilka* was in service until 1984, and *Junger Pionier* until 1987.

Sailings normally offered by the Dresden paddle steamers are:

From Dresden to Pillnitz return at 10:00, 12:00, 14:00 and 16:00
A 90-minute non-landing cruise at Dresden at 11:00, 11:30, 13:00, 15:00 and 17:00
3-hour non-landing trips from Dresden at 11:30 and 15:30
A return trip from Dresden to Bad Schandau at 10:30
A return trip from Bad Schandau to Dresden at 09:30, returning from Dresden at 13:30
A return trip downstream from Dresden to Seusslitz at 09:45
A return trip from Pirna to Decin at 09:30

These all operate daily from the beginning of May to early October, although the last 90-minute trip only operates Thursday to Saturday. There are also a two large diesel vessels in the fleet, which normally take the 08:30 and 09:15 return sailings to Königstein and a couple of small motor vessels which may from time to time operate sailings advertised as steamer sailings. In recent years there have been more sailings on the section between Bad Schandau, Königstein and Pirna, but these are not operating in 2006, which is not to say they may not return in future summers.

There are special 'parade of steam' events on 1 May and 19 August in 1996, when all the steamers parade in formation from Dresden to Pillnitz and back. These are normally held around the same dates, although on occasion there has been a similar event on the 'Day of German Unity' at the beginning of October.

PS DIESBAR

Diesbar with funnel lowered approaching a bridge, 1991.

Length: 52.72m   Gross tonnage: 108
Propulsion: Paddle Steamer
Engine type: 2-cylinder simple expansion oscillating, 110hp
Built: 1884   Rebuilt (most recent): 1988
Passenger capacity: 170
Body of water: River Elbe   Home port: Dresden
Frequency of operation: Normally reserve
Period of operation: Early April to 2 November
Website address: www.saechsische-dampfschiffahrt.de/index11_en.html
Builders: Werft Blasewitz, Dresden
Engine builder: John Penn & Son, London, 1841, from *Bohemia*
Owner: Sächsische DS GmbH
Former names: *Pillnitz* 1927
Remarks: Coal-fired

1884: 15 May: Entered service as **Pillnitz**. Built using the second-hand oscillating machinery from the previous **Pillnitz**, built as **Stadt Meissen** in 1857, which had been scrapped in the previous year. This machinery had originally been installed in **Bohemia** of 1841, the first steamer to operate to Prague. The crankshaft bears the inscription *Gussstahl-10 Jahre Garantie – Krupp bei Essen – 1853* (Cast steel – 10 year guarantee – Krupp of Essen – 1853).

1926: Tiller steering altered to a manual steering wheel on the bridge.

1927: Renamed **Diesbar**.

1928: Fitted with a steam steering engine, wheelhouse, and electric lighting.

1945: Used for several months as a ferry between Altstadt and Neustadt in Dresden, following the destruction of the bridges in the allied air raids.

1946-49: Undergoing post-war repairs, delayed because of a shortage of material. Wooden paddle floats replaced with metal floats.

1959: New boiler fitted.

1976: Chartered to Tschechoslowakische Elbe-Oderschiffahrt for service on the Czechoslovakian section of the Elbe from Decin.

1978: Laid-up in Dresden-Neustadt harbour.

1985: Listed as Technical Monument.

1985-89: Restored at Laubegast.

1986: Moored at Dresden to commemorate the 150th anniversary of Dresden steamers.

1989: 21 October: Return to service in 1927 condition with engine totally overhauled.

1992: Partially modernised as part of the fleet modernisation. Bow rudder installed. Plumbing and galley brought up to date. Remained coal-fired.

Diesbar sees less service than the remainder of the Dresden fleet, and is often lying in steam as a reserve steamer at Dresden.

PS DRESDEN

Dresden off Pillnitz, 2002.

Length: 68.70m   **Gross tonnage:** 160
Propulsion: Paddle Steamer   **Engine type:** Compound Diagonal, 300hp
Built: 1926   **Rebuilt** (most recent): 1993
Passenger capacity: 400
Body of water: River Elbe   **Home port:** Dresden
Frequency of operation: Daily   **Period of operation:** Early April to 2 November
Website address: www.saechsische-dampfschiffahrt.de/index11_en.html
Builders: Werft Laubegast, Dresden   **Engine builder:** WUMAG, Dresden Übigau
Owner: Sächsische DS GmbH

1926: 28 April: launched.
  29 June: entered service.

1946: 18 June: gutted by fire in Loschwitz harbour after surviving the war unscathed.

1949: 7 June: re-entered service after major rebuild.

1969: Ship and engine overhauled. New paddleboxes and wheelhouse fitted.

1978: 1 June: Collision with Czech stern-wheel tug *Sumava* after a failure in the latter's steering equipment.

1979-82: Major overhaul.

1989: May: Ground-breaking voyage across the Iron Curtain down the Elbe to Hamburg for the port city's 800th Harbour Birthday Celebration.

1992: 3 December to 27 May 1993: Major rebuild for new owners. Inner passenger accommodation rebuilt.

Dresden can often be found on the service from Dresden to Pillnitz.

PS KRIPPEN

Length: 56.04m   **Gross tonnage:** 120
Propulsion: Paddle Steamer
Engine type: 2-cylinder simple expansion horizontal, 110hp
Built: 1892   **Rebuilt** (most recent): 1994
Passenger capacity: 250
Body of water: River Elbe   **Home port:** Dresden
Frequency of operation: Daily   **Period of operation:** Early April to 2 November
Website address: www.saechsische-dampfschiffahrt.de/index11_en.html
Builders: Werft Blasewitz, Dresden

Krippen at Bonn, during her wanderings in October 1996.

Owner: Säschische DS GmbH
Former names: *Tetschen* 1946

1892: 21 June: Entered service. **Tetschen** was the first steamer in the fleet to have electric lighting installed.

1928: Steam steering gear installed. Wheelhouse added.

1945: Used as an accommodation ship for the occupying Red Army after the end of the war.

1946: Renamed **Krippen**. Re-entered service.

1970s: Used as reserve steamer, only seeing occasional service.

1979: Withdrawn from service. Laid-up in Neustädter harbour.

1982: Sold to Kloschwitz on the River Saale for static use.

1983: Moved to the Saale at a period of high water.

1986: Pulled up on the bank. Little work on restoration done.

1988: Sold to Stolpe, Lüneburg. Planned to be used in the Netherlands.

1991: Brought back to the Laubegast yard.

1992: Rebuild commenced. New boiler fitted.

1993: Purchased by Historische Dampfschiffs-Reederei Meissen Junghans & Steuer GmbH, Meissen.
  December. Towed to Lauenburg. Hull split into three parts and taken by barge to the Brand-Werft at Oldenburg via the River Elbe, North Sea, and River Weser

1994: 28 April. Trial trip after extremely fast rebuild. Lower deck aft converted to a restaurant. Converted to oil-firing. Sailed back to Meissen via the River Weser, Mittelland Canal and River Elbe.
  7 May: Entered service at Meissen. Operated short non-landing trips from there.

1995: October to Autumn 1996: Visited various places on the River Elbe and Rhine and their tributaries, including Prague, Berlin, Hamburg, and Stuttgart. Eventually laid-up at Frankfurt on Main in late 1996.

1997-99: Chartered to KD-Line for use on short sailings at Frankfurt.

1999: November: Sold to Sächsichen Dampfschiffahrt, becoming the ninth paddle steamer in their fleet, the largest fleet of paddle steamers in the world.

2000: Took her place in regular service from Dresden, often operating the downstream cruise to Meissen and Seusslitz.

PS KURORT RATHEN

Length: 55.66m
Propulsion: Paddle Steamer   **Engine type**: Compound Oscillating, 140hp
Built: 1896   **Rebuilt** (most recent): 1994
Passenger capacity: 290
Body of water: River Elbe   **Home port**: Dresden
Frequency of operation: Daily   **Period of operation**: Early April to 2 November
Website address: www.saechsische-dampfschiffahrt.de/index11_en.html
Builders: Werft Blasewitz, Dresden   **Engine builder**: Kette, Dresden–Übigau
Owner: Säschische DS GmbH
Former names: *Bastei* 1956

1896: May: Entered service as **Bastei**. She was the last flush-decked steamer to join the Dresden paddle steamer fleet.

1912: Electric lighting installed.

1926: Steam steering gear and wheelhouse installed.

1928: Upper deck and deck saloons fitted. Steam heating fitted. Paddle boxes rebuilt and wooden floats replaced by steel floats.

1934: Sunk near Rathen after striking a rock. Raised and repaired.

1956: Renamed **Kurort Rathen**.

1968: Rebuilt: Deck saloons rebuilt with deeper windows.

1974: Collided with a bridge pillar at Meissen.

1978: Withdrawn from service with boiler damage.

1980: New boiler-dome fitted. Returned to service.

1989: Boiler failure. Laid-up.

1993: Modernised. New oil-fired boiler fitted.

Kurort Rathen is normally in service on the sailing between Bad Schandau and Pillnitz or Dresden.

PS LEIPZIG

Leipzig at Dresden, 2004. (A. Blackler)

Length: 70.05m   **Gross tonnage:** 163
Propulsion: Paddle Steamer   **Engine type:** Compound Diagonal, 325hp
Built: 1929   **Rebuilt** (most recent): 1993
Passenger capacity: 429
Body of water: River Elbe   **Home port:** Dresden
Frequency of operation: Daily   **Period of operation:** Early April to 2 November
Website address: www.saechsische-dampfschiffahrt.de/index11_en.html
Builders: Werft Laubegast, Dresden   **Engine builder:** WUMAG, Dresden Ubigau
Owner: Säschische DS GmbH

1929: 25 March: Launched; 11 May: Entered service. She was the sixty-eighth and final paddle steamer to be built for the Dresden fleet and is a slightly longer (1m) sister of **Dresden**.

1939-45: Chartered by the Third Reich.

1943-45: Used as a hospital ship, moored behind the island at Pillnitz.

1945: 3 March: Hit aft by a bomb during the aerial bombardment of Dresden. 15 March: Sank.

1945: 24-25 December: Raised and towed to the Laubegast yard.

1947 7 June: Returned to service after repairs.

1967: Major overhaul. Both paddle boxes replaced.

1970: Wheelhouse replaced by an aluminium one.

1988: Withdrawn for overhaul and boiler replacement, which was delayed because of lack of money.

1992-93: Rebuilt and modernised at Laubegast yard. Deck saloons totally rebuilt.

1993: 20 July: Returned to service.

Leipzig can often be found on the Dresden to Pillnitz service.

PS MEISSEN

Meissen off Pillnitz racing a canoeist, 2002.

Length: 64.35m   **Gross tonnage**: 131
Propulsion: Paddle Steamer   **Engine type**: Compound Oscillating, 230hp
Built: 1885   **Rebuilt** (most recent): 1993
Passenger capacity: 277
Body of water: River Elbe   **Home port**: Dresden
Frequency of operation: Daily   **Period of operation**: Early April to 2 November
Website address: www.saechsische-dampfschiffahrt.de/index11_en.html
Builders: Werft Blasewitz, Dresden
Engine builder: Sächsische Maschinenbauanstalt, Dresden-Neustadt
Owner: Säschische DS GmbH
Former names: *Sachsen* 1928, *König Albert* 1898

1885: Beginning of summer season: Entered service as *König Albert*. Described as 'elegant and comfortable'.
1898: Renamed *Sachsen*.
1913-14: Low pressure oscillating engine rebuilt as compound. Steam steering machine fitted. Trunk boiler replaced by a cylindrical boiler.
1927-28: Hull lengthened by 3.66m aft of the boiler, upper deck and aft deck saloon added. Steam heating added. Wooden paddle floats replaced by steel floats. Renamed *Meissen*.
1943: 28-29 July: Sailed to Hamburg to evacuate 350 wounded from air raids and take them to Magdeburg.
1967-68: Upper deck lengthened and fore saloon added. Paddle boxes renewed.
1981: Out of service because of boiler damage.
1983-85: Major overhaul at Laubegast. New boiler fitted. Deck saloons renewed.
1985: May: Returned to service for her centenary.
1992-93: Modernised by Werft Genthin, Brandenburg (towed there by *Sachsenwald*): converted to oil firing.
1993: 26 July: Returned to service.

Meissen is often used on charters and special sailings, and is also on the trips from Dresden to Saxon Switzerland (Königstein, Bad Schandau).

PS PILLNITZ

Length: 64.18m   **Gross tonnage**: 130
Propulsion: Paddle Steamer   **Engine type**: Compound Oscillating, 230hp
Built: 1886   **Rebuilt** (most recent): 1993
Passenger capacity: 277
Body of water: River Elbe   **Home port**: Dresden
Frequency of operation: Daily   **Period of operation**: Early April to 2 November
Website address: www.saechsische-dampfschiffahrt.de/index11_en.html
Builders: Werft Blasewitz, Dresden
Engine builder: Sächsische Maschinenbauanstalt, Dresden-Neustadt
Owner: Säschische DS GmbH
Former names: *Weltfrieden* 1993, *Pillnitz* 1952, *Diesbar* 1927, *Köningin Carola* 1919

1886: Entered service as **Köningin Carola**. Built as a sister of **König Albert** (see **Meissen**). Built as a Jubilee-ship for the 50th anniversary of her operators.

1911-12: Low pressure oscillating engine rebuilt as compound. Steam steering machine fitted. Trunk boiler replaced by a cylindrical boiler.

1919: Renamed **Diesbar** following the end of the Monarchy.

1923: Transferred to NDBE (Neue Deutsch-Böhmische Elbschiffahrt) for express freight service to Hamburg. Proposals to rebuild her, fortunately, did not come to fruition.

1924: Returned to SBDG.

1926-27: Lengthened by 3.66m, upper deck and aft deck saloon added. Wooden paddle floats replaced by steel floats. Renamed **Pillnitz**.

1943: End July: Sailed to Hamburg to evacuate wounded and homeless from air raids.

1945: 15 February: Slightly damaged by a bomb during the aerial bombardment of Dresden.

1952: 1 May: Renamed **Weltfrieden** (World Peace).

1956: Upper deck lengthened by 3.00m.

1967: Forward deck saloon added.

1979: Out of service after a boiler failure.

1981-83: Rebuilt at Laubegast. New boiler fitted.

1992-93: Modernised at Werften Genthin, Magdeburg, towed there by steam tug **Sachsenwald**.

1993: 10 July: Returned to service. Renamed **Pillnitz**.

Pillnitz is mainly employed on the sailings between Pirna and Bas Schandau.

PS PIRNA

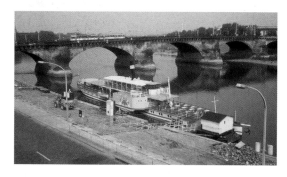

Pirna at Dresden 1994.

Length: 55.74m   **Gross tonnage:** 111
Propulsion: Paddle Steamer   **Engine type:** Compound Oscillating, 140hp
Built: 1898   **Rebuilt** (most recent): 1994
Passenger capacity: 290
Body of water: River Elbe   **Home port:** Dresden
Frequency of operation: FX   **Period of operation:** Early April to 2 November
Website address: www.saechsische-dampfschiffahrt.de/index11_en.html
Builders: Werft Blasewitz, Dresden   **Engine builder:** Kette, Dresden-Übigau
Owner: Sächsische DS GmbH
Former names: König Albert 1919

1898: Entered service as the express steamer **König Albert** with first-class aft saloon and upper deck for the service from Dresden to Aussig (now Usti). Painted with a sand-coloured upper hull rather than the green of the normal steamers. In this year the SBDG carried a record total of 3.6 million passengers, many of these on Dresden commuter services which were supplanted by trams in later years.

1919: Renamed **Pirna** after the end of the monarchy.

1928: Paddleboxes replaced. Steam heating added. Wooden paddle floats replaced by steel floats. Converted to a one-class steamer.

1943-45: Requisitioned by the Third Reich. Used as a floating office at the Junkers aircraft factory at Dessau.

1961: Fore saloon fitted.

1972: 7 October: Engine room and electrical circuitry seriously damaged by a coal-bunker fire.

1973: Returned to service after repairs.

1974-75: Boiler replaced with a second-hand one from the canal tug *Unscha*.

1986: Out of service because of crew shortage.

1989-90: Back in service.

1990: September: Withdrawn from service because of boiler failure.

1993-94: Rebuilt and modernised at Laubegast. New boiler fitted.

1994: 29 April: Returned to service. Kiosk erected on after deck for duty-free trips to Decin (Czech Republic).

Pirna is mainly employed on the sailings in Saxon Switzerland, based at Bad Schandau or Königstein, and has often been used on the sailings to Decin in recent years because of her duty-free kiosk. The ending of duty-free in 2004, following the admission of the Czech Republic to the EU, may mean that other steamers could be allocated to this duty.

ST SACHSENWALD

Sachsenwald at Stadt Wehlen, 2002.

Length: 30.5m
Propulsion: Single Screw   **Engine type**: Triple Expansion, 225hp
Built: 1914   **Passenger capacity**: 60
Body of water: River Elbe   **Home port**: Stadt Wehlen
Frequency of operation: Charters   **Period of operation**: May to October
Website address: www.elbeschiffahrt-frenzel.de
Builders: Wiemann, Brandenburg
Owner: Personenschiffahrt Oberelbe Bernd Frenzel, Pirna
Former names: *Ida-Erna* 1935
Remarks: Coal-fired

1914: Entered service as the tug *Ida-Erna* for G. Helmeke, Altenplatow, near Genthin. Operated on the Elbe from Magdeburg to Hamburg, later also on the Mittellandkanal.

1934: Sold to W. Bernau, Marienwerder.

1935: Renamed *Sachsenwald*. Fitted with a Kort Nozzle around the screw about this time. Also operated on the River Oder.

1972: Laid-up at Burg, near Magdeburg, on the Elbe-Havel Canal.

1979: Purchased by Bernd Frenzel, Pirna.

1980: Towed to Königstein. Lay for a number of years in a side-arm of the River Elbe near there.

1990: December: Rebuild commenced at Laubegast. New boiler fitted.

1991: 6 August: Return to steam. Operated passenger trips from Stadt Wehlen.

1992: Towed paddle steamers *Meissen* and *Weltfrieden* to the repair yard at Genthin.

1995: Chartered to Havel-Dampfschiffahrt Potsdam for five years, to operate passenger trips out of Potsdam.

2001: Replaced by **Gustav** at Potsdam.

2002: Returned to service on the upper Elbe in Saxon Switzerland.

2004: Lengthened by 5m aft of the funnel at the Laubegast yard, Dresden to make her draw less water and so be more suited to low water levels on the Elbe.

Sachsenwald is normally operated on charters but once a year (in 2006 from 20 to 24 May) makes a return trip to Prague and on to Slapy Dam taking four days in each direction, with overnights spent at hotels in Litomerice, Melnik and Prague, with a bus return or a bus outward for the return voyage.

PS STADT WEHLEN

Stadt Wehlen on the Elbe, 2002.

Length: 57.92m   **Gross tonnage**: 108
Propulsion: Paddle Steamer   **Engine type**: Compound Oscillating, 180hp
Built: 1879   **Rebuilt** (most recent): 1994
Passenger capacity: 300
Body of water: River Elbe   **Home port**: Dresden
Frequency of operation: Daily   **Period of operation**: Early April to 2 November
Website address: www.saechsische-dampfschiffahrt.de/index11_en.html
Builders: Werft Blasewitz, Dresden   **Engine builder**: Ruston, Prague, 1857
Owner: Sächsische DS GmbH
Former names: **Mühlberg** 1962, **Dresden** 1926

1879: 18 May: Entered service as **Dresden**. She was fitted with the simple oscillating machinery and boiler from the previous **Dresden** of 1857, which had been scrapped in the previous year.

1893: New boiler fitted.

1895: Lengthened by 2m aft of the boiler.

1915: Engine rebuilt as a compound. New boiler, steam steering gear, replacing the previous tiller steering, and electric lighting installed.

1926: Renamed **Mühlberg** when present **Dresden** delivered.

1949-50: Upper deck added. Steam heating added. Wooden paddle floats replaced by steel floats. Cabin windows enlarged.

1963: Renamed **Stadt Wehlen**.

1977: Collided with **Pirna** and the Augustusbrücke in Dresden after a log got jammed in the paddles. No passengers injured.

1978: Autumn: Laid-up due to boiler failure.

1982: New boiler fitted. Returned to service.

1993: 4 July: last day in service in the former DDR condition.

1993-94: Rebuilt and modernised. Converted to oil firing.

Stadt Wehlen is normally employed on the 90-minute sightseeing cruises in Dresden with several departures daily.

SS WEHLEN-BASTEI

Wehlen-Bastei at Bad Schandau, 2004.
(A. Blackler)

Length: 15.50m   **Gross tonnage**: 23.5
Propulsion: Single Screw   **Engine type**: Compound, 45hp
Built: 1925   **Rebuilt** (most recent): 1994
Passenger capacity: 40
Body of water: River Elbe   **Home port**: Bad Schandau
Frequency of operation: Charters
Website address: http://www.ovps.de/Dampfer01.html; wehlen-online.de/Faehre-Wehlen/default.htm
Builders: Schiffswerft, Maschinen- und Kesselfabrik Übigau, Dresden
Owner: Oberelbische Verkehrsgesellschaft Pirna-Sebnitz GmbH (OVPS)
Former names: *Stadt Wehlen-Bastei* 1995, *Pötzscha-Wehlen Bastei* 1939
Remarks: Coal-fired

1925: Built as a River Elbe passenger ferry.
1928: Purchased by Herold & Mathes, Wehlen for the ferry service from Wehlen to the station on the other side of the river. Named *Pötzscha-Wehlen-Bastei*. Used as a passenger ferry and to tow a vehicle-carrying barge.
1939: Renamed *Stadt-Wehlen-Bastei*.
1945: Ferry services nationalised with the formation of the DDR.
Late 1960s: Now owned by the town of Stadt Wehlen. Cabin rebuilt from wood to steel and fitted with rectangular windows.
1980s: Only occasionally in service in times of high water.
1983–85: Overhauled at Laubegast.
1987: Now owned by VEB Kraftverkehr Pirna.
1991: Boiler out of certificate and removed, laid-up at Laubegast.
1992: Taken over by OVPS (Oberelbische Verkehrsgesellschaft Pirna-Sebnitz GmbH).
1994: Owners commenced restoration work. New coal-fired boiler fitted. Wood cladding added to outside of deck saloons. Modified for two-man operation with bridge control of engine.
1995: 27 April returned to service, named *Wehlen-Bastei*.

Wehlen-Bastei has seen scheduled service in some seasons since 1995, but is now operated on occasional charters from her base at Bad Schandau.

River Elbe: Lauenburg

PS KAISER WILHELM

Length: 57.20m   **Gross tonnage**: 86
Propulsion: Paddle Steamer   **Engine type**: Compound Diagonal, 168hp
Built: 1900   **Passenger capacity**: 350

Kaiser Wilhelm at Hitzacker, 1980.

Body of water: River Elbe   **Home port**: Lauenburg
Frequency of operation: Approximately alternate SuO
Period of operation: End May to end September
Website address: www.raddampfer-kaiser-wilhelm.de/kaiser/Inhalt.htm
Builders: Dresdner Maschinenfabrik und Schiffswerft AG, Dresden-Neustadt
Owner: Verein zur Förderunng des Lauenburger Elbschiffahrtsmseum e.V
Remarks: Coal-fired

1900: 18 May: Left the builder's yard for the delivery voyage down the Elbe, through the North Sea and up the Weser to Hameln.
24 May: Entered service for Oberweser-Dampfschiffs-Gesellschaft, Hameln between Hameln and Hannoversch-Münden.
1910: Returned to Dresden for lengthening by 5m, in two sections fore and aft of the engines, and the installation of steam steering. Made the journey both ways via the North Sea, as the Mittelland Canal was not then open.
1954: New boiler fitted.
1970: 26 September: Final sailing on the Weser.
28 September: Sold to Verein zur Förderunng des Lauenburger Elbschiffahrtsmseum e.V for service on the Elbe.
15 October: Sailed to Minden, and via the Mittelland Canal and the Elbe to Lauenburg.
November: First sailing from Lauenburg. She was the first operating preserved German steamer.
Early-1980s: Repairs to hull.
1991: 6-7 July: Made an upstream sailing to Wittenberge, the first since the reunification of Germany.
Mid-1990s: New paddle wheels fitted.

Kaiser Wilhelm sails out of Lauenburg on approximately alternate weekends each summer, mainly upstream to Bleckede, with occasional sailings continuing to Hitzacker. Calls have been possible at Boizenburg only since the reunification of Germany, as that town was previously in the DDR. In fact the sailings used to run along the border, which ran along the middle of the river. About once a year, a sailing is offered downstream to Hoopte. As she is operated with a volunteer crew, sailings cannot be offered on a more frequent basis.

RIVER RHINE AND TRIBUTARIES

SS EXPRESS

Length: 29.26m
Propulsion: Single Screw   **Engine type**: Compound, 80hp
Built: 1884   **Rebuilt** (most recent): 200?
Passenger capacity: 272, (formerly)
Body of water: Dotrmund-Ems Canal   **Home port**: Waltrop
Frequency of operation: Awaiting restoration
Builders: Forges & Ateliers de Paris à St Denis

Express awaiting restoration
at Heinrichenburg, 2004.

Owner: Westfalische Industriemuseum
Remarks: Coal-fired

1884: Entered service as a *bateau-mouche* on the River Seine in Paris.
1929: Sold for service in Belgium on the River Meuse at Liège.
1937: Withdrawn from service, used as a floating office at Liège.
1962: Sold to an American enthusiast for use as a houseboat at Liège.
1990: Sold to the Westfalische Industriemuseum at the Heinrichenburg ship-lift at Waltrop, near Dortmund.

Restoration has started on **Express**, but other priorities and a lack of funds mean that her return to service is likely to be a long-term project.

PS GOETHE

Goethe on the Rhine.

Length: 83.25m   **Gross tonnage**: 522
Propulsion: Paddle Steamer   **Engine type**: Compound Diagonal, 700hp
Built: 1913   **Rebuilt** (most recent): 1996
Passenger capacity: 900
Body of water: River Rhino   **Home port**: Koblenz
Frequency of operation: Daily   **Period of operation**: 1 May to 3 October
Website address: www.k-d.com
Builders: Gebr. Sachsenberg, Köln-Deutz
Owner: Köln-Düsseldorfer Deutsche Rheinschiffahrt AG

1913: Entered service for Köln-Düsseldorfer Rheinschiffahrt AG on the Rhine as a passenger–cargo
  steamer with an open foredeck, used for freight, and no fore saloon.
1925: Rebuilt with fore saloon and upper deck throughout.
1942: 29 July: Two bombs exploded near the steamer when moored at Koblenz. Twenty-one injured.
1945: 3 March: Sunk near Oberwinter in an air raid. Seriously damaged.
1949: Towed to Schiffswerft Christoph Ruthof, Mainz. Rebuilt, lengthened by 6m, new superstructure
  built. New streamlined funnel fitted.
1953: 11 May: Returned to service.

1976: Repainted in 'old-timer' livery.
1989: Withdrawn from service.
1995-96: Rebuilt at the Dutch yard 'De Biesboch' at Dordrecht. Traditional steamer-type funnel fitted. Bow thruster fitted.
1996: 28 August: Re-entered service.

Goethe is normally now employed on a daily round trip departing Koblenz at 09:00 for Rüdesheim with a number of intermediate calls en route, including Boppard, St Goar, St Goarshausen, Oberwinter, Assmanshausen and Bingen.

ST GREDO

Gredo on the Main.

Length: 15.54m
Propulsion: Single Screw   **Engine type:** Compound, 62hp
Built: 1916   **Passenger capacity:** 12
Body of water: River Main   **Home port:** Hanau-Grossaunheim
Frequency of operation: Charters
Builders: Bodan Werft, Kressbronn
Owner: Förederverien Dampfmaschinenmuseum Hanau e.V

1914: Built as the tug **Christl** for service in Dortmund harbour.
1946: Sold for use on the River Main: Renamed **Gredo**, after the names of the two daughters of the former owner, GREtha and DOra. Superstructure rebuilt in present form. Operated by Wasser und Schiffahrtsamt Mannheim und Karlsruhe.
Late 1960s: Operated by Preuss, Andernach as Rhine tug.
1986: Withdrawn from service.
1989: Returned to steam after a three-year restoration project at Bingen.
2006: Sold to cureent owners.

Gredo is operated for charters and special trips on the River Main from Hanau or Gemünden.

SS NIXE

Length: 24.30m   **Gross tonnage:** 38
Propulsion: Twin Screw   **Engine type:** Triple Expansion, 110hp
Built: 1939   **Passenger capacity:** 58
Body of water: Dotrmund-Ems Canal   **Home port:** Waltrop
Frequency of operation: Very occasional public trips
Builders: Werft Nobiskrug, Rendsburg
Engine builder: Schiffswerft Dresden-Übigau
Owner: Westfälische Industriemuseum
Remarks: Coal-fired

Nixe at Heinrichenburg, 2004.

1939: Built for the Preussische Maschinenbauamt Magdeburg-Rothensee as a combined tug and river/canal inspection steamer for the River Elbe and Mittelland Canal.

1945: Taken over by Wasser- und Schiffahrtsamt Hitzacker West Germany.

Mid-1970s: Withdrawn.

1977: May: Sold to Netherlands owners.

1985: Purchased by Westfälische Industriemuseum for use at the preserved ship-lift at Heinrichenburg.

1987: Present at the 750th anniversary celebrations in Berlin.

1990s: Completely restored.

1998: Returned to steam.

2001: Not in service due to staff shortages.

It is not known if there are plans to offer public trips in the future with **Nixe** at Heinrichenburg. She is one of a large number of preserved vessels there. Other steamers, non-passenger carrying, located there are the former Dutch Police launch **Cerberus** (1930), tugs **Fortuna** (1909) and **Teniers** (1909) and steam river tanker **Phenol** (1904).

RIVER WESER

PS WAPPEN VON MINDEN

Wappen von Minden at Minden, 2002.

Length: 54.07m   Gross tonnage: 120
Propulsion: Paddle Steamer   Engine type: Compound Diagonal, 153hp
Built: 1941-9   Rebuilt (most recent): 2000
Passenger capacity: 230
Body of water: River Weser   Home port: Minden
Frequency of operation: Daily?   Period of operation: April to October
Website address: www.mifa.com
Builders: Praga Yard, Prague   Engine builder: CKD, Prague, 1939
Owner: Stadt Minden   Operator: Mindener Fahrgastschiffahrt (MiFa)
Former names: *Labe* 2001

1941: Building started, but this was delayed by the war. She was the sister of ***Vltava***, and was intended to be the second of a group of five sister ships.

1949: Steamer completed as ***Labe*** for CSPL for river service at Prague, also sailing upstream to Stechovic, and from 1955 to Slapy Dam.

1977: Aft deck saloon added.

1986: Withdrawn at the end of the season and laid-up. By this time, she was the last coal-fired steamer in the Prague fleet.

1995: Moves started by Arbeitsamt Minden to purchase a paddle steamer for service on the Weser.

1997: August: Sunk at her moorings.

1998: 23 June: Purchased by present owners. One week later, towed to the Laubegast yard at Dresden, where the boiler was removed, and repairs made to the hull.

End October: Towed to Minden via the Mittelland Canal. Restoration work continued there, aided by a group of unemployed youth. Totally rebuilt Schottel-pump bow thruster added for greater manueverability on the River Weser. Wooden deck laid. Superstructure renewed. New oil-fired boiler fitted.

2001: 13 April: Returned to service on the Weser at Minden, renamed ***Wappen von Minden***. Chartered to Mindener Fahrgastschiffahrt.

Wappen von Minden offers a variety of trips from Minden:

2-hour trips up the Weser to Porta Westfalica at 11:30 and 14:30, generally on Tuesdays, Wednesdays, Thursdays and Saturdays when she is otherwise unengaged.

One-way day trips, normally on the third Wednesday of each month, downstream to Dörverden, leaving at 10:00 and returning by train. These continue to Bremen on a second day, back to Nienburg on the third day and back to Minden on the fourth day.

Return day trips on the fourth Sunday of each month upstream to Rinteln, leaving at 09:00.

Return day trips east along the Mittelland Canal to Lüdersfeld, on the second Sunday of each month, departing at 09:30.

One-way day trips to Hameln on the first Sunday of each month, departing at 09:00 with return by bus, or by steam train from Rinteln, these continue on consecutive days to Polle, Bad Karlshafen, Hannoversche Münden, and return with overnight stops at Holzminden and Hameln. Each sector has a bus return to the starring point for that day, or overnight stays in hotels are possible.

11 Netherlands

Preserved steamers in the Netherlands are mainly tugs. The best place to see and travel on these is at one of the major steam rallies, the principal of which is Dordt in Stoom, held at Dordrecht in even-numbered years in mid-May. A number of the preserved tugs are owned by museums and others by private individuals and enthusiast groups.

PASSENGER STEAMERS

PS DE MAJESTEIT

Length: 81.30m   Gross tonnage: 536
Propulsion: Paddle Steamer   Engine type: Compound Diagonal
Built: 1926   Rebuilt (most recent): 1997
Passenger capacity: 600
Body of water: River Maas   Home port: Rotterdam
Frequency of operation: 2 F/S evg per month   Period of operation: Year round
Website address: www.raderstoomboot.nl

De Majesteit off Dordrecht
during *Dordt in Stoom*, 2004.

Builders: Gebr Sachsenberg, Köln-Deutz
Owner: Nederlands Raderstoomboot Maatschappij
Former names: *Rüdesheim*, *Rheinland*

1926: 1 June: Entered service as *Rheinland* for Köln-Düsseldorfer Line.

1945: Sunk by artillery fire near Kaiserswerth.

1950: Raised and rebuilt at the Berninghaus yard at Köln-Deutz. New superstructure and modern funnel fitted.

1951: Returned to service.

1956: Boiler converted to oil firing.

1965: Renamed *Rüdesheim*.

1979: Repainted in 'Old-timer' colours with wide orange band along top of hull.

1982: Withdrawn from service. Used for a number of years as a floating landing stage at Köln.

1993: Sold to present owners. Rebuilding began.

1999: 15 June: Entered service as a party-boat for trips and charters out of Rotterdam.

She normally operates a public evening cruise year round on one Saturday per month.

PS HANSA

The hull of *Hansa* awaiting restoration at
Rotterdam. (Rederij K.J. Key)

Length: 68.60m
Propulsion: Paddle Steamer   **Engine type**: Compound Diagonal, 700hp
Built: 1886   **Rebuilt** (most recent): 200?
Home port: Rotterdam
Frequency of operation: Awaiting restoration
Website address: www.stoomvaart.nl/site_eng.htm
Builders: L. Smit & Zoon, Kinderdijk
Engine builder (if different from builder): Gebr. Sachsenburg, Rosslau, 1910, from *Kronprinsessin Cecilie* still to be fitted
Owner: Nederlands Raderstoomboot Maatschappij

1886: Entered service on the Rhine for Köln-Düsseldorfer Line.

1920-1923: used by occupying troops.

1924: Sold to W. Peters, Köln. Used as a boathouse near Köln.

1930: Sold for use as a restaurant at Düsseldorf-Vollmerswerth. Engines, boiler and, latterly, one paddle box, removed.

2000: Sold to present owners, towed to Rotterdam.

Plans call for her to have the engine formerly in the KD steamer **Kronprinsessin Cecilie** (built 1910, withdrawn 1974, scrapped 1984) fitted in her, and to be rebuilt for excursion work out of Rotterdam. At the time of writing work has ceased because an expected government subsidy has not bee forthcoming.

TSS SUCCES

Length: 38.40m
Propulsion: Twin Screw   **Engine type**: 2 Triple Expansion, 500hp
Built: 1897   **Rebuilt** (most recent): 1990
Passenger capacity: 110
Body of water: Ijsselmeer   **Home port**: Kampen
Frequency of operation: Charters
Website address: www.faim.nl
Builders: Boele, Slikkerveer   **Engine builder**: H.J. Koopman, Dordrecht 1916
Owner: Rederij Faim & Co., Marknesse
Former names: *Succes I*, *Sleipnir* 1973, *Succes* 1916
Remarks: Also has diesel

1897: Built by Machinefabriek Huiskens en van Dijk, Dordrecht, with the hull being built by P. Boele, Slikkerveer and machinery by Huiskens & van Dijk, as the twin screw Rhine tug **Succes** for Abraham van Dordt, Rotterdam (other sources state Otto Kriens, Dordrecht).

1916: Taken over by Nederlandse Transport Maatschappij, renamed **Sleipnir**. Used for towing from Rotterdam to the Ruhr. Re-engined.

1952: Sold to Nederlandse Rijnvaart Vereniging.

1957: Sold to Vacuum Cleaning, Rotterdam and rebuilt as a tank cleaning steamer. Converted to oil-firing. Renamed **Succes I**.

1973: Withdrawn from service. Laid-up.

1976: Sold to A Rijsdijk-Boss & Zonen B V, Henrik Ido Amdacht for scrapping.

1985: Purchased for preservation by Joop Moos, Enkhuizen.

1986: Work commenced on rebuilding her as a passenger steamer.

1989: Rebuilding completed in the style of then old Zuider Zee steamer **de Bosman**. Diesel engines also fitted, ostensibly for emergency use.

1996: Sold to Rederij Faim & Co., Kampen for use in the party charter trade.

Succes mainly operates on her diesel machinery. There is a glass portion in her saloon floor, through which the steam engines can be seen to be not working when the ship is underway under diesel power.

SL WOLK

Length: 21.75m
Propulsion: Single screw   **Engine type**: Compound, 90hp
Built: 1917   **Rebuilt** (most recent): 2003
Passenger capacity: 50
Body of water: Amsterdam area   **Home port**: Amsterdam
Frequency of operation: Charters

Wolk in the Amsterdam canals.
(Henk Jan Buchel)

Website address: www.denederlanden.com/wolk.htm
Builders: van Schouten, Muiden   **Engine builder**: Escher-Wyss 1889, from *Riesbach*, Zürichsee
Owner: Rederij de Nederlanden

1917: Hull built. The history of this hull is obscure at the moment.
2002-04: Rebuilt by Ocean Affairs, Amsterdam, fitted with the old steam engine of the Zürichsee steamer *Riesbach* (1892). *Wolk* has been reconstructed as a loose replica of *Riesbach*. The engine was latterly, until *c*.1967, working as a donkey engine on a sand barge. *Wolk* is propelled by a hybrid steam/electric system.

Wolk is used for luxury charters on the Amsterdam canals.

TUGS

ST ADELAAR

Adelaar at *Dordt in Stoom*, 2004.

Length: 20.62m
Propulsion: Single Screw   **Engine type**: Triple Expansion, 150hp
Built: 1925   **Rebuilt** (most recent): 1975
Body of water: Ijsselmeer   **Home port**: Beverwijk
Frequency of operation: Rallies
Website address: www.stoomvaart.nl/site_eng.htm
Builders: werf 'Hubertina' v/h. Jacobs, Haarlem
Owner: B van Gulik, Beverwijk
Former names: *Botlek* 1973, *Adelaar* 1965
Remarks: Coal-fired

1925: Built by N V werf Hubertina v/h Jacobs Machinefabrik of Haarlem for N V Stoomsleepdienst 'Maas', P Boudewijs, Rotterdam as a harbour tug.

1965: Sold to 's Gravenhaagsche Sleepdienst, Vlaardingen, renamed **Botlek**.
1973: Sold to P. Molendijk, Vlaardingen. Renamed **Adelaar**.
1977: Sold to the B.H. van Gulik, Beverwijk, for preservation.

ST CHRISTIAN BRUNINGS

Christian Brunings outside Amsterdam Maritime Museum, 1998.

Length: 31.25m
Propulsion: Single Screw   **Engine type:** Compound, 375hp
Built: 1900   **Rebuilt** (most recent): 1964
Passenger capacity: 100
Body of water: Amsterdam harbour   **Home port:** Amsterdam
Frequency of operation: Occasional public trips
Website address: www.stoomvaart.nl/site_eng.htm
Builders: Jan Meursing, Amsterdam
Engine builder (if different from builder): Hollandse Ijssel, Oudewater 1926
Owner: Nederlands Scheepvaart Museum, Amsterdam
Remarks: Coal-fired

1900: Built by Jan Meursing, Amsterdam, for the government agency, Rijkswaterstaat, as a director's ship and icebreaker.
1926: New engine and boiler fitted.
1967–68: Withdrawn from service.
1968: 31 January: Donated to Amsterdam Maritime Museum.

ST DOCKYARD IX

Dockyard IX at *Dordt in Stoom*, 2004.

Length: 25.06m   **Gross tonnage:** 230
Propulsion: Single Screw,   **Engine type:** 4-cylinder compound, 500hp
Built: 1940, **Rebuilt** (most recent): 199?
Body of water: Rotterdam harbour   **Home port:** Rotterdam
Frequency of operation: SuO

Period of operation: End May to early September
Website address: www.stoomvaart.nl/site_eng.htm
www.buitenmuseum.nl/publiekservice/stoomvaarten.html
Builders: Rotterdamse Droogdok Maatschappij
Engine builder (if different from builder): Lentz design
Owner: Maritime Museum Prins Henrik, Rotterdam
Remarks: Lenz engine; coal-fired

1940: Built by Rotterdam Droogdock Maatschappij as a dockyard tug for their own use.
1942: 15 January: Entered service.
1978: 25 September: Withdrawn from service, sold to Maritime Museum 'Prins Hendrik', Rotterdam.
1994: 25 May: Owners became Stichting Buitenmuseum Leuvehaven, Rotterdam.

Dockyard IX shares with *Dockyard V*, *Pieter Boele* & *Vollharding 1* a series of Sunday afternoon trips round Rotterdam harbour in the summer months.

ST DOCKYARD V

Length: 25.10m   Gross tonnage: 230
Propulsion: Single Screw   Engine type: 4-cylinder compound, 500hp
Built: 1947   Rebuilt (most recent): 1980
Body of water: Rotterdam harbour   Home port: Rotterdam
Frequency of operation: SuO
Period of operation: End May to early September
Website address: www.stoomvaart.nl/site_eng.htm;
www.buitenmuseum.nl/publiekservice/stoomvaarten.html
Builders: Rotterdamse Droogdok Maatschappij
Engine builder (if different from builder): 1947, Lentz design
Owner: Maritime Museum Prins Henrik, Rotterdam
Remarks: Coal-fired; Lenz engine; shares roster with *Dockyard V*, *Pieter Boele* & *Vollharding I*

1942: Hull built as a dockyard tug for the builders' own use.
1946: Completed after delays due to the war.
1947: 7 May: Entered service.
1978: December: Withdrawn from service. Sold to Vereningen Dockyard V, Leiden.
1980: March: Returned to service after restoration.
1994: 25 May: Taken over by Stichting Buitenmuseum Leuvehaven, Rotterdam.

Dockyard V shares with *Dockyard IX*, *Pieter Boele* & *Vollharding 1* a series of Sunday afternoon trips round Rotterdam harbour in the summer months. (See colour photograph 20.)

SS ELFIN

Length: 33.00m
Propulsion: Single Screw   Engine type: 2 Compound, 250hp
Built: 1933   Rebuilt (most recent): 1996
Body of water: Ijsselmeer   Home port: Wormerveer
Frequency of operation: Rallies
Website address: www.stoomvaart.nl/site_eng.htm
Builders: J.S. White, Cowes
Owner: Stichting tot Behoud van het Stoomschip
Former names: *TCA 1* 1995, *HOM 7* 198?, *Droogdock 18*, HMS *Nettle* 1958, HMS *Elfin* 1941

Elfin off Dordrecht at *Dordt in Stoom*, 2004.

1933: Built by J. Samuel White & Co., at Cowes, Isle of Wight as **HMS *Elfin***, a torpedo recovery vessel and tender for the Royal Navy. Based at Portland as a tender to **HMS *Titania***, depot ship of the 6th Submarine Flotilla.

1934: 16 January: Launched.

1940:. Based at Blyth, still with the 6th Submarine Flotilla, working along the eastern coast of England.

1941: 20 August: Renamed **HMS *Nettle***.

1943: July: Serving at Rothesay at this time.

1946: Moved back to Portland.

1957: 14 August: Sold to Pound's of Portsmouth for scrapping. Used at this time in filming the movie *The Key*, starring Sophia Loren, William Holden, and Trevor Howard.

1958: Sold to Amsterdam Droogdock Maatschappij, renamed *Droogdock 18*, converted to a tank cleaning steamer. Used in Amsterdam harbour.

Unknown date: Renamed ***H.O.M.7***.

198?: Renamed ***TCA 1***.

1989: Withdrawn from service.

1995: Purchased for preservation by present owners.

Restoration has been gradual, but by 2004, she had been restored to her original outward appearance, with the interior accommodation still to be restored.

ST FINLAND

Finland at *Dordt in Stoom*, 2004

Length: 22.48m
Propulsion: Single Screw   **Engine type**: Triple Expansion, 225hp
Built: 1921   **Rebuilt** (most recent): 1976
Passenger capacity: 50
Body of water: Dutch rivers & canals   **Home port**: Dordrecht
Frequency of operation: Rallies

Website address: www.stoomvaart.nl/site_eng.htm
Builders: De Groot & van Vliet, Slikkerveer
Engine builder (if different from builder): P. Smit Jr, Rotterdam
Owner: Stoomstichting Nederland
Former names: *Hercules* 1976, *Delfshaven* 1974, *Hercules* 1965, *Finland* 1949,
Arabe 1936, *Finland* 1931
Remarks: Coal-fired

1931: Built by P. Smit Jr, Rotterdam for NV Nederlandshe Stoomsleepdienst v/h. van Piet Smit Jr. as the harbour tug *Finland*.
Chartered to Anglo-Algerian Coaling Co., renamed *Arabe*.

1936: Charter ended. Returned to her original name.

1937: Chartered to Pontonniers for use in the Oosterschelde in Zeeland.

1943: Used as a transport from Lemmer to Amsterdam.

1949: 22 March: Sold to Steenkolen Handelsvereeniging N.V., renamed *Hercules*.

1955: Owners became Utrecht N.V. Transport-en Handelsmaatschappuij Steenkolen, Utrecht.

1965: Purchased by Gravenhaagsche Sleepdienst, Vlaardingen, renamed *Delfshaven*. Used as a steam harbour tug at Vlaardingen.

1974: 29 May: Sold to Hevenrenigings-en Transportbedrijf B.V., Vlaardingen.

1976: Purchased for preservation by D.C. Vastenhout, Rotterdam. Operated by Stoomstichting Nederland. Renamed *Finland*.

ST FURIE

Furie at *Dordt in Stoom*, 2004.

Length: 30.26m   Gross tonnage: 416
Propulsion: Single Screw   Engine type: Triple Expansion, 450hp
Built: 1916   Rebuilt (most recent): 1978
Body of water: New Waterway   Home port: Maasluis
Frequency of operation: Occasional public trips
Website address: www.stoomvaart.nl/site_eng.htm
Builders: Bodewes, Martenshoek   Engine builder: Fulton, Martenshoek
Owner: Stichting Hollands Glorie, Maasluis
Former names: *Jan van Gent* 1976, *Holmvik* 1976, *Holmen III* 1969, *Gebrs. Bodewes VI* 1919

1916: Launched as the tug *Gebrs. Bodewes VI*.

1918: Sold to Holmen Bruks & Fabriks, Norrköping, Sweden, renamed *Holmen III*.

1969: Sold to Gustav A Åkerlund, Stockholm, renamed *Holmvik*.

1976: Purchased by A V R O Hilversum, for use in making the Dutch TV series *Hollands Glorie*, renamed *Jan van Gent*.
When filming finished, sold to Gebrs Heise, Zaandam, renamed *Furie*.

1978: Sold to present owners. Moved to Maasluis, moored at the Dutch National Tug Museum.

ST GABRIELLE

Gabrielle at Dordt in Stoom, 1996.

Length: 19.50m
Propulsion: Single Screw   **Engine type:** Compound, 125hp
Built: 1903   **Rebuilt** (most recent): 1973
Body of water: Alkmaardermeer   **Home port:** De Woude
Frequency of operation: Occasional public trips
Website address: www.stoomvaart.nl/site_eng.htm
Builders: Wiemann, Brandenburg
Owner: Koema, De Woude
Former names: *Amelie* 1937, *Odette*, *Rachael*, *Willy*
Remarks: Coal-fired

1903: Built by Gebr. Wiemann, Brandenburg as a tug for A. Shulze, also of Brandenburg for use on rivers and canals in the Berlin area.
Unknown date: Sold to L. Barriere, Antwerp, renamed *Rachael*.
Unknown date: Sold to an unknown owner in Liege, renamed *Odette*.
Unknown date: Renamed *Amelie*.
1937: Renamed *Gabrielle*, at this time under the ownership of H Baelen, Bree, Belgium. Used on the Albert Canal.
1941: Sold to Fa. Closset Zand en Grints bagger, Maastricht (a dredging company).
Up to 1968: Chartered in winter by the Rijkswaterstaat for the measuring of water levels.
1972: Sold to Walburg, Henrik Ido Ambacht for scrap.
1973: Sold on to J. Toebes, Heemskerk for preservation.
1980: Sold to C. Aaij, Hoorn.
1981: New boiler fitted.
1988: Sold to J. Th. Mos, Enkhuizen.
1991: Sold to Koema, De Woude.
2003: 30 June: Sold to P. van Leeuwen.

ST GEBROEDERES BEVER (known as GEBR. BEVER)

Length: 25.06m
Propulsion: Single Screw   **Engine type:** 4-cylinder Compound, 500hp
Built: 1941   **Rebuilt** (most recent): 1981
Passenger capacity: 55
Body of water: River Maas   **Home port:** Dordrecht
Frequency of operation: Rallies
Website address: www.stoomvaart.nl/site_eng.htm
Builders: Rotterdamse Droogdok Maatschappij

Gebr Bever at her berth in Dordrecht inner harbour, 2004.

Engine builder (if different from builder): Lenz Design
Owner: S. Beltman, Dordrecht
Former names: *Dockyard III* 1981
Remarks: Lentz engine

1941: Launched as **Dockyard III** for Rotterdamse Droogdok Maatschappij. Was sunk throughout the war years, later raised and construction completed.
1946: 16 June: Entered service for her builders.
1962: Converted from coal to oil firing.
1981: Withdrawn from service.
  16 November: Sold to Stolk's Handelsondermening BV, Henrik Ido Ambacht.
  25 November: Sold to present owner, renamed **Gebroeders Bever**, normally known as **Gebr Bever**.

Gebr Bever has been laid-up at Dordrecht for many years because boiler repairs or a new boiler are required.

ST HARDI

Hardi in the early stages of restoration, Dordrecht, 1996.

Length: 41.50m
Propulsion: Single Screw
Engine type: Triple Expansion + exhaust turbine, 350hp
Built: 1948
Body of water: River Maas   **Home port**: Dordrecht
Frequency of operation: Sunk but raised
Website address: members.lycos.nl/hardi/
Builders: Marine Arsenal yard, Cherbourg, France
Owner: Stommmuseumschip Hardi
Former names: *Anke Langenberg* 1994, *Ronny* 1984, *Hardi* 1970

1946: Built at the naval shipyard in Cherbourg as one of a group of eighteen steam tugs for French operator CFNR for service on the Rhine, Named **Hardi**. Built with a Bauer-Wach exhaust steam turbine. Designed at the 'De Biesboch' yard in Dordrecht.

1956-58: Withdrawn from service and laid-up when replaced by modern diesel tonnage.

1970: Sold to Unitas, and rebuilt as the steam tank cleaning ship **Ronny**. Lengthened by 6 metres, new, large, boiler fitted.

1984: Purchased by Tank Cleaning Rotterdam (TCR). Renamed **Anke Langenberg**. Based in Rotterdam harbour.

1994: Sold to South American owners, but when they did not take delivery, sold to Scheepssloperij Nederland, 's Gravendeel for scrapping.

1995: 24 February: Sold to Vereniging Pieter Boele for preservation for 1 guilder. Moved to Dordrecht and renamed **Hardi**.

Work has been progressing slowly in the restoration of **Hardi** at Dordrecht; she is unique in being probably the last surviving reciprocating-engined steamer with an exhaust steam turbine.

ST HERCULES

Hercules, with *Adelaar* inside her, Hellevoetsluis, 1991.

Length: 21.70m   **Gross tonnage**: 25
Propulsion: Single Screw   **Engine type**: Compound, 225hp
Built: 1915   **Rebuilt** (most recent): 1983
Body of water: Dutch rivers & canals   **Home port**: Schiedam
Frequency of operation: Rallies
Website address: www.sshercules.nl
Builders: Bodewes, Martenshoek
Engine builder (if different from builder): A.S. Fulton, Martenshoek
Owner: Stichting Carolische Werktuigen
Former names: *Ditte Hastrup* 1979, *Fremad II* 1964, *Fremad* 1917, *Gebroeders Bodewes III* 1915
Remarks: Coal-fired

1915: Built by G. & H. Bodewes, Martenshoek as the sea-going tug **Gebroeders Bodewes III** for their own use.

1915: 3 December: Sold to the Danish Navy, renamed **Fremad**.

1917: 28 January: Renamed **Fremad II**.

1964: 16 December: Sold to J. Hastrup, Copenhagen, was to be renamed **Ditte Hastrup**. Used as a houseboat in Copenhagen, later laid-up and became derelict and stripped of many fittings.

1979: Sold to J. Th. Mos, Enkhuizen. Moved to Enkhuizen for preservation.

  Sold to G.C. Boekweit. Renamed **Hercules**. Restoration work continued for the next five years.

1983: 4 August: Returned to steam.

1985: 21 January: Taken over by Stichting Carolische Werktuigen, Schiedam.

ST HUGO

Hugo. (De Fotoboot)

Length: 18.50m
Propulsion: Single Screw   **Engine type**: Compound, 150hp
Built: 1929   **Rebuilt** (most recent): 197?
Body of water: Dutch rivers & canals   **Home port**: Zaandam
Frequency of operation: Rallies
Website address: www.stoomsleepbootdehugo.nl/
Builders: Botje & Ensing, Groningen   **Engine builder**: builders, 1926
Owner: Stichting Stoomsleepboot D
Former names: *Hugo Hedrich* 1985
Remarks: Coal-fired

1929: Built by C.V. Scheepswerf en Machinefabrik v/h Botje & Ensing & Co., Groningen fro J.H. Steffen, Hamburg as the harbour tug *Hugo Hedrich*. Fitted with an engine manufactured in 1926 by her builders.

1977: Sold to S.C. Heisse, Zaandam for preservation.

1985: Sold to A. de Leeuw, Voorburg, near Zaandam. Renamed *Hugo*.

2002: September: Boiler failed, withdrawn from service.

2004: December: Boiler replaced.

ST JACOB LANGEBERG

Jacob Langenberg.

Length: 26.75m   **Gross tonnage**: 170
Propulsion: Single Screw   **Engine type**: Triple Expansion, 700hp
Built: 1902
Body of water: Dutch rivers & canals   **Home port**: Wormerveer
Frequency of operation: Undergoing restoration
Website address: www.stoomvaart.nl/site_eng.htm
Builders: Schichau, Elbing (now Elblag)

Owner: Vereningen Stoomvaart
Former names: *Bot* 1969, *Von Bötticher* 1969
Remarks: Coal-fired

1902: Built for Imperial Kanalamt Kiel as the icebreaking tug *Von Bötticher* for use on the Kiel Canal.
1904: Owners became Wasserstrassenmechinenamt Rendsburg.
1933: Rebuilt, so she could function as an icebreaker. Teak deck replaced by steel deck.
Late 1950s: Wheelhouse move up to the top of the boiler housing.
1969: Sold to Langeberg Cleaning, Netherlands, Renamed *Bot* for the delivery voyage. Renamed *Jacob Langeberg*. New bridge built around the wheelhouse.
1977: Boiler failed.
Early 1980s: Second-hand boiler obtained, old boiler was removed and it was found that the new boiler did not fit in the space.
1993: Another second-hand boiler obtained from Navy tug *Y8262*. After this was obtained the owners went out of business. Ship acquired by Vereningen Stoomvaart for preservation.
1999: Boiler fitted in ship.

Funding is still awaited to replace various steam pipes and fit a new funnel. It is planned that she be rebuilt in her 1933 appearance.

ST JAN DE STERKE

Jan de Sterke off Dordrecht, *Dordt in Stoom*, 1996.

Length: 14.37m
Propulsion: Single Screw   Engine type: Compound, 65hp
Built: 1913   Rebuilt (most recent): 1977
Body of water: Dutch rivers & canals   Home port: Gorinchem
Frequency of operation: Rallies
Website address: www.stoomvaart.nl/site_eng.htm
Builders: van Straaten & Van den Brink, 's Gravenhage
Engine builder: Kreber, Vlaardingen
Owner: Gorcumse Stoomboot Stichting 'De Compound', Gorinchem
Former names: *Hendrina II* 1995, *Mariette* 1977, *Snel* 1949
Remarks: Coal-fired

1913: Built as the tug *Snel* for Stoomsleepdienst Vollharding, Rotterdam for use in Rotterdam harbour.
1949: Sold to the Duliette family, Namur, Belgium for use on the River Meuse. Renamed *Mariette*.
1970: Sold to German owners.
1973: New boiler fitted.
1977: Sold to H. van Duuren, Leeuwarden for preservation, Renamed *Hendrina II*. Engine totally restored.
1995: Sold to Gorcumse Stoomboot Stichting 'De Compound', Gorinchem, renamed *Jan de Sterke*.

ST JOHANNES

Johannes. (From a postcard in the author's collection)

Length: 15.54m
Propulsion: Single Screw   **Engine type:** Compound, 95hp
Built: 1908   **Rebuilt** (most recent): 1973
Passenger capacity: 34
Body of water: North Sea Canal   **Home port:** Westzaan
Frequency of operation: SuO
Website address: www.stoomvaart.nl/site_eng.htm
Builders: Wollheim, Cosel near Breslau
Owner: P. van Leeuwen
Former names: *Schill* 1949
Remarks: Coal-fired

1908: Built as the tug ***Schill*** for Berliner Lloyd AG for use in the harbours of Hamburg and Stettin, later used in Berlin.

1917: Owners became Schlesische Dampfer-Compagnie-Berliner Lloyd.

Mid-1930s: Rebuilt at the yard of Schlesische Dampfer-Compagnie, Zarkau near Glogau on the River Oder.

1939-45: Used as an icebreaker and tug in Berlin and at Furstenberg/Oder.

1945: 18 March: Damaged and holed by an allied air attack, towed to Berlin Spandau with a pump on board.

1946: Returned to service for AGB, Berlin.

1948: Moved to Potsdam, then back to Berlin.

1949: Renamed ***Johannes***.

1950: Became part of the nationalised DSU tug fleet of East Germany (DDR).

1957: Owners became VEB-Binnenreederei, Berlin.

1968: New boiler fitted.

1971: Taken out of service, then sold to A. Richter, Hamburg.

1973: Sold to S. Visser, Westzaan, Netherlands for preservation. Sunday excursions offered from Westzaan to the Cruquius steam mill museum. These were marketed by Thalassa Travel, Amsterdam. At some stage a small passenger deck cabin had been built aft.

2003: Spring: Sold to P. Van Leeuwen. At this time she was in a poor state.

ST MAARTEN

Maarten at *Dordt in Stoom,* 1996.

Length: 19.46m   **Gross tonnage:** 9
Propulsion: Single Screw   **Engine type:** Triple Expansion, 150hp
Built: 1926   **Rebuilt** (most recent): 1980
Body of water: Dutch rivers & canals   **Home port:** Leeuwarden
Frequency of operation: Rallies
Website address: www.stoomvaart.nl/site_eng.htm
Builders: Van de Werf, Deest (Gelderland)
Engine builder: I.A. Kreber, Vlaardingen
Owner: Stichting Stoomboot Maarten, Leeuwarden
Former names: *Ido II* 1970, *Luisse* 1967, *Holland* 1959, *Cor-Adri* 1943

1926: 20 November: Built as the tug ***Cor-Adri*** for Sleepbootmaatschappij Cor C. Bos, Dordrecht.
1940: 31 May: Sold to NV Sleepboot Juliana, Rotterdam.
1943: 10 November: Renamed ***Holland***.
1958: 1 July: Sold to D van Zwol, Amsterdam.
1959: 9 October. Renamed ***Luisse***. Purchased by H. Kawaters, Duisburg, Germany, chartered to Fa. Gruyter & Co., Duisburg.
1965: 17 March: Sold to NV Ijzer-en Mateelhander Walburg, Zwijndrecht.
1967: Sold to J. & J. Kramer, Rotterdam and Zaandam.
   27 December: Purchased by A Rijsdijk-Boss & Zn., Henrik Ido Ambacht renamed ***Ido II***.
1970: Sold to D.L.H. Smit, Kinderdijk. Restoration began at his yard. Renamed ***Maarten***.
1975: Purchased by N. Bekkema, Epe.
1980: Sold to H.J. van Duuren, Leeuwarden.
1981: 2 November: Taken over by Stichting Stoomboot Maarten, Leeuwarden.
Early 1990s: Converted from coal to oil firing.

ST NOORDZEE

Noordzee at the Flensburg Dampf Rundum 1995.

Length: 22.80m
Propulsion: Single Screw   Engine type: Compound, 320hp
Built: 1922   Rebuilt (most recent): 1976
Body of water: Ijsselmeer   Home port: Medemblik
Frequency of operation: Rallies
Website address: www.stoomvaart.nl/site_eng.htm
Builders: Janssen & Schmilinsky, Hamburg
Engine builders: Blohm & Voss, Hamburg
Owner: C.P. Jonger, Twist
Former names: *Nordsee* 1976, *Taucher Sievers IV* 1970, *B & V XII* 1959
Remarks: Coal-fired

1922: Built by Janssen & Schmilinsky at Hamburg for shipbuilders Blohm & Voss AG, Hamburg as the sea-going tug *B & V XII*.
1948: Laid-up.
1959: 3 October: Sold to Taucher and Bergungsgesellschaft Sievers, Cuxhaven, renamed *Taucher Sievers IV*.
1970: Sold to Reederei Nordsee, renamed *Nordsee*.
1975: Sold to Handelsonderneming A.C. Slooten, Wormer.
1976: Resold to C.P. Jongers, Medemblik, renamed *Noordzee*.

Noordzee is a regular visitor to steam rallies, and has made trips outside the Netherlands, e.g. to the *Dampf-Rundum* in Flensburg in 1995.

ST PIETER BOELE

Length: 30.95m
Propulsion: Single Screw   Engine type: Triple Expansion, 300hp
Built: 1893   Rebuilt (most recent): 1987
Passenger capacity: 50
Body of water: Rotterdam harbour   Home port: Rotterdam/Dordrecht
Frequency of operation: SuO
Period of operation: Late May to early September
Website address: www.stoomvaart.nl/site_eng.htm;
www.buitenmuseum.nl/publiekservice/stoomvaarten.html
Builders: P Boele Pzn, Slikkerveer
Engine builder (if different from builder): Koopman, Dordrecht 1924
Owner: Stichting Buitenmuseum Leuvehaven, Rotterdam   Operator: Stichting Dordt in Stoom
Former names: *Speculant* 1970, *Mathilde* 1927, *Direktor Johann Knipscheer* 1919,
Wacht am Rhein VIII 1903
Remarks: Coal-fired; shares roster with *Dockyard V*, *Dockyard IX* and *Vollharding I*

1893: April: Entered service as the Rhine tug *Wacht am Rhein VIII* for J. Hüttner & D. Burgerhout, Rotterdam.
1901: 9 July: Sold to J. Wolteshoff Ruhrort & D. Burgerhout, Rotterdam.
1903: Sold to J. Knipscheer, Duisburg, renamed *Director Johann Knipscheer*.
1919 Sold to W. Tijssen, Rotterdam, renamed *Mathilde*.
1924: 8 May: Renamed *Speculant*. Rebuilt. Wheelhouse raised to the roof of the saloon. Re-engined.
1939: 29 December: Owner now W.R. Tijssen, Rotterdam.
1948: 21 January: Sold to Coöperatieve Vereniging van Sleepbooteigenaren E.U., Rotterdam.
1949: 21 January: Sold back to W.R. Tijssen, Rotterdam.
1965: Withdrawn from service.
1968: 11 October: Sold to S Heijden, New Jersey for preservation.
1970: Sold to Boele's Scheepswerven, Bolnes, renamed *Pieter Boele*. Restored and new boiler fitted.

Operated occasional passenger trips and charters out of Dordrecht after restoration.

1987: 24 February: Taken over by Maritiem Museum Prins Hendrik, Rotterdam. Operated by Stichting Dordt in Stoom.

1994: 15 June: Owners now Stichting Buitenmuseum Leuvehaven, Rotterdam.

Pieter Boele shares with **Dockyard V**, **Dockyard IX**, & **Vollharding 1** a series of Sunday afternoon trips round Rotterdam harbour in the summer months.

ST ROEK

Roek in Dordrecht inner harbour, *Dordt in Stoom*, 2004.

Length: 20.25m
Propulsion: Single Screw   Engine type: Triple Expansion, 165hp
Built: 1930
Body of water: Ijsselmeer   Home port: Enkhuizen
Frequency of operation: Rallies
Website address: www.stoomvaart.nl/site_eng.htm
Builders: Gebr van der Windt, Vlaardingen   Engine builder: I.A. Kreber, Vlaardingen, 1956
Owner: Joop Mos, 'Hawser Holland', Enkhuizen
Former Names: *Jacomien* 1960

1930: Built by Gebr. Van de Windt, Vlaardingen for Scheepvaart Mij Maas & Waal (Fa. Fransen), Dordrecht as the tug **Jacomien**.
1960: Sold to W. van Driel, Rotterdam, renamed **Roek**.
1970: Sold to Kauffeld, Roermond, rebuilt as motor tug.
1972: Sold to R. Visser, Amsterdam.
1979: Sold to J. Th. Mos, Enkhuizen
1980: 1956 (1930 according to some sources) steam engine and second-hand boiler, built in 1946, installed.
1983: Sold to W.P. Murphy, Jr., Miami, FL, USA. Did not leave the Netherlands.
1988: Sold to Hawser Holland, Enkhuizen.
2006: Summer: Placed up for sale.

ST ROSALIE

Length: 19.00m
Propulsion: Single Screw   Engine type: Compound Diagonal, 95hp
Built: 1873   Rebuilt (most recent): c.1985
Body of water: Ijsselmeer   Home port: Enkhuizen
Frequency of operation: Charters
Website address: www.stoomvaart.nl/site_eng.htm
Builders: F. Smit, Kinderdijk
Owner: Joop Mos, Enkhuizen. Operator: M. & K. Steamcharters, Enkhuizen
Former names: **Willem IV** 1972, **Willem III** 1965, **Jacoba** 1961, **Rosalie** 1940, **Nieuwe Zorg** 1927, **Den Briel** 1924
Remarks: Coal-fired

Rosalie in Dordrecht inner harbour,
Dordt in Stoom, 2004.

1873: Built as the tug **Den Briel** by Fop Smit, Kinderdijk for the torpedo service of the Ministry of War, Den Brielle.

1922: Home port changed to Gorkum.

1 April: Used as a Royal Yacht for one day.

1924: Sold to J.G. de Boer, Schiedam, renamed **Nieuwe Zorg**.

1927: Sold to A.J.J. de Groot, Schiedam, renamed **Rosalie**.

1928: Sold to R. Steenbeck, 's Hertogenbosch.

1940: Sold to W.G. Maas, Steen, renamed **Jacoba**.

1961: Renamed **Willem III**.

1965: Renamed **Willem IV**.

1972: Sold to R. Visser, Amsterdam for preservation. Steamed to the Kromhout yard, Amsterdam.

1976: Renamed **Rosalie**. Moved to the Verschure shipyard, Amsterdam. Used again for towing.

1980: Towing ceased. Returned to the Kromhout yard. Placed up for sale.

1983: 22 November. Sold to an E. Hoheitzel, Zürich, Switzerland for use on the Zürichsee. Sale was not completed after the prospective owner realised he would not be able to move **Rosalie** there by land because road bridges and tunnels en route were too low.

1987: Sold to present owner. Towed to Enkhuizen by **Roek**.

Rosalie is currently chartered to M. & K. (Mos & Kok) Steamcharters, and operates charters out of Enkhuizen.

ST SCHEELENKUHLEN

Scheelenkuhlen at *Dordt in Stoom*, 1996.

Length: 21.40m   Gross tonnage: 12
Propulsion: Single Screw,   Engine type: Compound, 200hp
Built: 1927   Rebuilt (most recent): 1976
Body of water: Dutch rivers & canals   Home port: Zaandam
Frequency of operation: Rallies

Website address: www.stoomvaart.nl/site_eng.htm
Builders: J. Oelkers, Neuhof/Hamburg
Engine builder: Christiansen & Meyer, Hamburg-Harburg
Owner: P. Visser, Westzaan
Remarks: Coal-fired

1927: Built as a tug for Wasser- und Schiffahrtsamt, Cuxhaven. Used as a a tug and icebreaker in the
  mouth of the Elbe in the Brunsbüttel and Cuxhaven areas.
1974: Withdrawn from service, laid-up.
1976: Sold to Handelsondermening A C Slooten, Wormer.
  November: Sold to P. Visser, Zaandam for preservation.
1980s: Restored and returned to service.

ST VOLLHARDING I

Vollharding I at Rotterdam Maritime Museum, 2004.

Length: 20.25m
Propulsion: Single Screw   Engine type: Triple Expansion, 174hp
Built: 1929   Rebuilt (most recent): 1978
Passenger capacity: 46
Body of water: Rotterdam harbour   Home port: Rotterdam/Alblasserdam
Frequency of operation: SuO
Period of operation: Late May to early September
Website address: www.stoomvaart.nl/site_eng.htm
      www.buitenmuseum.nl/publiekservice/stoomvaarten.html
Builders: De Hoop, Hardinxveld   Engine builder Vlaardinshce Maschinfabrik
Owner: Stichting Maritiem Buitenmusum Leuvehaven, Rotterdam
Former names: *Harmonie VI* 1951
Remarks: Coal-fired; shares roster with *Dockyard V*, *Dockyard IX* and *Pieter Boele*

1929: Built by Scheepsbouwerf de Hoop, Hardinxveld as the tug *Vollharding I* for Reederij de
  Sleepdienstonderneming P van Loon, Vreeswijk.
1930: 2 January: Registered at Dordrecht as *Harmonie VI*. Used until 1940 towing barges between
  Dordrecht and the Ruhr.

1951: Sold to Veereenigde Onafhankelijke Sleepdienst, Rotterdam. Renamed **Vollharding I**.

1953-55: Used in the building of dykes in Zeeland.

1967: Withdrawn from service, laid-up. In her final years in service she had been used as a source of steam.

1969: Sold to Maritiem Museum Prins Henrik, Rotterdam for preservation for the symbolic price of 1 Guilder.

1969-71: Restored by Van de Giessen-de Noord, Alblasserdam.

1978: Charteree by Vereniging Vollharding I.

1994: Owners now Stichting Maritiem Buitenmusum Leuvehaven, Rotterdam.

Vollharding I operates Rotterdam harbour cruises on summer Sundays on a roster with **Dockyard V**, **Dockyard IX**, and **Pieter Boele**.

12 Switzerland

Switzerland is notable for its white paddle steamers, which have become very much part of the tourist image of the country. These have survived in operation on five lakes, and have been constantly updated and rebuilt, while retaining their traditional external appearance and classic wood-panelled dining saloons. There are also a couple of small screw steam vessels in operation, and some modern steam launches.

The website swissitalianpaddlesteamers.com has a complete listing of Swiss paddle steamer sailings with any special sailings noted.

BRIENZERSEE (LAKE BRIENZ)

PS LÖTSCHBERG

Length: 55.60m   **Gross tonnage**: 260
Propulsion: Paddle Steamer   **Engine type**: Compound Diagonal, 450hp
Built: 1914   **Rebuilt** (most recent): 2002
Passenger capacity: 800
Body of water: Brienzersee   **Home port**: Interlaken
Frequency of operation: Daily
Period of operation: Early May to mid-September
Website address: http://www.bls.ch/schiff/flotte_loetschberg_d.html
Builders: Escher Wyss, Zürich
Owner: BLS, Interlaken

1914: 31 March: Launched; upper strake of hull painted red-beige.

25 July: Entered service, but laid-up after a few days due to the outbreak of war.

1915-22: Laid-up.

1923: Back in service for the summer season.

1950: A totally enclosed wheelhouse replaced the previous one, which was open at the back.

1967-68: Converted from coal to oil firing.

1975: Part of the upper deck glazed in to form a panorama saloon.

1979: Major overhaul: Upper deck glazing extended aft. Hull painted white all over.

2000-01: Major overhaul. New boiler fitted. Bow rudder converted from mechanical to electro-hydraulic operation. Upper strake of hull now painted green.

Lötschberg normally operates two return trips at 11:16 and 14:25 from Interlaken Ost to Brienz, on

Sundays from the beginning of May to late June, then daily until early September, continuing on Sundays until towards the end of September. The sailings connect at Giessbach with a vintage funicular up to the large hotel there, and at Brienz Bahnhof with the steam-hauled rack railway up the Brienzer Rothorn.

SL STEAMCHEN

Steamchen at Brienz.

Length: 7.17m
Propulsion: Steam Launch   **Engine type**: 2-cylinder simple, 6hp
Built: 1995   **Passenger capacity**: 8
Body of water: Lake Brinez   **Home port**: Brienz
Frequency of operation: Occasional Public trips
Period of operation: summer months
Website address: www.steamchen.com
Builders: Otto Thomson, Mühlheim a/d Ruhr, Germany
Engine builder: R. Mallinson, Windermere, UK
Owner: IG Brienzersee Dampfboote

1995: Built as a private launch for her builder. Visited the UK and Switzerland for steam meets.
1996: October: First steamed.
2002: March: Sold to present owners.

Steamchen operates occasional passenger trips on Lake Brienz and elsewhere on the Swiss Lakes.

SL VALHALLA

Valhalla on the Brienzersee.

Length: 6.20m
Propulsion: Single Screw   Engine type: 2-cylinder simple, 7.5hp
Built: 1986   Passenger capacity: 5
Body of water: Brienzersee   Home port: Iseltwald
Frequency of operation: Was in service 2003
Website address: www.steamchen.com
Builders: David Young, GB
Owner: IG Brienzersee Dampfboote

Valhalla is a modern steam launch that operates from Iseltwald on Lake Brienz, with public passenger sailings on selected dates each summer.

LAC LÉMAN (LAKE GENEVA)

PS HELVÉTIE

Helvétie on Lake Geneva, 1977.

Length: 78.00m   Gross tonnage: 429
Propulsion: Paddle Steamer
Engine type: 3-cylinder simple expansion diagonal
Built: 1926   Rebuilt (most recent): 1977
Passenger capacity: 1,500
Body of water: Lac Léman (Lake Geneva)   Home port: Geneva
Frequency of operation: Laid-up
Website address: www.cgn.ch; mypage.bluewin.ch/jvernet;
www.vapeurs-leman.com
Builders: Sulzer, Winterthur   Engine builder: To be built
Owner: CGN, Lausanne
Remarks: Currently diesel-electric, possibly to be converted back to steam

1926: 4 March: Launched for current owners.
  15 September: Entered service.
1930: Part of upper deck glazed in as smoking saloon.
1960-61: Winter: Converted from coal to oil firing.
1969-70: Partial rebuild. Upper deck glazing extended towards stern.
1974: November: Withdrawn from service because a new boiler was required.
1975-76: Engines and boiler removed. Engines placed in Musée de Léman, Nyon. Diesel electric machinery formerly in the Danube tug *Goliath* (1954) installed.
1977: Spring: Return to service as diesel-electric paddle ship. This conversion was not successful and she has seen little service, in the main lying at Geneva as reserve vessel, with occasional evening cruises offered from there.
2001: 31 December: Final sailing.

2002: Laid-up at Lausanne at end of season. It is proposed that a new steam engine, similar to that installed in **Montreux**, be fitted in **Helvétie**. Lack of funds has delayed this plan, although it is still a possibility, unlike the proposed return to steam of **Italie** and **Vevey**, which has been abandoned.

PS LA SUISSE

La Suisse on Lake Geneva, 1977.

Length: 78.00m   **Displacement tonnage:** 461
Propulsion: Paddle Steamer   **Engine type:** Compound Diagonal, 1,450hp
Built: 1910   **Rebuilt** (most recent): 1971
Passenger capacity: 1,350
Body of water: Lac Léman (Lake Geneva)   **Home port:** Geneva
Frequency of operation: Daily
Period of operation: Mid-May to late September
Website address: www.cgn.ch mypage.bluewin.ch/jvernet;
        www.vapeurs-leman.com
Builders: Sulzer, Winterthur
Owner: CGN, Lausanne

1908: 10 September: Ordered by present owners.
1910: 25 May: Entered service.
1931: Middle part of upper deck glazed in as a smoking saloon.
1943–48: Laid-up because of the Second World War.
1959–60: Converted from coal to oil firing.
Her regular service for many years incorporated a morning cruise from Lausanne to Thonon, and an afternoon anti-clockwise circuit of the upper lake from Lausanne via Evian, St Gingolph and Montreux. However she has in recent seasons, offered a day-long sailing from Geneva to Lausanne, Montreux and St Gingolph, the outward sector of which is marketed as the 'Rhône Express'.
2006: Following a major recasting of Lake Geneva timetables, placed on the 10:00 Geneva to Vevey return service via the Swiss shore in both directions.

La Suisse is probably the most magnificent paddle steamer in Europe.

PS MONTREUX

Length: 66.30m   **Displacement tonnage:** 323
Propulsion: Paddle Steamer   **Engine type:** Compound Diagonal, 1,100hp
Built: 1904   **Rebuilt** (most recent): 1999
Passenger capacity: 900
Body of water: Lac Léman (Lake Geneva)   **Home port:** Lausanne
Frequency of operation: Daily   **Period of operation:** Late June to end August
Website address: www.cgn.ch; mypage.bluewin.ch/jvernet; www.vapeurs-leman.com

Montreux leaving Geneva. (Simplon Postcards)

Builders: Sulzer, Winterthur   **Engine builder**: SLM, Winterthur
Owner: CGN, Lausanne

1903: 7 December: Launched.

1904: 12 May: Entered service.

1905: Fitted with a navigating bridge (she had previously just had a wheelhouse without bridge wings).

1909: Engine-room telegraphs installed.

1922: Upper deck awning replaced by an aluminium cover.

1931: Smoking cabin on upper deck removed and replaced by glazed-in portion of that deck.

1957: Withdrawn from service because the boiler needed replacement.

1959-60: Steam engine and boiler replaced by new diesel-electric machinery from Sulzer. Tall steamer funnel replaced with squat 'motorship-type' funnel.

199? Funnel replaced by tall steamer-type funnel.

1999-2001: Diesel-electric machinery replaced by new steam engine and boiler.

2004: Offered a lunch trip from Lausanne to Evian, an anti-clockwise afternoon circuit of the upper lake from Lausanne via Evian, St Gingolph, and Montreux, and an evening return from Lausanne to Yvoire, connecting there with the diesel-electric paddler *Vevey* back to Geneva.

2006: Following the recasting of the timetable, continued operating the 12:30 lunch cruise to Evian, then a 14:05 sailing to Morges, returning along the Swiss shore to Lausanne at 15:25 and on to Villeneuve, back to Lausanne, with an evening return sailing at 18:05 to Yvoire, going out via the Evian and Thonon and returning via Morges and ports on the Swiss shore.

2007: Afternoon sailing now only sails as far as Chateau de Chillon, evening sailing is now at 20:40.

PS RHÔNE

Rhône leaving Yvoire, 1983.

Length: 66.00m   **Displacement tonnage**: 407
Propulsion: Paddle Steamer   **Engine type**: Compound Diagonal, 900hp
Built: 1927   **Rebuilt** (most recent): 1969
Passenger capacity: 850
Body of water: Lac Léman (Lake Geneva)   **Home port**: Lausanne
Frequency of operation: Daily
Period of operation: Mid–May to late September

Website address: www.cgn.ch; mypage.bluewin.ch/jvernet; www.vapeurs-leman.com
Builders: Sulzer, Winterthur
Owner: CGN, Lausanne

1926: 29 March: Launched.
1927: Entered service for the Wine Festival in Vevey.
1939-46: Laid-up because of the war.
1959-60: Converted from coal to oil firing.
1968-69: New boiler fitted.
   Her sailings switched in recent years between shorter cruises from Geneva to the Petit-Lac and long all-day trips from Geneva to Montreux and St Gingolph. However, in 2004 she offered sailings alternating daily between a morning sailing from Geneva to St Gingolph, returning only as far as Lausanne, and a sailing the following day from Lausanne to St Gingolph and returning all the way to Geneva.
2006: Scheduled for two Upper-Lake Express sailings from Lausanne to St Gingolph and back at 09:30 and 12:30, and a third trip to Vevey at 15:40, although these may be offered by a motor vessel for part of the high season.
2007: Sailings altered to a 10:35 return from Lausanne to Geneva by the Swiss shore, returning at 15:00 and sailing onwards to Vevey, with a direct return to Lausanne.

PS SAVOIE

Savoie on Lake Geneva.

Length: 66.00m   Displacement tonnage: 367
Propulsion: Paddle Steamer   Engine type: Compound Diagonal, 900hp
Built: 1914   Rebuilt (most recent): 2005
Passenger capacity: 1000
Body of water: Lac Léman (Lake Geneva)   Home port: Lausanne
Frequency of operation: Daily   Period of operation: July to September
Website address: www.cgn.ch; mypage.bluewin.ch/jvernet; www.vapeurs-leman.com
Builders: Sulzer, Winterthur
Owner: CGN, Lausanne

1914: 7 January: Launched.
  23 May: Maiden Voyage.
1927: Middle portion of upper deck glazed in.
1928: Awning on upper deck replaced by aluminium cover.
1959: Converted from coal to oil-firing.
1962-63: Withdrawn from service because the boiler was worn out.
1966-67: Boiler replaced.
2003-05: Major overhaul and rebuild.
2006: 20 May: Re-entered service after rebuild.
   Summer: Scheduled to operate a lunch cruise from Geneva to Hermance at 12:20 and an afternoon and evening return from Geneva to Yvoire at 14:15 and 18:45.

In recent years, she has mainly been on the clockwise afternoon upper lake circuit from Lausanne via Vevey, Montreux, St Gingolph and Evian.

PS SIMPLON

Simplon on Lake Geneva, 1992.

Length: 78.00m   **Displacement tonnage**: 474
Propulsion: Paddle Steamer   **Engine type**: Compound Diagonal, 1,450hp
Built: 1914-20   **Rebuilt** (most recent): 1967
Passenger capacity: 1,500
Body of water: Lac Léman   **Home port**: Lausanne
Frequency of operation: Daily
Website address: www.cgn.ch; mypage.bluewin.ch/jvernet; www.vapeurs-leman.com
Builders: Sulzer, Winterthur
Owner: CGN, Lausanne

1914: 28 July: Construction began, but was delayed because of the First World War.
1915: 1 April: Launched.
1920: 23 June: Entered service.
1928: Replacement of upper deck awning with aluminium cover.
1932: Part of upper deck glazed-in.
1939-45: Saw little service because of the Second World War.
1958-59: Winter: Converted from coal to oil-firing.
1965: Withdrawn at end of the season because of the condition of her boiler.
1966-67: Major overhaul and rebuild. Fitted with new boiler.
2003: 18 August: Explosion in the furnaces. Withdrawn from service for repairs.
2005: 2 July: Returned to service.
2006: Scheduled to operate a 10:35 return trip from Lausanne to Geneva, sailing by the Swiss shore each way and incorporating a double Yvoire to Nyon crossing on the return sailing.
2007: Scheduled to operate at 09:30 from Lausanne direct to Le Bouveret, returning via Montreux and Vevey with another similar sailing at 12:30, and a 15:30 return from Lausanne to Montreux.

In recent years **Simplon** has seen little scheduled service, She is normally held in reserve at Lausanne and sails on charters, or to replace one of the other lake vessels which may have a charter or be out of service.

The diesel-electric paddler **Italie** (1908), dieselised in 1958, was withdrawn at the end of 2005.
     The similar **Vevey** (1907), dieselised in 1955, was scheduled to be withdrawn at the end of 2006, but. has been retained in service, including spells of winter service. Both will be laid-up at Lausanne in the meantime, in the hope that money will be available at some stage to have them re-engined and return to service.
The diesel-electric paddler **Genéve** (1896), which was dieselised in 1934, is in static use at Geneva as a youth centre.

It had been planned that the small launch **MG2** at Geneva, part of the fleet of the local Geneva operator Mouettes Genevoises, will be returned to steam. As of August 2005, however, the owners had not managed to obtain a suitable steam engine

VIERWALDSTÄTTERSEE (LAKE LUCERNE)

SL CAMPAGNORA

Steam launch *Campagnora* on Lake Lucerne, 2005. (Beat Bolzern)

Length: 5.40m
Propulsion: Single Screw   **Engine type:** 1-cylinder, 1.4hp
Built: 1979   **Rebuilt** 1988
Passenger capacity: 4
Body of water: Lake Lucerne   **Home port:** Vitznau
Frequency: Charters
Website address: www.dampfei.ch
Builder: Honnor Marine, Totnes, UK   **Engine builder:** Antony Bever
Owner: Walter Bünter, Vitznau

1979: Hull built as a rowing boat.
1988: Sold to Swiss owners and rebuilt as a steam launch.
*c.*2004: Sold to present owner.
2006: June: Scheduled to spend the month on Lake Lugano.

Campagnora is a tiny steam launch operated by the owner of the larger **Uranus** and available for charter

PS GALLIA

Gallia on Lake Lucerne, 1998.

Length: 62.90m   **Gross tonnage:** 328.9
Propulsion: Paddle Steamer   **Engine type:** Compound Diagonal, 1,080hp
Built: 1913   **Rebuilt** (most recent): 2004
Passenger capacity: 900

Body of water: Vierwaldstätter See (Lake Lucerne)   Home port: Luzern
Frequency of operation: Daily
Period of operation: Late May to late September
Website address: www.lakelucerne.ch
Builders: Escher Wyss, Zürich
Owner: SGV, Luzern

1913: 2 June: Launched.

1913: 23 July: Official trials.

1926: Wheelhouse fitted.

1936–37: Masts shortened during annual overhauls. This enabled her to sail into the Alpnachersee until the opening bridge was replaced by a fixed bridge in 1960.

1939–45: *Gallia* saw little service during the war years.

1977–79: Major refurbishment over two winters.

2002–04: Major rebuild.

2004: 1 May: Return to service after rebuild.

2004: Operated a mid-morning return sailing from Lucerne Seedorf on Sundays and a lunch-time return to Flüelen in the remainder of the week.

2006: Ran the 10:00 return sailing from Lucerne the length of the lake to Flüelen daily.

SL MELISANDE

Length: 7.32m
Propulsion: Single Screw   Engine type: Compound, built 1980, 5hp
Built: 1985   Rebuilt (most recent) 1997
Passenger capacity: 4
Body of water: Lake Lucerne   Home port: Luzern/Vitznau
Frequency: Charters
Website address: www.dampfei.ch
Builder: Glyn Lancaster Jones, Port Dinorwic, Wales
Engine builder: P Lewis, Norton, England, Stuart Turner design
Owner: Walter Bünter, Vitznau

1980: Construction commenced at Todmorden, hull later moved to Port Dinorwic.

1985: Completed for David Strong.

1986: July: Steamed for the first time.

1987: Current engine fitted. This was formerly in the launch *Scylla of Messina*.

1996: Sold to I.E. Thomson and G.R. Thomson.

1997: Completely rebuilt and refitted. Used on Lake Windermere.

2003: Sold to present owner and moved to Switzerland. Used in conjunction with *Uranus* and available for charter. Because she is trailable, i.e. is small enough to be towed behind a car, she often appears at meets of steam launches elsewhere in Switzerland.

PL LIBERTY-BELLE

Length: 7.45m
Propulsion: Paddle Steamer   Engine type: single-cylinder diagonal, 2.5hp
Built: 1987   Rebuilt (most recent): 2005
Passenger capacity: 5
Body of water: Lake Lucerne   Home port: Vitznau
Frequency: Occasional public trips
Website address: liberty-belle.globotech.ch/index.html

Builder: Glyn Lancaster Jones, Port Dinorwic, Wales   **Engine builder:** B Bolzern, Emmenbrücke
Owner: Beat & Martha Bolzern, Emmenbrücke
Former name: *Minerva* 1992

1987: Completed as *Minerva* for William S. Roberts, Menai Straits.

1992: Sold to L.W. Penman, moved to Devon and renamed *Liberty Belle*.

1993: Sold to Herbert Schuler and moved to Lake Lucerne. Boat and engine rebuilt. Boiler converted from paraffin to diesel.

1994: 1 October: First floated in a swimming pool.

1995: Paddles rebuilt.

1996: Boiler enlarged.

2001: Boiler converted to wood/coal firing.

2004: August: Sold to present owners.

   November to May 2005: New engine, built by present owner, fitted.

2006: Public trips scheduled for a New Year steam on 1 and 2 January, and a Nostalgia Festival on 15 and 16 July, both events at Vitznau.

2007: January: Hull and engine rebuilt.

Public passenger trips are offered at special steam events throughout Switzerland and in nearby countries, e.g. in August 2005 she visited an event at Aix-les-Bains on the Lac du Bourget and also became the first paddle steamer on the Sarnersee. The majority of her time is spent on Lake Lucerne.

PS RIGI

Rigi in the garden of the Verkehrshaus der Schweiz.

Length: 37.49m
Propulsion: Paddle Steamer   **Engine type:** 2-cylinder oscillating, 155hp
Built: 1848   **Rebuilt** (most recent): 200?
Passenger capacity: 200
Body of water: Lake Lucerne   **Home port:** Lucerne
Frequency of operation: Awaiting restoration
Website address: www.dampfschiff.ch/webpac/media/Top_Aktuell.pdf
Builders: Ditchburn & Mare, London
Engine builder: Escher Wyss, fitted 1894
Owner: Verkehshaus de Schweiz, Luzern **Operator:** SGV, Lucerne

1846: Ordered from Ditchburn and Mare, London, with machinery from John Penn & Son, for the newly formed Postdampfchiffahrts-Gesellschaft. The other operator on the lake, Knörr, had an exclusive arrangement with Escher-Wyss to build steamers, hence the order from a London builder. Delivered to Lucerne in sections, she originally had 2-cylinder simple expansion oscillating machinery.

1848: 16 March: Launched at Lucerne.

   1 May: Maiden voyage to Flüelen and back.

1852: Morgan system feathering paddle wheels fitted.

1860: Lengthened by *c*.4m.

1862: New funnel fitted. Converted from wood to coal-firing.

1863: Funnel converted to a collapsible form, so as to get under the Acheregg Bridge.

1870: Owners merged with the other operator on the lake to form VDGV (Vereinigte Dampfschiffahrts gesellschaft der Vierwaldstättersee).

1872: New boiler fitted, built by Sulzer.

1885: Owners renamed DGV (Dampfschiffahrtsgesellschaft der Vierwaldstättersee).

1894: New compound machinery, boiler, and paddle wheels fitted.

1901: Was the final steamer on the Lake to be fitted with electric lighting.

1905: Deck saloon on the after deck greatly extended.

1915-20: Out of service due to the war.

1921: Wheelhouse fitted. A Hanomag diesel engine was purchased for her, but never installed.

1924: New paddle boxes, new saloon windows, and new (non-collapsible) funnel fitted.

1940-41: Steering position raised by about 40cm.

1952: 31 May: Withdrawn from service. To be used in a proposed new transport museum.

1958: Partially dismantled and moved to the new Verkehrshaus der Schweiz (Swiss Transport Museum). New deck saloon fitted.

2005: 19 January: Announcement made that **Rigi** is to be restored to operating condition and returned to service as a museum steamer on Lake Lucerne. The restoration is to be a joint venture between the Verkehrshaus der Schweiz, SGV (the operator of the steamers on the lake) and the Dampferfreunde Vierwaldstättersee (enthusiast organisation).

August: Floodwater reached the museum grounds and **Rigi** floated, but soon sank due to her hull condition. The deck saloon was damaged and had to be demolished.

Four options for her restoration were considered:

1) Original condition from 1848, which would mean she would be more or less a replica.

2) As rebuilt in 1873 with a new boiler but still with tiller steering. Problem - at that time she still had her original John Penn engine.

3) As rebuilt in 1894 when her present oscillating engine built by Escher Wyss was fitted, still flush-decked. This is the favoured option.

4) As she finally appeared in service when withdrawn in 1953, with an aft deck saloon. This would give more passenger comfort but would not have the historic appearance befitting such a veteran.

It is planned that she offer public passenger trips on ten to twenty weekends per year but she would not have the speed to be able to work in the current SGV service. She would either run from Lucerne to Vitznau to connect with the preserved steam train on the Rigi railway, or to Alpnachstad to connect with a still-to-be-restored steam unit on the Pilatus railway.

2006: 27 March: It was announced that, due to the poor hull condition and possible stability problems, the proposed restoration to service would not be proceeded with and **Rigi** would remain in the Verkehrshaus, but be converted back to a flush-decked steamer and moved to a more visible position at the front of the maritime hall.

2007: 8 March: Hull moved to a new location in the museum grounds, using the most powerful crane in Switzerland.

PS SCHILLER

Length: 63.00m **Gross tonnage:** 320

Propulsion: Paddle Steamer **Engine type:** Compound Diagonal, 830hp

Built: 1906 **Rebuilt** (most recent): 2000

Passenger capacity: 800

Body of water: Vierwaldstätter See **Home port:** Luzern

Frequency of operation: Daily **Period of operation:** Late May to end September

Website address: www.lakelucerne.ch

Builders: Sulzer, Winterthur **Owner:** SGV, Luzern

1906: 17 February: launched.
  21 May: Entered service.
*c.*1920: Wheelhouse fitted.
1951–52: Converted from coal to oil firing.
1976–77: Major overhaul.
1998–2000: Major rebuild. New boiler fitted.
2004: Offered a morning return from Lucerne to Küssnacht on Sundays, followed by an afternoon return to Flüelen, and a 10:00 return to Flüelen on weekdays.
2006: **Schiller** ran the 13:20 return from Lucerne to Flüelen.

PS STADT LUZERN

Stadt Luzern on Lake Lucerne, 1998.

Length: 63.50m   **Gross tonnage:** 415
Propulsion: Paddle Steamer
Engine type: 3-cylinder simple expansion diagonal, 1,600hp
Built: 1928   **Passenger capacity:** 1,200
Body of water: Vierwaldstätter See   **Home port:** Luzern
Frequency of operation: Daily   **Period of operation:** May to September
Website address: www.lakelucerne.ch
Builders: Sachsenberg, Rosslau/Elbe   **Engine builder:** Sulzer, Winterthur 1929
Owner: SGV, Luzern

1927: 14 December: Launched.
1928: 13 March to 5 April: Trials. Engine defective.
  24 June: Entered service for one day only.
1928–29: Original 2-cylinder engine removed and new 3-cylinder Sulzer machine with automatic oiling installed.
1929: 6 July: Finally entered service.
1932: Only in service on Sundays because of the Depression.
1939–45: The paddle steamers on Lake Lucerne saw very little service during the war years. Because of a shortage of coal, they were fired by wood.
1940: 25 July: Carried General Henri Guisan and the highest officials of the Swiss army to Rütli for a meeting, which led to the 'Rütlirapport' which protected Swiss neutrality in the war. A brass plaque on the steamer commemorates this.
1953–54: Converted from coal to oil firing.
1980: 2 May: Made a special sailing with HM Queen Elizabeth II on board, to commemorate the 40th anniversary of the 'Rütlirapport'.
1985–89: Major rebuild over three to four winters. Upper deck saloon renewed and upper deck awning extended towards stern. Dining saloon restored to original art deco style.
2006: Operates a daily 11:25 return sailing from Lucerne to Flüelen. This is marketed at the 'William Tell Express' with a train connection onwards to Lugano and Locarno.

PS UNTERWALDEN

Unterwalden off Lucerne, 1998.

Length: 61.00m   **Gross tonnage**: 294
Propulsion: Paddle Steamer   **Engine type**: Compound Diagonal, 650hpv
Built: 1902   **Rebuilt** (most recent): 1985
Passenger capacity: 800
Body of water: Vierwaldstätter See   **Home port**: Luzern
Frequency of operation: Daily
Period of operation: Late May to end September
Website address: www.lakelucerne.ch
Builders: Escher Wyss, Zürich
Owner: SGV, Luzern

1901: 12 November: Launched.
1902: 18 May: Entered service.
*c.*1920: Wheelhouse fitted.
1949: Converted from coal to oil-firing.
1961: Rebuilt with telescopic funnel and masts, and lowering wheelhouse to pass under the new Acheregg Bridge and maintain sailings to Alpnachatad. After awning on upper deck replaced by aluminium cover.
1977: Withdrawn at end of season. Plans to scrap her were thwarted by local enthusiasts.
1983–85: Major rebuild.
2006: **Unterwalden** offered two daily return sailings to Alpnachstad at 10:15 and 14:00, connecting with the rack railway up Pilatus, also an evening cruise at 19:15 on a Friday.

SL URANUS

Steam launch *Uranus* at Brunnen Harbour Festival 2005. (Beat Bolzern)

Length: 6.10m
Propulsion: Single Screw   **Engine type**: Compound, 10hp
Built: 1989   **Passenger capacity**: 8

Body of water: Brienzersee/Vierwaldstätter See   **Home port**: Vitznau/Weggis
Frequency of operation: 1–2x monthly   **Period of operation**: June to September
Website address: www.dampfei.ch
Builders: W Hasler, Stanstad
Engine builder (if different from builder): Newark, UK, manufactured 1980
Owner: Walter Bünter, Vitznau

1970: Original wooden hull built.
1980: Engine and boiler fitted.
1989: New replacement steel hull built.

Uranus has operated passenger trips on both Lake Brienz and Lake Lucerne in recent years. She is normally in public operation once a month on a Thursday.

PS URI

Uri on Lake Lucerne, 1998.

Length: 61.80m   **Gross tonnage**: 293.6
Propulsion: Paddle Steamer   **Engine type**: Compound Diagonal, 650hp
Built: 1901   **Rebuilt** (most recent): 1994
Passenger capacity: 800
Body of water: Vierwaldstätter See   **Home port**: Luzern
Frequency of operation: Daily   **Period of operation**: May to September
Website address: www.lakelucenre.ch
Builders: Sulzer, Winterthur
Owner: SGV, Luzern

1901: 19 January: Launched.
 4 May: Entered service.
1923: Wheelhouse fitted.
1949: Converted from coal to oil firing.
1961: Rebuilt with telescopic funnel and masts, and lowering wheelhouse to pass under the new Acheregg Bridge and maintain sailings to Alpnachstad. After awning on upper deck replaced by an aluminium cover.
1978–81: Major rebuild over three winters.
1991–94 Major rebuild. New boiler fitted. Aluminium cover to upper deck removed. Upper deck glazed in to make panorama restaurant. Upper deck extended forward over part of the foredeck. Telescopic funnel and masts converted to fixed ones, thus making her unable to sail under the Acheregg Bridge to Alpnachstad.
2006: *Uri* offered a 09:20 return to Flüelen and a 15:25 return to Vitznau, with a 19:20 sunset cruise to Vitznau on Tuesday evenings, also on Wednesday evenings in fine weather.

The paddle steamer *Wilhelm Tell*, built in 1908 and withdrawn after the 1970 summer season, survives, with her engine still intact, in use as a floating restaurant at Lucerne.

THUNERSEE (LAKE THUN)

PS BLÜMLISALP

Blümlisalp arriving at Interlaken, 1992.

Length: 63.40m   **Gross tonnage**: 350
Propulsion: Paddle Steamer   **Engine type**: Compound Diagonal, 600hp
Built: 1906   **Rebuilt** (most recent): 1993
Passenger capacity: 800
Body of water: Thunersee   **Home port**: Thun
Frequency of operation: Daily   **Period of operation**: Late April to mid-October
Website address: http://www.bls.ch/schiff/flotte_bluemlisalp_d.html
Builders: Escher Wyss, Zürich
Owner: Genossenschaft Vaporama, Thun   **Operator**: BLS, Thus

1906: 31 May: Launched.
  1 August: Entered service.
1914: Hull painted light green.
1915, 1917-22: Out of service.
1930: Upper strip of hull painted dark green.
1939: Hull painted white; upper strip beige.
1966: Painted white all over.
1971: Withdrawn from service.
1992: 28 May: Return to service after a major rebuild, including new boilers, following a major campaign by enthusiast over the previous twenty-one years. Now had the upper strip of her hull painted light blue.
2005-06: Major renovation and overhaul.

Blümlisalp offers a 12:38 return sailing from Thun to Interlaken West, with an 1838 from Thun as far as Beatenbucht and back Tuesdays to Saturdays.

PS HELVETIA

An artist's impression of the proposed new *Helvetia* on the Thunersee.

Propulsion: Paddle Steamer   **Engine type**: Compound Oscillating, 250hp
Built: 200?
Body of water: Lake Thun   **Home port**: Thun
Frequency of operation: Proposed newbuilding
Builders: to be built
Engine builder: Escher-Wyss, Zürich, from *Giessbach*, 1899, fitted 200?
Owner: Vaporama, Thun

2003: New half-salon steamer proposed by steam museum Vaporama, Thun, using the engines from the
  Lake Brienz steamer *Giessbach*. These had been built in 1899 to replace the previous machinery in the
  steamer, which dated from 1859, and were preserved when she was scrapped in 1959.

ZÜRICHSEE (LAKE ZÜRICH)

PS STADT RAPPERSWIL

Stadt Rapperswil at Zürich, 1967.

Length: 59.10m   **Gross tonnage**: 262
Propulsion: Paddle Steamer   **Engine type**: Compound Diagonal, 500hp
Built: 1914   **Rebuilt** (most recent): 1986
Passenger capacity: 850
Body of water: Zürichsee   **Home port**: Zürich
Frequency of operation: Daily   **Period of operation**: May to September
Website address: www.zsg.ch/raddampfer
Builders: Escher Wyss, Zürich
Owner: ZSG, Zürich

1914: 14 March: Launched.
  31 May: Entered service.
1947: Rebuilt with telescopic funnel to enable her to sail into the Obersee to Schmerikon.
1955: Converted from coal to oil firing.
1952: Upper deck after awning replaced by an aluminium cover.
1972-73: Major overhaul.
1985-86: Major overhaul. New boiler fitted.
2005-06: Major overhaul.

Stadt Rapperswil and *Stadt Zürich* offer, between them, three return sailings from Zürich to Rapperswil
Sundays excepted, leaving Zürich at 09:30, 10:30 and 14:30, with an additional sailing as far as Männedorf
at 14:40.
    On Sundays, the 09:30 and 14:30 to Rapperswil operate, and there is a 12:30 sailing to Schmerikon on
the Obersee, passing under an extremely tight railway bridge en route.
    All sailings are normally only operated by a paddle steamer in fine weather.

PS STADT ZÜRICH

Stadt Zürich at Schmerikon, 1998.

Length: 59.10m   **Gross tonnage:** 262
Propulsion: Paddle Steamer   **Engine type:** Compound Diagonal, 500hp
Built: 1909   **Rebuilt** (most recent): 1990
Passenger capacity: 850
Body of water: Zürichsee   **Home port:** Zürich
Frequency of operation: Daily   **Period of operation:** May to September
Website address: www.zsg.ch/raddampfer/
Builders: Escher Wyss, Zürich
Owner: ZSG, Zürich

1909: 8 May: Launched.
  12 June: Maiden voyage.
1950: Upper deck after awning replaced by an aluminium cover.
1951: Converted from coal to oil firing.
2003–04: Major overhaul.

OTHER LAKES

SS GREIF

Greif on the Greifensee.

Length: 13.30m   **Gross tonnage:** 9
Propulsion: Single Screw   **Engine type:** Compound, 10hp
Built: 1895   **Rebuilt** (most recent): 1989
Passenger capacity: 22
Body of water: Greifensee   **Home port:** Maur

Frequency of operation: SuO 2 per month
Period of operation: Late April to mid-October
Website address: www.sgg-greifensee.ch/greif.htm
Builders: Escher Wyss, Zürich
Owner: SGG, Maur
Remarks: Coal-fired

1895: 12 October: Launch and maiden voyage.
1916: Rebuilt with Daimler petrol engine. The steam engine was installed in a gravel dredger in the Zürcher Obersee.
  21 August: Entered service as motor vessel.
1943: New motor fitted.
1984–88: Restoration and return to steam and original condition, using the original engine and a new boiler.
1988: 3 September: First public trip as a steamer again.

Greif normally offers three trips from Maur to Greifensee on the one or two Sundays per month that she is in operation, with four non-landing sailings from Uster one Sunday per month from June to September.

SL GUSTAV PRYM

Gustav Prym out of service at Kreuzlingen, 2005.

Length: 12.50m   Gross tonnage: 10.5
Propulsion: Single Screw   Engine type: Triple Expansion, 25hp
Built: 1916   Rebuilt (most recent): 1998
Passenger capacity: 12
Body of water: Bodensee   Home port: Kreuzlingen
Frequency of operation: SuO   Period of operation: Mid-April to end October
Website address: www.gustavprym.ch
Builders: Hamburg   Engine builder: Sissons, Swindon 1906
Owner: Karl Sailer: Operator: Historische Schifffahrt Bodensee

1916: Built as motor passenger launch for harbour service at Konstanz, Bodensee.
1963: Withdrawn.
1966: Converted to fire-boat, still at Konstanz.
1985: Finished service as fire-boat.
1986: Restoration began. Steam engine fitted.
1998: Restoration complete, entered service at Bodman running tourist trips on occasional dates during the summer months.
2003–04: Chartered to Olagomio, Murten: Moved to Murtensee/Lac de Morat at Murten/Morat to offer trips on the Murtensee.

2005: 24 April: Chartered by Historische Schifffahrt Bodensee. Moved back to the Bodensee, to Kreuzlingen.

In the summer of 2005 **Gustav Prym** offered 1-hour public cruises on one Sunday per month out of Kreuzlingen. Profits from the operation of **Gustav Prym** are going towards the raising and restoration of **Jura**.

PS JURA

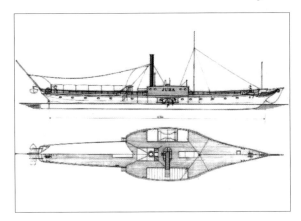

A profile of the paddle steamer *Jura*.

Length: 46.3m
Propulsion: Paddle Steamer
Engine type: 2-cylinder oscillating, 45hp
Built: 1854
Passenger capacity: 400 (originally)
Body of water: Bodensee
Frequency: to be raised and restored
Website address: http://www.todi.ch/jura.htm
Builder: Escher-Wyss, Zürich
Owner: Historische Schifffahrt Bodensee
Remarks: Wooden-hulled. Sank 1862, to be raised and restored

1854: Built as a flush-decked wooden-hulled paddle steamer for Sociètè des bateaux à vapeur du Lac de Neuchâtel for service on Lake Neuchâtel from Neuchâtel to Yverdon.

27 July: Launched.

7 September: Maiden voyage, a special trip to Estavayan.

1861: 19 September: Sold to Dampfboot-AG, Lindau for use on the Bavarian section of the Bodensee after an abortive sale to Lucerne earlier in the year. Moved to the Bodensee via Lucerne by horse-wagon. She was purchased to replace **Ludwig**, which had been sunk in a collision with the Swiss paddle steamer **Stadt Zürich**.

1864: 12 January: Sank in 45m of water off Bottighofen near Kreuzlingen after a collision in fog with the same steamer **Stadt Zürich** which had sunk her predecessor. One sailor lost his life but the passengers and the reminder of the crew managed to scramble onto the **Stadt Zürich** and were saved.

1953: Wreck found by a scuba diver. The wreck became very popular amongst divers and has been damaged over the years.

2000: Badly damaged by the anchor of a scuba dive boat.

2004: Declared as a historic site by the Thurgau regional government.

Historische Schifffahrt Bodensee formed to raise and restoree the steamer at a cost of around 8 miullion Swiss Francs.

If the group manages to raise and restore **Jura** she will be a unique example of a mid-nineteenth-century wooden paddle steamer, and the second oldest steamer in the world, after **Rigi**.

PS NEUCHÂTEL

Neuchâtel as a restaurant ship at Neuchâtel, 1987.

Length: 48.50m   **Tonnage:** 153
Propulsion: Paddle Steamer   **Engine type:** Compound, 360hp
Built: 1912   **Passenger capacity:** 550
Body of water: Lake Neuchâtel   **Home port:** Neuchâtel
Frequency of operation: static
Website address: http://www.trivapor.ch/Indexd.htm
Builders: Escher-Wyss, Zürich   **Engine builder:** Maffei, Munich, 1926
Owner: Trivapor, Neuchâtel
Remarks: Return to steam proposed

1912: 9 May: Launched.
   15 June: Entered service for Sociéte de Navigation sur les Lacs de Neuchâtel et Morat SA. Operated from Neuchâtel to Yverdon, Biel and Morat.
1949: Major overhaul: New aluminium awning over aft deck replaced previous canvas one.
1954: Converted to oil-firing.
1969: Withdrawn from service.
1970: Used as floating restaurant at Neuchâtel. Engine and boiler removed.
1999: Up for sale, preservation organisation Trivapor founded.
2003-04: Proposal to return her to steam using the engine formerly in the Chiemsee (Bavaria) paddle steamer ***Ludwig Fessler***, which had been removed in 1973 when she was dieselised.
2005: Engine arrived at Neuchâtel.
2007: 12 February: Finally purchased by Trivapor after much negotiation.

The Lake Neuchâtel paddle steamer ***Fribourg***, built in 1913 and withdrawn in 1965, survives at Portalban on the other side of the lake from Neuchâtel. She is used as an annexe to a restaurant, and one paddle box and wheel have been removed to make an under-cover access to her. Her engines and boiler have also been removed.

PS WENGI

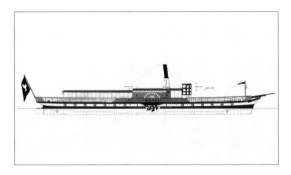

A profile of the paddle steamer
Wengi as proposed.

Length: 41.00m
Propulsion: Paddle Steamer   **Engine type:** Compound
Built: 1912 (?)   **Rebuilt** (most recent): 1956
Body of water: River Aare   **Home port:** Solothurn
Frequency of operation: Undergoing restoration
Website address: www.ds-wengi.ch
Builders: Danubius, Budapest   **Engine builder:** Escher-Wyss, Zürich
Owner: Verein Freunde der Dampfschifffahrt auf den Juragewässern
Former names: *Giurgiu* 1955, ***Locotenent Comandor Demetriade*** 1945, ***Zupa*** 1944, ***Locotenent Comandor Demetriade*** 1944, *?* 1919

1889: Built by Escher Wyss, Zürich for unknown owners.

1919: Ceded to Rumania following the First World War. Used by the Romanian Navy. Renamed ***Locotenent Comandor Demetriade***.

1944: Requisitioned by the Russian navy as a minesweeper. Later sunk and raised, taken over by the Yugoslav Navy, renamed ***Zupa***.

1945: Returned to Romania, regained the name ***Locotenent Comandor Demetriade***.

1955: Transferred to NAVROM, state owner of all Romanian ships, for civilian use. Renamed ***Giurgiu***.

1956: Rebuilt at Giurgiu and converted to a tug and long-range river inspection steamer. Used for river protection control, also as a buoy tender.

1970s (probably): Placed in reserve. Laid-up at Canalul Plantelor.

1996: After all the brass on board had been stolen, moved to Tulcea.

1999: Purchased by Verein Freunde der Dampfschifffahrt auf den Juragewässern, who plan to rebuild her as a replica of *Wengi*, (1856) the first steamer to run on the River Aare from Solothurn.

2001: Slipped, hull found to be in good condition. Engine removed and rebuilt in Switzerland. It is the intention that restoration be carries out at Mulhouse, in France.

This preservation project has had a bumpy ride, with a report erroneously stating that she would be too big for the river, and the resignation of the chairman of the preservation committee at one time. It seems now to be back on track, but the prospect of restoring an extremely corroded hull and bringing it from Rumania to Switzerland is immense. When, and if, restoration is completed it is planned that she run on the River Aare from Biel to Solothurn.

13 Hungary

The paddle steamer **Petofi** (1926) was taken out of service in 1983, and no news has been heard about her restoration for many years. It seems very unlikely she will ever return to service as a steamer.

The paddle steamer **Kossuth** (1914) is a statically moored floating restaurant at Budapest with a small museum on her lower deck.

The type 737 paddle steamer **Budapest** (1960), of the same class as the paddle steamers on the River Lena, is reported still to be in existence, but has been laid-up for many years.

The two-funnelled paddle steamer **Szoke Tisza** (1917), ex **Felszabadulas**, ex **Szent Imre**, originally **IV Karoly**, has been in static use at Szeged on the River Tisza since 1979. She was in service on the Danube until 1974.

At Neszmély, on the Danube in western Hungary there is a ship museum with two statically preserved paddle tugs, **Zoltan** of 1869, and **Neszmély**, ex **Bakony** of 1957, one of the class 732 steam tugs built at Budapest, mainly for the USSR, in the mid-fifties.

14 Poland

ST NADBOR

Nadbor at Wroclaw.

Engine type: 250hp
Built: 1947-9
Body of water: River Oder   Home port: Wroclaw
Frequency of operation: awating restoration; currently in static use
Website address: www.nadbor.pwr.wroc.pl/en_nadbor.php
Builders: Netherlands
Owner: Funacja Otwartego Muzeum Tekniki (Foundation of Open Museum of Techology)

1947-49: Built as a river tug for the River Oder, as part of a large order for twenty-two tugs for the River Oder. Used for towing barges between Kozle/Gliwice and Wroclaw.
1968: Withdrawn from service, used as a floating boiler for the shipyard of Zegluga na Odrze (the Oder Navigation).
1975: No longer used, later moved to the Czech Republic to supply steam and electric energy in a lock and weir building project.
1982: Abortive attempt to use her as an icebreaker at Wroclaw, which failed because she did not have an icebreaker bow.
1985: Moved to Osobowice to lay up.
1990s: ODTATRANS and the Foundation of Open Museum of Technology made efforts to preserve **Nadbor**.
1998: Overhaul and restoration commenced.
2001: Made a return trip to Rotterdam.
Nadbor is now in static use as a floating classroom by the Open Museum of Technology at Wroclaw.

15 Romania

The steamers of Romania have always been rather elusive, especially in Communist times, when details of both civil and military steamers were considered a state secret. With the end of communism in 1989, details have been more accessible, but there are a lot of old steamers laid-up there, and it is possible that others may, at some stage, be restored and moved elsewhere in Europe.

PS BORCEA

Borcea laid-up in Braila harbour 2004.
(Dr Cristian Craciunoiu)

Length: 38.00m
Propulsion: Paddle Steamer   **Engine type**: Compound Diagonal
Built: 1914   **Passenger capacity**: 200
Body of water: River Danube   **Home port**: Braila
Frequency of operation: Laid-up
Website address: www.danube-research.com/histships.html
Builders: Unknown, Turnu Severin
Engine builder: (if different from builder): Sachsenberg, Rosslau/Elbe
Owner: Casa Copiilor (Children's House) Braila

1914: Built as a passenger steamer at Turnu Severin. Used on the route from Cernavoda to Calarasi.
1914-18: Used as a workshop steamer, towing a barge.
1918-39: Used extensively as a passenger steamer throughout the Romanian stretch of the Danube.
1945: Became part of Sovromtransport (Soviet-Romanian Transport Co.). When that organisation ceased to exist, became part of the fleet of nationalised operator NAVROM.
Early 1980s: About to be scrapped, purchased by the Young Pioneers, Braila as a floating classroom.
Post 1989: With the end of communism, taken over by the Children's House of Braila.
1999: Laid-up.

PS REPUBLICA

Republica in operation and dressed overall at
a Romanian Navy Day, Spring 2005.
(Dr Cristian Craciunoiu)

Length: 54.00m
Propulsion: Paddle Steamer   **Engine type:** 500hp
Built: 1916,
Body of water: River Danube
Builders: Ganz-Danubius, Budapest
Owner: Romanian Navy
Former names: *Locotenent Comandor Vasile Paun* 2003, *Republica* 1991, *Capitan Comandor Paun*
1944, *Arad*, *Csobanc* 1918

1916: Built as **Csobanc** for MFTR, Budapest. Used as an armed steamer during the First World War. Used
as a guard ship near Orsova.
November: Used in raising sunken ships in the channel.
1917: 17 July: Released from military service and returned to MFTR.
1918: Captured by the Romanians whilst on the lower Danube, renamed **Arad**. Later taken over by the
Romanian Navy, renamed **Capitan Comandor Paun**.
1941 and 1944: Used as a command ship.
1944: Renamed **Republica**, continued to be used as a naval command ship.
*c.*1960: Used by Romanian president Gheorghiu Dej to inspect the Danube Flotilla several times. Based
at Braila.
1991: Renamed **Locotenent Comandor Vasile Paun**. This is in fact a historical error, as the First World War
hero whose name she commemorated in the 1918–44 era was Constantin Paun, and not Vasile.
1995: Used as command ship for an international naval manoeuvre on the Danube, carrying NATO
observers and journalists.
*c.*2003: Renamed **Republica**.

Republica is the last surviving paddle warship in the world.

PS TUDOR VLADIMIRESCU

Tudor Vladimirescu in winter lay-up at Galatz
shipyard, Spring 2006. (*Modelism* magazine)

Length: 65.80m
Propulsion: Paddle Steamer   **Engine type:** Compound Oscillating, 520hp
Built: 1854   **Passenger capacity:** 391
Body of water: River Danube   **Home port:** Braila
Frequency of operation: Occasional public trips
Website address: www.danube-research.com/Danube.html
Builders: Altofen Shipyard, Budapest   **Engine builders:** Escher Wyss, Zürich
Owner: NAVROM
Former names: *Grigore Manu* *c.*1945, *Sarmisgetuza* 1923, *Croatia* 1918

1854: Built as the tug **Croatia** for DDSG, Vienna. Used throughout the Danube region. Built with a 460hp
simple expansion oscillating engine.

1867: Engine compounded and power increased to 500hp.

1918: Given by Romanian operator NFR as war reparations following Austria-Hungary's defeat in the First World War. Renamed **Sarmisgetuza**. Rebuilt as a passenger steamer at Turnu Severin. Used on the Braila-Galati-Tulcea-Sulina service, and also on the Turnu Severin-Calafat-Giurgui-Oltenita-Tutucaia route.

1923: Renamed **Grigore Manu** Continued on the same routes.

1945: NFR merged with other operators to form NAVROM. Renamed **Tudor Vladimirescu** about this time.

1958: Modernised. New bridge and superstructure fitted. At this stage, a plate was placed on board, giving her building date erroneously as 1874. Used on cruises in the Danube Delta. In the winter her engines were used as a vibration laboratory for the students of the Naval Institute of Galati.

1990: Used as a floating restaurant at Tulcea.

1992-95: Refitted at Turnu Severin shipyard.

2000-02: Gutted pending a refit at the Galati Damen shipyard. Funds dried up when work was incomplete.

2002: September to August 2003: Work re-started and rebuild was completed at the Aker yard at Braila. Rebuilt to a more modern profile.

2003: 15 August: Returned to service. Used by the government-owned shipping company NAVROM for VIP cruises on the Danube and the Delta.

Tudor Vladimirescu is currently the oldest operating steamer in the world.

16 Russia

Surviving steamers in Russia are few and far between, but include the last surviving overnight passenger steamers not in tourist service. Information about Russian steamers was hard to obtain during the Soviet era, but it is understood some were in service on the Volga up to the 1980s.

PS BLAGOEVSHCHENSK

Blagoevschensk on the Lena.

Length: 71.41m   Displacement tonnage: 542
Propulsion: Paddle Steamer   Engine type: Compound Diagonal, 450hp
Built: 1959   Passenger capacity: 187 berths
Body of water: River Lena   Home port: Yakutsk
Frequency of operation: 2-3/monthly
Period of operation: Late May to end September
Website address: www.riverships.ru/english/types/737_specs.shtml
Builders: Schiffswerft Budapest, Obuda
Owner: Upper Lens Shipping Co., Kirensk

1959: Built at Budapest as one of the final members of the class 737 paddle steamers, of which some sixty-five were built for various river systems in the Soviet Union between 1951 and 1959.

1961: Entered service on the River Lena in eastern Siberia. It is not known if she was sailed there, via the Danube, Black Sea, thought the Russian waterways to Archangel and along the Arctic Coast, or if she was cut into sections and taken to the Lena by rail.

2005: It was reported that the River Lena paddle steamers would not be operating in the 2005 season According to some reports she was making short trips for tourists from Summer 2005 onwards.

Of the four type 737 allocated to the River Lena, **Blagoevschensk** and **Krasnoyarsk** remain in summer service on the Lena from Osetrovo, near Ust Kut to Yakutsk.

Irkutsk is still extant, but is laid-up, and **Khabarovask** sank in August 1999 and has never been raised. The service takes five days in each direction, and runs from the end of May to the end of September each year with six or seven departures each month. It is the only surviving overnight scheduled passenger service operated by a steam vessel in the world.

SS DUNKAN

Dunkan at Stockholm Harbour Festival, 1998.
(B. Worden)

Length: 21.50m
Propulsion: Single Screw   **Engine type**: Compound, 200hp
Built: 1901   **Rebuilt** (most recent): 1998
Body of water: Baltic Coast   **Home port**: Kalundborg
Frequency of operation: Sunk then raised
Website address: www.dunkan.de/
Builders: Unknown, Varkaus
Owner: Valentin Syromiatnikov
Former names: *Kolpino* 1998, *Leporello* 1902

1901: Built as the tug-cum-icebreaker **Leporello**.
1902: April: Sold to the steel factory 'Ishorskiie Zavodi', St Petersburg, Russia.
    12 September: Renamed **Kolpino**, placed in service from Kolpino to St Petersburg and Kronstadt.
1918: Used to carry ammunition from the military harbour at Kronstadt to St Petersburg.
1932: New boiler fitted.
1942: winter: No longer in regular service, used as a) tug, b) icebreaker, c) to transport fuel to other ships and d) as a supplier of steam to heat other ships.
1943-46: Major refit.
1956: Boiler converted to oil-firing.
1987: Withdrawn from service, to be scrapped.
1992: Purchased by present owner.
1992-98: Major restoration. New deck salon added aft, diesel auxiliary machinery fitted. Renamed **Dunkan**.
1994: Return to steam in the St Petersburg area.
1998-2002: Operating to various ports in the Baltic, visiting various steam festivals, including Stockholm in 1998, and Vejle in 2002. Based at Rostock from 2000 to 2002.
2002: 22 July: Ran aground whilst en route from Vejle to Copenhagen near Kongstrup, Kalundborg Fjord, Sjaelland, Denmark.

26 July: A tug attempted to pull Dunkan free, but she capsized and sank in 15m of water.

2003: 9-10 April: Raised by the floating crane Samson, and taken to Kalundborg where she was placed on the quay. Restoration started, supported by the newly formed organisation 'Dunkan's Venner'.

PS IRKUTSK

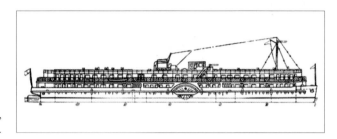

A profile of a type 737 paddle steamer, of the same class as *Irkutsk*.

Length: 71.41m   **Displacement tonnage:** 542
Propulsion: Paddle Steamer   **Engine type:** Compound Diagonal, 450hp
Built: 1959
Body of water: River Lena   **Home port:** Yakutsk
Frequency of operation: Laid-up
Website address: www.riverships.ru/english/types/737_specs.shtml
Builders: Schiffswerft Budapest, Obuda
Owner: Upper Lens Shipping Co., Kirensk

1959: See **Blagoevschensk**.

PS KRASNOYARSK

Krasnoyarsk in service on the Lena.
(B. Worden collection)

Length: 71.41m   **Displacement tonnage:** 542
Propulsion: Paddle Steamer   **Engine type:** Compound Diagonal, 450hp
Built: 1959   **Passenger capacity:** 250 berths
Body of water: River Lena   **Home port:** Yakutsk
Frequency of operation: 2-3/monthly
Period of operation: Late May to end September
Website address: www.riverships.ru/english/types/737_specs.shtml;
http://travel.independent.co.uk/low_res/story.jsp?story=430527&host=2&dir=33
Builders: Schiffswerft Budapest, Obuda
Owner: Upper Lens Shipping Co., Kirensk

1959: See **Blagoevschensk**.

2005: It was reported that the River Lena paddle steamers would not be operating in the 2005 season. According to some reports she was making short trips for tourists from Summer 2005 onwards.

PS LOMONOSOV

Lomonosov on the Volga *c.*1960. (From the book whose title translates as *Paddle Steamers on the Volga*)

Length: 102.40m
Propulsion: Paddle Steamer
Built: 1905
Body of water: River Volga　　**Home port:** Nr Nizhny Novgorod
Frequency of operation: Laid-up since 1965
Builders: Unknown, Russia

1905: Built for service on the River Volga.
1940: Lengthened to 102.4m.
1965: Withdrawn from service. Laid-up at a yard near Nizhny Novgorod.

PS N V GOGOL

N V Gogol at Brin-Navolok on the Northern Dvina, 2002. (B. Worden)

Length: 70.70m
Propulsion: Paddle Steamer　　**Engine type:** Triple Expansion Diagonal, 360hp
Built: 1911　　**Rebuilt** (most recent): 1941
Passenger capacity: 53
Body of water: Severnaya Dvina River　　**Home port:** Archangel
Frequency of operation: Weekly　　**Period of operation:** Summer
Builders: Sormovo, Nizhni Novgorod
Owner: Emterprise Zwezdotchka, Severodvinsk, near Archangel

1911: Built for Severnoe Parokhodnoe Obshchetvo 'Kotlas-Archangelsk-Murman' for service on the Northern Dvina. Originally carried 695 passengers. After building cut into three sections and moved to Weliki Ustyug, where she was reassembled. Initially operated from Vologda to Archangel, later from Ustyug and Kotlas to Archangel, and then from Kotlas to Archangel.
1918: Owners nationalised. Used to evacuate archives and civilian and military property from Archangel to Ustyug during the Revolution.
1919: laid-up for repairs.
1921: Returned to service from Archangel to Vologda.
1939-41: Major rebuild, new longer hull fitte'.

1941: 2 August: Return to service after overhaul.

1945: Now in service from Archangel to Kotlas.

Early 1950s: Boilers converted from wood-firing to oil-firing.

1958-59: Major refit at Veliki Ustyug, new boiler fitted.

1972: Sold to the Zvezdochka shipyard, Severodvinsk.

1972-73: Rebuilt. Passenger capacity now 140. Funnel now collapsible to enable her to pass under a bridge to the shipyard at Severodvinsk. Now used for holiday cruises for employees of her owners. Also used to transfer 'Young Pioneers' to riverside camps.

1994-96: Refitted at Zvezdochka shipyard, Severodvinsk.

1998: Eight-day cruises from Archangel to Weliki Ustyug advertised by Intourist Travel Ltd, London, although these never took place.

A number of other type 737 paddle steamers are in static use, mainly on the River Volga, while the icebreaker **Krasin**, built in 1916 by Armstrong Whitworth on the Tyne, is a museum at St Petersburg. The paddle steamer **Sviatitel Nikolai** (1897) is a museum at Krasnoyarsk on the River Yenisei.

17 Greece

Greece has not seen steam propulsion used in the routes to the Aegean and other islands for many years, but two turbine-powered cruise ships survive in Greek waters.

TSS AEGEAN II

Aegean II as *Ausonia* off Limassol, 2004.
(Bruce Peter)

Length: 159.26m   **Gross tonnage:** 12,609
Propulsion: Twin Screw,   **Engine type:** 4 Turbine, 17,400hp
Built: 1957   **Rebuilt** (most recent): 1984
Passenger capacity: 620
Body of water: Aegean Sea   **Home port:** Piraeus
Frequency of operation: 3 and 4 day cruises
Period of operation: May to October
Website address: www.louiscruises.com/au.htm
Builders: C. Riunuti Adriatico
Engine builder (if different from builder): Adriatico
Owner: Louis Cruise Line
Former names: *Ausonia* 2005, **Ivory** 2007

1956: 5 August: Launched.

1957: 23 September: Delivered by her builders to Adriatica Line. Used on the service from Trieste to Beirut via Venice, Brindisi (Bari on the homeward voyage), and Alexandria. Initially operated along with **Esperia** (1949), providing a weekly service between the two vessels.

1978-79: Converted for cruising at Arsenal Triestino SpA, San Marco. Passenger Capacity increased from 529 to 690.

1979: Sold to Italia Crociere International (ICI). Ran Mediterranean Cruises. Some sources erroneously state that she was chartered to Chandris in this year.

1980: Chartered to Grimaldi and made cruises for ICI-Siosa cruise for two seasons.

1983: Sold to Ausonia Crociere SpA, Naples, part of the Grimaldi-Siosa group.

1984: Rebuilt at La Spezia. Ocean deck extended aft. Passenger numbers increased from 690 to 750.

1986: Rebuilt at Fincantieri, Palermo. Extra superstructure added forward of the bridge on the Ocean deck.

1998: 5 May: Sold to Louis Cruise Line of Limassol, Cyprus. Used for short two- and three-day cruises from Cyprus to Egypt, Israel or Rhodes with some seven-day cruises in September or October.

1999: April: Chartered to First Choice cruises for Mediterranean Cruises. Laid-up at Eleusis at end of 2000 season, and not used until 2004.

2004: Used for short cruises from Limassol to Beirut, and from Beirut to Limassol and the Greek Islands.

2005: It was announced she would be renamed **Ithaca** for three- and four-day Aegean cruises from Piraeus, but this did not take place.

Summer: Operated five-day cruises out of Cyprus to the Greek Islands.

October: Operated two cruises from Limassol to the Adriatic.

2006: May: Renamed **Ivory**.

May and June: Operated three- and four-day Aegean cruises out of Piraeus.

July to mid-September: Operated five-day cruises from Limassol to the Aegean each Sunday and two-day cruises from Limassol to Beirut each Sunday. The Aegean cruises have varying itineries.

2007: Chartered to Golden Star Cruises, renamed **Aegean II**, operated three- and four-day Aegean cruises from Piraeus and four each Friday and Monday respectively from late March to early September.

TSS THE EMERALD   Bahamas Flag

The Emerald at Ajaccio, 2002. (Bruce Peter)

Length: 182.10m   **Gross tonnage:** 26431
Propulsion: Twin Screw   **Engine type:** 4 Turbine, 22,000hp
Built: 1958   **Rebuilt** (most recent): 1993
Passenger capacity: 1174
Body of water: Caribbean/Adriatic   **Home port:** Santo Domingo/Corfu
Frequency of operation: Cruises   **Period of operation:** All year
Website address: www.simplonpc.co.uk/SantaRosa.html
Builders: Newport News SB & Drydock Co., Newport News
Engine builder (if different from builder): General Electric
Owner: Louis Cruise Lines. **Operator:** Thomson Cruises
Former names: *Emerald*, *Regent Rainbow*, *Diamond Island*, *Santa Rosa*

1957: 28 August: Launched.
1958: 12 June: Delivered as **Santa Rosa** for Grace Line, New York, USA.
26 June: First trip from New York to Central America.

1959: 26 May. Collided with tanker *Valchem* off Atlantic City.

1970: Sold to Prudential Grace Line, New York.

1971: 22 January: Laid-up in Hampton Roads.

1975: Taken over by US Department of Commerce. Remained laid-up.

1976: Taken over by Vintero Corp., New York. Moved to Baltimore, remained laid-up.

1989: Sold to Coral Cruise Line.

  12 December: Towed to Chalkis, Greece by tug *Zamtug IV*.

1990: March to 1992: Rebuilt at Chalkis.

1992: Renamed *Rainbow* for Rainbow Cruises.

1993: January: Sold to Regency Cruises, Nassau, Bahamas, renamed *Regent Rainbow*.

1996: 27 November: Arrested at Tampa, USA.

  December: Sold to Louis Cruise Lines, Limassol, Cyprus, renamed *The Emerald*.

1997: May: Chartered to Thomson Cruises for Mediterranean Cruises.

1999: Transferred to Bahamas flag, port of registry Nassau.

The Emerald offers seven-day Adriatic cruises from Corfu, calling at Koper, Venice, Zadar, Brindisi and Dubrovnik.

18 Italy

Cruise Ship

TSS SKY WONDER

Sky Wonder as *Pacific Sky* off Isle of Pines, New Caledonia, 2004. (Jonathan Boonzaier)

Length: 240.31m   **Gross tonnage:** 46,087
Propulsion: Twin Screw   **Engine type:** 4 Turbine, 29,501hp
Built: 1984   **Rebuilt** (most recent): 1992
Passenger capacity: 1,585
Body of water: Adriatic   **Home port:** Venice
Frequency of operation: Cruises   **Period of operation:** All year
Website address: www.pullmanturcruises.com/sky.html
Builders: Chantiers de Nord et del la Mediterranée, La Seyne, France
Engine builder: CNIM, La Seyne, to a General Electric design
Owner: Pullmantur Cruises, Spain
Former names: *Pacific Sky* 2006, *Sky Princess* 2000, *Fairsky* 1988

1982: 6 November: Launched.

1984: 12 April: Delivered to Sitmar Cruises.

  2 May: Entered service cruising from the US West Coast to Alaska.

1988: 14 September: Sitmar taken over by P & O. Renamed *Sky Princess*. Operated for Princess Cruises.

2000: Cruising from Australian ports. Renamed *Pacific Sky*.

2005: December: Sold to Pullmantur, Spain.

2006: February: Operated seven-day cruises out of Singapore to Malaysian and Thai ports under the marketing name of Cruise Asia. These cruises alternated between an eastern and a western itinerary, sailing as far as Phuket and Bangkok respectively.

6 May: Scheduled to be handed over to Pullmantur, the remainder of the cruise season from Singapore, which had been advertised to continue until November, being cancelled. Renamed *Sky Wonder*.

10 May: Left Singapore for Piraeus. Now registered in Malta.

12 June: First cruise scheduled from Piraeus to Venice. She is to offer alternate one-way cruises from Piraeus and Venice, sailing each Monday. Calls will be made at Dubrovnik, Corfu, Rhodes and Mykonos southbound or Santorini northbound.

December to March 2007: Scheduled for cruises from Santos, Brazil.

2007: 18 January: Ran aground on a sandbank in the Rio de le Plata, while heading for Punta del Este, Uruguay. Managed to free herself after 20 hours aground.

Coast

ST PIETRO MICCA

Pietro Micca at Naples 1974. (Author's collection)

Length: 29.11m   **Gross tonnage:** 134
Propulsion: Single Screw   **Engine type:** Triple Expansion, 500hp
Built: 1895   **Rebuilt** (most recent): 1997
Passenger capacity: 30
Body of water: Mediterranean   **Home port:** Fiumicino
Frequency of operation: charters
Website address: www.tecnomar.net/pietromicca/presenti.htm
Builders: Rennoldson & Son, South Shields
Owner: Associazone amici delli Navi a Vapore G L Spinelli
Former names: *Dilwara* 1905

1895: Built as the harbour tug *Dilwara* by Rennoldson & Son, South Shields, Tyneside, England, for the United Steam Tug Co., Gravesend.

1907: Sold to Impresa Giuseppe Fogliotto, Naples. Renamed *Pietro Micca*.

22 March: left Gravesend on her delivery voyage.

5 April: Arrived at Naples after stops en route at Falmouth and Oran.

c.1914–c.1918: Used as an auxiliary minesweeper.

c.1939–43: Used as an auxiliary minesweeper.

1943: At this time owned by Giuseppe Merlino, Naples.

12 October: Requisitioned by British Forces for naval service in the Mediterranean.

1946: 16 January: Returned to her owners.

1952: Boilers converted from coal to oil firing.

1960s: Now owned by Francesco Merlino, Naples.

1970s: Sold to S.AR.GE.NAVI (Societa Armamento Gestione Navi Marittima Srl), Naples.

1987: Major refit. Latterly she was used to provide steam to US warships whilst their own boilers were under repair.

1993: On the sale list. Retained and preservation started by a volunteer group, led by Pierpaolo Giua.

1996: Sold to Associazone amici delli Navi a Vapore G.L. Spinelli, owned by the above volunteer group, for preservation. Restored and now moored at the Tecnomar shipyard at Fiumicino (Rome). G.L. Spinelli was a young volunteer who was killed in a road accident.

1997 and 1999: Made trips to Monte Carlo for a classic boat festival.

1997-2000: Refurbished at the Tecnomar yard at Fiumicino.

Pietro Micca is available for charter both for towage and for passenger trips.

Lakes

PS CONCORDIA

Concordia approaching Como, 2002.

	Length: 53.77m **Tonnage:** 286
Propulsion: Paddle Steamer	**Engine type:** Triple Expansion Diagonal, 600hp
	Built: 1926 **Rebuilt** (most recent): 1977
	Passenger capacity: 600
	Body of water: Lake Como **Home port:** Como
	Frequency of operation: SuO **Period of operation:** July & August
	Website address: www.navigazionelaghi.it/album/flotta/como/concordia.htm
	Builders: Odero, Sestri Ponente
	Owner: Ministero di Trasporti Gestione Navigazione
	Operator: NLC (Navigazione Lago do Como)
	Former names: *28 Ottobre* 1943

1926: Built by Odero, Sestri Ponente. Shipped in sections to Dervio on Lake Como and assembled there as the half-saloon steamer **28 Ottobre** for Società Lariana for service on that lake. Unusually for a steamer, she and **Patria** have Caprotti valve gear on their triple expansion machinery.

2 November: Launched. Towed to Tavernola for fitting out.

1943: 25 July: Renamed **Concordia**.

1944: November: Laid-up under camouflage netting at Isola Comacina, along with seven other steamers, to protect them from the advancing allied troops and allied air raids.

1950: Boilers converted to oil firing.

1952: 21 August: Lake steamers nationalised. Present owners took over.

1973: Not in service.

1974: 18 February to 25 June 1977: Major refit. Aft deck saloon with restaurant added.

Concordia does not see daily service, but is normally used on the 12:00 sailing from Como to Colico on Thursdays in July and August. She also on occasion offers peak season sailings on Sundays, and is available for charters.

PS PATRIA

Patria approaching Bellagio, 1983.

Length: 52.50m   **Gross tonnage:** 329
Propulsion: Paddle Steamer   **Engine type:** Triple Expansion Diagonal
Built: 1926   **Rebuilt** (most recent): 2000
Passenger capacity: 600
Body of water: Lake Como   **Home port:** Como
Frequency of operation: Return to steam 200?
Website address: www.paddlers31.freeserve.co.uk/patria.htm;
    digilander.libero.it/lariana/versione%20inglese/Flotta/Flotta%20Odierna/Patria.htm
Builders: N. Odero, Sestri Ponente
Owner: Provincia di Como   **Former name:** *Savoia* 1943

1926: Built in sections at Odero, Sestri Ponente, and shipped in sections to Dervio. Erected there as the
    half-saloon steamer *Savoia* for Società Lariana for service on Lake Como.
    31 July: Launched.
1942: 16 October: Ran aground near Gravedonna, because of the wartime blackout.
1943: Renamed *Patria*.
1944: November: Laid-up and camouflaged at Isola Comacina, along with seven other steamers, to
    protect them from the allied air attack.
1945: 10 January: Damaged by allied air attack in mid-lake. Five passengers killed and seventeen
    wounded.
1951: 23 June: Return to service after major refit and conversion to oil firing. New shorter white funnel
    added, with a red band and top rather than the previous black one with a broad white band.
1952: August: Lake steamers nationalised. Present owners took over.
1972-73: Major refit.
1983: Short funnel replaced by tall black one with a broad white band.
1990: 28 October: Final trip before withdrawal from service for hull repairs. It was announced that
    she would possibly be converted to diesel propulsion. After considerable opposition, this idea was
    dropped.
1994: Dry-docked at Dervio for hull inspection. No work was done and over the years she got more
    and more derelict.
1999: 17 July: An agreement was signed by the owners, the local and regional governments, a national
    bank, and the Famiglia Comasca, the leading organisation campaigning for her preservation, to preserve
    Patria, retaining her steam machinery.
2004: A plan was announced to sell her to the Provincia de Como for a symbolic 1 Euro. The Provincia
    initially refused to accept this, but she was finally purchased by them late in 2005.
2006: September: Proposed that she be towed to Como to be an exhibit at the Centobarche exhibition
    there from 22 to 24 September but in the event this did not take place, ostensibly on the grounds that
    it would be 'too expensive and dangerous'.

PS PIEMONTE

Piemonte departing Locarno 1977.

Propulsion: Paddle Steamer

Length: 51.20m   **Gross tonnage**: 273
Engine type: Compound Diagonal, 440hp
Built: 1904   **Rebuilt** (most recent): 1974
Passenger capacity: 500
Body of water: Lake Maggiore   **Home port**: Arona
Frequency of operation: Sundays only
Website address: www.navigazionelaghi.it/album/flotta/maggiore/piemonte.htm
Builders: Escher Wyss, Zürich
Owner: Ministero di Trasporti Gestione Navigazione
Operator: NLM (Navigazione Lago Maggiore)
Former name: *Regina Madre* 1948

1904: Built by Escher Wyss, Zürich for service on Lake Maggiore.

1948: Renamed **Piemonte**.

1961–65: Major refit at the yard at Arona.

1973-74: August: Major refit at the yard at Arona.

1975: Used on the Arona to Locarno service.

1976, 1977: Used for lunch cruises from Locarno on several days per week.

1978 onwards: Mainly used for charters, with one annual public cruise on 15 August public holiday.

2001: October: Final sailing before major refit.

2006: 13 May: Returned to service on a special inaugutraion cruise not open to the general public.

    In Summer 2006, **Piemonte** was offering 3-hour cruises from Arona at 12:30 and 16:00 every Sunday in July and August.

There are five surviving formerly operational paddle steamers on the Italian Lakes, two in static use, two converted to paddle motor vessels, and one converted to a screw motor vessel:

Lombardia, built in 1904 and withdrawn in 1958, is in use as a restaurant at Arona on Lake Maggiore.

Plinio, built in 1903 and withdrawn in 1963, was for many years used as a yacht club headquarters at Colico, near the north of Lake Como, and is now a floating restaurant at Verceia on Lake Mezzola in a small lake a couple of miles north of the northern end of Lake Como.

Milano was built in 1904 as a paddle steamer for use on Lake Como. In 1926 she was converted to a screw motor vessel, yet retaining her sponsons, and in recent years has had her tall 'steamer' funnel reinstated, so that from a distance she looks like a paddle steamer.

G Zanardelli was built in 1903 for service on Lake Garda and was converted to diesel-hydraulic propulsion in 1980.

Italia was built in 1908 and was similarly converted in 1975-6.

Both Lake Garda paddlers see service on scheduled sailings, mainly at the south end of the lake from Desenzano and Sirmione to Maderno.

19 Monaco

TSY DELPHINE   **Registered in Madeira**

Delphine undergoing restoration at Bruges, 1998.

Length: 78.60m   **Gross tonnage**: 1,950
Propulsion: Twin Screw   **Engine type**: 2 Quarduple Expansion, 3,000hp
Built: 1921   **Rebuilt** (most recent): 2003
Passenger capacity: 28
Body of water: Mediterranean   **Home port**: Monaco
Frequency of operation: Charters
Website address: www.ssdelphine.com
Builders: Great Lakes Shipbuilding & Engineering Co., River Rouge, Mi., USA
Owner: Ineke Bruynooghe
Former names: *Dauntless* 1997, *Delphine* 1968, **HMS** *Dauntless* 1946, *Delphine* 1942

1920: Ordered as a private steam yacht for Horace Dodge of the Dodge automobile company. Named after his daughter and intended as a gift for his wife. The interiors were designed by Tiffany.

1921: 2 April: Launched. Sadly both Horace Dodge and his brother had died during the building period. *Delphine* was inherited by his widow Anna. She mainly sailed in the Great Lakes area, but occasionally sailed to the Atlantic Ocean and on to Florida, the Caribbean and even Hawaii for the winters. At that time, she was the largest vessel to pass through the Welland Canal and pre-Seaway St Lawrence River.

1926: Anna Dodge remarried, to Hugh Dillman.

21 September: Caught fire and sank whilst at New York when Mrs Dodge and her new husband were at the opera. Later raised and returned to service after a four-month refurbishment, and modernising of the internal décor, the original mahogany panelling giving way to flat white painted panels.

1940: Sank and was raised.

1942: 21 January: Acquired by the US Navy, renamed **USS Dauntless**. Used as the flagship of Admiral Ernest King, Commander in Chief of the US Fleet and chief of naval operations, mainly moored in Chesapeake Bay. President Roosevelt, Sir Winston Churchill, General Eisenhower and Josef Stalin were all reportedly on board at different times during this period.

1946: 22 May: Re-purchased by Anna Dodge. Refitted for use as a yacht. Renamed **Delphine**.

1957: Out of service, permanently docked at her private pier with only three of the former fifty-five crew members onboard.

1962: Laid-up at New London, Conn.

1968: Purchased by the Seafarer's Harry Lundeberg School of Seamanship, Piney Point, Maryland, renamed **Dauntless**, with the pennant number PG-61. Used as a training shop for merchant seamen.

1986: Sold to Travel Dynamics, New York City. Restoration planned but never commenced.

1989: Sold to Sea Sun cruises, a French-Singaporean company. Intended for cruises out of Singapore. Sailed to Malta. Major damage to the boiler tubes due to being fed with salt water during her Transatlantic crossing.

1993: Sold to Groupes Georges Michel. Moved to Marseilles. Still no restoration work done on her.

1997: September: Sold to Tiptoe Yachting, a Virgin Islands company, owned by Belgian Jacques Bruynooghe, towed to Bruges, Belgium for restoration. Renamed **Delphine**.

1998: February to July 2003: Restoration took place at Bruges by Longueville NV, including three trips to dry dock, once each at Ostend, Ghent, and Hansweert (NL). New boilers and bow and stern thrusters fitted. Interiors returned to something similar to her original condition, with wood veneer panelling.

2003: August: Steamed to her new home port, Monaco.

9 September: Re-baptised by Princess Stephanie of Monaco.

2004: Summer: Used on charter to Sicily, Corsica, Sardinia and Île d'Hyeres.

Delphine normally spend her winters moored at Monaco and is available for charter in the summer months. She is unique in having the last surviving operating large quadruple expansion engine, and is the largest surviving steam yacht in the world.

20 Spain

Coast

SS HIDRIA II

Hidria II at Pontevedra.

Length: 30.5m   **Gross tonnage:** 177.8

Engine type: Triple Expansion, 180hp

Built: 1965   **Rebuilt** (most recent): 2004

Passenger capacity: 120

Body of water: Galician Coast   **Home port:** Pontevedra

Frequency: Occasional public trips   **Period of operation:** Summer

Website address: www.hidria.net

Builder: Astillero do José Roberto e Jihos S.A., Teis-Vigo   **Engine builder:** Compania Trasmediterranea, Valencia, built 1922 for **Hidria I**

Owner: Vapores del Atlantico SL

Remarks: Wooden-hulled

1963-66: Built for Aljibes del Vigo as a water tanker, serving ships anchored there.

1997: Restoration started at Porto Veloxo (O Grove). Originally it was intended to restore her as a sailing ship, before it was decided to restore the steam engine.

2001: Towed to the shipyard of Joaquin Castro, Pontevedra for further work.

2005: Restored and returned to steam. Visited various places along the northern and north-western Spanish coast for special events, including Vigo, Muros and Porto Veloxo (O Grove). Normally based at Pontevedra.

2006: Hull colour changed to green.

Canary Islands

SS LA PALMA

La Palma awaiting restoration 1997.
(Salvador Cervantes)

Length: 67.1m   **Gross tonnage:** 894
Engine type: Triple Expansion, 140hp
Built: 1912   **Rebuilt** (most recent): pending
Passenger capacity: 190
Body of water: Canary Islands   **Home port:** Santa Cruz de Tenerife
Frequency: Undergoing restoration
Website address: www.correillolapalma.com/index.php?lang=2
Builder: W. Harkness & Son Ltd, Middlesbrough, England
Engine builder: McColl & Pollok, Sunderland
Owner: Cabildo Insular de Tenerife
Operator: Associacion pro Restauración Corriello 'La Palma'

1912: Built as **La Palma** for Cia de Vapores Correos Interinsulanos Canarios, Las Palmas, a subsidiary of Elder Dempster Lines. Used on inter-island and coastal mail, passenger and cargo services in the Canary Islands.

24 April: Arrived Las Palmas.

1930: Owners sold to Cia Trasmediterranea.

1936-38: Used as a transport during the Spanish Civil War. Made some sailings with troops from Santa Cruz de Mar Pequeña, Ifni (then under Spanish occupation, now in Morocco) to Vigo.

1938: Inter-island railings recommenced.

1950: October: Converted from coal to oil firing.

1951: Wheelhouse fitted.

1963: Passenger accommodation modernised with en suite facilities on some cabins.

1976: 17 March: Laid-up at Las Palmas after a boiler failure.

  12 November: Sold at auction to Mrs H. Flick.

1982: December: Reported moored in a marina at Las Palmas for possible use as a floating yacht club.

1986: 13 March: Donated to Cabildo Insular de Tenerife, intended to become the Museo de la Navegaceon Canarias. Towed to Santa Cruz de Tenerife and placed on land at the NUVASA yard there. Political changes meant that little work was done after the first year or so, and she lay for fourteen years becoming derelict.

2003: Associacion Pro Restauracion y Conservacion Corriello La Palma (Association for the restoration and conservation of the mail steamer La Palma) founded to lobby island authorities for the restoration of the steamer.

2005: June: Restoration to operating condition commenced. Bow thruster to be added. Restoration is expected to be completed by 2007.

Cruise Ships

TSS OCEANIC

Length: 238.44m   **Gross tonnage:** 38,772
Propulsion: Twin Screw   **Engine type:** 4 Turbine, 60,500hp
Built: 1965   **Rebuilt** (most recent): 1985
Passenger capacity: 1056
Body of water: Barcelona   **Home port:** Western Mediterranean
Frequency of operation: Cruises   **Period of operation:** March to December
Website address: www.pullmanturcruises.com/oceanic.html
Builders: Cantieri Riunuti del Adriatico.Monfalcone
Engine builder: De Laval
Owner: Club Vaccaciones   **Operator:** Pullmantur Cruises
Former names: (*Big Red Boat 1*), *Starship Oceanic* 1998, *Royale Oceanic* 1985, *Oceanic* 1985

1963: 15 January: Launched.
1965: 31 March: Maiden Voyage for Home Lines from Genoa to New York.
24 April: First cruise from New York to Bahamas.
1985: Sold to Premier Cruise Lines, Nassau; renamed *Royale Oceanic*, later that year *Starship Oceanic*.
1986: 25 April: First cruise for Premier from Port Canaveral to the Bahamas
1998: Renamed *Oceanic*. Marketed as *Big Red Boat 1*.
2000: September: Arrested at Freeport with bankruptcy of Premier Cruise Lines.
30 December: Sold to Pullmantur Cruises, Spain.
2001: May: First cruise for Pullmantur from Barcelona.

Oceanic offers weekly cruises around the Western Mediterranean from Barcelona from March to December, sailing each Monday with calls at Villefranche, Livorno, Civitavecchia, Naples and Tunis.

21 Turkey

SY GONCA

Gonca at Istinye on the Bosphorus, 2001.

Length: 33.00m   **Gross tonnage:** 270
Propulsion: Single Screw   **Engine type:** Triple Expansion, 350hp

Built: 1910   Rebuilt (most recent): 1997
Passenger capacity: 6
Body of water: Bosphorus   Home port: Istanbul
Frequency of operation: Charters
Website address: deneme.yore.com.tr/koc/www_setur2/english/gonca.html
Builders: Unknown, GB
Engine builder (if different from builder): unknown, UK
Owner: Rahmi M Koc Museum
Former name: *Selanik*

1909 or earlier: Built at an unknown UK yard for Selanik Liman Isletmesi as the tug *Selanik* for service
   at Selanik, now Salonika in Greece.
1911: September: Seized by the Ottoman navy, converted to a minelayer.
   December: Recommissioned, based at Selanik.
1912: 27 November: Left Selanik for Canakkale.
1924: Laid-up at Gölcük.
1927: Renamed *Gonca*, became a tender to the Turkish Navy. Used as a ferry to bring workers from
   Istanbul to and from the Gölcük naval base.
1959: Major refit.
c.1989: Out of service.
1992: Sold to Rahmi M. Koc. Camper and Nicholson, Gosport, UK, commissioned to oversee the design
   of a conversion to a charter yacht. Restoration continued at the Halic Yard.
1994: Moved to Tuzla.
1997: Returned to service as a charter yacht.
2004: Noted moored at the Rahmi M. Koc Industrial Museum. It has been reported that she is offering
   short cruises from there.

TSS GUZELHISAR

Guzelhisar departing Kocatas in her last year in
service as a Bosphorus ferry, 1986.

Length: 46.40m   Gross tonnage: 453
Propulsion: Twin Screw   Engine type: 2 Triple Expansion, hp
Built: 1911
Body of water: Bosphorus   Home port: Tuzla
Frequency of operation: Awaiting restoration
Builders: Hawthorn Leslie, Hebburn
Owner: Koc Industrial Museum

1911: Built for Sirket-I Hayriye for Bosphorus ferry service. Also known as **Bosphorus No 68**.

At some stage, a saloon was created on her open upper deck, firstly on the after section and then it was extended forwards to below the wheelhouse.

1944: 1 July: Company nationalised; owners became part of Turkish Maritime Bank.

1986: 12 December. Was the last of the tall-funnelled ferries from the early years of the twentieth century to remain in service. Laid-up at Pendik.

1991: Towed to Hasköy shipyard for reconstruction as a museum ship Hull stripped but no further work done.

1994: Purchased by Ramhi M. Koc Industrial Museum. Towed to Tuzla.

1996: Grounded and partly sunk by heavy weather at Tuzla.

1997: Refloated and laid-up at Tuzla. No further work carried out.

It is proposed that **Guzelhisar** be restored, although it is uncertain if this will be for static or operational use.

TSS INKILAP

Inkilap at Kadiköy, 2001.

Length: 69.87m   Gross tonnage: 780

Propulsion: Twin Screw   Engine type: Two 4-cylinder Compound, 1,600hp

Built: 1961   Rebuilt (most recent):

Passenger capacity: 1952

Body of water: Bosphorus   Home port: Istanbul

Frequency of operation: Daily   Period of operation: All year

Website address: http://www.clydeshipping.co.uk/viewalbum.asp?folder=Bosphorus+Ferries+from +Fairfield+1961

Builders: Fairfield, Govan   Engine builder (if different from builder):

Owner: Sehir Hatlari Isletmesi

1961: Built by Fairfield of Govan on the Clyde, as part of a group of nine twin-screw steamers for service on the Bosporus. All were fitted with four-cylinder compound machinery, designed by Christiansen and Meyer of Hamburg, and of the Fredrikstad steam motor type.

Normally operated on the Karakoy to Haydarpasa and Kadikoy route across the Bosphorus, a busy commuter route. Occasionally offered summer Sunday relief services to the Princes Islands.

2004: September: Laid-up in the Halic (Golden Horn) along with her three sisters.

2006: Owners privatised and taken over by Istanbul Deniz Otobusleri (IDO).

TSS KANLICA

Kanlica off Karaköy, 1991. (B. Worden)

Length: 69.90m   **Gross tonnage:** 780
Propulsion: Twin Screw   **Engine type:** Two 4-cylinder Compound, 1,600hp
Built: 1961   **Rebuilt** (most recent): 1995
Passenger capacity: 1952
Body of water: Bosphorus   **Home port:** Istanbul
Frequency of operation: Daily   **Period of operation:** All year
Website address: http://www.clydeshipping.co.uk/viewalbum.asp?folder=Bosphorus+Ferries+from
  +Fairfield+1961
Builders: Fairfield, Govan
Owner: Sehir Hatlari Isletmesi

1961: Built by Fairfield of Govan on the Clyde, as part of a group of nine twin-screw steamers for service
  on the Bosphorus. All were fitted with four-cylinder compound machinery, designed by Christiansen
  and Meyer of Hamburg, and of the Fredrikstad steam motor type.
Normally operated on the Karakoy to Haydarpasa and Kadikoy route across the Bosphorus, a busy
  commuter route. Occasionally offered summer Sunday relief services to the Princes Islands.
1993: 13 December: Major fire whilst moored at the Halic yard.
1995: Return to service.
2004: September: Laid-up in the Halic (Golden Horn) along with her three sisters.
2006: Owners privatised and taken over by Istanbul Deniz Otobusleri (IDO).

ST LIMAN 2

Liman 2 at the Rahmi M Koc Industrial
Museum, 2001.

Length: 19.00m   **Gross tonnage:** 50
Propulsion: Single Screw   **Engine type:** Triple Expansion, 170hp
Built: 1935   **Rebuilt** (most recent): 1991
Passenger capacity: 12
Body of water: Halic (Golden Horn)   **Home port:** Istanbul
Website address: www.rmk-museum.org.tr/english/exhibit/marine.html
Builders: Netherlands
Owner: Rahmi M Koc Museum

1935: Built as a harbour tug for TDI Istanbul Liman Isletmesi.

Now preserved at the Rahmi M Koc Museum on the Golden Horn in Istanbul and reportedly used for short tourist trips from there.

TSS TEGMEN ALI IHSAN KALMAZ

Tegmen Ali Ihsan Kalmaz at Karaköy, 2001.

Length: 39.87m   **Gross tonnage:** 780
Propulsion: Twin Screw   **Engine type:** Two 4-cylinder compund, 1,600hp
Built: 1961   **Rebuilt** (most recent):
Passenger capacity: 1952
Body of water: Bosphorus   **Home port:** Istanbul
Frequency of operation: Daily   **Period of operation:** All year
Website address: http://www.clydeshipping.co.uk/viewalbum.asp?folder=Bosphorus+Ferries+from +Fairfield+1961
Builders: Fairfield, Govan
Owner: Sehir Hatlari Isletmesi
Former name: *Ihsan Kalmaz*

1961: Built by Fairfield of Govan on the Clyde, as part of a group of nine twin-screw steamers for service on the Bosporus. All were fitted with four-cylinder compound machinery, designed by Christiansen and Meyer of Hamburg, and of the Fredrikstad steam motor type.

Normally operated on the Karakoy to Haydarpasa and Kadikoy route across the Bosphorus, a busy commuter route. Occasionally offered summer Sunday relief services to the Princes Islands.

Built as *Ihsan Kalmaz*, and later, at an unknown date, renamed *Tegmen Ali Ihsan Kalmaz*.

2004: September: Laid-up in the Halic (Golden Horn) along with her three sisters.

2006: Owners privatised and taken over by Istanbul Deniz Otobusleri (IDO).

TSS TURAN EMEKSIZ

Length: 69.87m   **Gross tonnage:** 780
Propulsion: Twin Screw   **Engine type:** Two 4-cylinder Compound, 1,600hp

Turan Emeksiz at Haydarpasa, 2001.

Built: 1961   **Passenger capacity**: 1952
Body of water: Bosphorus   **Home port**: Istanbul
Frequency of operation: Daily   **Period of operation**: All year
Website address: http://www.clydeshipping.co.uk/viewalbum.asp?folder=Bosphorus+Ferries+from
  +Fairfield+1961
Builders: Fairfield, Govan
Owner: Sehir Hatlari Isletmesi

1961: Built by Fairfield of Govan on the Clyde, as part of a group of nine twin-screw steamers for service on the Bosporus. All were fitted with four-cylinder compound machinery, designed by Christiansen and Meyer of Hamburg, and of the Fredrikstad steam motor type.

Normally operated on the Karakoy to Haydarpasa and Kadikoy route across the Bosphorus, a busy commuter route. Occasionally offered summer Sunday relief services to the Princes Islands.

2004: 8 September: Final service across the Bosphorus. Withdrawn and laid-up in the Halic (Golden Horn) alongside her three sisters.

2006: Owners privatised and taken over by Istanbul Deniz Otobusleri (IDO).

The steamer **Yalova**, one of a group of six steamers built in Holland in 1948, is laid-up at Samsun. She was sold there in 1997 for conversion to a static restaurant ship.

The steamer **Deniz Gûlu**, formerly **Buyukada**, was a restaurant ship in Zonguldak until recently, but is no longer there, with no information as to her fate.

The steamer **Ataköy**, one of the group of nine Fairfield-built steamers of 2001, was sold to KD-Eregli on the Black Sea Coast in 2000. It was intended she be converted to a restaurant ship, but permission was not granted to this, and on 22-23 February 2004, she ran aground, and was partially sunk and was broken up where she lay.

PART 2

THE REST OF
THE WORLD

22 Africa

Surviving steamers on the African continent are confined, as far as is known, to a handful on the Nile in Egypt, a very threatened trio on Lake Victoria and a modern steam launch at Cape Town.

Until recently, the steam tug *Alwyn Vincent* offered harbour trips at Cape Town, South Africa, but she has had a diesel engine fitted, although keeping her steam machinery in situ but non-operational.

The Belgian-built sternwheeler *Luama* was in operation from Ubundu to Kindu on the River Zaire in eastern Congo, then Zaire, at the time of the BBC *Great River Journeys* TV series in 1984, but there has been no more recent news of her, and it must be assumed that she is no longer in operation.

On Lake Malawi, there is a restoration project underway for the steamer *Chauncy Maples* (1899), but as far as is known, there are no plans to fit a steam engine in her.

There were steamers at one time on the River Niger, run by the United Africa Co., but since the end of their operations, there has been no news from there, and I understand all the so-called steamers operating there are diesel powered.

EGYPT

The surviving steamers in Egypt are all, or were all previously, used as overnight cruise steamers on the Nile. It has been difficult to research their history and details of the period between the end of the monarchy in 1952 and recent years are more or less non-existing. There is also a problem in that what the Egyptians may tell you about your history and the historical facts may be different. Most steamers are claimed to originally have been used by King Farouk or King Fuad, when in fact, they may merely have been owned by the governments of these kings.

A couple of working sternwheelers remain on the Nile, *Niagara* and *Indiana*. *Indiana* is now used for river maintenance work, and *Niagara* seems to be in static use. Both were originally in the fleet of the Anglo-American Nile and Tourist Co. which operated a fleet on Nile steamers used for charter work.

SWS IBIS

Ibis laid-up at Cairo, 1996. (B. Worden)

Length: 36.58   **Gross tonnage**: 118
Propulsion: Sternwheeler   **Engine type**: Horizontal
Built: 1885   **Rebuilt**: current
Passenger capacity: 28
Body of water: River Nile   **Home port**: Cairo
Frequency of operation: return to steam 200?
Builders: John Elder & Co., Govan   **Owner**: Seti First Travel

1885: Built for Thomas Cook & Son as part of a fleet of stern-wheelers for Wolseley's expedition to rescue

General Gordon from Khartoum. Initially used as a gunboat, later used to carry mails from Asyut to Aswan.

1899: Acquired by the Steamers and Boats Department of the Sudan Government and used on a twice weekly express service from Wadi Halfa to Aswan, as part of a through rail/steamer service from Cairo to Khartoum.

1903: Taken over by Sudan Railways.

1938-9: Used in the film *The Four Feathers* starring Ralph Richardson.

Unknown date: Withdrawn from service when replaced by a motor vessel.

   Laid-up at Cairo for many years.

1996: Noted laid-up at Cairo. She still has a steam chest cover bearing the builders' name.

*c.*1999: Purchased by Seti First travel for conversion to a luxury river cruise vessel.

2006: No longer appear on Seti First's website. Rebuild has been put on hold.

Karim on the Nile, March 2006. (Beat Bolzern)

QWS KARIM

Length: 45.80m   Displacement tonnage: 600
Propulsion: Quarter Wheeler   Engine type: 2 x Compound Horizontal
Built: 1917   Rebuilt (most recent): 1992
Passenger capacity: 34
Body of water: River Nile   Home port: Luxor/Aswan
Frequency of operation: Weekly cruises   Period of operation: October to April
Website address: www.beo-news.ch/dampf/Regaegyp.htm
www.vjv.com/destinations/africa/egypt/king-fuads-nile-steamer/index.html
Builders: Lytham Shipbuilding & Engineering Co. Ltd
Owner: Spring Tours, Cairo
Former names: *S61*

1917: Built as *S61*, part of a large class of S-class sternwheelers for the Inland Water Transport division of the Royal Engineers. These were built by several different builders.

1918: Towed out to the Persian Gulf, but was still at Alexandria when the war ended. Purchased by the Egyptian Government. Claimed to have been used as a royal yacht by King Fuad and King Farouk.

1952: Claimed to have been used by President Nasser after the overthrow of King Farouk. Latterly saw little service and condition deteriorated.

1991: Purchased by Spring Tours.

1992: Refitted: Put into the Luxor to Aswan cruise circuit and marketed in the UK by Voyages Jules Verne.

1997: Laid-up after the terrorist attack on tourists at Luxor.

2002: September: Returned to service.

Karim offers weekly cruises on the regular Nile cruise circuit from Aswan to Luxor and back.

PS MEMNON

Length: 39.93m   **Displacement tonnage:** 120
Propulsion: Paddle Steamer   **Engine type:** Compound Diagonal
Built: 1904   **Passenger capacity:** 80
Body of water: River Nile   **Home port:** Cairo
Frequency of operation: Undergoing restoration
Website address: http://www.setifirst.com/docs/pboats_memnon.htm
Builders: Unknown, UK   **Owner:** Seti First Travel

1904: Built for Thomas Cook Nile fleet. Probably used for private charter cruises.
1948: 31 October: Following the withdrawal of Thomas Cook from the Nile service, sold to H.E. Aly
   Maher Pacha. Her history for the next twenty-nine years is obscure.
1977: Used under the name **Karnak** in the film of the Agatha Christie novel *Death on the Nile*, featuring
   Peter Ustinov. Subsequently laid-up at Luxor.
Unknown date: Purchased by Seti First Travel.
1997: Moved to Cairo. Rebuilt as a floating restaurant, occasionally sailing.
2005: Rebuilding started.
2007: Expected re-entry to service as a cruise steamer.

TSS MISR

Length: 66m
Propulsion: Twin Screw   **Engine type:** Triple Expansion
Built: 1918   **Rebuilt** (most recent): 2005
Passenger capacity: 52
Body of water: Riven Nile   **Home port:** Luxor
Frequency: Weekly cruises   **Period of operation:** All year
Website address: www.vjv.com
Builder: Lytham Shipbuilding and Engineering, UK
Owner: Voyages Jules Verne

1918: Built as the twin screw tunnel tug **ET7**, for the Admiralty, for the Inland Water Transport fleet of
   the Royal Engineers in Egypt.
   18 July: Sailed for Alexandria.
   8 September: Arrived Alexandria.
After the war she was sold to the Egyptian Government, and at some stage renamed **Misr**. Her history
   is obscure after that. Like all other surviving Nile steames, she is claimed to have been used by King
   Farouk.
1939: Noted as being used for a reception for the Governor of Cairo on King Farouk's birthday.
1992: Noted in a history of Lytham Shipbuilding and Engineering as being under restoration at that
   time.
2005: Voyages Jules Verne announced that **Misr** was being fully restored by them and would be operating
   weekly cruises from Luxor to Aswan and back from 7 November.
   November: Cruises now scheduled to start in October 2006, the delay is claimed to be because of
   problems with the steam plant.
2006: 2 October: Weekly cruises scheduled to start. These will continue year-round.

An illustration of **Misr** indicates that she appears to be a modern Nile cruise ship built on an old hull.

PS NILE PEKING/TIME MACHINE

Time Machine at Aswan, 1996. (B. Worden)

Length: 42.00m   **Displacement tonnage:** 500
Propulsion: Paddle Steamer   **Engine type:** Compound Horizontal, 90hp
Built: 1908   **Rebuilt** (most recent): 1996
Passenger capacity: 38
Body of water: River Nile   **Home port:** Cairo
Frequency of operation: Twice daily
Website address: http://myweb.tiscali.co.uk/tramways/TimeMachine.htm
www.touregypt.net/featurestories/dinnercruise.htm
www.peking-restaurants.com/branches.html
Builders: Alley & McLellan, Glasgow, #525
Engine builder: Rankine, Birmingham 1908
Owner: S. Gummieh, Helipolis, Cairo
Former names: *Time Machine*, *T M Mahasen*

1908: Claimed to be built for the Egyptian Royal Family and later reportedly used by King Farouk as a yacht. Other sources claim she was built in 1906.

1952: Taken over by the Egyptian Government on the end of the monarchy. Used as a state yacht for Presidents Nasser and Sadat.

1982: Auctioned off, rebuilt as a river cruise ship. Used on tourist cruises from Luxor to Aswan, renamed *Time Machine*. Owners at this time were SS Time Machine Co., Heliopolis, Cairo.

1996-97: Marketed in the UK by Voyages Jules Verne.

1999: October: Moved to Cairo. Refitted as the Chinese restaurant *Nile Peking*, although this renaming may not be official. Believed to operate cruises up to twice a day.

PS SUDAN

Sudan at Esna, 1996. (B. Worden)

Length: 68.60m   **Displacement tonnage**: 519
Propulsion: Paddle Steamer   **Engine type**: Triple Expansion Diagonal, 500hp
Built: 1921   **Rebuilt** (most recent): 1994
Passenger capacity: 46
Body of water: River Nile   **Home port**: Aswan
Frequency of operation: Weekly cruises   **Period of operation**: All year
Website address: www.steam-ship-sudan.com;
      www.vdm.com/vdm/voyages/annonce/annonce-sudan.asp
Builders: Bow McLachlan, Paisley
Owner: Voyages du Monde, France
Remarks: Also has diesel thrusters with Schottel propulsion

*c.*1916: Construction started, but was presumably delayed by the war. (This is based on the yard number.)
1921: Built for Thomas Cook Nile fleet as a sister ship to **Arabia** (1912) and **Egypt** (1908), both built by Thornycroft. All three were used on the Cairo to Aswan service, the return voyage taking twenty days thus enabling a weekly service to be offered, sailing each Wednesday.
1939: Service withdrawn on the outbreak of war.
1950: 14 March: Following the withdrawal of Thomas Cook from Nile service, sold to H.E. Fouad Serag El Din Pasha (Egyptian Minister of Finance).
1950s: Sold to Mrs Zeinah El Wakil, wife of the Egyptian Prime Minister.
  Renovated in the shipyard of Ahmed Aboud.
1961: Taken over by the Egyptian Government, handed over to Egyptian Hotels Co. SAE.
Unknown date: Operated by tour company Eastmar.
Unknown date: Purchased by Anny International Co. for Touristic Investment, a sister company of Seti First Travel.
1992. Rebuild commenced.
1994: Rebuild completed. Diesel bow and stern thrusters added. Entered service on the Luxor to Aswan cruise circuit. Operated by Seti First Travel.
1997: Cruises offered by Tjaereborg Germany.
2003: Purchased by French tour operator Voyageurs du Monde.
2004: Used under the alias of **Karnak** in the ITV film of *Death on the Nile*, starring David Suchet.

Sudan operates alternate four and five day cruises from Luxor to Aswan and vice versa.

The owner's website erroneously states that **Sudan** was built in 1887, but there has been some confusion there with an earlier **Sudan**.

KENYA

ST KAVIRONDO

Length: 30.50m   **Gross tonnage**: 200
Propulsion: Single Screw   **Engine type**: Triple Expansion, 400hp
Built: 1912
Body of water: Lake Victoria   **Home port**: Kisumu
Frequency of operation: sunk
Builders: Bow McLachlan, Paisley
Owner: Kenya Railways

1912: Built in sections at Paisley by Bow McLachlan. Some sources state that she was built by Fleming and Ferguson, also situated at Paisley.

1913: Built for the Uganda Railway. Manufactured in Scotland in sections, shipped out to Kenya and re-assembled at Kisumu. Used as a tug-cum-passenger vessel on Lake Victoria, towing up to six lighters to serve the smaller settlements on the shores of the northern part of the lake.

1926: Owners renamed the Kenya Uganda Railway.

1927: December: Owners became the Kenya Uganda Railway and Harbours.

1948: Owners amalgamated with the Tanganyika Railway to form East African Railways & Harbours.

1969: Owners became East African Railways & Harbours Corporation.

1978: Owners became Kenya Railways.

1987: Withdrawn and laid-up at Kisumu, where she later sank at her moorings.

Kavirondo is believed to be currently for sale, but it is likely that, if sold, she would be converted to diesel propulsion or scrapped.

TSS NYANZA

Nyanza at Kisumu.

Length: 67.10m   Gross tonnage: 1146
Propulsion: Twin Screw   Engine type: Triple Expansion, 900hp
Built: 1907
Body of water: Lake Victoria   Home port: Kisumu
Frequency of operation: Occasional public trips
Website address: www.schoute.org/mvnyanza.htm
Builders: Bow McLachlan, Paisley   Engine builder: J.S. White, Cowes (unconfirmed)
Owner: Delship Ltd

1907: Built in Scotland in sections for the Uganda Railway, shipped out to Kenya and re-assembled at Kisumu. Used as a cargo steamer on Lake Victoria with accommodation on deck for third-class passengers.

21 December: Launched at Kisumu.

1926: Owners renamed the Kenya Uganda Railway.

1927: December: Owners became the Kenya Uganda Railway & Harbours.

1948: Owners amalgamated with the Tanganyika Railway to from East African Railways and Harbours.

*c.*1964: Fitted with the boilers from the **Robert Coryndon** (1930), which had run on Lake Albert. New, wider, funnel fitted.

1969: Owners became East African Railways and Harbours Corporation.

1977: Owners became Kenya Railways.

1978: Laid-up at Kisumu.

1995: Sold for scrap.

1996: Sold to present owners. Operated from Kisumu to Mwanza.

1998: March/April: Out of service after being replaced by a diesel vessel.

2004: Occasionally steamed, although her owner has plans to convert her to diesel. An unconfirmed report states that she in under conversion to diesel for use as an oil tanker.

SS USOGA

Length: 67.10m   **Gross tonnage:** 1,300
Propulsion: Single Screw   **Built:** 1912
Body of water: Lake Victoria   **Home port:** Kisumu
Frequency of operation: sunk
Website address: http://www.mccrow.org.uk/EastAfrica/EAR&H/EAR_Marine_Division/Marine_
  Division.htm
Builders: Bow McLachlan, Paisley

1913: Built for the Uganda Railway in Scotland in sections, shipped out to Kenya and re-assembled at
  Kisumu. Used on a clockwise round-the-lake passenger service from Kisumu along with sister **Rusinga**,
  which sailed in the opposite direction. She had accommodation for twenty-eight first-class passengers
  in double cabins, sixteen second-class in four-berth cabins and up to 250 deck passengers.
1926: Owners renamed the Kenya Uganda Railway.
1927: December: Owners became the Kenya Uganda Railway & Harbours.
1935: Major rebuild. First-class accommodation enlarged.
1948: Owners amalgamated with the Tanganyika Railway to form East African Railways & Harbours.
1961: Replaced on her round-the-lake service by the new motor vessel **Victoria**. Used on the service
  from Mwanza to Bukoba.
1969: Owners became East African Railways & Harbours Corporation.
1978: Owners became Kenya Railways. By this time **Usoga** was laid-up at Kisumu, where she still
  remains.
1995: Sold for projected use as a floating hotel.

There have been unrealised plans to restore **Usoga** as a museum, but latest reports state that she is in a
sunken condition.

SOUTH AFRICA

SL VICKY

Propulsion: Single screw
Built: SSuX   **Passenger capacity:** 40
Body of water: Cape Town harbour   **Home port:** Cape Town
Frequency of operation: Daily   **Period of operation:** All year (?)
Website address: www.wcities.com/en/record/,165405/147/record.html

Vicky is a small modern steam launch reportedly operating harbour cruises at Cape Town. She is claimed
to be a replica of the **African Queen**.

Surviving steamers in Asian waters are few and far between, with only a handful known to survive of the once numerous fleets of paddle steamers in the Indian sub-continent and in Myanmar (formerly Burma).

BANGLADESH

PS KIWI

Length: 71.60m **Gross tonnage**: 638
Propulsion: Paddle Steamer **Engine type**: Triple Expansion Diagonal, 1,059hp
Built: 1930
Passenger capacity: 1337
Body of water: Pudda River **Home port**: Dhaka
Frequency of operation: Occasional public trips
Builders: Denny, Dumbarton
Owner: Bangladesh Inland Waterways Transport Corporation (BIWTC)
Remarks: Operates in peak traffic times at religious festivals, Coal-fired

1930: Built for India General Navigation and Railway Co. as a sister of *Ostrich* (1929); Shipped from Dumbarton on 16 July. Had a capacity of over 1,300 passengers.
Shipped to India in sections and re-assembled at Garden Reach Workshops Calcutta.
1948: On the partition of India, ownership transferred to Pakistan River Steamers Ltd, Chittagong.
1972: 26 March: On East Pakistan becoming Bangladesh, the steamer fleets were nationalised under the ownership of Bangladesh Inland Waterway Transport Corporation. Operated in the 'Rocket Steamer Service' from Dhaka to Khulna.
*c.*1988: By this time, she was the last surviving steamer in Bangladeshi waters and was only utilised at times of high demand, at religious festivals.
2001: Photographed in a derelict state with her passenger accommodation stripped out.

There are four Denny-built dieselised paddle steamers in operation on the Rocket Steamer service: *Ostrich* (1928), *Mahsud* (1928), *Lepcha* (1937), and *Tern* (1948).

INDIA

Calcutta

TSS SEVA

Length: 73.92m **Gross tonnage**: 1,354
Propulsion: Twin Screw **Engine type**: 2 Triple Expansion
Built: 1963
Body of water: River Hooghly **Home port**: Calcutta
Frequency of operation: for sale
Builders: Simons-Lobnitz, Renfrew **Owner**: Calcutta Port Trust

1963: Built as a survey and salvage tug for use at Calcutta. Also used as a tender.
1999: Reported to be withdrawn from service and awaiting disposal.
2005: Still listed in Lloyds Register.

River Ganges

PS BENARES

Length: 51.80m   Gross tonnage: 281
Propulsion: Paddle Steamer   Engine type: Compound Diagonal, 500hp
Built: 1896   Passenger capacity: 1,400
Body of water: River Ganges   Home port: Munger
Frequency of operation: Occasional public trips
Builders: Bow McLachlan, Paisley
Owner: Unknown

In the 1980s this steamer was reported in the Swiss magazine *Dampfer Zeitung* to have been purchased for preservation and to be offering passengers rips from Munger, possibly renamed as **Prince of Wales**, or having previously been named **Prince of Wales**. No further information has come to hand.

SWS FALTA

Length: 47.50m   Gross tonnage: 200
Propulsion: Sternwheeler   Engine type: Compound Horizontal, 7hp
Built: 1928
Body of water: River Ganges   Home port: Bhagalpur?
Frequency of operation: in service?

JAPAN

SL MICHINOKU RHODE ISLAND

Length: 9.14m
Propulsion: Steam Launch   Engine type: Compound, 12hp
Passenger capacity: 12
Body of water: Japanese coast   Home port: Aomori
Website address: www.steamboating.com/page85.html; www.mtwbm.com/english
Builders: Beckmann Boatshop, Slocum, RI, USA
Engine builder: Strath Steam, Goolwa, Australia
Owner: Michinoku Traditional Wooden Boat Maritime Museum, Aomori

Michinoki RI is a modern launch, built in the USA for use at a the Michinoku Traditional Wooden Boat Museum in Japan. She has a fibreglass hull, painted to simulate wood planking.

SS THE TOPAZ   Panama Flag

Length: 195.10m   Gross tonnage: 32,327
Propulsion: Single Screw   Engine type: Turbine, 30,000shp
Built: 1956   Rebuilt (most recent): 1998
Passenger capacity: 1,364
Body of water: world-wide, based in Japan   Home port: Peace Ship
Frequency of operation: cruises   Period of operation: All year
Website address: www.peaceboat.org; www.maritimematters.com/topaz1.html;

The *Topaz* at Dover, 2001. (Bruce Peter)

www.simplonpc.co.uk
Builders: Fairfield, Govan   **Engine builder**: Pametrada
Owner: Topaz Investments   **Operator**: Peace Boat
Former names: *Olympic* 1997, *Fiesta Marina* 1994, *Carnivale* 1993, *Queen Anna Maria* 1975,
Empress of Britain 1964

1955: 22 June: launched by HM Queen Elizabeth II as **Empress of Britain** for Canadian Pacific Steamships Ltd, Liverpool.

1956: 3-10 March: Sea trials.

20 April: Maiden voyage Liverpool-Montreal.

1956-64: Summer service Liverpool-Greenock-Quebec-Montreal; winter service Liverpool-Saint John, NB.

1960: 15 January: First cruise, New York to West Indies.

1962: 13 February: First cruise from Liverpool.

1963: 23 October: Chartered to Travel Savings Association for cruises from UK and South Africa.

1964: 18 November: Sold to Greek Line, renamed **Queen Anna Maria**.

November to 6 March 1965: Rebuilt by Mariotti, Genoa, passenger capacity increased from 894 to 1,145.

1965: 24 March: First voyage Piraeus-New York, later ran from Haifa to New York. Also offered cruises.

1975: 22 January: Laid-up at Piraeus.

December: Sold to Carnival Cruise Lines, renamed **Carnivale**. Overhauled by Newport News Shipbuilding & Engineering, Newport News, maximum passenger capacity now increased to 1297. Panama flag.

1976: 7 February: First cruise out of Miami to the Caribbean.

1984: 26 May: First cruise from Miami to the Bahamas.

1990: June: Transferred to Bahamas flag; home port now Nassau.

1993: October: Operating for Fiestamarina Cruises, Nassau, a subsidiary of Carnival. Renamed **Fiesta Marina**.

1994: May: Sold to Epirotiki Lines, Piraeus. Renamed **Olympic**.

1996: Epirotiki merged with Sun Lines to form Royal Olympic Cruises.

1997: Sold to Thomson Cruises, renamed **The Topaz**.

1998: 19 January: Arrived at Skaramanga, Greece for rebuilding.

Registered owners now Topaz International Shipping. Panama.

Used on Mediterranean cruises.

2003: Summer: Chartered to Peace Boat, Japan.

2006: Charter extended to 2008.

The Disney Theme Park at Tokyo has a sternwheeler named **Mark Twain**, similar to the sternwheelers at Disneyland California, Disney World, Florida and Euro Disney, France. I have been unable to ascertain whether this is steam-powered, but have come across a comment that engine parts of the sternwheeler **Admiral Joe Fowler**, which was then being broken up, were shipped to Japan in 1980.

Two small 20ft open steam launches, **American Beauty** and **Courageous** were supplied to Disney Tokyo by Beckmann Boatshop of Maine, USA, but I have been unable to ascertain if they are in service and carrying passengers.

MYANMAR

PS MYAT YADANA

Myat Yadana at Bagan/Pagan, 2007.

Length: 62.36m   Gross tonnage: 427
Propulsion: Paddle Steamer   Engine type: Triple Expansion Diagonal, 98.5netthp
Built: 1948   Rebuilt (most recent): 2002
Body of water: River Ayeyarwady (Irrawaddy)   Home port: Bagan (Pagan)
Frequency of operation: dinner cruises
Website address: www.phwasawtravel.com
Builders: Yarrow, Scotstoun
Owner: Phwaw Saw Typical Village Travels and Tours (U Khin Maung)
Former names: *Minthamee*

1947: Built as **Minthamee**, one of a class of eight M-class sister ships built for the Irrawaddy Flotilla to replace steamers lost during the war. Four steamers were built by Dennys and four by Yarrows.
   December: Shipped to Rangoon. The machinery had been shipped in October.
1948: 4 January: Burma became independent. The steamers of the Irrawaddy Flotilla Co. were taken over by the Burmese Government.
1949: Entered service on the Rangoon to Mandalay Express service.
Unknown date: Renamed **Myat Yadana**.
1970s: The only one of its class to retain steam propulsion, the other steamers being converted to diesel, with Hydromaster units replacing the paddles.
Unknown date: Owned by General Ne Win and used as his private yacht and as a VIP steamer.
Unknown date: Sold to U Khin Maung.
2002: Restored at Simalike Dockyard, Yangon (Rangoon).
2004: Re-entered service on day and evening trips from Bagan (formerly Pagan).

SS SALIN

Length: 32.31m   Gross tonnage: 102
Propulsion: Single Screw   Engine type: Triple Expansion
Built: 1921
Passenger capacity: 92
Body of water: Peoples Oil Industry   Home port: Yangon
Builders: Fleming & Ferguson, Paisley
Owner: Peoples Oil Industry

This steamer is described in Lloyds Register as a passenger steamer. No further information is available.

NORTH KOREA

The paddle steamer **Pyongyang No 1** at Pyongyang, built as a copy of the Dresden steamer **Dresden**, has recently been confirmed to be diesel propelled.

24 Australia

COAST

Surviving steamers at ports on the Australian coast are mainly tugs, with a couple of replica paddle steamers, one large double-ended Scots-built ferry, which has had rather a chequered career since coming out of service over thirty years ago, one steam yacht and one passenger launch.

PS DECOY

Decoy at her berth in Perth. (Julia Deayton)

Length: 25.10m   Tonnage: 187dw
Propulsion: Paddle Steamer
Engine type: 2-cylinder simple expansion horizontal, 15hp
Built: 1987   Passenger capacity: 230
Body of water: Swan River   Home port: Perth
Frequency of operation: SuO, charters   Period of operation: All year
Website address: www.psdecoy.com
Builders: Australian Shipbuilding Industries, South Coogee
Engine builder: Ransome, Sims & Jeffries, Ipswich, UK 1905
Owner: Swan River Paddle Steamers Ltd

1987: Built as a replica of **Decoy** (I), which was built in 1878 at Renfrew, Scotland and shipped out to Australia in sections. She was designed as a harbour tug but on completion was sold for use on the Murray and Darling rivers, based at Mannum. Between 1902 and 1905, she was used as a tug in the South Australian Gulf, and then worked as an excursion steamer at Perth from 1905 to 1909. In the latter year, she was towed back to the Murray, where she was converted to a houseboat in 1932. She is still extant in derelict condition on the banks of the Murray at Mannum.
28 February: Launched.
6 April: Entered service on the Swan River.
1989: December: Sold.
1990: December: Repossessed by her original owners.
2007: 14 January: Rammed the Canning Bridge on the Swan River and got stuck under it for a while.

Decoy offers public Riverboat Jazz cruises each Sunday afternoon as well as charters. She is the first paddle steamer to operate on the Swan River since 1927.

SL ELIZABETH ANNE I

Elizabeth Anne I on the Yarra at Melbourne, 2005. (Roderick Smith)

Length: 12.10m
Propulsion: Single Screw   **Engine type:** Compound, 50hp
Built: 1993   **Passenger capacity:** 12
Body of water: Yarra River   **Home port:** Melbourne
Frequency of operation: Regular   **Period of operation:** Year round?
Website address: www.steamengine.com.au/steam/water/elizabeth_anne/
Builders: Devonport, Tasmania
Engine builder: Mare Island Naval base, San Francisco, Ca. USA, 1918
Owner: Melbourne River Cruises
Remarks: Wood-fired
Former name: *James Goodwin*

1993: Built as ***James Goodwin*** for Kevin Pearce for use on the Gordon River, Tasmania, in connection with his floatplane business. Fitted with a US Navy Tyne M Compound engine.
1999 (or earlier): Owners licence revoked due to competition with other operators.
2000: Purchased by Southgate River Tours for service on the Yarra River at Melbourne, after lying idle for a year.
2002: Sold to Melbourne River Cruises, although not operated as part of their excursion fleet.

Elizabeth Anne I is used on river tours on the Yarra River in Central Melbourne, with a 1-hour cruise upstream from Southbank at 11:00 daily.

SY ENA

Ena off Sydney Opera House.

Length: 30.50m   **Gross tonnage:** 65
Propulsion: Single Screw   **Engine type:** Compound, 24nhp
Built: 1901   **Rebuilt** (most recent): 1986

Passenger capacity: 45
Body of water: Sydney harbour   Home port: Sydney
Frequency of operation: Charters
Website address: www.enasteamyacht.com.au
Builders: Ford, Berry's Bay, Sydney   Engine builder: 1984
Owner: Marlou Mistral Incorporated
Former names: *Aurore*, *Ena* 1945, HMAS *Sleuth* 1921, *Ena* 1916

1901: Built as the steam yacht *Ena* for Sir James Dibbs. At that time, she was the largest steam yacht in Sydney harbour.

1916: November: Sold to the Royal Australian Navy. Renamed HMAS *Sleuth*. Used as a patrol ship in the Torres Strait.

1917: Used as a naval tender, serving the training ship HMAS *Tingira*. Also used to tow targets for gunnery practice.

1920: February. Purchased by Waterside Chandlery and Shipping Co. Ltd.

1921: Purchased by William Longworth and renamed *Ena*.

1933: Sold to a syndicate headed by Walter Driscoll of Hobart. Moved to Tasmania to carry apples from Huon to Hobart, later withdrawn from service and laid-up in Sandy Bay.

1940: Purchased by the Roche Brothers as a crayfishing boat.

1945: Steam engine removed and replaced by a diesel, but the steam machinery was stored at Hobart. Renamed *Aurore*. Later sold again for crayfishing.

1980: Sold for use as an abalone diver's boat.

1981: 4 March: Sank after hitting a submerged object in the d'Entrecasteux Channel, southern Tasmania. Raised after three months.

1982: February: Purchased by the Hartogen group and towed to Sydney.

1983: Restoration work began.

1986: Restoration work complete, renamed *Ena* and fitted with a new engine which included some parts from the engine of the Hobart River ferry *Excella*, which was similar to the original engine that had been fitted in *Ena*. Renamed *Ena*.

December to September 1987: Completed a circumnavigation of Australia.

1991: Sold at auction to present owners after being repossessed by the bank following financial difficulties of the then owners due to a stock market collapse.

Ena is an excellently restored luxurious steam yacht that is offered for charter in the Sydney area.

ST FORCEFUL

Forceful at Brisbane 2001. (Roderick Smith)

Length: 36.89m   Gross tonnage: 287
Propulsion: Single Screw   Engine type: Triple Expansion, 1,050hp
Built: 1925   Passenger capacity: 100

Body of water: Brisbane River　　**Home port**: Brisbane
Frequency of operation: SuO　　**Period of operation**: April to June
Website address: www.maritimemuseum.com.au/ships/forceful.htm
Builders: Alexander Stephen, Govan, Scotland
Owner: Queensland Maritime Museum, Brisbane
Former names: **HMAS** *Forceful* 1945, *Forceful* 1942
Remarks: Coal-fired

1925: 20 November: Launched for MacDonald Hamilton & Co., Brisbane as a tug.
　21 December: Departed the Clyde on her delivery voyage.
1926: 7 March: Arrived Brisbane. Also used occasionally as a salvage tug.
1927: Ownership transferred to William & Co.
1941: December: Chartered by the British Ministry of War Transport for service in the Middle East.
　22 December: Sailed from Brisbane for the Middle East.
1942: 14 January: Arrived at Freemantle. Due to the entry of Japan into the war, approval for her to sail from Australia was withdrawn and she lay at Freemantle until requisitioned by the Royal Australian Navy.
　16 February: Requisitioned by the Royal Australian Navy as **HMAS** *Forceful*. Based at Darwin, doing local work and towing lighters to Marauke, Dutch New Guinea.
1945: 11 October: Paid off by the navy and returned to her owners.
1961: April: Ownership transferred to Queensland Tug Co. Pty Ltd.
1970: 28 September: Withdrawn from service.
1971: 10 June: Handed over to the Queensland Maritime Museum Association for preservation.

Forceful operates a 6-hour City to Bay excursion most Sundays at 10:00 on two ten-week seasons each year, from April to June and from October to December, with some extra trips on Saturdays and public holidays.

SS JOHN OXLEY

John Oxley on the slipway, 2003. (Author's collection)

Length: 51.20m　　**Gross tonnage**: 544
Propulsion: Single Screw　　**Engine type**: Triple Expansion, 1,400hp
Built: 1927　　**Rebuilt** (most recent): 200?

Body of water: Sydney harbour   Home port: Sydney
Frequency of operation: Undergoing restoration
Website address: www.australianheritagefleet.com.au/JoOx/JoOx.html
Builders: Bow McLachlan & Co., Paisley, Scotland
Owner: Sydney Maritime Museum

1927: Built for Queensland Maritime Board for use as a buoy tender, to service the buoys in Moreton Bay and at other points along the Queensland Coast. Also used as a relief pilot vessel in Moreton Bay for ships using the port of Brisbane.
20 July: Launched.
1943: January: Requisitioned by the Royal Australian Navy.
1946: 24 July: Returned to her owners. Converted to oil-firing.
1968: Withdrawn from service.
1970: Donated to Sydney Maritime Museum.
1973: Last recorded steaming prior to restoration, for the opening of the Sydney Opera House.
1982: Restoration work commenced.
1997: January: Slipped for hull repairs, work which is ongoing on the hull plating at the time of writing.

SS LADY HOPETOUN

Lady Hopetoun with Sydney Harbour Bridge in the background.

Length: 23.50m   Gross tonnage: 38
Propulsion: Single Screw   Engine type: Triple Expansion
Built: 1902   Rebuilt (most recent): 1991
Passenger capacity: 25
Body of water: Sydney harbour   Home port: Sydney
Frequency of operation: Occasional public trips
Website address: www.australianheritagefleet.com.au/LdyHpt/LdyHpt.html
Builders: Ford, Berry's Bay, Sydney
Engine builder: Simpson Strickland, Dartmouth
Owner: Sydney Maritime Museum
Remarks: Coal-fired

1902: Built as a VIP launch for Sydney Harbour Trust. Passengers over the years included King George VI, the Duke of Windsor, The Queen of Thailand and Lord Montgomery of Alamein. Also used as a relief pay boat and a small tug.
1913: A state cabinet meeting was held aboard because of the threat of 'Potential leaks' by the then Premier, Mr Holman.
1916: Carried animals across the harbour to the then new Taronga Park Zoo.
1920s: New coal-fired boiler fitted.
1939-45: Requisitioned for use as a hospital boat in the event of an attack on Sydney.

1965: Replaced by a new vessel.

1966: 18 January: Acquired by the Lady Hopetoun and Port Jackson Marine Steam Museums, now the Sydney Maritime Museum, which had been formed to preserve her.

1965-70: Restoration work under way to make her complete for the 1970 Captain Cook bicentenary celebrations.

1990: Slipped for six months. Copped sheathing on hull removed, engine and boiler removed for complete overhaul.

1996: New boiler installed.

Lady Hopetoun is available for charter on Thursdays, Fridays, Saturdays and Sundays and normally performs a 4-hour cruise on Sydney harbour. Occasional public cruises are offered.

TST LYTTLETON II

Length: 37.50m   **Gross tonnage:** 303
Propulsion: Twin Screw   **Engine type:** 2 Triple Expansion, 1,250hp
Built: 1939   **Passenger capacity:** 200
Body of water: Port Philip Bay   **Home port:** Melbourne
Frequency of operation: For sale
Website address: www.baysteamers.com.au/lyttelton.htm
Builders: Lobnitz & Co., Renfrew
Owner: Bay Steamers Ltd, Melbourne
Former names: *Victoria* c.2004, *Lyttleton II* 1991
Remarks: Tug

1938-9: Built on the Clyde by Lobnitz & Co. Ltd, Renfrew, sailed for New Zealand on completion. Built for Lyttleton Harbour Board for service as a tug.

1939: 8 June: Arrived at Lyttleton after a three-month ten-day delivery voyage of 13,850 miles.

1979: Withdrawn and laid-up.

1981: April: Sold to the Pittwater and Broken Bay Ship Co-op Ltd, sailed across the Tasman Sea to Sydney, arriving on 2 May. Operated excursions from Sydney for a while, then laid-up.

1983: Owners put the ship up for sale.

1984: Owners name now Port Jackson (*Lyttleton II*) Steam Preservation Group Ltd.
Sold to Ned Dawson. Taken to Melbourne with a view of converting her to a cruising restaurant.

1991: Sold to the Victorian Steamship Association. Planned to be rebuilt as a passenger steamer and renamed **Victoria**. Dry-docked with extensive replacement of bottom plates. The name **Victoria** was painted on her hull.

2000: Owners renamed Bay Steamers Maritime Museum.

2004: Renamed **Lyttleton II**. Put up for sale.

DESS SOUTH STEYNE

South Steyne during her brief stay at Melbourne.
(Author's collection)

Length: 67.92m   Gross tonnage: 1203
Propulsion: One Screw each end
Engine type: 4-cylinder Triple Expansion, 3,250hp
Built: 1938   Rebuilt (most recent): 1988
Passenger capacity: 1781
Body of water: Sydney harbour   Home port: Sydney
Frequency of operation: Currently in static use
Website address: http://www.southsteyne.com.au/index1.htm
Builders: Robb, Leith   Engine builder: Harland & Wolff, Belfast
Owner: Brian McDermott
Remarks: 1 screw each end

1937: 14 October: Keel laid.

1938: 1 April: Launched.

18 July: Left Scotland on her delivery voyage.

19 September: Arrived at Sydney.

24 October: Entered service for the Port Jackson and Manly Steamship Co. Ltd on the service from Sydney to Manly. Over the next thirty-six years she made the crossing over 100,000 times, carrying over 92 million passengers.

1953: 1 November: Undertook her first regular ocean cruise, a trip to Broken Bay which she made each Sunday.

1973: 20 May: Final ocean cruise.

1974: 23 August: Final service run to Manly.

25 August: Suffered fire damage while awaiting a decision on her fate.

1975: April: Sold out of service. Sold a further three times prior to 1987, the final one of these being to Bob Kentwell.

1983: November: Towed to Ballina, NSW for restoration.

1988: It was planned that she start operating at Port Phillip. Moved briefly to Melbourne, but never operated there.

1990: December: Sold to Aspan Pty Ltd, Newcastle, NSW.

1991: January: Steamed from Sydney to Newcastle by members of the Victorian Steamship Association. Used at Newcastle as a function venue, and occasionally steamed.

1995: January: Moved to Sydney where she was used as a floating information centre for the 2000 Olympics.

1997: Mid-year: Ceased operating as an Olympics Information Centre.

c.2001: Opened as a restaurant next to Pyrmont Bridge in Sydney harbour.

South Steyne is still steamable but she has not sailed under steam since she was brought to Sydney in January 1995 although she was in steam in 2000 during the period of the Olympic Games, when her whistles and sirens were blown to the delight of the crowds on the quayside.

ST WARATAH

Waratah passing under Sydney Harbour Bridge.

Length: 33.10m   **Gross tonnage**: 132
Propulsion: Single Screw   **Engine type**: Compound, 275hp
Built: 1902   **Rebuilt** (most recent): 1997
Passenger capacity: 49
Body of water: Sydney harbour   **Home port**: Sydney
Frequency of operation: Occasional public trips
Website address: www.australianheritagefleet.com.au/Charter/NCharter.html
Builders: Cockatoo Docks & Eng. Co., Sydney
Engine builder: Ross & Duncan, Govan, Scotland
Owner: Sydney Maritime Museum
Former names: Burunda *c.*1919
Remarks: Coal-fired

1902: 22 May: Launched: Built as **Burunda** for the New South Wales Department of Public Works, based at Newcastle and used to tow dredgers and barges to various ports on the New South Wales Coast.

1906: From this date also used as a relief pilot boat at Newcastle and Sydney.

1914: 3 August: With the outbreak of the First World War she is used as an examination steamer at Newcastle, examining ships entering the port.
Early December: Transferred to Sydney, still used as an examination steamer.
8 December: Involved in a collision with pilot steamer **Captain Cook** off Sydney Heads. Beached at Camp Cove, near Watson's Bay, as she was in sinking condition. Floated off next morning after repairs, back in service within 8 days of the collision.

*c.*1919: Renamed **Waratah**. Now used to lay moorings in Coffs harbour and Byron Bay, also sailed as far afield as Nauru, laying moorings for the Phosphate Commissioners.

1936: From this date no longer used as a relief pilot vessel at Sydney, although she continued to do so at Newcastle.

1939: Again used as an examination steamer at Newcastle.

1940: Back to normal service.

1942: April: Fired on by local shore batteries when she entered Port Stephens. Two sailors wounded.

1948: Restricted to Newcastle harbour because of her age and condition.

1956: Received major refit for use as a buoy tender. New (third-hand) boiler dating from 1929 fitted. Large 3-ton winch and boom fitted. Due to her age and condition, confined to Newcastle harbour. Ceased pilotage duties in this year.

1968: 23 March: Purchased by Sydney Maritime Museum from the Department of Public Works when it was announced that she was to be sold for scrap.

1972: Laid-up at Blackwattle Bay because of lack of funds for her restoration.

1976: October: Slipped briefly at Cockatoo Island. A survey indicated the cost of the minimum repairs necessary would be more than the funds available.

1977: Docked at the museum's newly acquired and restored dry dock at Blackwattle Bay. Restoration work began by museum volunteers. 20% of the hull plating, 100% of the bulwarks and 60% of the deck structure were replaced.

1979: May: Taken out of dry dock.

1981: September: Steamed for the first time under preservation.

1993: January: Passenger certificate issued for forty-nine passengers.

Waratah is an excellently restored steam tug of a bygone era. She rarely offers public passenger sailings, but only charter trips.

ST WATTLE

Length: 24.70m   **Gross tonnage**: 100
Propulsion: Single Screw   **Engine type**: Compound, 300hp
Built: 1933   **Passenger capacity**: 65

Wattle arriving at Portarlington 1986.
(Roderick Smith)

Body of water: Port Philip Bay   **Home port**: Melbourne
Frequency of operation: ThSSuO   **Period of operation**: October to June
Website address: www.baysteamers.com.au
Builders: Cockatoo Docks & Eng. Co., Sydney
Owner: Bay Steamers Maritime Museum
Former name: *Codeco*
Remarks: Also daily in January

1933: Built as the tug **Codeco**, as a training exercise to enable the shipyard's apprentices to remain employed during the Depression.

27 June: Lifted into the harbour by floating crane **Titan**.

1934: Entered service for the Royal Australian Navy, based at Garden Island Dockyard, Sydney, manoeuvring barges within Sydney harbour, and towing targets out to sea during gunnery exercises. Later renamed **Wattle**.

1940: Used for scientific investigations to provide information on the degaussing of ships as protection against magnetic mines.

1969: Placed in reserve.

1971: 4 August: Acquired for preservation by the Lady Hopetoun and Port Jackson Marine Steam Museum, later Sydney Maritime Museum. Used for passenger excursions in Sydney harbour.

1978: September: Donated to the Victorian Steamship Association. Towed to Port Philip, Converted to carry fifty passengers.

2000: Victorian Steamship Association renamed Bay Steamers Maritime Museum.

2004: March Withdrawn from service because of the need of major hull re-plating.

Wattle normally operates an all-day Bay Excursion on Port Philip Bay on a Saturday to Portarlington, and 40-minute cruises from Williamstown hourly from 12:00 to 17:00 on Sundays and Public Holidays. In the summer school holidays she operates seal colony cruises from Rye Pier.

PS WILLIAM THE FOURTH

The *William the Fourth* replica when in service.
(Author's collection)

Length: 26.50m
Propulsion: Paddle Steamer   **Engine type:** Side Lever, 100hp
Built: 1988   **Passenger capacity:** 50
Body of water: Hunter River   **Home port:** Newcastle
Frequency of operation: Awaiting repairs
Website address: www.maritimeworld.net/sn.asp?PageNumber=65
Builders: Raymond Terrace (place), Williams River
Owner: Newcastle City Council & Port Stephens
Remarks: Replica of 1831 steamer, coal-fired

1985: Work commenced on a replica of the 1831 steamer **William the Fourth** for the Australian bicentennial celebrations. The original vessel had been one of the first steamers on the Australian Coast, sailing initially from Sydney to Newcastle and later south to Jervis Bay and north to the Clarence River. She sailed in Australian waters until 1867 when she was sold to China.

1987: 26 September: Launched.

1988: Entered service. She was fitted with telescopic masts and funnel to enable her to pass under low bridges. Ran occasional excursions along the Hunter River from Newcastle, with occasional visits to other places, such as Port Stephens, Port Macquarie and Sydney. At one time **William the Fourth** was providing public cruises on the third Sunday of each month.

2001: Late: Laid-up at Newcastle, needing repairs to the boiler, deck and mast. A group of volunteers was undertaking essential hull maintenance.

2002: December: Taken over by Newcastle City Council as a preservation project, but restoration work has progressed slowly since then. The deck has been replaced and many other parts of the ship restored.

2005: October: It was reported that *William the Fourth* was to be sold, leased or handed over to a community group to help stop her falling into further disrepair.

2006: At the time of writing plans were underway for her to be back in steam by late 2006 to coincide with the opening of a new Maritime Centre/Museum on the foreshore.

ST YELTA

Yelta at Adelaide, 1986. (Roderick Smith)

Length: 31.50m   **Gross tonnage:** 233
Propulsion: Single Screw   **Engine type:** Triple Expansion, 970hp
Built: 1949   **Rebuilt** (most recent): 1997
Passenger capacity: 60+A55
Body of water: Port River   **Home port:** Adelaide
Frequency of operation: four days per week
Period of operation: school holidays
Website address: www.history.sa.gov.au/maritime/vessels/yelta.htm
Builders: Cockatoo Docks & Eng. Co., Sydney
Owner: South Australian Maritime Museum

1949: Built as a tug for Ritch & Smith, Port Adelaide.

1976: November: Withdrawn from service and laid-up.

1980: Sold to Port Adelaide Branch of the National Trust of South Australia.

1985: May: Purchased by the South Australian Maritime Museum. Restoration commenced by volunteer groups.

1988: 13 September. Returned to steam. Slipped for hull repairs.

October: Re-entered water.

1995: September: Passenger certificate issued after further restoration, A passenger canopy and seating had been fitted. Passenger trips started.

Since 1995, **Yelta** has operated Dolphin Seeking cruises four days a week in each school holiday period with two 1-hour cruises each operating day.

Murray River

The Murray River has a good number of preserved paddle steamers, as noted below. The Murray paddlers were a very distinctive type. Propulsion was often by traction engine machinery with the boiler placed between the cylinders. The steamers were, in the main, not built as passenger steamers, but to carry cargo and supplies to the many isolated sheep stations along the length of the river, and to take bales of wool from these places to the railheads for onward transport to the cities. Some were used for towing barges and some for 'snagging', clearance of floating logs and tree branches from the river, a very necessary task on a river that flows through forest areas. The Murray River is navigable for over 1,400 miles from Goolwa to Albury, and over 1,000 miles of each of the tributaries, the Murrumbidgee and Darling, were also navigable.

PS ADELAIDE

Adelaide on the River Murray.
(Author's collection)

Length: 23.30m   Gross tonnage: 58
Propulsion: Paddle Steamer
Engine type: 2-cylinder Simple Expansion Horizontal, 36hp
Built: 1866   Rebuilt (most recent): 1987
Passenger capacity: 49
Body of water: Murray River   Home port: Echuca
Frequency of operation: Daily   Period of operation: Year round
Website address: www.portofechuca.org.au
Builders: Linklater, Echuca   Engine builder: Fulton & Shaw, Melbourne
Owner: Echuca City Council   Remarks: Wood-fired

1866: 27 June: Launched as a cargo-passenger steamer for J.G. Grassie, Poon Boon Station and S. & H. Officer, Murray Downs Station. Used to bring wool and passengers downriver from Swan Hill to Echuca. (According to some sources, the launch date was 27 July.)

1872: July: Sold to D. Blair & Geo McGrowther. Mainly used as a towing steamer, towing timber barges.

1891: June: Sold to Murray River Saw Mills.

1924: Rebuilt. Round paddle boxes replaced with square ones. Rear sunken cabin raised above deck.

1926: July: Sold to McCulloch Carrying Co.

1938: Boiler replaced for the second time.

1957: Taken out of service and laid-up, after the transportation of logs was transferred to motor vehicles.

1959: Sold to A. Rowe, Saw Miller, Paringa, South Australia. He intended to convert her to a sternwheel motor vessel, but fortunately, *Adelaide* was sold before this could be done to her.

1960: Sold to Echuca Apex Club and steamed to Echuca.

1963: Preserved on land at Hopwood Gardens, Echuca.

1982: Restoration commenced.

1984: 2 February: Refloated.

1985: October: Returned to service following full restoration and fitting with round paddle boxes again, operating tourist excursions from Echuca. Re-commissioning ceremony performed by HRH the Prince of Wales as part of the State's 150th anniversary celebrations.

1991: Taken to Barmah for ther 125th birthday. Soon after this, commenced offering passenger trips at Echuca, initially just with twelve passengers.

Adelaide operates 1-hour trips from the Port of Echuca five times daily at 10:15, 11:30, 13:15, 14:30 and 15:45, in conjunction with *Alexander Arbuthnot* and *Pevensey*.

PS ALEXANDER ARBUTHNOT

Alexander Arbuthnot leaving Echuca. (Roderick Smith)

Length: 23.20m   **Gross tonnage:** 46
Propulsion: Paddle Steamer
Engine type: 2-cylinder simple expansion horizontal, 4hp
Built: 1923   **Rebuilt** (most recent): 1994
Passenger capacity: 47
Body of water: Murray River   **Home port:** Echuca
Frequency of operation: Daily   **Period of operation:** All year
Website address: www.portofechuca.org.au
Builders: Felshaw, Koondrock
Engine builder: Ruston, Hornsby & Co., Grantham, UK. 1889 from *Glimpse*, fitted when built
Owner: Echuca City Council   **Remarks:** Wood-fired

1916: Built as a barge.

1923: Converted to a steamer by for Farmers and Citizens Trustee Co., as executors of the estate of A. Arbuthnot. Fitted with the engine and boiler of *Glimpse*. Built to tow log barges to the Arbuthnot Saw Mills.

c.1929: Sold to Arbuthnot Saw Mills, later to Evans Bros.

1942: Sold to Barmah Red Gum Charcoals Ltd, and was used to carry charcoal from the forests, 70 miles upstream at Yielima and Barmah, to Echuca. By this time, she was the last privately owned steamer operating out of Echuca.

1947: Sunk at Yielima.

1973: January: Refloated and moved downriver, then placed on a low loader and taken to Shepparton for preservation. Intended to make tourist trips from Shepparton International Village, but spent most of her time out of service in a small lake there.

1990: February: Purchased by Echuca City Council for the 'Port of Echuca' attraction.

1991: December: Mover to Echuca for restoration. New boiler fitted.

1994: 8 December: Entered service from the Port of Echuca.

1996: 8 June: Caught fire due to a spark from her funnel. Parts of her cabins destroyed.

2002: Withdrawn from service for major boiler repairs.

2004: April: Returned to service for the first time since the fire in 1996. *Alexander Arbuthnot* is now operating regularly from the 'Port of Echuca' and her sailings alternate with those *Adelaide* and *Pevensey*.

PS CANALLY

The hull of *Canally* awaiting the fitting of the paddle wheels and sponsons, 2004. (Roderick Smith)

Length: 28.04m   Gross tonnage: 93
Propulsion: Paddle Steamer
Engine type: 2-cylinder simple expansion horizontal, 20hp
Built: 1907   Rebuilt (most recent): 200?
Body of water: Murray River   Home port: Mildura
Frequency of operation: Undergoing restoration
Website address: www.sunraysia.vic.edu.au/riverboats/murray/Canally.html
Builders: R.W. Beer, Koondrock   Engine builder: Marshall, Gainsborough, UK
Owner: Chislett Families + River and Riverboat Preservation Society
Remarks: To be based at Euston

1907: Built for T.H. Freeman with a 14hp Marshall engine. Manly used as a cargo or towing steamer. Known as the 'Greyhound of the River'.

1922: Owned by W. Tinks.

1924: Owned by Francis & Tinks Ltd.

1925: Sold to Dept. of Public Works, NSW.

1935: Sold to N. Collins.

1942: Machinery removed, converted to a barge.

*c.*1953/4: Sold to Chislett Brothers. Normally towed by **PS Hero** to the owners' sawmill at Boundary Bend.

1957: Sunk at her moorings near Boundary Bend.

1997: Sold to a joint venture between the Chisletts and the Rivers and Riverboat Preservation Society.

1998: January: Hull raised and taken to Mildura for restoration.

2000: April: Restoration work commenced.

2004: July: Hull refloated. Towed to Euston by the replica **PS *Lady Augusta*** for the completion of restoration. A 20hp Marshall steam engine has been acquired for her.

PS CANBERRA

Canberra on the Murray, 1992. (B. Worden)

Length: 22.60m   **Gross tonnage**: 51
Propulsion: Paddle Steamer   **Engine type**: Horizontal, 14hp
Built: 1912   **Rebuilt** (most recent): 2003
Passenger capacity: 150
Body of water: Murray River   **Home port**: Echuca
Frequency of operation: Daily   **Period of operation**: All year
Website address:
    www.travelcentre.com.au/travel/airshows/DC3/photo_gallery_echuca.htm;
    www.emmylou.com.au/About%20Canberra.html
Builders: D Milne, Goolwa
Engine builder: Marshall & Sons, Gainsborough, UK 1923
Owner: Murray River Paddlesteamers Ltd

1912: Built as a fishing steamer for David Connors. Originally has a 12hp Marshall engine.

Prior to 1922: Now used as a cargo steamer out of Swan Hill.

*c.*1945: Sold to N. & M. Collins, Mildura, and converted to an excursion boat to run out of Mildura, later sold to a group from Renmark, who operated her there.

1950s: Used as a houseboat.

1963: Sold to Murray SS & Tourist Co., for passenger trips from Mildura.

1966: 19 November: Purchased by Echuca Tourist Promotion Council.

24 December: Moved to Echuca and commenced operating on excursions there the same afternoon.

1971: November: Diesel engine fitted but steam engine retained in situ. Upper promenade deck fitted.

2001: Sold to Murray River Paddlesteamers Ltd, the owners of ***Emmy Lou*** and the diesel paddler ***Pride of the Murray***.

2002-03: New steam engine fitted, similar to the original and built in 1923 by Marshall of Gainsborough. Diesel removed.

2003: 18 February: First cruise under steam since 1972.

Canberra offers 1-hour cruises from Echuca five times daily at 10:15, 11:30, 12:45, 14:00 and 15:15.

PS COLONEL

Colonel (to the left) undergoing restoration at Murray Bridge, 2003. (Roderick Smith)

Length: 24.10m **Gross tonnage**: 57
Propulsion: Paddle Steamer **Engine type**: to to be fitted
Built: 1895 **Rebuilt** (most recent): 199?
Body of water: Murray River **Home port**: Murray Bridge
Frequency of operation: Undergoing restoration
Builders: Permewan, Wright & Co.
Engine builder: Marshall & Sons, Gainsborough, UK
Owner: S.A. Moritz

1895: Entered service for Permewan, Wright & Co., Sydney as part of a large fleet of paddle steamers on the River Murray.
1919: July: Owners became part of Murray Shipping Ltd.
c.1938: Sold to M. Collins & N. Wallace, latter owned by N. Collins.
c.1942: Engine and boiler removed; hull sold to M. Hoffman for use as a houseboat, which was later moved to Renmark.
1974: September: Acquired by present owner in a sunken condition. Later raised and moved to Murray Bridge, floating on a plastic bag, for restoration on the same slipway on which **Oscar W** was restored.

PS CUMBEROONA

Cumberoona at Albury, 1993. (Roderick Smith)

Length: 25.20m **Gross tonnage**: 200
Propulsion: Paddle Steamer **Engine type**: 2x 2-cylinder horizontal, 16hp (200kw)
Built: 1986 **Passenger capacity**: 200
Body of water: Murray River **Home port**: Albury
Frequency of operation: SSuO **Period of operation**: October to Mid-April

Website address: http://www.cumberoona.com.au/?p1
Builders: Chapple Bros Engineering, North Albury
Engine builder: 2 Pitt Buffalo engines, 1906 & 1909
Owner: Murray River Steam Navigation Co.
Remarks: Wood-fired

1986: 1 March: Launched. Fitted with two second-hand engines on a split paddle shaft, One engine was previously in a portable engine and the other in a traction engine.
1987: 4 January: Entered service as a river cruise vessel based at Albury.

Cumberoona was designed to commemorate the Australian bicentennial in 1988. She normally operates on Saturdays and Sundays and daily in school holidays with three sailings, a 1-hour cruise at 10:00, a 90-minute cruise at 12:00 and a 1-hour trip at 14:00, but sailings can be cancelled if the river is too high or too low. Albury is the highest operating point for paddle steamers on the River Murray.

PS EMMYLOU

Emmylou near Echuca. (Author's collection)

Length: 34.50m   **Gross tonnage**: 92
Propulsion: Paddle Steamer
Engine type: 2-cylinder simple expansion horizontal
Built: 1982   **Passenger capacity**: 20
Body of water: Murray River   **Home port**: Echuca
Frequency of operation: 2-3 day trips   **Period of operation**: All year
Website address: http://www.emmylou.com.au/About%20Emmylou.html
Builders: Anthony Browell and friends, Barham
Engine builder: Marshall, Gainsborough, UK, 1906
Owner: Murray River Paddlesteamers Ltd
Remarks: Wood-fired

1980-82: Built to traditional style for Anthony Browell. Named after the Country and Western singer Emmylou Harris. Fitted with a Marshall engine that had formerly been in a sawmill. Initially used only privately.
1982: Featured in the TV series *All the Rivers Run*, bearing the name **Providence**.
1984: Purchased by Chas McG Carling, Moama, who formed Emmy Lou Enterprises and started using her as a passenger steamer out of Echuca.

Emmylou operates out of Echuca offering two-night cruises in the summer months on Wednesdays and Fridays upstream 65km to Barmah Lakes or downstream 70km to Perricota Station, and short 1-hour cruises at 10:00, 11:15, 13:00, 14:30 and 15:45 on Mondays or Tuesdays.

PL ETONA

Etona at Mannum in 2003. (Roderick Smith)

Length: 18.29m
Propulsion: Paddle Steamer   **Engine type:** 2-cylinder simple, 8hp
Built: 1899   **Rebuilt** (most recent): 1962-65
Body of water: Murray River   **Home port:** Echuca, Vic
Frequency: Private yacht
Website address: murray.anglican.org/murraymissionmemories.htm
Builder: Ross Family, Milang   **Engine builder:** Ransome, Sims & Jeffries, Ipswich
Owner: Rob Symons, Echuca   **Remarks:** Wooden-hulled, coal-fired

1898: Construction began.

1899: Completed for the Church of England Mission. Used as an itinerant floating church, operating between Morgan and either Mannum or Renmark, stopping at communities en route to hold services. Commanded by a minister-cum-captain. A small chapel was provided in the aft saloon. Later an extra cabin was built on the upper deck aft of the wheelhouse.

*c.*1900: The mission was split in two and *Etona* served the Mannum to Chowilla section of the river.

1912: Mission ceased as the river communities had become towns with permanent churches. The chapel equipment was removed and distributed to river-town churches. Sold to Capt. Archie Connor, Boundary Bend, Victoria. Used as a fishing boat on the Murrumbidgee and Lachlan Rivers and occasionally to carry cargo, often fruit during the fruit-picking season.

1930s: By this time the top deck had been removed and the main deckhouse reconfigured.

1944: Abandoned on the banks of the Murrumbidgee River, wheelhouse removed and used as a chicken house.

1956: Reactivated for mercy missions during flooding on the Murrumbidgee, which was at times up to 60 miles wide. Abandoned again after the floods had subsided.

1961: September: Purchased for preservation by Phil Symons and Ian Stewart from Echuca. Sailed to Echuca under her own power.

1965: Restoration completed. Restored to original condition externally, and internally with several cabins.

1999: Sailed to Milang to celebrate the centenary of her building.

2001: Was the only paddle steamer to do the whole Centenary of Federation cruise from Echuca to Goolwa.

Etona is normally moored at Echuca. She does not offer public passenger trips and is used as a private yacht by her owners.

PS GEM

Length: 40.00m   **Gross tonnage:** 228
Propulsion: Paddle Steamer   **Engine type:** Compound Horizontal, 40nhp
Built: 1876   **Rebuilt** (most recent): 2005

Gem at Swan Hill in 1963 before the channel from her basin to the river was filled in. (R. Smith collection)

Passenger capacity: 52
Body of water: Murray River   **Home port**: Swan Hill
Frequency of operation: Undergoing restoration
Website address: www.pioneersettlement.com.au/ps_gem.html
Builders: Air & Westergaard, Moama
Engine builder: Davey Bros, Ballarat 1877
Owner: Swan Hill Pioneer Settlement

1876: Built as a barge for E.C. Randell.

1877: Engines and superstructure fitted. Used as a cargo steamer, her first voyage being from Echuca to Goolwa and return.

1878: 25 September: Sold at auction to E.P. Sabine, who operated her as a cargo boat from Blanchetown to Wentworth via Morgan.

1879: April: Sold to Hugh King & Co., used for this year on the Darling from Wentworth to Wilcannia.

1882: February to June. Lengthened by 40ft at Goolwa. New superstructure with cabin accommodation for 100 passengers added. Operated a service from Morgan to Wentworth and Mildura between June and December.

1888: November: Engine compounded, new boiler fitter. Sold to Hugh King, who was the captain for many years, and G. Chaffey.
December: Sold to Murray River Navigation Co. and H. King.

1889: March: Murray River Navigation Co. now sole owners.

1909: 22 November: Gem Navigation Co. formed, joining the fleets of Benjamin Chaffey and Landseer and that of the Murray River Navigation Co.

1918: January: Sailing Murray Bridge to Renmark.

1919: 17 November: Gem Navigation Ltd joined with other firms to form Murray Shipping Ltd.

1939: Major rebuild to refit her for the tourist trade. Mainly used from Morgan to Mildura, sometimes in connection with coach tours. Laid-up at Morgan during the war years until 1946.

1948: November: Sank after she was snagged at Cal Lal.

1949: 26 September: Returned to service.

1953: August: On the liquidation of Murray Shipping Ltd, sold to A.H. Wilkins. Moved to Mildura and used as a boarding house.

1954: Laid-up.

1962: Towed to Swan Hill by **Oscar W** and placed on land to become the centrepiece of the Swan Hill Pioneer Settlement. Converted to a restaurant and Art Gallery in a small pool at the entrance to the museum.

1998: Restoration commenced. The eventual aim of this is to get her back into survey standard, which should mean that she will return to steam on the Murray.

PS HERO

Length: 28.10m   **Gross tonnage**: 82
Propulsion: Paddle Steamer
Engine type: 2-cylinder simple expansion horizontal, 28hp

Hero undergoing restoration at Echuca, 2003.
(Roderick Smith)

Built: 1874   **Rebuilt** (most recent): 2000
Body of water: Murray River   **Home port**: Echuca
Frequency of operation: Charters
Website address: www.steamengine.com.au/steam/water/hero/index.html
Builders: G. Linklater, Echuca   **Engine builder**: Still to be installed
Owner: G. Byland
Remarks: Raised from riverbed

1874: 16 September: Launched for J. Maultby for use on the upper Murrumbidgee as a towing and cargo steamer.

*c.*1891: Sold to D. Stratton & Co., later sold to Permewan Wright & Co. and returned to sail out of Echuca. Again later sold to Chislett Bros and used as a towing steamer for their sawmill at Boundary Bend, where she worked until the 1940s, when she was laid-up.

1956: Reactivated after a spell abandoned at Boundary Bend and used to rescue cattle during a major flood.

1957: 19 January: Burnt at Boundary Bend and was deliberately sunk to extinguish the fire.

1986: Sold to G. Byford, Strathmerton, to be raised, although no work was done on raising her.

1998: Raised and taken to Echuca for restoration on land.

2001: 13 September: Refloated. Restoration continued, with the re-building of the passenger accommodation and wheelhouse.

2002: 9 November: Boiler re-installed. After forty-one years submerged the engine was found to be unusable, and a new replica engine is to be built and installed.

2007: 31 May: Steamed for the first time since restoration.

It is reported that **Hero** will be used as a floating hotel when restoration is completed.

PS INDUSTRY

Industry at Clayton, 2004. (Roderick Smith)

Length: 34.10m   **Gross tonnage**: 91
Propulsion: Paddle Steamer
Engine type: 2-cylinder simple expansion horizontal, 30hp
Built: 1911   **Rebuilt** (most recent): 1991
Passenger capacity: 65
Body of water: Murray River   **Home port**: Renmark

Frequency of operation: First Sunday each month except May, which is 2nd Sunday
Period of operation: All year
Website address: www.renmarkparinga.sa.gov.au/site/page.cfm?u=136
Builders: G.B.Wilson, Goolwa
Engine builder: P.A. Roberts & Sons, Bendigo, Victoria
Owner: Corporation of the Town of Renmark
Remarks: Ex Govt Workboat, wood-fired

1911: January: Built as a workboat to the design of A.J. Inches for the Engineering and Water Supply Department of the South Australian Government for use in snagging (clearing tree trunks and logs obstructing the waterway), lock repairs and dredging.
1917: Taken over by the newly formed River Murray Commission.
1933: Extensively refitted and new boiler installed.
1969: October: Retired from service.
1970: Presented to the town of Renmark.
1975: August: Opened as a museum.
1989: Restored to steam, used in the film *River Kings*, disguised as **Lady Mabel**.
1995: 16 July: Commenced service carrying passengers, operated by a Friends Group.

Industry now makes passenger trips from Renmark at 11:00 and 13:30 on the first Sunday of each month, and is supported by 'Friends of the Industry'. At other times she is open to the public.

PS MARION

Marion with *Oscar W* behind her at Mannum, 2001. (Roderick Smith)

Length: 32.90m   **Gross tonnage**: 157
Propulsion: Paddle Steamer
Engine type: 2-cylinder simple expansion horizontal, 120 Ihp
Built: 1897   **Rebuilt** (most recent): 1994
Passenger capacity: 100
Body of water: Murray River   **Home port**: Mannum
Frequency of operation: approximately monthly   **Period of operation**: All year
Website address: www.psmarion.com
Builders: A.H. Landseer, Milang
Engine builder: Marshall, Gainsborough, UK 1900
Owner: Mannum Council
Remarks: Wood-fired, thirty berths

1896: Designed as a steamer for G.S. Fowler, Adelaide. He died before work was finished and she was completed as a barge for D. & J. Fowler Ltd but not used. Lay for sale at Milang.
1897: 16 February: Launched.

1900: Sold to William Bowling, who owned shops at Mildura and Wentworth. Moved to Echuca where the engine and superstructure were fitted.

13 October: Entered service as a hawking steamer (itinerant floating shop). Ran on the Darling River from Wentworth.

1908: 17 July: Sold to Benjamin Chaffey, Mildura. Converted to a passenger–cargo steamer by building up her superstructure, using many parts from the steamer *Pearl*, which was being dismantled at the time. She also carried cargo for the remote communities along the river, and bales of wool. She initially had sleeping accommodation for eight passengers.

22 November: Gem Navigation Co. formed. This was a merger of the Chaffey and Landseer fleets.

1910: September: On a fortnightly Morgan to Mildura service.

1914: Rebuilt as a pure passenger steamer, with accommodation for forty passengers.

1919: 17 November: Gem Navigation Ltd joined with other firms to form Murray Shipping Ltd.

1922: Now sailing from Morgan to Swan Hill.

December to 1923: June: Rebuilt on the slip at Echuca, the passenger accommodation was extended and more berths provided, her funnel moved towards the stern and her engine turned round.

1926: 28 November: Suffered a major fire in her cargo, including 125 cases of petrol stowed on the foredeck, whilst moored at Murray Bridge. Fortunately, there were no injuries and the fire was put out without all the petrol cans exploding. At this time, her service was from Murray Bridge to Berri and Renmark. Repaired after the fire on the slipway at Morgan.

1930: Murray Bridge to Renmark service discontinued. Operated from Morgan to Swan Hill.

1934: December: Made the first of what became regular summer cruises from Morgan, upriver to Renmark, down to Goolwa and back to Morgan.

1940: Major refit. New dining saloon on lower deck added.

1941: Laid-up at Morgan.

1946: Returned to service.

1949-50: 4 new cabins added.

1953: August: Sold to L.M. Arnold following the liquidation of Murray Shipping Ltd the previous year. No longer in regular service.

1958: October: Sold to A.H. Wilkins. Used as a boarding and lodging house at Morgan.

December: Sold to Murray Steamers Ltd. Moved to Berri. The new owners hoped to restore her and return her to service.

1963: 6-10 June: Sailed from Berri to Mannum. Sold to the National Trust of South Australia, placed in a specially built dry dock at Mannum, and used as a museum.

1990: July: Moved from the dock to enable a survey to be made and restoration to commence. Later moved back into the dock.

1994: 26 November: The first stage of her restoration complete, *Marion* was recommissioned and returned to service.

1996: Second stage of restoration completed.

1997: 13-16 March: First long cruise under restoration, from Mannum and Murray Bridge to Goolwa for a Wooden Boat Festival.

2004: Both paddle boxes rebuilt.

2006: May to August: Planned slipping for major hull restoration.

2007: June-July: Major upriver trip planned as far as Wentworth for *Ruby*'s centenary celebrations.

Marion makes both day trips from Mannum and occasional trips upriver of several days, details of which can be found on her website.

PS MELBOURNE

Propulsion: Paddle Steamer

Length: 29.90m   Gross tonnage: 69

Engine type: Compound Horizontal, 25hp

Built: 1912   Rebuilt (most recent): 1965

Passenger capacity: 300

Melbourne on the Murray, 1992. (B. Worden)

Body of water: Murray River   **Home port**: Mildura
Frequency of operation: Daily   **Period of operation**: All year
Website address: www.murrayriver.com.au/boating/paddlesteamers/melbourne-rothbury/
  melbourne.htm
Builders: Government Dockyard, Williamstown
Engine builder: Marshall, Gainsborough, UK
Owner: A.E. & F.O. Pointon, Mildura
Remarks: Ex Govt Workboat, wood-fired

1912: Built for the Victorian Government as a snagging steamer and workboat. (Snagging is the clearance of logs obstructing the waterway.) Based at Echuca and occasionally used for excursions.
1924: 19 November: Withdrawn from service and laid-up.
1939: Used to clear a log jam of 2,000 tons of logs at Torrumbarry Weir.
*c.*1940: Sold to Evans Brothers, Echuca Saw Mills. Used towing timber barges to and from the Barmah Forest.
1965: Sold to Albert Pointon, Mildura. Upper deck added and converted to a passenger steamer operating short river trips from Mildura.
1966: 3 January: Made first excursion trip from Mildura.

Melbourne offers cruises from Mildura at 10:50 and 13:50 daily with the exception of Saturday mornings (outside of the school holiday periods). Each cruise lasts 2 hours, 10 minutes.

PS OSCAR W

Oscar W at Goolwa, 2004. (Roderick Smith)

Length: 31.70m   **Gross tonnage**: 83
Propulsion: Paddle Steamer
Engine type: 2-cylinder simple expansion horizontal, 8nhp
Built: 1908   **Rebuilt** (most recent): 1987
Passenger capacity: 15
Body of water: Murray River   **Home port**: Goolwa

Frequency of operation: Occasional public trips
Website address: http://www.woodenboatfestival.com.au/oscarw/index.htm
Builders: Franz Wallin, Echuca   **Engine builder**: Marshall, Gainsborough, GB
Owner: Alexandrina District Council
Remarks: Wood-fired

1908: Built as a cargo and towing steamer for her builder Captain Franz Wallin, and named after his son, who was later killed in the First World War.

1915: Sold to Permewan Wright & Co. Ltd. Used to carry bales of wool.

1919: Owners merged with other operators to form Murray Shipping Ltd.

1942: Sold to Capt. G. Ritchie. Planned to be converted to a passenger steamer to operate out of Goolwa, but wartime restrictions curtailed these plans. Steamed from Echuca to Goolwa.

1943: Sold to P.W. Richards, R. Knox & T.C. Goode.

Sold to Highways and Local Government Department of South Australia, used as a workboat based at Morgan. Often used to take cross-river unpowered car ferries (punts) to Morgan where they were overhauled.

1945: Boiler converted to oil-firing.

1959: Withdrawn from service.

1960: Sold to P. & P. Hogg. Intended to be used as a passenger/cargo steamer out of Mildura. Occasionally operated excursions out of Echuca before settling down in the excursion trade at Mildura.

1962: Towed *Gem* from Mildura to Swan Hill. Due to low water levels she was unable to return upstream for 9 months, during which time she operated passenger trips out of Swan Hill or Echuca.

1964: September: Sold to A. & J. Moritz, then A.E. Moritz, who started major restoration work on the hull.

1975: Placed on the slip at Murray Bridge for re-planking. This work was hampered by lack of funds and the owners advancing years. Converted back to wood-firing.

1984: Owner died.

1986: Purchased by Tourism South Australia, initially for use as a static exhibit as the River Murray Interpretative Centre at Signal Point.

1987: 30 March: Returned to steam, sailed to Goolwa.

1991: Completed a round trip of 2,000 miles from Goolwa to Echuca (1,167 miles each way).

1992: Towed the barge *Dart* from Goolwa to Mildura in a record time of four days, 23 hours.

1996: New boiler fitted.

2001: Taken over by Alexandrina District Council. Three-stage restoration began with the replacement of the aft deck.

2003: Two thirds of the bottom planking and some frames replaced. Sailed to Mildura in September as part of the Randell Cadell 150th anniversary celebration.

2004: July: Remainder of bottom planking and stern post replaced. Sailed upstream to Wentworth for the Junction Rally.

2005: October: Reached Cadell for a school programme.

2007: March: Restoration planned to be completed for the Wooden Boat Festival.

Oscar W often operates with the barge *Dart*. She is supported by the group 'The Friends of the Oscar W'. At the time of writing the only major work remaining to be done is the repair or replacement of the steel upper hull. When back in service, it is planned to steam her once a month, with short day cruises or trips upstream from the lakes, e.g. from Wellington to Murray Bridge.

PS PEVENSEY

Length: 33.80m   **Gross tonnage**: 103
Propulsion: Paddle Steamer   **Engine type**: Compound Horizontal, 20hp
Built: 1910   **Rebuilt** (most recent): 1976
Passenger capacity: 100

Pevensey near Echuca. (Author's collection)

Body of water: Murray River   **Home port**: Echuca
Frequency of operation: Daily★   **Period of operation**: All year
Website address: www.portofechuca.org.au
Builders: Permewan, Wright & Co. Ltd, Moama
Engine builder: Marshall, Gainsborough, GB
Owner: Echuca City Council
Former name: *Mascotte* 1911
Remarks: ★Alternates with *Adelaide* and *Alexander Arbuthnot*, wood-fired

1910: Built for Permewan Wright & Co. Ltd as the barge *Mascotte* because the engine was still in transit from the UK.

1911: Rebuilt as a paddle steamer and renamed *Pevensey*. Used for towing wool barges.

1919: July: Owners became part of Murray Shipping Ltd.

1932: October: Almost destroyed by fire at Koraleigh Landing, near Swan Hill. The deckhouses were destroyed and the steamer partially sunk, but the engine and hull escaped major damage.

1933-35: Rebuilt at Morgan.

1939: Running a regular service from Morgan to Mildura.

1945: July: Sold to L.W. Mewett, Mildura.

1952: Steamed to Moorna Station to be used as the base for a fishing fleet.

1958: May: Laid-up at Renmark.

1962: November: Sold to B.J. Oxley, who planned to restore her as a floating museum at Mildura.

1967: Sunk by vandals at Mildura.

1968: Sold to Bill Collins, raised by him and his brother Norm, who later sold her to Mildura City Council.

1973: Sold to Echuca City Council to be restored as a museum exhibit.
 5 August: Arrived Echuca from Mildura under her own steam.

1974: Hauled on the slipway at Echuca for restoration.

1976: March: Restoration started after being delayed by several major floods.

1979: Entered passenger service from Echuca after restoration.

1982: Starred in the TV series *All the River Run*, named *Philadelphia* for it.

Pevensey operates 1-hour trips from the Port of Echuca five times daily at 10:15, 11:30, 16:15, 14:30 and 15:45, in conjunction with *Alexander Arbuthnot* and *Adelaide*.

PS RUBY

Length: 39.90m   **Gross tonnage**: 205
Propulsion: Paddle Steamer   **Engine type**: 2-cylinder simple expansion horizontal
Built: 1907   **Rebuilt** (most recent): 2005
Body of water: Murray River   **Home port**: Wentworth, NSW
Website address: http://www.psruby.com/index.php
Builders: David Milne, Morgan, SA

Ruby at Wentworth, 2004. (Roderick Smith)

Engine builder: Robey, Lincoln, UK, 1926, fitted 2005
Owner: Wentworth Shire Council

1907: Built for the Gem Line, owned by Captain Hugh King, Morgan. Operated as a passenger steamer from Morgan to Mildura and, when water levels permitted, to Swan Hill. Originally had a 20hp twin-cylinder Robey engine.

1909: Owners merged with the Ben Chaffey Steamboat Co. to from the Gem Navigation Co.

1911: New engine fitted from the paddle steamer ***Industry*** (not the present one).

1918: The engine and boiler from the paddle steamer ***Lancashire Lass*** (1878) were installed.

1919: Owners merged with other operators to form Murray Shipping Ltd.

1922: New engine installed, built by Horwood, Adelaide.

1930: Boiler replaced.

Early 1930s: Withdrawn from service.

1938: Sold to V Robbins, converted for use as a houseboat at Mildura.

1960: By this date, ***Ruby*** had been abandoned at Johnson's Bend, near Wentworth.

1969: Purchased by Wentworth Rotary Club. Towed to Wentworth by a speedboat. Restored for static display at Fotherby Park near Darling Bridge, Wentworth with engine, boiler and paddle wheels removed.

1996: Placed in the trusteeship of Wentworth Shire Council, which formed a committee to plan a complete restoration.

2002: 26 January: Refloated after the restoration of the hull.

2004: 10-11 July: Recommissioning ceremony performed at Wentworth.

2005: September: Engine (this was a 1926 Robey engine which had been acquired from an owner in Sydney some years previously), boiler shaft and paddles were in position but various ancillary items like the feedwater pump, gauges and lubricators still had to be fitted.

14-15 October: Towed to Mildura for a convention. This was her first visit to Mildura in around sixty years.

2007: June-July: Major event on the River Murray planned to celebrate ***Ruby***'s centenary. She will meet up again with the other large passenger steamers with which she cruised in the 1930s and 1940s, ***Marion***, which will come upstream on a cruise to Renmark, or Mildura if water levels permit, and she will pass by ***Gem*** at Swan Hill.

It is intended that when ***Ruby*** is back in steam she will make special eco-cruises along the river, with passengers using the restored cabins.

Other preserved and recently built Murray paddle steamers are purely used as private yachts by their owners, while some others are the subject of long-term restoration projects like ***Australien***, which is just an unrestored hull in poor condition lying on land at the moment, or ***Success*** which, although previously to be restored for operational use is now just being restored for static use.

There are a good number of diesel paddlers on the Murray, some offering passenger trips, and sum operated as private yachts. Traditionally-styled passenger diesel paddlers include ***Avoca*** (1877), ***Coonawarra*** (1950), ***Mundoo*** (1986) and ***Rothbury*** (1881) at Mildura, ***Mayflower*** (1884) at Morgan, ***Pride of the Murray*** (1976) at Echuca, and ***Pyap*** (1909) at Swan Hill. ***Coonawarra*** and ***Pride of the Murray*** were built on old barge hulls, and all the others were formerly steam-powered.

OTHER LAKES

PS CURLIP

The original *Curlip* on the Snowy River.
(Roderick Smith collection)

Length: 20m
Propulsion: Paddle Steamer
Passenger Capacity: 55
Body of Water: Snowy River, Victoria   **Home Port**: Orbost
Frequency: Under construcition
Website address: www.abc.net.au/landline/content/2006/s1757230.htm
Builder: owners   **Engine builder**:?, England, prior to 1930
Owner: Paddle Steamer Curlip Inc., Orbost
Remarks: Wooden-hulled

Mid-1990s: Project started to build a rough replica of **PS *Curlip***, which ran on the Snowy River as a tug from 1890 until wrecked in 1919. The original steamer towed barges between Orbost and Marlo at the mouth of the river, where the cargo was transferred to coastal vessels, and also on the Broderick River. She was 48ft long, rather than the 65ft of the replica.

2003: Paddle Steamer Curlip Incorporated formed to build the replica.

2006: April: $500,000 grant for the replica vessel made by the Victoria State Government. A similar amount has been donated by the Federal Government and about $200,000 donated by the local community.

July: Construction began. A boiler and engine have been sourced in the UK and shipped out to Australia, where it is being refurbished at Orbost Secondary College.

2007: October: Proposed launch date.

2008: late: Proposed completion.

PS ENTERPRISE

Enterprise on an operating day at Lake Burley
Griffin, 2006. (D. Bromage)

Length: 17.31m   **Gross tonnage**: 55
Propulsion: Paddle Steamer
Engine type: 2-cylinder simple expansion horizontal, 12hp
Built: 1878   **Rebuilt** (most recent): 1988
Body of water: Lake Burley Griffin   **Home port**: Canberra
Frequency: Demonstration steaming only
Website address:
www.theage.com.au/articles/2003/08/29/1062050655128.html?oneclick=true;
www.nma.gov.au and search for 'Enterprise'
Builder: Lynch and Moore, Echuca   **Engine builder**: Beverley Iron Works, UK
Owner: National Museum of Australia

1877: November: Launched.

1878: Completed for W.L. Keir, Echuca for use towing barges on the Edward and Murrumbidgee Rivers.

1897 or before: Sold to T.H. Freeman.

c.1903: Sold to Davie, Price & Co.

1911: Or prior: Converted to a hawking steamer operating out of Wentworth.

c.1919: Sold to A Creager, used as a fishing boat.

1945: Converted to a houseboat, later laid-up at Mannum.

1950s: Sold to Malcolm Phillip.

1973: Sold to G.L. Niehus and moved to Murray Bridge for restoration, after which she was based at Mannum.

1984: Sold to the Museum of Australia. Restoration to original appearance began.

1987: April: Moved by road to Echuca for restoration to continue. New boiler fitted, engine overhauled.

1988: April: Launched into the Murray River after work on the hull completed.

October: Moved by road to Canberra where she was placed in Lake Burley Griffin.

Enterprise is steamed on Lake Burley Griffin several times per year, although she is too small to carry paying passengers. She is crewed by volunteers.

The dieselised paddle steamer *Golden City* (1885) had been restored on the shores of Lake Wendouree at Ballarat, but was destroyed by fire on 3 March 2006.

The paddle steamer *Maid of Sker* (1885) has been statically restored on land at Nerang, Queensland since 1976 and a further restoration has recently taken place.

25 New Zealand and the Pacific Islands

Surviving steamers in New Zealand form an eclectic mix, with a couple of preserved tugs, several launches, one British-built paddle steamer which has recently been restored after many years sunk in a muddy riverbed, and a large twin screw steamer at one of New Zealand's premier tourist towns.

NORTH ISLAND

SL ALICE

As we go to press news has come to hand of the small steamboat *Alice*, which operates on Lake Taupo. She is understood to have been built between 1861 and 1879, and to have been re-launched in 2001. She is 10.67m long, and has a Semple Vee twin-cylinder engine, but no further details are available of her history.

SS ELIZA HOBSON

Length: 9.14m
Propulsion: Single Screw   Engine type: Compound, 15hp
Built: 1998   Passenger capacity: 14
Body of water: Kerikeri Inlet   Home port: Kerikeri
Frequency of operation: Twice daily SuX   Period of operation: September to May
Website address: www.steamship.co.nz
Builders: New Zealand Steamship Co.
Owner: Northern Steamship Co.   Remarks: Wood-fired

1996-97: Hull and engine built: Engine completed a few weeks after launching.
1998: Completed: Ran trips from the New Zealand National Maritime Museum, Auckland.
2002: 31 December: Sold to present owners and moved to Kerikeri.

Eliza Hobson is a small steamer designed as a replica of the small steamers which operated as water taxis in the waters around Auckland *c.*1900. She burns waste material from a sawmill in her boiler.
    She makes 1-hour sailings from Monday to Saturday from October to April at 11:00 and 14:00.

SL FIREFLY

Length: 7.62m
Engine type: Single Cylinder
Built: 1882   Rebuilt (most recent): 2002
Passenger capacity: 12
Body of water: Kerkeri inlet   Home port: Kerikeir
Frequency: Daily   Period of operation: September to May
Website address: www.steamboat.co.nz;www.steamlaunch.co.nz/Firefly.html
Builder: Auckland   Engine builder: ?
Owner: Northern Steamship Co.   Former name: *Boss Murphy* 2005

1882: Built.
2002: Was at this time a motor launch named *Boss Murphy*. Cabin removed and steam engine fitted.
    Operated on the Waipa River. Boiler heated by waste cooking oil.
2004: 27 November: Sold to present owners. Renamed *Firefly*.

Firefly operates in the cruises from Kerikeri along with *Eliza Hobson*.

SL JAMES TORREY

James Torrey.

Length: 10.97m
Propulsion: Single Screw   Engine type: Compound, 12hp

Built: 1993   Passenger capacity: 13
Body of water: Lake Tarawera   Home port: Near Rotorua
Frequency of operation: Regular scheduled   Period of operation: All year
Website address: www.steamboat.co.nz/jamestorrey.htm
Builders: G. Clark & B. Sharrock, New Plymouth   Engine builder: locally made
Owner: Tarawera Steamboat Excursions   Remarks: Coal-fired

1993: Built for current service.
1998: Started commercial service after government permission was granted

James Torrey sails at 10:00 from Boat Shed Bay to Hot Water Beach, a 45-minute sail, returning at 12:15.

SL PUKE

Puke in service at Auckland.
(NZ National Maritime Museum)

Length: 7.92m
Propulsion: Single Screw   Engine type: 1-cylinder,
Built: 1872   Rebuilt (most recent): 1977
Passenger capacity: 7
Body of water: Auckland harbour   Home port: Auckland
Frequency of operation: Occasional public trips
Website address: www.nzmaritime.org.nz/home.html
Builders: E. Thompson & Son, Aratapu, Kaipara harbour
Engine builder: A. & G. Price, *c*.1900
Owner: New Zealand National Maritime Museum

1872: Built.
1977: Restored by Alan Brimblecombe; fitted with current machinery, which was built *c*.1900 as a horizontal, enclosed crank, mill engine, which had been converted to a vertical engine in the 1970s and fitted with Fink reversing gear when fitted to *Puke*.
1988: Used as the official boat of the New Zealand Expo Commission, Brisbane, Australia.
1989: Sold to the New Zealand National Maritime Museum, from where she operates some passenger sailings.

SWS SPIRIT OF WAIKATO

Length: 45.72m
Propulsion: Sternwheeler   Engine type: 1-cylinder,
Body of water: Waikato River   Home port: Hamilton

An artist's impression of the proposed sternwheeler *Spirit of Waikato*.

Frequency of operation: Proposed newbuilding
Builders: To be built
Owner: Leighton Collins

This is a proposed new sternwheeler, to be built by a local steamer enthusiast as a tribute to the stern-wheelers, which used to run in this area up to the 1920s or later.

SS TOROA

Toroa awaiting restoration at Auckland, 1990. (Author's collection)

Length: 39.90m   **Gross tonnage**: 308
Propulsion: Single Screw   **Engine type**: 2 Triple Expansion, 51nhp
Built: 1925   **Passenger capacity**: 1221
Body of water: Auckland harbour   **Home port**: Auckland
Frequency of operation: Return to steam 200?
Website address: www.toroa.org.nz/index.html
Builders: G. Nicoll, Auckland
Engine builder: Aitchison and Blair, Clydebank, Scotland
Owner: *Toroa* Preservation Society, Auckland
Remarks: One screw each fore and aft, coal-fired

1925: 20 April: Launched.
  7 July: Trials.
  12 July: Commenced service from Auckland across the harbour to Devonport. She had a certificate for 1,250 passengers.
1960s: Following the opening of the Auckland Harbour Bridge in 1959, she was mainly used for weekend trips and charters, also rush hour relief sailings.
1980: 8 August: Survey expired. Laid-up at St Mary's Bay with a cracked fire box.
1985: Taken over by the *Toroa* Preservation Society. Restoration commenced.
1988: 1 August: Slipped for hull inspection and application of antifouling paint.
1990: 25 February: Moved from Westhaven to Birkenhead Wharf. Restoration continues by a small volunteer group.

1996: By this time, the overhaul of the engine was 90% complete, and replanking of the upper deck was 70% complete. It was hoped to have her back in service for the America's Cup in September 1999, but this was not able to be done.

1998: 1 June: Sank at her moorings during a storm.

1 July: Raised, towed across the harbour and slipped.

2001: 17 November: Pulled up a slipway and placed on a trailer for restoration work to continue on land.

Restoration work continues on ***Toroa***, although no definite timetable can be made for a return to steam.

PS WAIMARIE

Waimarie on the Whanganui River, 2005.
(Wayne Duncan)

Length: 31.10m   **Gross tonnage**: 80
Propulsion: Paddle Steamer   **Engine type**: 2-cylinder simple expansion, 86hp
Built: 1900   **Rebuilt** (most recent): 1999
Passenger capacity: 150
Body of water: Whanganui River   **Home port**: Wanganui
Frequency of operation: Daily   **Period of operation**: November to April
Website address: www.riverboat.co.nz
Builders: Yarrow & Co., Poplar, London
Owner: Waimarie Riverboat Restoration and Navigation Trust
Former names: *Aotea*

1899: Built by Yarrow, Poplar, for the Whanganui Settlers' River Steamship Co., as ***Aotea***. Shipped out to New Zealand in sections.

1900: March: Assembled at Whanganui.

29 June Maiden voyage. Used as a passenger and cargo steamer from Whanganui upriver to Pipiriki.

1902: October: Sold to A. Hatrick & Co., following the liquidation of her owners. Renamed ***Waimarie***. Continued on the same service, also carrying mails.

1928: Sold to Whanganui River Services Ltd, also owned by a member of the Hatrick family.

1949: July: Withdrawn from service and laid-up.

1952: April: Sank at her moorings, leaving only her port paddle housing and bridge above water. Some years later these were removed as hazards to navigation and the remains disappeared in the mud.

1990: 14 February: Whanganui Riverboat Restoration and Navigation Trust former to raise and restore her.

1993: 25 January: Refloated after being raised from her muddy grave. Restoration and rebuilding commenced. New replica boiler built and fitted.

1999: 15 May: Relaunched.

2000: 1 January: Returned to service as a tourist cruise steamer on the Whanganui River.

Waimarie is a unique example of the small steamers built in Britain for export to the far corners of the British Empire. Her restoration is extensive and she is well worth a visit. She sails daily during the summer season from late October to the end of April at 14:00, and during the winter season at 13:00 on Saturdays, Sundays, and Public Holidays from May to July and from the beginning of September to late October, with daily sailings during the school holidays in the last week of September and the first week of October. Lunch and dinner cruises are also offered for a minimum of thirty passengers. All cruises last 90 minutes or 2 hours.

TST WILLIAM C DALDY

A night shot of *William C Daldy* at Auckland, 2002. (Roderick Smith)

Length: 36.30m   **Gross tonnage**: 349
Propulsion: Twin Screw   **Engine type**: 2 Triple Expansion, 1,950hp
Built: 1935   **Passenger capacity**: 100
Body of water: Auckland harbour   **Home port**: Auckland
Frequency of operation: Occasional public trips
Website address: www.daldy.com
Builders: Lobnitz, Renfrew
Owner: Auckland Harbour Board, leased to the Steam Tug *William C. Daldy* Preservation Society
Remarks: Coal-fired

1935: 1 October: Launched as a tug for Auckland Harbour Board.
   30 October: Sea Trials held in the Firth of Clyde.
   Sailed from Glasgow on her delivery voyage.
1936: 30 January: Arrived at Auckland, where she was used as a harbour tug with occasional passenger trips for the Harbour Board chairman and invited guests.
1977: March: Replaced by a new motor tug and withdrawn from towage service and laid-up.
1978: October: leased to the 'Steam Tug *William C. Daldy* Preservation Society'. Used for passenger sailings in Auckland harbour.
2000: November 10: Returned to service after major refit lasting seven weeks.
2002-03: Ran public passenger trips in connection with the America's Cup races. Otherwise she is almost entirely devoted to charters.

SOUTH ISLAND

TSS EARNSLAW

Length: 51.20m   **Gross tonnage**: 330
Propulsion: Twin Screw   **Engine type**: 2 Triple Expansion, 500hp
Built: 1912   **Passenger capacity**: 747
Body of water: Lake Wakatipu   **Home port**: Queenstown
Frequency of operation: 6x daily exc. June

Earnslaw on Lake Wakapitu, 1989.
(Author's collection)

Period of operation: July to mid-May
Website address: http://www.realjourneys.co.nz/Main/earnslawcruises
Builders: John McGregor & Co. Ltd, Dunedin
Owner: Real Journeys
Remarks: Coal-fired

1911: 4 July: Keel laid at McGregor's shipyard in Dunedin. Built in numbered sections, which were taken by rail to Kingston where she was re-erected on the lake shore.

28 November: Keel laid at Kingston.

1912: 24 February: Launched.

3 August: First Trials trip.

18 October: Entered service for New Zealand Railways on a railway connection service from Kingston to Queenstown. Also operated to Glenorchy at the head of the lake.

1935: The first road was opened from Kingston to Queenstown. The rail passenger service to Kingston was withdrawn the following year. Passenger trips by *Earnslaw* after this were mainly operated in the summer months.

1936: Promenade deck covered and curtains fitted round the sides. Provision of hot meals ceased.

1962: Road opened from Queenstown to Glenorchy. End of the thrice-weekly scheduled steamer service from Queenstown to Glenorchy.

1968: New Zealand Railways announced they were to cease operating *Earnslaw*.

1969: 1 January: Leased to Lake Wakapitu Steamship Co.

12 December: Leased to Fiordland Travel Ltd. Used for short cruises round the lake.

1971: December. Regular cruise to Kingston in connection with the *Kingston Flyer* steam train commenced. This was not successful and only lasted one season.

1982: Sold to Fiordland Travel Ltd.

1984: Major refit. The sides around the promenade deck aft were glassed in and a wheelhouse was fitted at this time. Bar fitted in the former second-class saloon forward. Original dining saloon converted to a souvenir shop. Engine room skylights on promenade deck replaced by balustrades to allow passengers to see the engines in action.

1991: Regular cruises to Walter Peak High Country Farm commenced.

2002: Fiordland Travel Ltd renamed Real Journeys.

The winch at the slipway at Kinloch where *Earnslaw* is slipped for overhaul every two years has been powered since 1922 by the boiler and engines from the paddle steamer ***Antrim*** (1868).

Earnslaw normally operates six 90-minute cruises daily with a call at Walker Peak sheep station, with three of these operating all year round, and three from October to mid-April.

TST LYTTLETON

Length: 38.10m **Gross tonnage**: 292
Propulsion: Twin Screw **Engine type**: 2 Compound, 1,000hp

Lyttleton at Lyttleton, 2005. (Roderick Smith)

Built: 1907   Rebuilt: 1973
Passenger capacity: 150
Body of water: Lyttleton harbour   Home port: Lyttleton
Frequency of operation: SuO   Period of operation: September to June
Website address: www.steam.co.nz/lyttleton.htm
Builders: Ferguson Bros, Port Glasgow
Owner: Lyttleton Harbour Board, leased to the Tug *Lyttleton* Preservation Society
Former names: *Canterbury* 1911
Remarks: Coal-fired

1907: Built on the Clyde as the harbour tug *Canterbury* for Lyttleton Harbour Board: Sailed out to New
    Zealand under her own steam.
  11 September: Delivered.
1911: Renamed *Lyttleton*.
1943: Made a sailing to Bluff to pick up the hulk of the former government steam yacht *Hinemoa* (1875),
    which she later towed to a point 60 miles north-east of Lyttleton, where *Hinemoa* was sunk in 120
    fathoms of water.
1970: Withdrawn from service.
1972: Taken over by the Tug *Lyttleton* Preservation Society.
1973: Passenger sailings commenced after restoration work.

Lyttleton normally operates a Sunday afternoon harbour tour from September to June, in addition to
charters.

SD TE WHAKA

Te Whaka at Dunedin, 2005. (Roderick Smith)

Length: 38.43   Gross tonnage: 324
Engine type: Compound, 295hp
Built: 1910   Rebuilt (most recent): Pending
Passenger capacity: 120-150
Body of water: Otago harbour   Home port: Dunedin

Frequency: awaiting restoraiton and conversion
Website address: http://www.bondstore.co.nz/nzhistoricships/qs/table/Te%20Whaka.htm
Builder: Ferguson Bros, Port Glasgow
Owner: Te Whaka Maritime Heritage Trust

1910: Built as a steam grab dredger for Lyttleton Harbour Board. Sailed out to New Zealand via the Suez Canal, Colombo, Djakarta, Freemantle, and Melbourne.
1965: Boiler replaced with one from the tug **Kumea**. Steam grab crane replaced by a Priestman diesel crane.
1987: Withdrawn from service and laid-up.
1993: Sold to present owners for preservation and proposed conversion to a passenger-carrying steamer.
1994: March. Towed to Dunedin, where the crane was later removed.

Lack of funding has meant that major restoration work has not commenced on **Te Whaka**.

Recently restored is the small paddle vessel **Tamati**, built in 1902 for service on Lake Taupo and now operating on Lake Ianthe on the west of South Island.

MICRONESIA

SS THORFINN

Length: 58m   **Gross tonnage**: 599
Propulsion: Single Screw   **Engine type**: 4-cylinder Compound, 2,500hp
Built: 1952   **Rebuilt**: 1995-6
Passenger capacity: 22 berthed
Body of water: Truk Lagoon   **Home port**: Truk, Caroline Islands
Frequency of operation: Weekly seven-day cruises
Period of operation: All year
Website address: www.thorfinn.net
Builders: Stord Verft   **Engine builder**: Fredrikstad MV
Owner: Seaward Holdings Micronesia, Chuuk, Micronesia
Former names: *Chester* 1978, *Thorfinn* 1966

1952: Built as the steam whaler **Thorfinn** for Thor Dahl, Sandefjord, Norway. Designed by Fredrikstad Mekaniske Verksted, who built the engines, but built by Stord Verft.
1955-57: Used as a whale catcher for the factory ship **Thorshammer**, in Antarctic waters.
1957-61: Used with factory ship **Thorshavet**.
1962-66: Used with factory ship **Thorshovdi**.
1966: June: Sold to Karlsen Shipping, Halifax, Nova Scotia. Renamed **Chester**. Used as a whaler and in the Newfoundland seal hunts.
1970: Owners now MV Tem Ltd.
1975: Feb: Sold to E.L. Higgs and D.M. Mercier, Halifax.
1978: March: Ownership transferred to Seaward Holdings Ltd, (owned by E.L. Higgs), Vancouver, B.C. Renamed **Thorfinn**. Converted to a fish camp for sport fishermen and used on the coast of British Columbia.
1982: Again converted for use as a mini-cruise vessel. Cabins installed in place of the hold space in the lower deck forward.
1987: Moved to Truk.
1995: 24 December: Resumed service after a $850,000 major refit.

Thorfinn normally runs week-long cruises for divers to view the the Second World War wrecks in Truk Lagoon, but in June she offers fourteen-day Pan Micronesia Cruises to Yap and back.

GREAT LAKES

SL NOTTINGHAM CASTLE

Nottingham Castle at Sault Ste, Marie.
(Purves Marine)

Length: 18.30m   **Gross tonnage**: 40
Propulsion: Single Screw   **Engine type**: Compound
Built: 1943   **Passenger capacity**: 20
Body of water: St Mary's River   **Home port**: Sault Ste Marie, ON
Frequency of operation: Charters   **Period of operation**: Summer months
Website address: www.purvismarine.com/other_info.html
Builders: Hancock, Pembroke Dock
Engine builder (if different from builder): LNER Cowlairs Works, Glasgow
Owner: Purvis Marine
Former names: *Cresset, 298*
Remarks: Wooden hull

1943: Built as the British Admiralty harbour launch **HSL298**, also known as **Cresset**.
1960s: Withdrawn.
1965-67: Converted to a private yacht. Cruiser stern fitted, lengthening her by about 7ft. Wheelhouse added. Renamed **Nottingham Castle**.
1969: Sold to John Player & Sons, the tobacco company, as part of a small fleet of steam launches that they then operated.
1975: Sold to a group of Canadian steam enthusiasts and moved to Toronto.
1979: Used as Ontario Government Flagship during the yachting Olympics at Kingston.
1981: Moved to Lake Rousseau, one of the Muskoka Lakes. Owned by Pagnton House Hotel, Minnett and used as a hotel yacht for excursions from there.
1990s: Laid-up out of service.
1999: Rebuilt. Purchased by Purvis Marine for use on charters at Sault Ste Marie. Ontario.

SS PUMPER

Length: 18.60m
Propulsion: Single Screw   **Engine type**: Compound, 75hp
Built: 1903   **Rebuilt** (most recent): 1994
Passenger capacity: c.90
Body of water: Rideau Canal   **Home port**: Kemptville, Ontario
Frequency of operation: Out of service, laid-up

Pumper as *Bytown Pumper* at Ottawa. (J.E. Roue)

Website address: www.pumper.ca
Builders: Buffalo, NY
Engine builder (if different from builder): Doty, Goderich, Ont., 1895
Owner: Doug Pettit & Family
Former names: *Bytown Pumper* 1997, *Racey* 1990, *Paul Evans* 1980, *Racey*, 1957, *Planet* 1909
Remarks: Wood-fired

1903: Built as the steam fishing boat *Planet*, for use at Buffalo.

1909: Seized by the Canadian Coast Guard for breaching border controls and taken to Port Dover, Ont. Sold at auction to James Lowe, renamed *Racey*.

1913: Sold to Harry Ansley, Port Dover.

1935: Sold to F.S. James, Meldrum Bay.

1945: Now owned by Hindman Transportation Co., Owen Sound. Used as a tug and icebreaker.

1957: Renamed *Paul Evans*, still at Owen Sound. Fitted with a diesel engine.

1975: Sold to Owen Sound Historical Society.

1980: Sold to H. Gamble, Port Dover, renamed *Racey*.

1989: Purchased by Rideau Steamships Ltd. Second-hand Doty steam engine, dating from 1895, and boiler dating from 1900, previously in *Islanda*, fitted at Port Dover. The engine was built for *Mary Ellen* in 1888 on the Karwatha Lakes, which was rebuilt as *Majestic* in 1897 and rebuilt again as *Islanda* (I) in 1909, *Islanda* (I) burnt in 1910, and the engine was installed in *Islanda* (II) the same year. She was out of service in 1944, and the engine and boiler were removed in 1952, and then placed in storage.

1990: July: Returned to steam. Renamed *Bytown Pumper* and used for excursions out of Ottawa. Operated trips on the Rideau Canal in conjunction with coach tour operator Gray Line.

1994: Sponsons added for stability and to increase passenger capacity.

1997: Sold to Doug Pettit and family. Moved to Niagara-on-the-Lake. Operated cruises from there. Renamed *Pumper*.

1999: New wood-burning boiler fitted.

2003: Withdrawn at end of season. The owner of *Pumper* announced in October 2003 that *Pumper* would not operate in 2004. The main reasons for this were stated to be the lack of signs for her departure point, and the excessive berthing fees charged by the Canadian Parks Service.

2004: Laid-up near Kemptville, Ont.

PS TRILLIUM

Length: 45.70m   **Gross tonnage**: 611
Propulsion: Paddle Steamer   **Engine type**: Compound Diagonal, 350hp
Built: 1910   **Rebuilt** (most recent): 1976
Passenger capacity: 500
Body of water: Toronto harbour   **Home port**: Toronto
Frequency of operation: Peak summer SSuO

Trillium at Toronto, 1996.

Period of operation: July/August
Website address: www.greatlakesschooner.com
Builders: Polson Iron Works, Toronto
Owner: Municipality of Metropolitan Toronto, Parks and Recreation Department
Remarks: Double-ended

1910: Built as a double-ended passenger ferry for the Toronto Ferry Co. for service to the Toronto Islands. She was a copy of *Bluebell* (1906). Mainly ran to Hanlan's Point and Centre Island.
  18 June: Launched.
1919: Chartered for a trip by the Prince of Wales and his party.
1926: Ferry service taken over by Toronto Transportation Commission. From now on, *Trillium* mainly served Centre Island, with occasional trips to Ward's Island and Hanlan's Island.
1940: Major conversion undertaken.
1952: Withdrawn from service. From now on placed on standby, to be used as an emergency ferry. Laid-up at one of the islands.
1957: Complete withdrawal from service and berthed on a lagoon on the Toronto Islands. Deteriorated and was badly affected by dry rot over the ensuing years, sinking once or twice.
1973-76: Complete rebuild at Port Colborne to original 1910 appearance. New oil-fired boiler fitted. Wooden decks replaced by steel decks, Wooden wheelhouses replaced by aluminium ones.
1976: 19 May: Returned to service.
1990: Operated regular cruises from Toronto. These were not successful, and she returned to charter sailings only.

Trillium is mainly operated on charter cruises, but in the peak summer season she is used as a relief ferry on the routes to the islands. Her charters are marketed by the Great Lakes Schooner Co.

The steam tug *Ned Hanlan* (1932) is statically preserved on land at Toronto. In the late 1990s there was a plan to return her to steam but this has been postponed indeifintely.
  The cargo/passenger steamer *Norisle* (1946) is in static use as a restaurant and museum at Manitowaning on Manitoulin Island. She was in service from Tobermory to Manitoulin Island until 1974.

MUSKOKA LAKES

SS BIGWIN

Length: 20.12m   **Gross tonnage**: 25
Propulsion: Steam Launch
Built: 1910   **Rebuilt** (most recent): 2005
Passenger capacity: c.20
Body of water: Lake of Bays   **Home port**: Dorset, Ont.

Bigwin. (Owners)

Frequency of operation: Undergoing restoration
Website address: www.bigwinsteamboat.com
Engine builder (if different from builder): Polson
Owner: Lake of Bays Marine Museum and Navigation Society
Former name: *Ella Mary* 1925
Remarks: Wooden-hulled

1910: Built as the steam yacht **Ella Mary** for use around Belle Island north of Beaumaris in northern Lake Muskoka. Fitted with a triple expansion Polson engine.

1925: Purchased by Huntsville Navigation Co. for the Bigwin Inn, a large resort hotel on Bigwin Island on the Lake of Bays. Renamed **Bigwin**. Mainly used for the 10-minute crossing from Norway Point to Bigwin Island, but sailed to Glenmount for Sunday church services and offered occasional excursions on the Lake of Bays.

1928: Ownership transferred to the Bigwin Boat Livery Co. Ltd.

*c.*1943: Steam engine replaced by a diesel engine.

1970: Withdrawn from service when the Bigwin Inn ceased to be a hotel. Laid-up at Norway Point. Later sank at her berth after many years of neglect.

1991: Purchased by the Lake of Bays Marine Museum and Navigations Society. Raised and taken to South Portage where she was stored in the open in a field at Dwight.

2002: 3 August: Returned to Dorset for restoration on land. Her original engine has survived and will be re-installed in her.

2008: Probable completion of restoration.

It is planned that, when restoration is complete, she be moored at Dorset where the owners are restoring a store as a museum. **Bigwin** will be moored there, and will offer charters and, hopefully, occasional public trips.

TSS SEGWUN

Length: 37.50m   **Gross tonnage**: 308
Propulsion: Twin Screw   **Engine type**: 2 Compound, 33nhp
Built: 1887   **Rebuilt** (most recent): 1980
Passenger capacity: 99
Body of water: Muskoka Lakes   **Home port**: Gravenhurst
Frequency of operation: Daily
Period of operation: Mid-June to mid-September
Website address: www.muskokasteamships.com
Builders: Unknown, Clyde
Engine builder (if different from builder): Doty Engine Co., Goderich, Ont. 1 from 1907, 1 from 1914
Owner: The Muskoka Steamship & Historical Society
Operator: The Muskoka Lakes Navigation & Hotel Co.
Former name: *Nipissing* (II) 1925
Remarks: Coal-fired

Segwun at Gravenhurst, 1996.

1887: Built as the paddle steamer **Nipissing** (II) for A.P. Cockburn for passenger, freight and mail service on the Muskoka Lakes. Iron hull built at a so far unknown yard in Glasgow, Scotland. Shipped out to Gravenhurst in sections. The walking beam engine, built by Davidson and Doran of Kingston, Ontario, from **Nipissing** (I) of 1871, which had burnt and sank in the summer of the previous year, was used. Spring: Launched at Gravenhurst. Operated until 1893 from Port Cockburn to Lake Joseph.

1899: Dining room widened to the full width of the hull. Engine and paddlewheels lowered.

*c.*1905: Roof on second deck widened to the full width of the hull and pilothouse moved from the second to the third deck.

1914: Summer: Crankshaft broke at Milford Bay. Steamer was pushed the 2 miles to Beaumaris by a nine-year-old boy in a small 4hp motorboat. Steamer withdrawn and laid-up because of the poor state of her machinery.

1925: Hull of **Nipissing** rebuilt as a twin screw steamer using two second-hand compound engines. These came from different unidentified steamers and were not a matched pair, and one is installed backwards: this is so that the two propellers can rotate in opposite directions and cancel each other's torque. New funnel and boiler fitted. New wooden superstructure fitted. Renamed **Segwun**. Small steam generator from **Nipissing** (II) retained.

6 July: Maiden voyage as **Segwun**. Operated mainly from Bracebridge to Bala, connecting with the northbound steamers at Beaumaris, and the Canadian Pacific Trains at Bala.

*c.*1943: Aft lounge converted into two staterooms.

1946: Second deck cabins rebuilt to width of hull and six new very small staterooms installed. Former after lounge with its two staterooms removed. Forward cabin extended aft.

1949: April: Muskoka Lakes Line founded to operate the Muskoka Lakes Steamers.

1950: Now sailed on the 100-mile cruise from Gravenhurst.

1951: February: Muskoka Lakes Line bankrupt. Steamer repossessed by Muskoka Lakes & Hotel Co.

1955: February: Taken over by Gravenhurst Steamship Ltd.

1958: 5 August: Ran aground on an unmarked shoal off Walker's Point, damaging both propellers. Withdrawn from service and laid-up.

1962: Purchased by the town of Gravenhurst, with enthusiast support, and opened as the Segwun Steamboat Museum, moored at Gravenhurst. All except one stateroom replaced by a picture gallery.

1969: Restoration to operating condition commenced.

1973: Muskoka Steamship & Historical Society formed, under the leadership of the Ontario Roadbuilders Association. Segwun purchased for $1.00.

August: Slipped for a year. Iron hull plates below the waterline replaced by steel plates. Damaged hull and props repaired.

1974: 1 June: Re-launched by Prime Minister Pierre Trudeau.

1981: Restored to operating condition. The 'Ladies Lounge' forward on the second deck survives from **Nipissing** (II). The staterooms aft on that deck have been removed and that area is now a bar.

Muskoka Lakes Hotel & Navigation Co. re formed by a group of Gravenhurst residents to operate her because government funding for the restoration required that she be operated by a commercial company. This company leased **Segwun** from the Historical Society.

27 June: Re-entered service on the Muskoka Lakes.

1985: Following five unprofitable seasons, the Muskoka Steamship & Historical Society assumed ownership of the shares of the Muskoka Lakes Hotel & Navigation Co.

1997-2002: The Society replaced all the external wood on **Segwun**.

2003: Spring: Freight deck rebuilt with the forward end becoming the eighteen-seat 'Islander Dining Room'.

Segwun operates cruises from Gravenhurst three to five times daily from early June to Canadian Thanksgiving day in October. On Mondays she operates an 9-hour cruise through the locks at Port Carling to Lake Joseph. In spring and fall weeks, there are overnight cruises, with the night being spent in a resort hotel on the lake shore.

SY WANDA III

Wanda III at Gravenhurst, 1996.

Length: 30.80m   Gross tonnage: 60
Propulsion: Single Screw   Engine type: Triple Expansion, 27nhp
Built: 1915   Rebuilt (most recent): 1996
Passenger capacity: 24
Body of water: Muskoka Lakes   Home port: Gravenhurst
Frequency of operation: Undergoing repairs
Website address: www.segwun.com
Builders: Polson Iron Works, Toronto
Owner: The Muskoka Steamship & Historical Society
Operators: Muskoka Steam & Classic Yachts Ltd
Remarks: Coal-fired

1915: Built for the Timothy Eaton family as a private yacht for use from the family's summer home on Lake Windermere to the railway at Muskoka Wharf (Gravenhurst). Built with the same type of engine as those used in Canadian Navy minesweepers in the First World War, and as a result was able to steam at 24mph. Sailed to the Eaton estate at Kawandag, near Rousseau.

1930: Sold to the Bigwin Inn, for use on the Lake of Bays as a hotel yacht for the aforementioned hotel. Moved overland to the Lake of Bays.

1949: Sold to David Cameron Peck, a collector of several steam yachts and steam memorabilia.

1955: Reverted to the ownership of the Bigwin Inn after Peck fled the revenue authorities.

1970: Following closure of the hotel, sold to various other owners on the Lake of Bays. Eventually fell into disrepair.

1971: Purchased by Sandy Thomson, of Hamilton. Restored and returned to steam on the Lake of Bays. He found the cost and time required for continual restoration more than he could afford.

1993: Acquired by the Muskoka Lakes Navigation & Hotel Co. Returned to Gravenhurst for restoration.

1996: August Restored completed to 1915 condition. Rededicated by Primer Minster Jean Chretien. Returned to service as a charter steamer, leased to the wholly owned subsidiary, Muskoka Steam and Classic Yachts Ltd.

2004-05: Out of service for hull renovations.

It is expected that ***Wanda III*** will return to service in Summer 2006 or 2007. She will have a passenger certificate for twenty-four and it is likely that will be used for 45-minute cruises, departing hourly from Gravenhurst.

WEST COAST

ST MASTER

Master at Vancouver. (Marpole Winter)

Length: 21.60m   **Gross tonnage:** 95
Propulsion: Single Screw   **Engine type:** Triple Expansion, 150hp
Built: 1922   **Rebuilt** (most recent): 1980
Body of water: Strait of Georgia   **Home port:** Vancouver
Frequency of operation: Occasional public trips (check website)
Website address: www.ssmaster.org
Builders: Arthur Moscrop, False Creek, Vancouver
Engine builder: Beardmore, Speedwell Works, Coatbridge, Scotland 1916
Owner: SS Master Society/Vancouver Maritime Museum
Remarks: Wooden-hulled

1922: Built as a tug for Capt. Herman Thorsen. Fitted with an engine built by William Beardmore in
   Scotland and intended for a Royal Navy Minesweeper which was incomplete at the end of the war.
1927: Sold to the Master Towing Co. Worked for Fraser Mills and was later chartered to the Lamb
   Logging Co., used to tow logs and timber barges from coastal ports to the sawmills at False Creek and
   elsewhere.
1940: Sold to Marpole Towing Co.
1944: New boiler fitted.
1947: Control of Marpole Towing Co. passed to Evans, Coleman, and Evans.
*c.*1951: Now part of the operations of the Gilley Bros, fleet, another subsidiary of Evans, Coleman, and
   Evans.
1959: Decommissioned. Laid-up at the mouth of the Brunette River and abandoned
1962: 14 August: Acquired by the Western Canada branch of the World Ship Society. Restoration
   commenced.
1963: 23 April: Back in steam.
1971: April: Transferred to the Society for the Preservation of the Steam Towboat *Master*.
1980: Total rebuild began.
1985: May: Owners' name changed to SS Master Society.
1986: May: Served as the flagship of Expo 86.

Two former Canadian Pacific Railway-owned steam sternwheelers survive in static use the Canadian
Rockies, *Moyie* (1898) at Kaslo on Kootenay Lake, and *Sicamous* (1914) at Penticton on Okanagan Lake.
The latter is also the location of the tug *Naramata* (1913), also a museum.
   In the Yukon, sternwheelers *Klondike* (1936) and *Keno* (1922) are museums at Whitehorse and Dawson
City respectively.

27 The United States

The United States has a wide variety of currently extant passenger steamers, ranging from small modern launches, through classic sternwheelers, to large excursion boats and a couple of laid-up former transatlantic liners.

The classic Mississippi stern-wheeler has become so symbolic that replicas crop up everywhere. Only six steam-powered sternwheelers survive on the Mississippi system, but hundreds of diesel copies, some with powered stern-wheels, and many more with dummy stern wheels, are in service throughout the country.

CRUISE SHIPS

TSS OCEANIC

Independence in service at Honolulu.
(Ed Lafferty, from a Chantry Classics postcard)

Length: 208.01m   Gross tonnage: 23,719
Propulsion: Twin Screw   Engine type: 4 Turbine, 55,000hp
Built: 1950   Rebuilt (most recent): 1994
Passenger capacity: 1,077
Body of water: Norwegian Cruise Lines   Home port: San Francisco
Frequency of operation: Laid-up
Website address: www.maritimematters.com/independence.html
Builders: Bethlehem Steel, Quincy, Mass.
Owner: Norwegian Cruise Line
Former names: *Independence* 2005, *Oceanic Independence* 1982, *Sea Luck 1* (proposed 1976), *Independence* 1974

1950: 3 June: Launched for American Export Lines.
  1 December: Trials commenced.
1951: 10 February: Maiden Voyage: eight-week Mediterranean cruise from New York.
  12 April: First line voyage New York to Genoa. Her regular route was from New York to Naples, with intermediate calls at Gibraltar (Algeciras from 1956), .Cannes and Genoa. Operated alongside sister ship **Constitution** on the route.
1959: February: Wheelhouse, bridge wings, and navigation rooms moved forward 21ft and raised 8ft. New first-class passenger accommodation built behind them.
1960: Repainted with all-white hull.
1968: March: Rebuilt from three-class to one-class ship. Painted with psychedelic sunburst pattern on hull. The centre of this was intended to represent Jean Harlow's eyes.
  July: Regained previous colours.
  November: Extensive refit with private facilities installed in all the former tourist-class cabins. Post-refit cruise from New York in December cancelled due to a docker's strike. **Independence** never sailed again for American Export.

1969: 13 March: Laid-up in Baltimore.

1974: January. Sold to Atlantic Far East Lines (C.Y. Tung).

1975: 17 March: Renamed **Oceanic Independence**. Registered at Monrovia, Liberia.

23 March: Left Baltimore on a positioning cruise to Durban.

24 April: Made first cruise from Durban.

September: Chartered to the South African Government to make three voyages from Walvis Bay to Lisbon to evacuate Portuguese nationals escaping from Angola

1976: 19 November: laid-up in Hong Kong. There were unfounded rumours that she was to be sold as a gambling ship in the Middle East and renamed **Sea Luck 1**.

1979: Sold to American Hawaii Cruises, Honolulu. Rebuilt by Kawasaki Shipyards, Kobe, and then in Taiwan until June 1980.

1980: June: Entered service on seven-day Hawaii cruises from Honolulu, with an annual cruise to San Francisco en route to refit. Returned to US registry.

1982: Regained name **Independence**.

1994: Major refit at Newport News Shipbuilding, Virginia. Funnels repainted in Hawaiian flower motif.

2001: 20 October: Laid-up in Honolulu following bankruptcy of owners.

November. Moved to San Francisco and laid-up in the Maritime Administration Fleet in Suisun Bay.

2003: 14 April: Purchased by Norwegian Cruise Lines for possible cruises along the US Coast. Moved to the former Mare Island Naval base at Vallejo.

2004: 26 July: Moved back to San Francisco, Pier 70 complex, for lay up. This is about 3 miles south of Fisherman's Wharf.

2005: 25 October: Renamed **Oceanic**. Ownership transferred to California Manufacturing Co., based at the same address as Norwegian Cruise Lines. It is uncertain if the name has been painted on her hull or not.

It is uncertain at the time of writing **Independence** will ever return to commercial service, and if so, it is extremely likely she will be re-engined.

QSS UNITED STATES

United States departing Southampton in 1966.

Length: 301.80m   **Gross tonnage:** 53,329
Propulsion: Quadruple Screw   **Engine type:** 4 Turbine, 241,000hp
Built: 1952   **Rebuilt** (most recent): 2005+
Passenger capacity: 1,928
Body of water: Norwegian Cruise Lines   **Home port:** Philadelphia, PA
Frequency of operation: Return to service 200?
Website address: www.ssunitedstates.org
Builders: Newport News SB & Drydock Co., Newport News, Va.
Engine builder: Westinghouse Electric Corporation, Pittsburgh, Pa.
Owner: Norwegian Cruise Line

1951: 23 June: Floated out after building in a dry dock at the Newport News shipyard.

1952: 26 March: The first of three days of sea trials.

22 June: Delivered to United States Lines.

3 July: Maiden Voyage New York to Southampton. Broke North Atlantic speed record (Blue Riband), which still stands for a full-sized liner, with a crossing from Ambrose Lightship to Bishop Rock in three days, 12 hours, 12 minutes. Service extended to Bremerhaven in the winter months.

1962: Caribbean and longer cruises began to supplement the transatlantic sailings, which were beginning to be affected by the advent of jet aircraft.

1969: 8 November: Withdrawn from service. Laid-up at Newport News, later in Hampton Roads.

1973: February. Moved to Norfolk, Va. Now owned by the United States Maritime Administration.

1978: Sold to United States Lines, Seattle (Richard Hadley).

1984: October: Fittings, furniture, crockery, etc. auctioned off.

1989: 4 March. Moved to Newport News.

1992: 27 April. Sold at auction to Marmara Marine, New York.

4 June: Towed to Tuzla, near Istanbul for proposed rebuilding.

1993: 1 November: Towed to Sevastopol, Ukraine, for removal of asbestos, lifeboats and davits.

1994: 15 May: Towed back to Tuzla. Interiors stripped out but lack of funds meant that the rebuilding was not completed.

1996: 25 July: Towed back to Philadelphia, where she has remained laid-up ever since.

Sold at auction to Edward Cantor, New York.

1997: 25 January: Sold to Fred Mayer.

2003: 14 April: Purchased by Norwegian Cruise Lines for possible cruises along the US Coast. It is uncertain at the time of writing if these will ever take place, and if so, it is extremely likely she will be re-engined.

2006: May: Star Cruises (parent company of Norwegian Cruise Line) chairman announced that the rebuild of **United States** would definitely go ahead.

EAST COAST

SL AFRICAN QUEEN

African Queen safely out of the water at Key Largo, 2004.
(Melanie Deayton)

Length: 9.10m
Propulsion: Single Screw   Engine type: Compound, 20hp
Built: 1912   Passenger capacity: 12
Body of water: Connecticut River/Florida Keys
Home port: Old Saybrook, Cn/Key Largo, Fa.
Frequency of operation: Daily?   Period of operation: All year
Website address: keylargoprincess.com/queen.htm;
www.steamboating.net/page31.html

Builders: Unknown yard, north-east England   Engine builder: Unknown, USA
Owner: ? Hendricks
Former name: *Livingstone* 1951

1912: Built as **Livingstone** for the British East Africa Railway Co., later known as the Uganda Railway for service on Lake Albert. She was shipped in sections to Port Florence, now Kisumu, on Lake Victoria, then on to Jinja, and by rail to Masindi Port on Lake Kioga, and was then carried down to Butiaba on Lake Albert. Used mainly for short trips from Butiaba to the Murchison Falls. She is reputed to have been built at a 'yard on the north-east coast'. Some sources state she was built by Lytham Shipbuilding and Engineering, but that is disproved in the history of that yard.

1926: Owners renamed the Kenya Uganda Railway.

1927: December: Owners became the Kenya Uganda Railway and Harbours.

1948: Owners amalgamated with the Tanganyika Railway to from East African Railways and Harbours.

1951: Used by Joe Hoesli, assistant director, for use on the film *African Queen*, starring Humphrey Bogart and Katherine Hepburn. By this time, she was abandoned, her steam engine having at some stage been replaced by a diesel, which had later been removed. She was fitted with a new diesel and a dummy steam engine for use in the film.

1967: Sold at auction to Mr Wilson, later to Fred Reeve, San Francisco. Used for the American Cancer Society in fund raising drives.

1982: Found abandoned in a cow pasture at Ocala, Fa. Purchased and restored by James Hendricks, used on trips from Holiday Inn, Key Largo.

1996: Moved to Old Saybrook, Connecticut in the summer months for trips on the Connecticut River. It is not certain if this continues, or if she is based at Key Largo all year round.

James Hendricks died a few years ago, and his son now runs **African Queen**. She spends much of the time hauled up out of the water under a canopy. An outboard motor has been installed in addition to the steam engine.

ST BALTIMORE

Tug *Baltimore* at Baltimore. (B. Worden)

Length: 26.70m   Gross tonnage: 81
Propulsion: Single Screw   Engine type: Compound, 202hp (originally 330)
Built: 1906   Rebuilt (most recent): 1985
Passenger capacity: 36

Body of water: Chesapeake Bay   **Home port**: Baltimore, Pa.
Frequency of operation: Occasional public trips
Website address: www.steamtug.org
Builders: Skinner Shipyard & Drydock Co., Baltimore
Owner: Baltimore Museum of Industry   **Remarks**: Coal-fired

1906: Built for Baltimore Harbor Board as a harbour inspection tug. Used for several purposes, including towing barges, as an auxiliary fireboat, as an icebreaker during the summer months, and as a VIP launch for the Harbor Commissioners.
8 December. Sea Trials.

1916: July: Received the German cargo-carrying submarine *Deutschland*. (Note: at this point the USA was still neutral in the First World War.

1922: Tug damaged during the launching of a ship when the ship being launched capsized on top of her, damaging or destroying the wheelhouse and funnel. During repairs, a new boiler was fitted.

1956: Baltimore Harbor Board dissolved. Maryland Port Authority established and ownership transferred to the latter.

1957: Converted to oil firing.

1963: Withdrawn from service. Sold to Alexander Luckton, Jr, a bookshop owner who planned to use her to tow a barge with 100,000 books to educate the populace of Puerto Rico.
When Mr Luckton's health failed, sold to Harbor Towing Co. of Baltimore. Coast Guard certification lapsed

1963/4: Sold to S.F. DuPont. Registered as a private yacht.

1979: Sunk at her moorings in Sassafree River.

1981: Donated to the Baltimore Museum of Industry. Raised and restored, converted back to coal-firing.

1989: Restoration completed. Back in operating condition.

Baltimore is open as a museum ship at Baltimore and offers public cruises three or four times a year.

SS JOHN W. BROWN

John W Brown in the Cape Cod Canal, 1995.
(Richard I. Weiss, from a Simplon Postcards postcard)

Length: 128.80m   **Gross tonnage**: 7,176
Propulsion: Single Screw   **Engine type**: Triple Expansion, 2,500hp
Built: 1942   **Passenger capacity**: 730
Body of water: Chespapeake Bay   **Home port**: Baltimore, Pa
Frequency of operation: Occasional public trips
Website address: www.liberty-ship.com
Builders: Bethlehem Fairfield Shipyard, Baltimore
Owner: US Government   **Operator**: Project Liberty Ship

1942: 7 September: Launched as one of over 2,700 Liberty Ships. These were part of an emergency shipbuilding programme, and designed to be built simply and quickly.

29 September: Maiden voyage for US Navy from Baltimore to New York to load tanks, jeeps, ammunition etc. for the Persian Gulf.

1943: June: Converted to a limited capacity troopship for up to 500 troops or POWs in addition to cargo.

1943-45: Made seven voyages from the United States to North Africa, Italy, Belgium and France. Participated in the invasion of southern France.

1945-48: Made five peacetime voyages to France, Italy, Denmark, Germany and the UK.

1948: Started use as a school ship in New Jersey, preparing high school students for seagoing careers.

1978: May: Project Liberty Ship founded to restore **John W Brown** as a maritime museum and as a memorial to the shipyard workers, merchant mariners, and US Navy armed guard crews who built, sailed and defended Liberty Ships during the Second World War.

1982: Use as a school ship ceased.

1983: 31 July: Joined the National Defense Reserve Fleet anchored in the James River, Virginia.

1985: 1 March: Listed on the National Register of Historic Places.

1988: August 13: Towed to Baltimore, where she was restored.

1991: August 24: Restored to steaming condition and wartime grey livery. Ran trials in Chesapeake Bay. 21 & 22 September: Inaugural cruise on Chesapeake Bay.

1994: Coast Guard Certification received for coastwise ocean voyages. Coastal cruises as far as Halifax, Nova Scotia.

John W. Brown normally makes three one-day public Living History cruises each year from Baltimore on Chesapeake Bay.

TSS LILAC

Lilac at New York awaiting restoration, 2004.

Length: 52.73m   **Gross tonnage:** 779
Propulsion: Twin Screw   **Engine type:** 2 Triple Expansion, 800hp
Built: 1933   **Rebuilt** (most recent): 2003
Body of water: Hudson River   **Home port:** New York
Frequency of operation: Undergoing restoration
Website address: www.steamerlilac.org
Builders: Pusey & Jones, Wilmington, Delaware
Owner: *Lilac* Preservation Project   **Former name:** **USLHT** *Lilac*

1931: Originally contracted to Hampton Roads Shipbuilding of Portsmouth, Va., and to be named **USLHT Azalea**, but a lower contract was accepted from Pusey and Jones.

1933: 26 May: Launched as **USLHT** (United States Light House Tender) **Lilac**. She was the second of two lighthouse tenders in the Violet class for the United States Bureau if Lighthouses. Based at Edgemont, De, working the Delaware River and Bay.

1939: July: United States Bureau if Lighthouses became part of the US Coast Guard.

1973: Withdrawn from service, by which time she was the last steam lighthouse tender in the US. Donated to the Barry Lundeberg Seafarers International Union seamanship school in Maryland for use as a training ship for engine room personnel

1988: Sold. Laid-up in a fresh water creek at Richmond, Va.

2003: Purchased by *Lilac* Preservation Project. Towed to Brooklyn, New York. Restoration commenced. 31 December: Moved from Brooklyn to Pier 40, Manhattan.

PS NORTH RIVER OF CLERMONT (replica)

The 1909 replica of *North River of Clermont*. (Author's collection)

Length 45.72m
Engine type: Single Cylinder,
Built: 2007
Body of water: Hudson River   **Home port**: Saugerties, NY
Frequency: Proposed replica
Website address: www.fultonsteam.com
Builder: Saugerties

It is proposed that for the 2007 bicentenary of the world's first commercial steamship, a steam-powered replica of Robert Fulton's **North River of Clermont**, popularly known as **Clermont**, be built. As drawings of the original do not exist, it is likely that this will be a replica of the 1909 replica named **Clermont** which was built for the centenary. The original steamer operated from New York to Albany on the Hudson River.

If not completed for the 2007 celebrations, the steamer will feature in a major celebration in 2009 of the 400th anniversary of Henry Hudson's and Samuel de Champlain's explorations. Initial plans call for her to sail from Saugerties to Tivoli and Clermont State Historic Site.

SS SABINO

Sabino at Mystic Seaport, 1992. (B. Worden)

Length: 17.40m   **Gross tonnage:** 25
Propulsion: Single Screw   **Engine type:** Compound, 75hp
Built: 1908   **Rebuilt** (most recent): 1973–80
Passenger capacity: 100
Body of water: Mystic River   **Home port:** Mystic Seaport, CN
Frequency of operation: Daily
Period of operation: Mid-May to early September
Website address:
     www.mysticseaport.org/index.cfm?fuseaction=home.viewPage&page_id=BE6B81E4-BCFB-
     F236-6B115D74422A6FEE;
     www.mysticseaport.org/index.cfm?fuseaction=home.viewpage&page_id=B41A9814-9BB3-
     DAAF-E910B083A80D0941
Builders: W. Irving Adams & Son, East Boothbay, Maine
Engine builder: James H. Paine & Son, Noank, Conn.
Owner: Mystic Seaport Museum Inc., Mystic
Former name: *Tourist* 1922
Remarks: Wooden hull, coal-fired

1908: 7 May: Launched for the Damariscotta Steamboat Co. as *Tourist*. Fitted with a three-year-old boiler.

25 June: First voyage for the Damariscotta Steamboat Co. for the mail steamer service on the Damariscotta River and Linekin Bay in Maine, about 50 miles north of Portland. This was a year-round service, apart from the depths of winter, when ice restricted operation. Originally, her main deck was open-sided and the pilothouse was only 4ft above. In her early years, she did not have a canopy over the upper deck.

1915: New boiler from Bath Iron Works fitted.

1918: 26 August: Was swept into a nearby bridge while approaching Cotrell's Wharf, Damariscotta after the engineer fell into the engine, injured his arm, and was unable to get the engine into reverse for berthing. Steamer capsized and sank. The engineer was drowned, but the nineteen passengers on board and the remaining crew were saved without serious injuries. *Tourist* was repaired and was back in service after six weeks.

19 December: Leased by Capt. Oscar C Randell for service on Casco Bay for 10 days whilst his own steamer, also named *Tourist*, was undergoing repair

1920: Damariscotta Steamboat Co. dissolved. *Tourist* out of service, due to competition from motor cars, which also now carried the mails.

1921: 8 October: Sold to Popham Beach Steamboat Co., for service on the Kennebec River. Renamed *Sabino*. Rebuilt with main deck partly closed in and pilot house raised to height of upper deck.

1927: 23 July: Sold to Harry P Williams, Portland, Maine, for use on Casco Bay.

1927-28 winter: Sponsons added to improve the stability of the steamer.

1933: Line renamed Island Evening Line. *Sabino* from now was running summer afternoon and evening trips from Portland to Peaks Island.

1935: 25 July: Sold to Casco Bay Lines. Same service continued.

1940-41 winter: New Almy boiler fitted. Funnel heightened by 6ft.

*c.*1942: Bow closed in between main and upper decks (this was removed after she left Casco Bay). Loading area added on hurricane deck on top of canopy.

1952: Laid-up as reserve steamer, by now the last steamer in the Casco Bay Lines fleet.

1956: July: Reactivated on the evening run to Peaks Island after her replacement, *Sunshine*, ran aground and was wrecked.

1957 and 1958: Operated on the day run to Bailey Island.

1959: For sale.

1961: March 14: Sold to Captain 'Red' Slavit of Haverhill, Mass. Steamer slipped and hull found to be rotten. Sold on to Edward Lamb, then on 19 April to Philip J. Corbin. Sailed to Newburyport, Mass., after temporary hull repairs.

Operated excursions on the Merrimac River out of Newburyport.

1962: autumn: Major refurbishment/rebuild commenced after she sank at her moorings. This took place on a home-made marine railway (slipway) at the owner's home on Rings Island. Stairways installed on either side of the pilothouse. New engine room ventilators fitted, originally on *Emita* (1880).

1967: September 8: Restoration completed, re-launched and re-entered service from Salisbury to Haverhill.

1971: Sold to SS Sabino Inc. (Philip Corbin, C. Bruce Brown and Joseph Pulvino, Newburyport).

1973: May 5: Leased to Mystic Seaport, Conn. Steamed part of the way to Mystic, and was towed the rest by the fishing boat *Silver Star*.

Summer: Started operating seven trips per day, six half-hour daytime trips and a 2-hour evening cruise, from Mystic Seaport. Restoration continued during the winter months until 1980.

1974: Sold to Mystic Seaport.

1992: Listed as a National Historic Landmark.

Sabino is the last survivor of the once numerous small local steamboats that operated on the New England coast. She sails daily from mid-May to early October, with half-hour sailings on the hour from 10:30 to 15:30, then a 90-minute sail down past Noank, where her machinery was built, at 16:30.

SWS SPLASH

Splash in the Delaware River. (Owners)

Length: 19.80m   Gross tonnage: 15
Propulsion: Sternwheeler
Engine type: 2-cylinder simple expansion horizontal, 12hp
Built: 1970, Rebuilt: 2004
Body of water: Delaware River   Home port: New Hope, NJ
Frequency of operation: Floating classroom, charters
Website address: www.gsenet.org/library/11gsn/2000/gs00526-.php; http://www.steamboat-classroom.org/
Builders: Unknown, Cincinatti
Owner: Delaware River Steamboat Floating Classroom Inc.
Former name: *Shawnee Princess* 2004

1970: Built as **Shawnee Princess** for use at Grand Rapids, Ohio, on the Maumee River.

1977: Entered service.

1980: New boiler installed, pilot house raised half a deck and sponsons added

1995: Out of service and laid-up.

*c.*2000: Sold to Bart Hoebel: Moved on a flatbed to his farm at Rocky Hill, NJ,

2001: Moved to C. & F. Metal Fabricators near Hillsborough, NJ for rebuilding, including a new hull. Rebuilt as a replica of an 1850s workboat.

2004: May 8: Re-entered service as **Splash** at New Hope, PA., on the upper reaches of the Delaware River. Used as a floating classroom for environment-based learning in partnership with the Delaware River Greenway Partnership. **Splash** is an acronym for **S**tudent **P**articipation in **L**earning **A**quatic **S**cience and **H**istory.

GREAT LAKES

TSS BADGER

Badger at Ludington, 1996.

Length: 125.15m   **Gross tonnage:** 4244
Propulsion: Twin Screw   **Engine type:** 2 x 4-cylinder unaflow, 8000hp
Built: 1953   **Passenger capacity:** 620, with 42 staterooms
Body of water: Lake Michigan   **Home port:** Ludington, Mi.
Frequency of operation: Daily   **Period of operation:** Mid-May to end October
Website address: ssbadger.com
Builders: Christy Corporation, Sturgeon Bay, WI
Engine builder: Skinner Engine Co., Erie, PA
Owner: Lake Michigan Carferry Co.
Remarks: Also carries 180 cars, coal-fired

1952: 9 September: Launched, on the same day as her sister **Spartan**.

1953: 21 March: Entered service for the Chesapeake and Ohio Railroad on the railway wagon, passenger, and car service across Lake Michigan from Ludington to Milwaukee, Manitowoc, and Kewaunee.

1963: The C&O merged with the Baltimore and Ohio Railroad to form B&O/C&O.

1980: October 6: Milwaukee service ceased. The rail service on this route had ceased earlier in the year.

1982: 9 January: Final crossing on Manitowoc service.

1983: 1 July: Taken over, along with the surviving routes, by Michigan-Wisconsin Transportation Corporation. Summer passenger and car service operated Ludington to Milwaukee. This only ran for two seasons.

1990: November 16: Final run from Ludington to Kewaunee. Laid-up at Ludington along with **Spartan** and **City of Midland 41**.

1991: July: Purchased by Charles E. Conrad.

November: Deal declared null, when the owner of Michigan-Wisconsin Transportation Corporation was declared bankrupt.

1992: February: Bankruptcy court awarded ownership to Conrad's company, Lake Michigan Carferry Service.

15 May: Summer only passenger and car service from Ludington to Manitowoc restarted. *Badger* had been refurbished prior to this. 16 inside staterooms removed and replaced by a gift shop, an exhibit area/museum, a movie lounge and an amusement arcade.

1996: Spring: Additional car deck fitted to increase car capacity from 120 to 180.

Badger is unique on two fronts, both in being the last steam-powered car ferry in operation worldwide, and in being the largest surviving coal-fired steamer in the world. Sister ship *Spartan* has been laid-up at Ludington since 1982, and has been used for parts to keep *Badger* going. *City of Midland 41* was converted to the barge *PM41* in 1997.

Badger sails each morning from mid-May to mid-October at 09:00 returning at 14:00, or departing at 08:00 from June to the beginning of September, returning at 13:15, when she also has an evening service at 19:55 with an overnight return.

SWS CHAUTAUQUA BELLE

Chautauqua Belle at Mayport, 1996.

Length: 19.80m
Propulsion: Sternwheeler
Engine type: 2-cylinder simple expansion horizontal, 40hp
Built: 1976   **Passenger capacity**: 122
Body of water: Lake Chautauqua   **Home port**: Mayfield, NY
Frequency of operation: Daily
Period of operation: Memorial Day to Labor Day
Website address: www.chautauquabelle.com
Builders: J. Webster, Mayville, NY   **Engine builder**: H. McBride
Owner: Chautauqua Lake Historic Vessels Co.

1975-76: Built at Mayville on Lake Chautauqua in what was basically a home-built operation by Jim Webster, who was to be he first operator. Built with a steel hull and aluminium superstructure.

1979: Hull widened to improve stability.

1980s: Sold to Sea Lion Project.

2004: Out of service for major repairs. Did not run at all in this season.

2007: 14 April: To be auctioned.

Lake Chautauqua, although only a few miles from Lake Erie, drains south into the Allegheny River, and thus into the Ohio, the Mississippi, and ultimately the Gulf of Mexico. *Chautauqua Belle* operates from Mayville at the northern end of the lake, and normally offers three cruises daily at 11:00, 13:15 and 15:00.

SS COLUMBIA

Columbia when in service, 1990. (B. Worden)

Length: 65.84m   **Gross tonnage:** 968
Propulsion: Single Screw   **Engine type:** Triple Expansion, 1,217hp
Built: 1902
Passenger capacity: 2,566 as of 1991. Built to carry as many as 4,500
Body of water: Detroit River and connecting waterways   **Home port:** Detroit, Mi
Frequency of operation: Awaiting restoration
Website address: www.boblosteamers.com/start.html;   www.sscolumbia.org
     www.freep.com/apps/pbcs.dll/article?AID=/20060116/NEWS02/601160399
Builders: Detroit Ship Building, Wyandotte, Mi.
Owner: Steamer Columbia Foundation

1902: Built for the Detroit, Belle Ile and Windsor Ferry Co. for service from Detroit to Bois Blanc Island, serving the Amusement Park there. Built with a steel hull and main deck and wooden superstructure. Designed by Frank E. Kirby.
  8 July: Entered service.
1908: From about this date Bois Blanc Island was known as Bob-Lo Island.
  Boat deck extended to stern.
1911: Boat deck extended forward from the pilothouse creating passenger space. This deck was not previously open to passengers. Bridge wings relocated.
1930s: Owners name changed to the Bob-Lo Excursion Co.
*c.*1941: Funnel modernised with lowered height and teardrop section.
Post-1945: Modern lifeboats and Wellin Davits installed replacing originals.
1991: autumn: Service withdrawn. Laid-up at the Nicholson Terminal and Dock Co. at Ecorse, Michigan. Sold to a Chicago nightclub operator.
1996: Ownership passed to Steamer Columbia Foundation. Moved to the former Great lakes Engineering Works property, Ecorse, Mi.
2003: Rumours of plan to move *Columbia* to New York and restore her for use on the Hudson River.
2004: Feasibility study undertaken to keep *Columbia* in Detroit and return her to service there.
  August dry-docked at Nicholson Terminal for survey.
  12 November: Towed to Nicholson Terminal to be shrink-wrapped to protect her from the ravages of the winter weather. This was funded by the Detroit Riverfront Conservancy.
2006: January: Detroit Riverfront Conservancy announced it would withdraw its funding by the spring.
  12 May: Sold to SS Columbia project, who intend to restore her and move her to New York to run on the Hudson River from New York to Bear Mountain.
  10 October: $150,000 grant awarded by New York State Office of Parks, Recreation and Historic Preservation.

Columbia has been slowly deteriorating over the years she has been laid-up while various plans were mooted to preserve her. She and *Ste Claire* are is the last unaltered survivors of the many passenger steamers designed by Frank E. Kirby (*Milwaukee Clipper* was designed by Kirby as *Juniata*, but was extensively rebuilt, and the hull of *City of Mackinac* of 1883 survives), and the last survivors of the large propeller-driven excursion steamers of inland America. It is to be hoped that one or other of the plans to preserve and restore her are successful.

SL LOUISE

Louise on Lake Geneva, Wisconsin.
(Virgil Wuttke, from a postcard)

Length: 22.90m
Propulsion: Single Screw   **Engine type**: Compound, 120hp
Built: 1902   **Rebuilt** (most recent): 1978
Passenger capacity: 50
Body of water: Lake Geneva   **Home port**: Lake Geneva, Wi
Frequency of operation: Charters   **Period of operation**: May to October
Website address: www.genevalakecruiseline.com/louise.php
Builders: Racine Boat Works
Engine builder: Plenty, Newbury, UK 1926, from *HSL???*, fitted 1978
Owner: Gage Marine. Williams Bay, Wi.

1902: Built for John J. Mitchell for service on Lake Geneva as a steel-hulled steam yacht. (Some sources say that she was built in 1900.)

1930s: Sold to the Wisconsin Transportation Co., operator of passenger services on the lake. Triple expansion stem engine replaced by a gasoline engine.

1965: Withdrawn from service. Hull stripped and moved a mile overland for storage.

Later: Acquired by Gage Marine.

1975: Restoration commenced by Gage Marine, owners of Geneva Lake Cruise Line.

1978: July: Re-entered service, with a steam engine fitted which had originally built in 1926 for a Royal Navy Harbour Service Launch (HSL) and a new boiler.

In recent years **Louise** has been offered for charters only, although occasional public passenger sailings have been offered in earlier seasons since restoration.

SS MARINE STAR

Aquarama when in service leaving Cleveland,
c.1960. (Richard I. Weiss collection, from a
postcard)

Length: 150.28m   **Gross tonnage**: 12,773
Propulsion: Single Screw   **Engine type**: Turbine, 9,900shp
Built: 1945   **Rebuilt** (most recent): 1962
Passenger capacity: 2,500
Body of water: Lake Ontario   **Home port**: Buffalo, NY
Frequency of operation: Laid-up, for sale
Website address: continuouswave.com/boats/aquarama;
wnyheritagepress.org/photos_week_2005/aquarama/aquarama.htm

Builders: Sun Shipbuilding & Dry Dock Co., Chester, PA
Engine builder: General Electric
Owner: Empire Cruise Lines, St Thomas, On.
Former names: *Aquarama*, 1995, *Marine Star* 1955

1945: Built as a standard C4-S-B5 cargo steamer for the United States Maritime Commission. Made one transatlantic return trip before the war ended, then laid-up.

1955: Sold to Sand Products Corporation, Detroit, Mi. Rebuilding to a car and passenger ferry started at Todd Shipyards, Brooklyn. Then towed to Chicago via the Atlantic Ocean, Gulf of Mexico, Mississippi and Illinois Rivers. Renamed *Aquarama*.

Mid-1955: Entered service on day cruises from Chicago.

1956: Offered cruises from Chicago to Detroit and Cleveland.

1957: In regular service from Cleveland to Detroit.

1962: Withdrawn from service, laid-up at Muskegon, M.

1987: Sold to Canadian owners and towed to Sarnia, Ont., where some of her interiors were gutted. It was proposed that she be moved to Port Stanley and used as a floating convention centre, but this never materialised.

1989: June: Towed to Windsor, Ont.

1995: 1 August: Towed to Buffalo, NY. Plans for use as a floating casino. Renamed *Marine Star*.

1997: Mover to Cargil Pool Elevator Pier.

It is extremely unlikely that *Aquarama* will ever steam again, having been laid-up for thirty-three years with little work having been done on her in that period.

PL PRINCESS

Princess at her berth at Bay City, Mi.
(C. Dougherty)

Length: 11.58m
Propulsion: Paddle steamer   **Engine type**: 1-cylinder walking beam, 20hp
Built: 1984   **Passenger capacity**: 6
Body of water: Saginaw River   **Home port**: Bay City, Mi.
Frequency: Charters
Builder: Millerick Bros, Coastal Marine, San Francisco
Engine builder: Sarlin Steamworks
Owner: Princess Steamboat Co. (Capt Ed Morris)
Former name: *Tule Princess*

1984: Built for use at San Francisco as the private yacht *Tule Princess* by David Sarlin, who built the engine himself to blueprints of an 1857 walking-beam engine.

1996: Following the death of David Sarlin, sold to Ed Morris, moved to her present location and renamed *Princess*. Offered for charters on the Saginaw River.

Princess is the only operating steamer in the world with a walking-beam engine, once very popular in American side-wheel paddle steamers.

SS STE CLAIRE

Ste Claire when in service, 1990. (B. Worden)

Length: 55.20m **Gross tonnage**: 870
Propulsion: Single Screw **Engine type**: Triple Expansion, 1,083hp
Built: 1910 **Passenger capacity**: 2414
Body of water: **Home port**: Lorain, Ohio
Frequency of operation: Undergoing restoration
Website address: www.bobloboat.com
Builders: Toledo Ship Building, Toledo, Ohio
Owner: St Claire Foundation (Ohio)

1910: Built for the Detroit, Belle Ile and Windsor Ferry Co. as a smaller sister of **Columbia** for the service from Detroit to the amusement park at Bob-Lo Island. Designed by Frank E. Kirby.

7 May: Launched.

1930s: Company now known as the Bob-Lo Excursion Co.

*c.*1941: Funnel modernised with lowered height and teardrop cross-section.

1940s: Extensive modernisation of the superstructure, including new pilothouse and associated crew's quarters in streamlined style, enclosure of main deck fore and aft with large circular openings.

1991: Autumn: Service withdrawn. Laid-up at the Nicholson Terminal and Dock Co., Ecorse, Michigan. Sold to a Chicago nightclub owner.

1996: Sold to Steamer Ste Claire Foundation (Michigan).

2001: Sold to Steamer Ste Claire Foundation (Ohio). Principals are Diana Evonne and her husband John Belko. Moved to Toledo for dry-docking and restoration. Occasionally opened to the public for tours; used as Halloween 'haunted house' prior to 31 October each year.

2003: Autumn: Moved to Lorain, Ohio, used as Halloween 'haunted house' prior to 31 October each year. Later moved to Belanger Park, River Rouge, Ohio where restoration continues.

SWS SUWANEE

Length: 18.30m
Propulsion: Sternwheeler **Engine type**: Horizontal
Built: 1927 **Rebuilt** (most recent): 1989
Passenger capacity: 60
Body of water: Dearborn Village pond **Home port**: Dearborn, Mi
Frequency of operation: Daily **Period of operation**: Year round
Website address: www.wrenscottage.com/gvm/transportation/suwanee.php
Builders: Henry Ford Museum, Dearborn
Owner: Henry Ford Museum and Greenfield Village, Dearborn, MI
Remarks: Coal-fired

1927: Built. The engine was built using parts of an earlier **Suwanee** which had been long since sunk in Florida's Suwanee River.

1930: New boiler built by Henry Ford.

1935: Superstructure added.

Suwanee at Dearborn Village, 1996.

1954: New boiler fitted.

1968: Original wooden hull replaced.

1988: Rebuilt with a steel hull.

2006: According to unconfirmed reports she had ceased operating due to the high costs of operating expenses and insurance.

Suwanee operates trips around Suwanee Lagoon, a pond at Greenfield Village, adjacent to the Henry Ford Museum at Dearborn, Ill. Greenfield Village is a collection of old buildings from various parts of the USA, many with historical connections to famous Americans, which have been re-erected in an open-air museum.

SL WINDERMERE

Length: 6.71m

Propulsion: Steam Launch   **Engine type**: Compound

Built: 1987   **Passenger capacity**: 12

Body of water: Walloon Lake   **Home port**: Wallonn Lake, Mi

Frequency of operation: in service

Website address: www.steamboating.net/page75.html

Builders: Beckmann Boatyard   **Engine builder**: Semple

Owner: David Beier

Windermere is a modern steam launch that operates in connection with her owner's restaurant on Walloon Lake in northern Michigan.

On the Great Lakes, the former Canadian Pacific steamer **Keewatin** is a museum at Douglas, Michigan. She is a unique survivor of the pre-1914 overnight passenger steamer.

The steam train ferry, **City of Milwaukee** (1931) is a museum at Manistee, Michigan, while **Milwaukee Clipper**, built in 1908 as **Juniata** is at Muskegon, Michigan.

There are many steam-powered 'lakers' (cargo vessels), still in service on the Great Lakes, almost all with turbine propulsion, although a couple, **Southdown Challenger** (1906) and the Canadian-owned **James Norris** (1952), still have reciprocating steam engines of the Skinner Unaflow variety. There are a number of such vessels in static preservation, but these are outside the scope of this volume.

GULF OF MEXICO

SS AMERICAN VICTORY

Length: 133.20m   **Gross tonnage**: 7,612

Propulsion: Single Screw   **Engine type**: 2 Turbine, 6,000hp

Built: 1945   **Rebuilt** (most recent): 2003

American Victory at her berth in Tampa.

Passenger capacity: 700
Body of water: Florida Coast   **Home port**: Tampa, Fl.
Frequency of operation: Occasional public trips
Website address: www.americanvictory.org
Builders: California Shipyards, Los Angeles   **Engine builder**: Allis Chalmers
Owner: American Victory Maritime Memorial and Museum Ship

1945: Built for the United States War Shipping Administration as one of a large fleet of emergency-built Victory Ships.

20 June: Launched.

June to September: Carried ammunition and other cargo for the US Army from Los Angeles and other US West Coast ports to Southeast Asia.

November: Sailed to Calcutta and Port Said, returning to New York.

1946: Made one sailing from New York to the Caribbean and South America.

June: Chartered to American Export Lines, carrying cargo, mainly from New York to Europe, Russia and the Near East in connection with the Marshall Plan.

1947: January: Led a convoy of several ships out of Odessa into the Black Sea through ice-choked seas against the advice of the captain of the local icebreaker.

December: Charter ended, laid-up in the Hudson River Reserve Fleet.

1951: 15 February: Chartered to the US Navigation Co.

1952: 21 February: Again chartered to the US Navigation Co., this time for service from United States and Japanese ports supporting the US troops in the Korean War.

30 December: Chartered to Dichmann, Wright and Pugh Inc., carrying military cargoes to the Korean War.

1953: March: Used to return the bodies of 370 GIs who had lost their lives in the Korean War.

1954: 6 January: Laid-up in the Sabino River Reserve Fleet, Texas.

1963: A plan to convert *American Victory* as one of fifteen Victory Ships designated as 'Forward Depot Ships' was never proceeded with. If this had gone ahead, she would have become *USNS Carthage*.

1966: 19 July: Chartered to the Hudson Waterways Corporation to support the Vietnam War effort under Military Sealift Command, carrying bombs, military equipment and supplies to South Vietnam and Thailand.

1967: September: Severely battered by Typhoon Diana en route from Japan to South Vietnam.

1969: 24 October: Deactivated, laid-up in the James River Reserve Fleet.

1985: 13 March: Chosen as part of the Victory Ship Validation Program. Brought back to full operational status and ran sea trials for 26 hours.

24 June: Returned to the James River Reserve Fleet.

1999: April: Acquired by The Victory Ship, Inc.

September: Towed to her new homeport of Tampa for preservation as a Memorial and Museum Ship.

2003: 20 September: First sailing under preservation with about 700 passengers.

American Victory makes several day cruises each year, leaving Tampa at 09:00.

MISSISSIPPI AND TRIBUTARIES

SWS AMERICAN QUEEN

Length: 127.40m   Gross tonnage: 4,700
Propulsion: Sternwheeler
Engine type: 2 tandem Compound Horizontal, 1,500hp
Built: 1995
Passenger capacity: 436
Body of water: Mississippi & tributaries   Home port: New Orleans, LA
Frequency of operation: Period of operation: All year
Website address: www.majesticamericanline.com
Builders: McDermott Shipyard, Morgan City, LA
Engine builder: Unknown builder *c.*1930, from dredger *Kennedy*
Owner: Majestic American Steamboat Company
Remarks: Also has 2 diesel screws

1994: Built, with a new hull, but using the engines (*c.*1930) from the dredger *Kennedy*.
1995: 27 June: Entered service for Delta Queen Steamboat Co. *American Queen* is the largest steam sternwheeler ever built, and the most elaborately decorated. Her steam-powered stern wheel is supplemented by two diesel-powered thrusters or propellers. Her funnels are hinged to pass through bridges, and her pilothouse can be hydraulically lowered for the same reason.
2001: October: Laid-up after the bankruptcy of her owners parent company, American Classic Voyages.
2003: January: Returned to service after Delta Queen Steamboat Co. was purchased by Delaware North Companies.
2005: 1 September: Home Port moved temporarily to Memphis because of the devastation in New Orleans by Hurricane Katrina.
  16 September: Withdrawn from service because of Hurricane Katrina.
2006: Owners merged with American West Steamboat Company to form Majestic American Steamboat Company.
2007: 9 March: First post-Katrina sailing scheduled, a nine-day cruise from New Orleans.

American Queen normally operates for most of the year on three and four night cruises from New Orleans to Baton Rouge, with longer seven-day one-way sailings to Memphis and vice versa in the summer months.

SWS BELLE OF LOUISVILLE

Belle of Louisville departing Louisville, 1996.

Length: 51.10m   Gross tonnage: 350
Propulsion: Sternwheeler
Engine type: 2-cylinder simple expansion horizontal, 400hp

Built: 1914   **Rebuilt** (most recent): 1968
Passenger capacity: 1,153
Body of water: Ohio River   **Home port**: Louisville, Ky
Frequency of operation: FSSuO
Period of operation: Memorial Day to Labor Day
Website address: www.belleoflouisville.org
Builders: James Rees & Sons, Pittsburgh
Engine builder: James Rees, Pittsburgh 1889-90
Owner: Louisville-Jefferson County Metro Government
Operators: Hornblower Marine Services
Former names: *Avalon* 1962, *Idelwild* 1947

1914: Built as *Idelwild* for the West Memphis Packet Co.

8 October: Launched.

1915: 8 January: Departed Pittsburgh for Memphis. Used as a passenger and freight ferry across the Mississippi River from Memphis, Tennessee to West Memphis, Arkansas.

Early 1920s: According to some sources, used for tramping (offering cruises for a few days each from different ports) in the entire Mississippi, Ohio, Illinois and Missouri River systems.

1925: 7 November: Sold to the Tri-State Ferry Co. of Cairo, Ill., for ferry service between Cairo and Bird's Point, Missouri.

1926: Used for excursions from St Louis on the upper Mississippi and Illinois Rivers.

1927: 30 August: Sold to Caesare Maestri, brother of the then Mafia boss in New Orleans, for use in New Orleans.

1928: Sold to New St Louis and Calhoun County Packet Co., of Hardin, Illinois, for use as a packet from St Louis to the Illinois River, also on excursion service on the Illinois and Ohio Rivers. Texas (topmost) deck roof extended for almost the entire length of the boat. Calliope (steam organ) and extensive gingerbread trim added. Most of second deck cabin bulkheads removed to provide large open, but covered, passenger area. Lights added to outline all four decks and pilot house at night. Based at Louisville.

1931: Chartered by the Rose Island Co. for excursions out of Louisville.

1934: Used for regular excursion service out of Louisville.

1938: Used to deliver a large electric dredger and its accompanying pontoons from Meredonia, Ill., to Island 8, near Hickman, Ky.

1941-45: Used during the Second World War to tow (push) oil barges. Also served as a floating USO nightclub for troops stationed at military bases along the Mississippi, and continued her excursion service during the summer months.

1945: January: New paddlewheel shaft fitted.

1947: Sold to J. Herod Gorsage, Peoria, Illinois and returned to the excursion trade.

1948: Renamed *Avalon* to honour the deathbed wish of her then master, Ben Winters, who had begun his career on an earlier steamer with that name. Used for tramping on the Mississippi, St Croix, Illinois, Kanawha, Ohio and Cumberland Rivers.

13 April: Sold to Ernst A. Meyer. (Other sources state 1950.)

1953: Fitted with the oil-burning boilers formerly in *Gordon C. Greene*, replacing the original coal-fired boilers, along with other engine room equipment, life jackets, life floats, linen, crockery, etc. from that boat. Texas deck shortened by 30ft.

1954: Sponsons added to the hull. Later based at Cincinatti.

By early 1950s: Main and second decks enclosed by boxy sheet metal bulwarks with rows of windows. Funnel shortened and pilothouse dome removed to clear low bridges. Mesh railings replaced by solid steel plate. Skylight windows covered over, leaving only three each end. Interior painted yellow, brown and pink.

1961: Laid-up at Cincinatti and badly vandalised.

1962: Out of service. Sold at auction, after the bankruptcy of her owners, to Jefferson County, Kentucky, later joined by the Louisville city authorities. Restored to operating condition.

14 October: Renamed *Belle of Louisville*.

1963: 30 April: Returned to service on excursions out of Louisville. New funnels fitted, Pilothouse dome re-fitted.

1965: New boilers installed, which were unsatisfactory.

1968: Hull widened by 5ft by the addition of sponsons. Lengthened by 10.2ft by the installation of a new bow. New roof fitted over the Texas deck. A further set of new boilers installed.

1998: 24 August: Sank at her moorings after a valve connected to the mains water supply was left open after filling the steamer's fresh water tanks. Raised a week later and towed to Jeffboat Shipyards for inspection and repairs.

2001: Hornblower Marine Services took over day-to-day operation, although the steamer is still owned by the local authorities. This was initially on a one-year contract, but a five-year contract was awarded to them in April.

2002: Marketing was improved by them, and the greater passenger numbers cut the losses the city was making on the operation of the steamer.

After 2002: Daily sailings reduced to weekends only.

Belle of Louisville is the last survivor of the Mississippi River day passenger steamers of the early twentieth century. She takes part in an annual steamboat race with *Delta Queen* and is a regular visitor to the *Tall Stacks* event at Cincinatti, a gathering of sternwheelers, both steam and diesel, public and privately owned. *Belle of Louisville* offers a 12:00 sailing FSO, a 14:00 sailing SuO, and evening cruises at 19:00 ThO and 20:00 FO, this latter being a 3-hour dance cruise, with the others being 2-hour trips.

SWS DELTA QUEEN

Delta Queen on the Mississippi River, probably in the sixties, from a postcard. (Author's collection)

Length: 86.90m   **Gross tonnage**: 1,650
Propulsion: Sternwheeler   **Engine type**: Compound Horizontal, 2,000hp
Built: 1926   **Rebuilt** (most recent): 1949
Passenger capacity: 174
Body of water: Mississippi & tributaries   **Home port**: New Orleans, LA
Frequency of operation: Cruises   **Period of operation**: All year
Website address: www.majesticamericanline.com
Builders: Denny, Dumbarton, superstructure Stockton, Ca.
Owner: Majestic American Steamboat Company

1925: Hull and engine built in sections by Denny, Dumbarton, Scotland. Reassembled at Stockton, California, where the superstructure was built. A number of US references erroneously give the builders name as Isherwood, but there was never a shipyard on the Clyde named Isherwood. Built for the California Transportation Co./River Lines for the overnight service from San Francisco to Sacramento. 9 March: Hull sections shipped from Dumbarton.

1927: 20 May: Completed. When in service in California, she had a large cover over the sternwheel.

2 June: Maiden voyage from San Francisco to Sacramento opposite sister ship *Delta King*, which had entered service a day earlier. On these trips she spent the day moored at Sacramento, but at San Francisco, after disembarking passengers, she moved to various cargo piers to offload and load freight consignments. She also carried passengers' cars at this period.

1932: California Transportation Co. merged with two other concerns to form River Lines.

1935: July: Dry-docked for inspection of hull and fitting of sprinklers following the Morro Castle disaster. Out of service for nine months.

1936: 1 April: Re-entered service.

1940: 29 September: Final trip from San Francisco to Sacramento, a special end-of-season daytime trip. October: Chartered to the US Navy as a receiving ship for Naval Reservists at Yerba Buena Island, San Francisco.

1941: April: Moved to Treasure Island.
November: Charter ended. Moved to Stockton and returned to owners. Sold to Isbrandtsen Steamship Co., New York for a proposed service on the Hudson or Mississippi. Boarded up for proposed delivery voyage. Early December: Again used by the Navy, this time to carry wounded from Pearl Harbor from the ships which had brought them from Hawaii to the naval hospital at Mare Island. Purchased by the US Navy. Assigned the Pennant Number YHB-7, the letters YHB denoting Yard House Boat.

1942: Loaned to the US Maritime Service for use as an officer's training school at Government Island, Oakland, followed by a brief stay at the former Neptune Beach Amusement Park at Alameda.

1943: Used as a military ferry in San Francisco Bay.

1944: 5 July: Belatedly reclassified as YFB-56, the prefix denoting Yard Ferry Boat.

1945: 23 April to 26 June: Used to take delegates to the United Nations Founding conference on sightseeing trips in San Francisco Bay.
After 2 September (VJ Day), used for ferrying returning servicemen from their ships to shore installations in the San Francisco Bay area.

1946: 20 August: Completed naval service, delivered to the mothball fleet in Suisun Bay. She was the only one of the large fleet of ships there that had arrived under her own power.
20 November: Purchased at auction by Greene Line for service on the Mississippi.

1947: February. Towed to Fulton's yard, Antioch to be prepared for the tow to the Mississippi. Paddle wheel removed. Lower two decks boarded up completely.
19 April: Left Antioch, towed by the tug **Osage**, passing through the Panama Canal on 10 May and arriving at the mouth of the Mississippi on 18 May.
19 May: Towed by two more tugboats up the Mississippi and Ohio Rivers to Cincinatti, where she arrived on 27 July.
August: Overhauled by Dravo Corporation, Pittsburgh. At this time the cover that was over her sternwheel in Californian waters was removed.

1948: 28 February: Left Pittsburgh for Cincinatti.
30 June: Left Cincinatti on her first cruise.

1969: Greene Line purchased by Overseas National Airways (ONA).

1970: Listed on National Register of Historic Places.
12 October: Made what was advertised as her farewell cruise from St Paul to New Orleans. It was planned that she be withdrawn because of SOLAS regulations that banned overnight passenger sailings on ships with a wooden superstructure.
31 December: Bill passed by US Congress to exempt **Delta Queen** from the above legislation. This was initally until 1973 and has been periodically extended.

1972: Made first cruises on the Arkansas River, to Little Rock, and the Illinois River, to Peoria.

1973: Company renamed The Delta Queen Steamboat Co. Five-year extension to exemption passed.

1974: April: Company sold to the Coca-Cola Bottling Co. of New York following the crash of two ONA aircraft and increased costs in building **Mississippi Queen**.

1976: Extension to legislation, covering 1978-83, passed.

1979: 17 August: President Jimmy Carter and his family sailed on **Delta Queen**.

Early 1980s: Control of company taken by Sam Zell and Bob Lurie, of Chicago. Exemption extended to 1988, later to 1993 and 1998.

1990: December to 1991: March: New wider hull fitted to increase buoyancy and fuel capacity.

1993: First cruises to Atchafalaya, on the Red, Old, and Atchafalaya Rivers.

1995: First cruise on the Intracoastal Waterway to Galveston, First cruise on the Arkansas River beyond Little Rock to Tulsa.

2001: October: Laid-up after the bankruptcy of her owners' parent company, American Classic Voyages.

2002: Returned to service after Delta Queen Steamboat Co. was purchased by Delaware North Companies.

2005: 1 September: Home port moved temporarily to Memphis because of the devastation in New Orleans by Hurricane Katrina.

2006: Owners merged with American West Steamboat Company to form Majestic American Steamboat Company.

Delta Queen is an important survivor, being the only historic overnight passenger sternwheeler in North America. She has a complex variety of sailings, those include: New Orleans east to Mobile and Pensacola; west to Galveston, sailings on the Cumberland River to Nashville, the Tennessee River to Chatanooga, on the Mississippi as far as St Paul, on the Ohio as far as Pittsburgh, and from Mobile to Chatanooga on the Tennessee-Tombigbee Waterway.

SWS JULIA BELLE SWAIN

Julia Belle Swain, 2003. (B. Worden)

Length: 32.90m   **Gross tonnage:** 98
Propulsion: Sternwheeler
Engine type: 2-cylinder simple expansion horizontal, 350hp
Built: 1971   **Passenger capacity:** 400
Body of water: Mississippi River   **Home port:** La Crosse, Wi.
Frequency of operation: MTWX   **Period of operation:** June to October
Website address: www.juliabelle.com
Builders: Dubuque Boat & Boiler Works
Engine builder: Gillette & Eaton, 1915 from **City of Baton Rouge**
Owner: Grand River Steamboat Co.
Remarks: 1- and 2-day trips

1971: Built as the last vessel built by Dubuque Boat & Boiler Works for service on the Illinois River at Peoria. Built using a 1915 engine from the ferryboat **City of Baton Rouge**. Designed by Capt Dennis Trone, who was her original owner.

1995: Spring: Sold to Grand River Steamboat Co. Moved to La Crosse, Wisconsin.

Julia Belle Swain's sailings include, about once a month, a one-way cruise to Winona, Minnesota and sometimes on the Wabasha, Minn., and back, as well as short Morning and evening cruises from La Crosse. Other one-way cruises go to Prairie du Chien, Wisconsin and Dubuque, Iowa, and to Lansing, Iowa. On the longer trips she offer short cruises from Winona, Dubuque or other ports on the river.

SWS MISSISSIPPI QUEEN

Length: 116.40m   **Gross tonnage:** 4,500
Propulsion: Sternwheeler
Engine type: 2 tandem Compound Horizontal, 2,000hp
Built: 1976   **Passenger capacity:** 422
Body of water: Mississippi & tributaries   **Home port:** New Orleans, LA
Frequency of operation: Laid-up   **Period of operation:** All year

Mississippi Queen from a postcard.
(Author's collection)

Website address: www.majesticamericanline.com
Builders: Jeffboat, Jeffersonville, Ind
Engine builder: Pine Tree Eng. Co., Brunswick, Maine
Owner: Majestic American Steamboat Company

1973: Construction began for Delta Queen Steamboat Co. Initially conceived as a replacement for **Delta Queen** prior to the latter's exemption from SOLAS regulations. Engines built to the design of the towboat **Jason**, to a Marietta Manufacturing Co. design. Because of modern anti-fire regulations, built entirely of metal, with no wood used in her construction or fitting out.

1974: Delta Queen Steamboat Co. was purchased by Coca-Cola Bottling Co. because of increasing costs in the construction of **Mississippi Queen**.

30 November: Launched.

1976: 20 July: Entered service alongside **Delta Queen**.

2001: October: Laid-up after the bankruptcy of her owners parent company, American Classic Voyages.

2002: 7 May: Returned to service after Delta Queen Steamboat Co. was purchased by Delaware North Companies.

2005: 1 September: Home port moved temporarily to Memphis because of the devastation in New Orleans by Hurricane Katrina.

2006: Owners merged with American West Steamboat Company to form Majestic American Steamboat Company.

Mississippi Queen operates a similar variety of cruise to **Delta Queen**, with seven-day cruises our of New Orleans, single trips to Memphis and back, an annual eleven-day trip to St Louis, billed as the 'Great Steamboat race', when she sails alongside **Delta Queen**, and sailings to and from St Louis, St Paul, Nashville, Chattanooga, Cincinatti, and Pittsburgh.

SWS NATCHEZ

Natchez at New Orleans.
(John Elk III from a postcard)

Length: 80.80m   **Gross tonnage**: 1,384
Propulsion: Sternwheeler
Engine type: 2 tandem Compound Horizontal, 1,500hp

Built: 1975   **Passenger capacity**: 1,600
Body of water: Mississippi River   **Home port**: New Orleans, LA
Frequency of operation: Three times daily   **Period of operation**: All year
Website address: steamboatnatchez.com
Builders: Bergeron Shipyard, Brathwaite, LA   **Engine builder**: From *Clairton*, 1925
Owner: New Orleans Steamboat Co.

1975: Built, with all-metal construction, for the New Orleans Steamboat Co. to operate excursions out of New Orleans. Also occasionally known as *Natchez IX* because she is the ninth vessels of that name on the Mississippi system. Fitted with the 1925 vintage machinery that was originally installed in the towboat *Clairton*, ex *Youghiogheny* of US Steel Co. The only wood in her is in the main bar, and the paddle floats (buckets in US parlance).
8 March: Launched.
2 April: Ran trials.
1982: Made a voyage to Louisville for a race with *Belle of Louisville* which she won. Gained the sobriquet 'Racehorse of the Western Rivers'.
2005: 28 August: Moved to Baton Rouge to escape Hurricane Katrina. Sailings cancelled unto 30 November. 19 October to 23 November: Made a River Relief 'tramping' tour on the Mississippi and Ohio Rivers. Visited Cincinatti, Louisville, Evansville, Paducah, Vicksburg and Baton Rouge, with cruises from each port. There were a races against the diesel sternwheeler *Belle of Cincinatti* at Cincinatti and *Belle of Louisville* at Louisville, both of which she won.

Natchez operates a 14:30 daily cruise, with a lunch cruise at 11:30 SSuO and an evening cruise at 19:00 FSO. All cruises last 2 hours.

There are a good number of Mississippi sternwheelers in static preservation, most of them former towboats. The most original is probably *William P Snyder Jr* at Marietta.

OTHER LAKES AND RIVERS

SWS GRACEFUL GHOST

Length: 15.20m
Propulsion: Sternwheeler   **Engine type**: 2-cylinder horizontal, 20hp
Built: 1990   **Passenger capacity**: 30
Body of water: Caddo Lake   **Home port**: Uncertain, TX
Frequency of operation: Daily
Period of operation: Late March to July; Labor Day to November
Website address: www.caddolake.com/steamboat.html
Builders: Joe Babcock, Plantersville, TX   **Engine builders**: Scripps Foundry and Machine Shop, Fredericksburg, Texas
Owner: Caddo Lake Steamboat Co.
Remarks: Wood-fired

1990: Built for Lexie Palmore as a private steamer to a design taken from a 1901 catalogue of Chicago Marine Iron Works.
1993: Public cruise started on Caddo Lake at Uncertain, Texas.

Main season sailings by *Graceful Ghost* are a daily evening cruise at 19:00, with three additional daytime sailings at 11:00, 13:00 and 15:00 each Saturday from May to July, with the 11:00 not running in March, April, September, October and November, no evening cruise in Novmber, and no sailings at all in August.

Scripps Foundry and Machine Shop have a small sternwheeler, **Rio Colorado** (1997), which operates on Lake Buchanan in Texas. She does not carry passengers and is used as a demonstration steamer for their stem engines.

SWS LIBERTY BELLE

Liberty Belle at Disney World, Florida.
(Melanie Deayton)

Length: 34.40m
Propulsion: Sternwheeler **Engine type:** 1-cylinder horizontal, 80hp
Built: 1973 **Passenger capacity:** 450
Body of water: Disney World **Home port:** Orlando, Fa.
Frequency of operation: Daily **Period of operation:** All year
Website address: www.mouseplanet.com/dtp/wdwguide/6_Parks/Magic_Kingdom/liberty_belle_photo_tour.htm
Builders: Todd Shipyards, Sarasota **Engine builder:** MAPO
Owner: Walt Disney World
Former names: *Richard F Irvine* 1996

1973: Built as **Richard F Irvine** for the Disney World Theme Park. Like the two **Mark Twains** at Los Angeles and Disneyland Paris, she moves round a pond in Frontierland, powered by her steam engine, but steered by underwater rails. There were originally also two walking-beam engine steam-powered side-wheelers, **Ports O'Call** and **Southern Seas** at Disney World, but they have been broken up in recent years as has the stern wheeler **Admiral Joe Fowler**.

Unknown date: Most of the wood on board replaced by fibreglass due to rapid deterioration because of the humid climate in Florida.

1996: Renamed **Liberty Belle**.

Liberty Belle operates many times each day on the 16-minute sail round Tom Sawyer's Island in Frontierland.

SS MINNEHAHA

Length: 21.30m
Propulsion: Single Screw **Engine type:** Triple Expansion, 200hp
Built: 1906 **Rebuilt** (most recent): 1996
Passenger capacity: 130
Body of water: Lake Minnetonka **Home port:** Excelsior, Minnesota
Frequency of operation: SSuO **Period of operation:** Summer
Website address: www.steamboatminnehaha.org

Builders: Twin City Rapid Transit Co., Minneapolis
Engine builder: O'Conner, *c.*1944, fitted 1994
Owner: Museum of Lake Minnetonka
Remarks: Sank 1926, raised 1980; coal-fired

1906: Built for Twin Cities Rapid Transit Co. (TCRT) as one of six express steamboats connecting with the Minneapolis streetcar system. Known as the 'streetcar boats.' Built in a streetcar (tram) workshop to a streetcar-like appearance. Used not only on commuter service connecting with the streetcars, but also to serve an amusement park on Big Island.
    May: Entered service.
1911 (or before): Canopy added on the upper deck.
1926: Scuttled in the lake north of Big Island after service ended due to the expansion of the road network to the lakeside communities.
1980: 29 August: Raised from the bottom of the lake. Taken to Niccum's boat yard. Lay outdoors rotting for ten years.
1990: Taken over by Minnesota Transportation Museum. Restoration and rebuilding began.
1996: 25 May: Restoration completed. Returned to service. Triple expansion engine from *c.*1944 fitted. Public cruises started in connection with a preserved streetcar line.
2005: Sold to the Museum of Lake Minnetonka.
2006: 5 August: Started operating again after a major refit and work on the hull.

Minnehaha operates on Saturdays, Sundays and public holidays with 1-hour non-landing trip at 10:20 and 17:20 and return trips to Wayzata (an hour each way) at 11:40 and 14:30. There is also a Wednesday evening concert cruise to Wayzata at 18:00 from mid-June to the beginning of August.

SWS MINNE-HA-HA

Minne-ha-ha on Lake George. (Owners)

Length: 31.40m
Propulsion: Sternwheeler
Engine type: 2-cylinder simple expansion horizontal, 127hp
Built: 1969   **Rebuilt** (most recent): 1998
Passenger capacity: 300
Body of water: Lake George   **Home port:** Lake George
Frequency of operation: 8-10 x daily
Period of operation: 1 May to Labor Day
Website address: www.lakegeorgesteamboat.com/minnehaha.html
Builders: Lake George Steamboat Co., Lake George Village, NY
Engine builder: Semple Engine Co., St Louis, unknown date, fitted 1994
Owner: Lake George Steamboat Co., Lake George Village, New York

1969: Built for present owners in a dry dock at Baldwin, N.Y., and towed to Lake George Village for completion.

1 August: Entered service.
1994: New engine fitted.
1998: December: Lengthened by 30ft.

Minne-Ha-Ha offers 1-hour cruises on the southern half of Lake George seven times daily from mid-June to Labor Day with five weekend trips each Saturday or Sunday outside the main season from mid/late May to mid-June and from the end of the main season in early September to early October. Peak season sailings are at 10:00, 11:30, 13:30, 15:00, 16:30, 18:00 and 19:30.

TSS TUSCARORA

Length: 23.16m
Propulsion: Twin Screw. Engine not yet installed
Built: 1900   Rebuilt (most recent): 200?
Body of water: Blue Mountain Lake   Home port: Prospect House
Frequency of operation: Undergoing restoration
Builders: A.C. Brown & Sons, Tottenville, Staten Island, New York
Owner: Peter Halsch   Remarks: Wooden-hulled

1900: Shipped in parts to Blue Mountain Lake and re-assembled there at Steamboat Landing.
   26 June: Launched. Later entered service for the Blue Mountain and Raquette Lake Steamboat Line, owned by W.W. Durrant.
1902: Owners now known as Raquette Lake Transportation Co.
1929: Service ceased. Purchased by Robert Graham, pulled out of the water and converted to a summer residence. Engine removed.
1998: Land on which the steamer lay purchased by Peter Halsch.
1999: Restoration started.

It is not certain at this stage if **Tuscarora** will be restored to operating passenger-carrying condition, although it is hoped that a steam engine will be re-installed.

The former Lake Champlain steamer **Ticonderoga** (1906), preserved on land at the Shelburne Museum at Burlington, Vermont, is the sole survivor of the once numerous walking beam steamers, with a large beam engine protruding above the superstructure which appeared to 'walk' when in operation.

WEST COAST

SL BURMAH QUEEN

Burmah Queen. (Capt. Wolfgang Schlager)

Length: 17.07m
Propulsion: Single Screw   Engine type: Compound, 149hp
Built: 1926   Rebuilt (most recent): 2003
Passenger capacity: 14
Body of water: Puget Sound   Home port: Seattle, Wa.
Frequency of operation: Charters and occasional public trips
Website address: www.raddampfer-kaiser-wilhelm.de/verein/Mitgleiderbericht/Burmah/seite-
    1_u.htm
Builders: Schiffswerft M C Stülcken & Sohn, Hamburg, Germany
Owner: Jerry Ross
Former names: *Clutha*, *Wasserschutzpolizei 5*

1925: 30 September: Launched.
1926: 29 April: Delivered to the Port Police in Hamburg, Germany as *Wasserschutzpolizei 5*.
1962: August: Withdrawn from service.
1964: Sold to David Rose and moved to California as deck cargo on a HAPAG freighter. Renamed
    Clutha. Based at Newport, Ca.
1968: Donated to San Francesco Maritime Museum. Renamed *Burmah Queen*. Sailed to San Francisco
    by Scott Newall. Lay at the Maritime Museum and was only occasionally steamed.
1976: Sold to Robert Blake, owner of boatyard General Engineering, to make space at the museum for the
    paddle tug *Eppleton Hall*. Occasionally steamed in San Francisco Bay and up to the Sacramento Delta.
    On the death of Robert Blake sold, possibly twice, to owners who did not operate her
1995: February: Sold to Jerry Ross, of Hansville, Wa, a volunteer stoker on *Virginia V*.
1996: September: Following some restoration work, towed to Seattle by the tug *Coast Pilot*.
    2 November: First steaming at Kingston Wa. Normally moored at Lake Washington, Seattle.
2001: Out of service awaiting a new boiler.
2006: Expected return to steam following the fitting of a new boiler.

SY CANGARDA

Cangarda at the Pusey and Jones Dock in 1901.
(A. Deayton collection)

Length: 39.60m   Gross tonnage: 116
Propulsion: Single Screw   Engine type: Triple Expansion, 300hp
Built: 1901   Rebuilt (most recent): 200?
Passenger capacity: 20
Body of water: In pieces   Home port: Fairhaven, Mass
Frequency of operation: Charters
Website address: www.powerandmotoryacht.com/features/0203cangarda;
    http://www.tricoastal.com/Cangarda/Cangarda.html
Builders: Pusey & Jones, Wilmington, De.
Engine builder: Sullivan
Former names: *Magedoma*, *Cangarda* 1903

1901: Built as a steam yacht at Wilmington for Charles Canfield and his wife Belle Gardner of Chicago,
    her name containing part of each surname.

20 May: Maiden cruise. Charles Canfield committed an 'indiscretion' with a female passenger, resulting in a America's most expensive divorce (at that time). He only made one cruise in **Cangarda**, and then put her up for sale.

1903: Sold to George and Mary Fulford, Brockville, Ontario. He was a Canadian Senator who had made his fortune selling 'Dr Williams' Pink Pills for pale people'. Renamed **Magedoma** after his wife Mary, and children George, Dorothy and Martha. Based on the St Lawrence River in the Thousand Islands area.

1905: George T .Fulford killed in Canada's first fatal motor accident. **Magedoma** inherited by his widow.

1927: Carried the Prince of Wales, later Edward VIII, the Duke of Kent, UK Prime Minster Ramsay MacDonald and the Canadian Prime Minister.

1939-45: Used by the Canadian Navy as a training ship on the Great lakes.

1948: Sold to J. Gordon Edmiston, Toronto.

1956: Purchased by S.B. Smith, Toronto. Taken to Rochester, NY for proposed restoration. During his ownership her steam engine was never used.

1983: Purchased by Richard Reedy. Towed to Boston, Mass, for restoration and proposed use as a charter vessel. Engine and boiler removed for restoration and rebuilt at Kew Bridge Steam Museum, London. Interior fittings stripped out.

1999: Sank at her moorings in Boston. Donated to J. Class Events, Newport, R I. Raised and taken to Fairhaven, Mass, for restoration. Rebuilt at Rutherford's Boatshop, Richmond, California.

2003: Sold.

2006: September: Reported to be undergoing a rebuild using a new hull with many of the old fitments and to be back in steam by 2007.

Cangarda is noteworthy in being probably the only surviving clipper-bowed steam yacht.

ST HERCULES

Hercules at San Franciso Maritime Museum, 1980.

Length: 41.15m   Gross tonnage: 409
Propulsion: Single Screw   Engine type: Triple Expansion, 1,000hp
Built: 1907
Body of water: San Francisco Bay   Home port: San Francisco
Frequency of operation: Occasional public trips
Website address: www.nps.gov/safr/local/herc.html
Builders: John H. Dialogue & Sons, Camden, NJ
Owner: San Francisco Maritime Historical Park

1907: Built for the Red Fleet, named because of their funnel colour, of San Francisco-based Shipowners and Merchants Tugboat Co. Sailed out to California through the Straits of Magellan along with sister

ship **Goliath**. Used for towing barges, sailings ships and log rafts between ports on the Pacific Coast of
the USA and Canada and to Hawaii.

1924: Sold to the Western Pacific Railroad Co. Used for towing railroad car barges across San Francisco
Bay.

1962: Withdrawn from service. Laid-up.

1975: Acquired by California State Park Foundation for San Francisco Maritime Museum. Restoration
commenced.

1977: Taken over by National Park Service.

1986: Designates a National Historic Landmark.

*c.*1992: Returned to steam.

Hercules sees occasional operation on trips in San Francisco Bay with a volunteer crew. Otherwise she is
an exhibit at San Francisco Maritime Museum.

SS JEREMIAH O'BRIEN

Jeremiah O'Brien at her berth in San Francisco.
(Marvin Jensen from a postcard)

Length: 127.30m   **Gross tonnage**: 7,176
Propulsion: Single Screw   **Engine type**: Triple Expansion, 2,500hp
Built: 1943   **Rebuilt** (most recent): 1979
Passenger capacity: 700
Body of water: San Franciso Bay   **Home port**: San Francisco, Ca.
Frequency of operation: Occasional public trips
Website address: www.ssjeremiahobrien.org;
        www.geocities.com/jeremiahobrien/obrien.html
Builders: New England Shipbuilding Corporation, South Portland, Me
Owner: US Government   **Operator**: National Liberty Ship Memorial Co.

1943: 19 June: Launched as one of over 2,700 Liberty Ships, These were part of an emergency shipbuilding
programme, and designed to be built simply and quickly

1944: June to December: Made eleven trips from the UK to Normandy as part of the D-Day invasion
force, including one trip from Belfast.

1945: Laid-up in the National Defense Reserve Fleet in Suisun Bay.

1966: Set aside by the United States Maritime Administration to be saved for future preservation.

1979: Taken out of mothballs and restored to operating condition.

1994: Sailed to Europe for the 50th anniversary of the D-Day landings.

Jeremiah O'Brien is normally berthed at Pier 45 at Fisherman's Wharf in San Francisco, and normally
makes two memorial sailings annually in May and October. She is one of only two surviving Liberty
Ships in the USA and is the only unaltered one.

2006 saw a visit to Sacramento in April, with the return sailing from Sacramento to San Francisco on sale
to passengers, and a visit to San Diego at the end of September for Fleet Week.

SS LANE VICTORY

Lane Victory at her berth at San Pedro, Los Angeles, 2004.

Length: 133.05m   **Gross tonnage**: 7,612
Propulsion: Single Screw   **Engine type**: 2 Turbine
Built: 1945   **Passenger capacity**: 800
Body of water: Pacific Ocean   **Home port**: Los Angeles
Frequency of operation: Occasional public trips
Website address: www.lanevictory.org
Builders: California Shipbuilding Corp., Los Angeles, Ca.
Owner: US Merchant Marine Veterans of the Second World War

1945: Built at part of a fleet of Victory ships for the US Maritime Administration. Used in the closing stages of the Second World War.

2 July: Maiden voyage for American President Lines.

1946 March: Chartered by American President Lines for use in the Marshall Plan.

1948: 11 May: Laid-up in the Suisun Bay Reserve Fleet.

1950: October: Used in the Korean War. Used in the Choisin Reservoir operation.

5 December: Rescued over 7,000 Korean civilians.

1953: 30 October: Laid-up in the Suisun Bay Reserve Fleet.

1965: September: Used in the Vietnam War.

1971: 17 February: Laid-up in the Suisun Bay Reserve Fleet.

1988: 18 October: President Reagan signed a bill donating **Lane Victory** to the US Merchant Marine Veterans of the Second World War.

1989: 12 June: Towed to Los Angeles Harbor, where restoration began.

1990: 14 December: Designated a National Historic Landmark. **Lane Victory** had steam up on this date and blew her whistle.

1992: 30 April: Dry-docked.

10 September: Sea Trials.

3 & 4 October: Inaugural cruise under preservation.

1994: Los Angeles Harbor Department built a permanent home for **Lane Victory** at Berth 94, next to the World Cruise Terminal and the Catalina terminal in San Pedro.

Lane Victory has been restored to wartime condition with grey hull and superstructure, and makes occasional cruises, about two each on a Saturday and Sunday in July, August and September, from her base at San Pedro, Los Angeles. These cruises include the capture of a 'spy' on board, an attack by enemy aircraft, and a memorial service.

SL LIBERTY BELLE

Length: 9.14m   Displacement tonnage: 9.2
Propulsion: Steam Launch   Engine type: Compound, 10hp
Built: 2001   Passenger capacity: 18
Body of water: Swinomish Channel   Home port: LaConner, Washington
Frequency of operation: 7 trips TX
Period of operation: 1 April to 15 September
Website address: www.steamboating.net/page84.htmll
Builders: Beckmann Boatshop, Slocum, Rhode Island
Engine builder: Strath Steam Works, Goolwa, Australia
Owner: Liberty Belle Steamship Co.
Former name: *Zebedee* 2005

2001: Built as *Zebedee* for 1-hour harbour trips at Port Townsend, Washington. Built with a fibreglass hull painted to simulate wood planking.
2005: Sold to present owner, moved to La Conner, and started operating trips out of there.

Liberty Belle operates cruises every hour daily except Tuesday from 11:00 to 17:00 from LaConner through the Swinomish Channel.

SWS MARK TWAIN

Mark Twain at Disneyland in 1980.

Length: 32.90m   Gross tonnage: 150
Propulsion: Sternwheeler
Engine type: 2-cylinder simple expansion horizontal
Built: 1955   Passenger capacity: 400
Body of water: Disneyland   Home port: Anaheim, Ca.
Frequency of operation: Daily   Period of operation: All year
Website address: allearsnet.com/dlr/tp/dl/twain.htm
Builders: Todd Shipyards, Los Angeles Division, San Pedro
Engine builder: Walt Disney Productions
Owner: Disneyland, Burbank, Ca.

1955: Built for the pond at Disneyland amusement park, the first Disney attractions park. Walt Disney and his wife celebrated their 30th wedding anniversary on board three days before the park opened. Money to complete her came from Walt Disney personally after funding ran out. Initially there was no maximum passenger capacity and on occasion she almost capsized, when passengers crowded to one side to see one of the other attractions in Disneyland. A capacity limit was imposed after that.

Although there is a large ship's wheel, she is guided round the pond by an underwater guide rail rather than by steering.

According to some reports, she was not built in 1955, but in 1956 to replace the first Disney sternwheeler, ***River Belle***, which had sunk on the opening day, 17 July 1955, off Tom Sawyer Island after being overloaded.

SY MEDEA

Medea off San Diego.
(Dale Frost, from a postcard)

Length: 33.40m
Propulsion: Single Screw   **Engine type**: Compound, 254hp
Built: 1904
Body of water: San Diego harbour   **Home port**: San Diego, Ca.
Frequency of operation: Occasional public trips
Website address: www.sdmaritime.org/contentpage.asp?ContentID=54
Builders: Stephen, Linthouse, Govan, Glasgow, Scotland
Owner: Maritime Museum Assn of San Diego
Former names: *Corneille* 1919, *Medea* 1917

1904: 29 August: Launched, after only fifty-one days under construction. Built as a steam yacht for William McAllister Hall, Laird of Torrisdale Castle, Carradale, Scotland. Based at Campbeltown, she was used for carrying hunting and shooting parties round the West Coast of Scotland, and was normally laid-up at Greenock in the winter months.

1911: 7 November: Sold to Frederick G. Todd, Troon, Scotland.

1914: Sold back to the chairman of her builders, John Stephen, Linthouse, Govan, Glasgow.

1917: On his death, offered to the Red Cross as a hospital ship.

24 April: Sold to the French Navy and renamed ***Corneille***. Converted to a patrol boat on anti-submarine warfare duties.

15 June: Entered service for the French Navy, based at Cherbourg. Used to escort sailing ships.

1918: 1 September: Now used as a boarder and minesweeper.

1919: 21 June: Sold at auction to M. Grahame-White, Warsash House, Warsash, Hants, England. Based at Glasgow. Electric light installed. Regained the name ***Medea***.

1921: Sold to H. Dudley-Ward, MP, London. Based at Southampton.

1922: Sold to the Rt Hon. F.E. Guest, MP, Roehampton, England. Still based at Southampton.

1923: Sold to A.M. Symington, Lisbon. Home port now Gibraltar.

1927: Sold to B.H. Piercy, London. Based at Cowes, Isle of Wight.

1929: Sold to Fred J Stephen, Rhu, Scotland, chairman of Stephens if Linthouse, and the original designer of the yacht. Used as commodore vessel of the Royal Northern Yacht Club.

1932: December: Fred Stephen died. A major rebuild and lengthening he had planned for ***Medea*** was never carried out.

1933: Put up for sale by the executors of Fred Stephen's estate.

1934: Sold to A.A. Paton, Liverpool.

1935: Sold to J.L. Wild, London. Spent her time between Brightlingsea and the Isle of Wight. Sailed under the flag of the Royal Motor Yacht Club, Sandbanks, Poole.

1941: April: Requisitioned by the Royal Navy as a barrage balloon vessel on the Thames Estuary, based at Sheerness.

1942: 25 September: Used as an accommodation vessel at Peterhead, Scotland.

1 December: Taken over by the Royal Norwegian Navy. Peterhead was one of the bases for the 'Shetland Bus,' fishing cutters running clandestine missions carrying arms and ammunition into occupied Norway. Used as an accommodation ship for maintenance crews for these craft.

1943: March: Transferred back to the Royal Navy.

1945: 9 August: Laid-up.

November: Sold back to J.L. Wild, now of Kenley, Surrey. In static use on a mud berth at the Aldous Successors Ltd shipyard, owned by Mr Wild, at Brightlingsea.

1962: Following the death of Mr Wild in 1960, sold to C.E. Reffitt, London. Returned to steam.

1964: Converted from coal to oil firing. Major refit at Bideford, Devon.

1965: early: Sold to Captain N.P.S. Millar, Padstow, Cornwall, England. Used as a charter yacht. Based at the McGruer yard at Roseneath, on the Gareloch, Scotland

1967: Boiler retubed.

1969: Sold to Capt. K.L. Holmberg, Jarnforsen, Sweden. Home port now Las Palmas, Gran Canaria, under the Panama flag.

1971: early: Berthed at Oskarshamn, Sweden, in use as a floating art gallery.

Sold to N. Paul Whittier, Goudge Island, BC, Canada. Sailed to Rotterdam, and then taken as deck cargo on German container ship **Riederstein** to Los Angeles.

October: Offloaded at Long Beach, Los Angeles. Steamed to Goudge Island, her owner's private island, for restoration.

1973: June 29: Following restoration and a return to her 1904 condition, including removal of the wheelhouse and a post-war extension to the aft cabin, steamed from Victoria, BC, to Sam Diego.

July 14: Donated to the Maritime Museum Association of Sam Diego.

1977: Flag changed from Panama to the USA. Certified by the US Coast Guard for harbour excursions.

1990: Dry-docked and work done on preservation of hull.

Medea is one of only a handful of surviving steam yachts worldwide. She is normally a static exhibit at San Diego Maritime Museum but operates VIP trips about two days a month.

SWS PORTLAND

Portland on the Columbia River at Portland, Oregon.

Length: 66.70m   Gross tonnage: 923
Propulsion: Sternwheeler
Engine type: 2-cylinder simple expansion horizontal, 1,800hp
Built: 1947   Rebuilt (most recent): 1993
Passenger capacity: 12(?)
Body of water: Columbia and Willamette Rivers   Home port: Portland, Oregon
Frequency of operation: Occasional trips
Website address: www.oregonmaritimemuseum.org;
        www.meic.com/Newsletters/2003/Spring03.htm
Builders: Northwest Marine Iron Works
Owner: Port Authority of Portland
Operator: Oregon Maritime Center and Museum (OMCM)

1947: Built as a port tug for Portland. She was the last steam-powered stern-wheeled tug to be built in the United States.

1981: Withdrawn from service.

1990: Restoration began by volunteers.

1993: June: Steamed again under her own power.

1994: Disguised as a Mississippi gambling boat in the film *Maverick*, starring James Garner, Jodie Foster and Mel Gibson.

Portland is normally berthed in downtown Portland on the Willamette River, and makes occasional excursions, As she does not have a passenger certificate, due to her not getting approval for the use of her boiler, which is the original one from building, passengers are selected at random from OMCM members.

SS RED OAK VICTORY

Length: 133.20m   Gross tonnage: 7612
Propulsion: Single Screw   Engine type: Turbine
Built: 1944
Body of water: San Franciso Bay   Home port: Richmond, Ca.
Frequency of operation: Undergoing restoration
Website address: www.ssredoakcitory.com
Builders: Kaiser Shipyards, Richmond, Ca.
Owner: United States Government, MARAD

1944: 5 December: Acquired by the US Navy from the US Maritime Commission, and commissions as the cargo ship **USS Red Oak Victory**.

1945: 11 January: Departed San Francisco for Pearl Harbor on her maiden voyage. Later departed Hawaii for service as an ammunition ship, operating out of the Philippines, carrying ammunition to various ships of the US Fleet in the Pacific.

1946: 12 June: Returned to the US Maritime Commission.

1947: In service for the Luckenbach Gulf Steamship Co., Seattle.
Laid-up in Suisun Bay Reserve Fleet.

1951: 12 February to 14 April: In service for the Luckenbach Steamship Co.

1953: 11 November: Laid-up in Suisun Bay Reserve Fleet.

1956: Operated one voyage with emergency bulk grain shipments to India and Pakistan.

1957: Operated by the Merchant Marine Administration.
Laid-up in Suisun Bay Reserve Fleet.

1965: 31 December: Leased to American Mail Lines.

1966: 27 January: Sailed from West Coast USA to South East Asia ports carrying supplies for the Vietnam War.

1968: 18 December: Withdrawn from service. Laid-up in Suisun Bay Reserve Fleet.

1998: 20 September: Towed to Richmond for preservation. The restoration project is part of the Richmond Museum of History, and she is being restored to her original as-built condition. Initial restoration is for use as a static museum/war memorial, but the long term aim it to restore **Red Oak Victory** to operational condition.

2006: 19 March: Opened as a museum.

SS VIRGINIA V

Length: 35.30m   Gross tonnage: 99
Propulsion: Single Screw   Engine type: Triple Expansion, 400hp
Built: 1922   Passenger capacity: 328

Virginia V at Seattle 1987. (Author's collection)

Body of water: Lake Union   **Home port**: Seattle, Wa.
Frequency of operation: Occasional public trips
Period of operation: May to December
Website address: www.virginiav.org
Builders: M. Anderson & Sons, Maplewood, Washington
Engine builder: Heffernan Engine Works, Seattle, 1898 from *Virginia IV*
Owner: Steamer Virginia V Foundation
Remarks: Wooden hull

1922: Built for the West Pass Transportation Co. as one of the 'Mosquito fleet' of small steamers operating on Puget Sound, using the engines from her predecessor *Virginia IV*, ex *Tyrus*, which had been sold and fitted with a diesel. Built for the West Pass route from Seattle to Tacoma. The engine had been built for the US Government, and installed in *Tyrus* when she was built in 1904.

5 March: Launched.

11 June: Maiden voyage on the Seattle to Tacoma route via Colvos Passage (the West Pass).

1926: April: US Mail contract awarded.

1931: 31 May: Schedule doubled to two round trips daily, one via the West Pass, and one via the East Pass, i.e. west and east of Vashon Island respectively.

1934: 21 October: Superstructure severely damaged whilst docking at Ollala in a 70mph storm. No injuries. Hull undamaged, however. Rebuilt at Lake Washington Shipyard, Houghton.

1938: January to April: *Virginia V* laid-up for the winter for the first time.

1940: Served the forts at the entrance to Puget Sound under a contract from the United States Army.

1942: 2 April: Moved to the Columbia River: Operated from Portland to Astoria.

6 August: Arrested because of unpaid debts. Laid-up at Vancouver, WA. Later sold at auction at Tacoma to Harbor Island Ferries, Seattle, but remained laid-up at Vancouver.

1943: 27 December: Sold to Jack S. Katz of Anacortes and Seattle and Captain Howard Parker.

1944: February. Moved to Seattle. Operated on the East Pass route.

1947 onwards: Operated excursions trips out of Seattle, to the San Juan Islands at weekends, and round Bainbridge Island on Wednesdays and Fridays.

1954: 5 January: Controlling interest sold to Captain Philip Luther of Puget Sound Excursion Lines, as Captain Parker was now seventy-five and about to retire.

1956: Controlling interest sold to Charles McMahon.

1958: Controlling interest sold to James F 'Cy' Devenny.

1968: Sold to the Northwest Steamship Co. Continued in excursion service.

1973: Placed on the National Register of Historic Places.

1976: Virginia V Foundation founded to work with Northwest Steam.

1978: Some restoration work done to meet US Coast Guard requirements, part funded by the US National Park Service.

1980: 30 September: Sold to the Virginia V Foundation.

1992: 5 October: Listed as a National Historic Landmark.

1996: Passenger certificate withdrawn. Used as a private yacht by Foundation members.

30 October: Major restoration work begun.

2002: 18 June: Returned to passenger service following restoration.

Virginia V operates a variety of charters and occasional public trips from Seattle, her normal run being a 3-hour cruise on Lake Union and Lake Washington. She is the sole survivor of the once numerous vessels of the 'Mosquito Fleet'..

ALASKA

SWS ALASKA QUEEN

Alaskan Queen at Sacramento when in service.
(Mrs M. Wilmunder)

Length: 43.90m   Gross tonnage: 375
Propulsion: Sternwheeler
Engine type: 2-cylinder simple expansion horizontal, 250hp
Built: 1984   Passenger capacity: 350
Body of water: Alaskan coast   Home port: Ketchikan
Frequency of operation: Twice daily   Period of operation: May to September
Website address: members.tripod.com/~Write4801/riverboats/e.html#ELOUI
Builders: Rancho Cordova, Ca.
Engine builder: Haslup Engine and Machine Co., Wheeling, WV, 1884 (from tug *Detroiter*)
Owner: Alaska Travel Adventures
Remarks: Has a bow thruster and two Honda outboard motors that serve as stern thrusters
Former name: *Elizabeth Louise*, 2007

1975: Construction commenced in the owner's backyard at Rancho Cordova, about 21 miles from Sacramento. The engine was built in 1884 for **Andy Hatcher**, and were late used in **Ray**, then in a floating sawmill, the paddle freighter **W.F. Smith** and finally the towboat **Coppertory**, which was later renamed **Detroiter**, in which they were in operation until 1971.

1981: 29 January: Launched in the Sacramento River near Elkhorn.

1985: 13 September: Entered service after fitting out.

2003: Hal Wilmunder, the seventy-eight-year-old owner, fell into the river and was drowned whilst undergoing repairs to damage caused by vandals to the steamer.

2006: Sold to Alaskan Travel Adventures.

2007: Moved to Foss Maritime Co., Seattle, for two months refurbishment including the installation of larger windows on the main deck and the fitting of a calliope. Renamed **Alaskan Queen**.

April: Arrived at Ketchikan after a ten-day voyage.

Alaskan Queen offers two two-hour cruises from Ketchikan daily. These are offerd as part of the shore excursion programme for most cruise ships calling at Ketchikan. The trips go south as far as Saxmar village. She is up for sale at the time of writing.

SL TEDIMAE

Length: 9.14m
Engine type: Compound, 12hp
Built: 2005
Passenger capacity: 12?
Home port: Ketchikan, Al
Frequency: new steamer
Builder: Beckman Boatshop, Slocum, Rhode Island
Engine builder: Strath Steam Works, Goolwa, Australia
Remarks: Wood-fired

2005: Built to a standard Tourboat 30 design by Beckmann Boatshop, a sister of **Laurie Ellen**. Originally fitted with a Semple engine, which was replaced by a Strath Swan before delivery. Due to the Alaskan climate the engine is totally enclosed within the cabin.
2006: April: Ran sea trials. Delivered.

SL LAURIE ELLEN

Length: 9.10m
Propulsion: Single Screw   Engine type: Compound V-shaped, 10hp
Built: 1999   Passenger capacity: 18
Body of water: Alaskan Coast. Hope Port: Juneau, Alaska
Frequency of operation: 6x SuX
Website address: www.juneausteamboatco.com
Builders: Beckmann Boatshop Ltd, Slocum, Rhode Island   Engine builder: Semple
Owner: Juneau Steamboat Co., Juneau

1999: Built for steamboat enthusiast Randy Flood, and operated hour-long public trips five times daily in the peak season out of Castine, Maine on Penobscot Bay for his Castine Steamboat Co.
2005: Sold to present owners and moved by land to Juneau, Alaska. In 2005 trips were offered daily except Sundays at 09:00, 10:30, 12:00, 13:30, 15:00 and 16:30, with the first two sailings omitted on Mondays.

In static preservation on the West Coast are the San Francisco Bay ferries **Eureka** (1923) at the San Francisco Maritime Museum and **Berkeley** (1898) at the San Diego Maritime Museum, the **Delta King** (1926), sister ship of the **Delta Queen**, which is a hotel at Sacramento, and **Eppleton Hall** (1914), a British paddle tug, also at the San Francisco Maritime Museum. There are a number of former San Francisco ferries, much altered, in a community of houseboats at Sausalito. The sternwheeler **Nenana** (1933) is in static preservation at Fairbanks, Alaska.

28 Latin America

Survivors in Latin America are rare, but they include three notable steamers: a two-funnelled naval tug, a wood-burning sternwheeler, and a typical coastal passenger-cargo steamer from the thirties, although of a design going back to the nineteenth century, on Lake Titicaca. Three small steam lunches have been recently 'discovered' on the Internet, and it is possible that more survive in this vast continent.

ARGENTINA

PS EXEQUIEL RAMOS MEJIA

Exequiel Ramos Mejia, with *Roque Saenz Pena* behind her, at Posadas, when in service prior to 1990. (C. Mey collection)

Length: 60.84m   **Gross tonnage**: 820
Propulsion: Paddle Steamer   **Engine type**: Unknown, 520hp
Built: 1911
Body of water: River Parana   **Home port**: Posadas
Frequency of operation: Occasional public trips
Website address: www.histarmar.com.ar/Infgral/FerriesHistPosadas.htm
Builders: A. & J. Inglis, Pointhouse, Glasgow
Owner: Ferrocarril Nacional General Urquiza

1911: Built in Scotland. It is uncertain whether she was steamed out to Argentina or shipped in sections.

1913: 18 October: Entered service for the Ferrocarril Nordeste Argentino, for the train ferry service from Posadas, Argentina to Pacú-Cuá, Paraguay on the main railway line from Buenos Aires to Asuncion. 6 coaches or 10 wagons could be carried.

1926: 20 September: Following a major cyclone one of these two train ferries was taken to Itapúa, the regional capital, where 400 had been killed and many injured, to serve as a floating hospital.

1932-35: Sent to Paraguay as a relief ship during the war between Paraguay and Bolivia.

Unknown date: Taken to Formosa with supplies during flooding of the Paraguay River.

1948: 21 October Ferrocarril Nordeste Argentino merged with the Ferrocarril Entre Rios to become Ferrocarril Nacional General Urquiza.

1990: 8 March: Crossing replaced by a rail bridge. Ferries laid-up at Posadas. Later donated to the city of Posadas.

2003: One ferry turned into a museum, the other maintained on a care and maintenance basis.

Neither ferry is currently operational.

PS ROQUE SAENZ PENA

The train deck of *Roque Saenz Pena* shortly after she ceased service, 1990. (Trains Unlimited Tours)

Length: 60.84m   Gross tonnage: 820
Propulsion: Paddle Steamer   Engine type: Unknown, 520hp
Built: 1911
Body of water: River Parana   Home port: Posadas
Frequency of operation: Occasional public trips
Website address: www.histarmar.com.ar/Infgral/FerriesHistPosadas.htm
Builders: A. & J. Inglis, Pointhouse, Glasgow
Owner: Ferrocarril Nacional General Urquiza

1911: Built in Scotland. It is uncertain whether she was steamed out to Argentina or shipped in sections.

1913: 12 September: Entered service for the Ferrocarril Nordeste Argentino, for the train ferry service from Posadas, Argentina to Pacú-Cuá, Paraguay on the main railway line from Buenos Aires to Asuncion. 6 coaches or 10 wagons could be carried.

1926: 20 September: Following a major cyclone one of these two train ferries was taken to Itapúa, the regional capital, where 400 had been killed and many injured, to serve as a floating hospital.

1932-35: Sent to Paraguay as a relief ship during the war between Paraguay and Bolivia.

Unknown date: Taken to Formosa with supplies during flooding of the Paraguay River.

1948: 21 October Ferrocarril Nordeste Argentino merged with the Ferrocarril Entre Rios to become Ferrocarril Nacional General Urquiza.

1990: 8 March: Crossing replaced by a rail bridge. Ferries laid-up at Posadas. Later donated to the city of Posadas.

2003: One ferry turned into a museum, the other maintained on a care and maintenance basis.

Neither ferry is currently operational.

BRAZIL

SS ARY PARRIERAS

Length: 119.44m   Gross tonnage: 4,879
Propulsion: Single Screw   Engine type: 2 Turbine, 4,800hp
Built: 1957   Rebuilt (most recent): 2,000
Passenger capacity: 497
Body of water: South Atlantic   Home port: Rio de Janeiro
Frequency of operation: Troopship
Website address: www.naviosdeguerrabrasileiros.hpg.ig.com.br/A/A106/A106.htm
Builders: Ishikawajima, Tokyo
Owner: Brazilian Navy

The Brazilian troopship *Ary Parreiras*.

1956: Built as part of a group of four steam turbine powered troopships-cum-cargo ships for the Brazilian Navy, the others being **Custódio de Mello** (withdrawn 2002), **Soares Dutra** (withdrawn 2001), and **Barroso Periera** (withdrawn 1995).

24 August: Launched.

1957: May: Arrived at Rio de Janeiro. Used as a naval transport ship.

1978: 9 January: Inaugural trip as a training ship for the Merchant Navy Officers Training School. Later reverted to use as a troopship.

2000: Major overhaul, including refurbishment of the machinery.

SWS BENJAMIN GUIMARÃES

Benjamin Guimarães on the Rio Sao Francisco.
(Author's collection)

Length: 38.10m   Gross tonnage: 321
Propulsion: Sternwheeler
Engine type: 2-cylinder simple expansion horizontal
Built: 1913   Rebuilt (most recent): 2004
Passenger capacity: 26
Body of water: Rio Sao Francisco   Home port: Pirapora
Frequency of operation: Weekly
Website address: www.primotur.com.br/detalhes_roteiro.asp?id=208
Builders: J. Rees, Sons & Co., Pittsburgh, Penn., USA
Owner: Cia de Navegaceo Sao Franciso, Pirapora
Remarks: Wood-fired

1913: Built by Rees of Pittsburgh as part of a large group of sternwheelers for the Amazon. Original name unknown.

1926: Sold to Júlio Mourão Guimarães and named after his father. Moved to the Rio São Francisco and used mainly for cargo on the river.

1963: Operated by Unitour Travel Agency, Belo Horizonte on thirteen-day cruises on the 1400km stretch from Pirapora to Juazeiro.

1964: Taken over by Servico da Comissão de Vale São Francisco (CVSP).

Mid-1980s Several dams built on the river, limiting use to the section from Pirapora to São Francisco.

1985: First unsuccessful attempts to restore her and retain her in service.

1988: Operated by Unitour on five-day cruises from Pirapora to São Francisco.

1991: Used by Focus Tours, Belo Horizonte on twice weekly cruises (Friday to Sunday and Sunday to Thursday) from Pirapora.

*c.*1992: Boiler failure: Out of service and laid-up.

1994: Sold to a Bahian entrepreneur. No work done on her and she was allowed to become derelict and be vandalised.

2002: January: Restoration started, funded by the tourism ministry of the state of Minas Gerais and Embratur (The Brazilian Institute of Tourism). It was decided to retain the wood-fired steam engine rather than replace it with a diesel. Hull rivets replaced by welding. Boiler repaired.

2004: 22 July: Restoration completed. In operation again on cruises from Pirapora sailing on a five-day trip with departures every Sunday.

[A Brazilian website claims that she was built in 1898 in Toronto for service on the Stikine River, as part of an all-Canadian route to the Klondike gold rush, but that she was never completed and was sold for use on the Amazon, moving to the Rio São Francisco in 1913. Canadian sources do not bear this story out, however.]

TST LAURINDO PITTA

Preserved tug *Laurindo Pitta* at Rio.
(Rogerio Cordeiro)

Length: 39.00m   **Gross tonnage:** 271
Propulsion: Twin Screw   **Engine type:** two 4-cylinder Compound, 850hp
Built: 1910   **Rebuilt** (most recent): 2000
Body of water: Guanabara Bay   **Home port:** Rio de Janeiro
Frequency of operation: MTWX, 2x daily   **Period of operation:** Year round
Website address: www.naviosdeguerrabrasileiros.hpg.ig.com.br/L/L009/L009.htm;
        https://www.mar.mil.br/sdm/pitta/pitta.htm
Builders: Vickers, Sons & Maxim, Barrow-in-Furness, England
Owner: Brazilian Navy
Operator: Naval Museum Friends League
Remarks: Naval tug

1910: Built for the Brazilian navy DNGO (Operations Naval Division) as a deep-sea tug.

1918: Based at Dakar, West Africa as mobile logistics support.

Later: Used as a harbour tug and at Rio de Janeiro naval base.

1969: Rebuilt.

1997: Restoration began.

2000: Restoration completed by the Naval Museum Friends League and used on trips round Guanabara Bay from the Espaco Cultural da Marinha (Navy Cultural Centre).

Laurindo Pitta is the only two-funnelled steam tug to survive in the world. She has an exhibition on board commemorating the involvement of the Brazilian Navy in the First World War.

CHILE

SS CHUCAO

Chilean steamer *Chucao*.

Length: 17.50m
Propulsion: Single Screw   **Engine type:** Compound, 45hp
Built: 1991
Body of water: Lago de Villarica   **Home port:** Pucon
Frequency of operation: 10x daily   **Period of operation:** All year?
Website address: www.vaporchucao.cl
Builders: Philippe Mérien
Engine builder (if different from builder): R. Holtz, Hamburg 1905
Owner: Vapor Chucao
Remarks: Coke/wood fired

1991: Built for passenger tourist service eon the Lago de Villarica, using a new hull, an engine built at Hamburg in 1905 and a boiler by her engine builders, built in 1925.

Chucao operates 1-hour cruises and 2-hour evening cruises on the lake from Bahia La Poza at Pucon.

SS COLLICO

Collico at Valdivia. (Norman Brouwer)

Length: 18.30m
Propulsion: Single Screw,   **Engine type:** 2-cylinder
Built: 1906   **Rebuilt** (most recent): 1999
Passenger capacity: 22

Body of water: Cruces River   **Home port:** Valdivia
Frequency of operation: Regular   **Period of operation:** All year?
Website address: www.tuerca.cl/noticias/n8/collico/
Builders: Dresdner Maschinenfabrik & Schiffswerf Ubigau, Dresden
Owner: Enrique Gigoux   **Operator:** Floating restaurant 'Camina de Luna'
Remarks: Wood-fired

1907: Built at Dresden for service at Valdivia, running up to 400km upstream on the rivers there. Shipped out to Chile in three sections.
1910: Entered service for the Kunstmann sawmill. Used for towing wood barges on the Calle-Calle rivers.
*c.*1960: Sold to Capitan Rosas, used for passenger and cargo services on the Valdivia River.
1980: Withdrawn from service.
*c.*1999: Restored for excursions up the Valdivia and Cruces Rivers from Valdivia.

SS ENCO

Enco rusting on the sands at Choshuenco on the shore of Lake Panguipulli.

Built: *c.*1900
Passenger capacity: was 300
Body of water, Lago Panguipulli   **Home port:** Choshuenco
Frequency: Undergoing restoration
Website address: www.chile.com/tpl/articulo/detalle/ver.tpl?cod_articulo=56017

*c.*1900: Built for service on Lago Panguipulli, probably between Panguipulli and Choshuenco.
*c.*1990: Withdrawn from service and laid-up on the lake shore at Choshuenco.
2005: Purchased by the owners of **Collico**, and restoration started. The original engine was found and is being restored.

MEXICO

SL AFRICAN QUEEN

Length: 7.92m
Propulsion: Single Screw   **Engine type:** Single Cylinder, 5hp
Built: 1998   **Passenger capacity:** 12
Body of water: Rio Salado   **Home port:** Nuevo Vallarta
Frequency of operation: Daily   **Period of operation:** All year
Website address: http://www.sunworx.com/sailing/

Builders: Mazatlan Sin, Mexico (1955)
Owner: Captain Vladivar Kostlivy

1998: 31 December: Built by Frederick H. Semple with a 1955 fibre-glass hull and a 1953 engine, manufactured by Semple.

African Queen is a modern canopied open steam launch named after the star of the 1951 film of that name, and operates daily cruises at 10:30 from the Hotel Paradise Village Marina, Nuevo Vallarta.

SS CATALINA

Catalina, sunk at Ensenada, 1998. (David Engholm)

Length: 86.90m   **Gross tonnage**: 1,766
Propulsion: Single Screw   **Engine type**: Triple Expansion, 4,000hp
Built: 1924   **Passenger capacity**: was 2,100
Body of water: Pacific Ocean   **Home port**: Ensenada
Frequency of operation: Half-sunk, awaiting restoration
Website address: www.sscatalina.org; www.escapist.com/sscatalina
Builders: Los Angeles Shipbuilding & Dry Dock Co., Los Angeles
Owner: Unknown

1924: 30 June: Maiden voyage from Wilmington, California to Avalon, Santa Catalina Island. Built for the Wilmington Transportation Co., owned by William Wrigley (of chewing gum fame).

1942: 25 August: Used as a naval transport in San Francisco Bay

1946: April 15: Ceased military service having carried a total of 820,199 troops, more than any other US Naval transport during the war.

1948: Owners' name changed to Catalina Island Steamship Line.

1964: Both masts removed. Lifeboats removed by life rafts. Benches installed in new space made available and passenger certificate raised from 1950 to 2100.

1975: Withdrawn from service, having carried 2.4 million passengers during her working life. In this year used in a movie as a rescue freighter, which saved the **Queen Ann**, played by the **Queen Mary**.

1976: Placed on the National Register of Historic Places.

1977: Auctioned and purchased by Hymie Singer as a gift for his wife. Lay off Long Beach for some years. Intended to be used as a private yacht, but she has never sailed since.

1985: Moved to Ensenada, Mexico.

1997: December: Partially sunk by high winds.

1998: February: Aground and listing to port. **Catalina** currently lies sunken at the Mexican port of Ensenada. There are plans to raise her and bring her back to Wilmington. Although these are supported by the City of Los Angeles, they are dependent on private funding for her restoration. The SSCPA (SS *Catalina* Preservation Association) and SOHO (Save Our Heritage Organization) are promoting her rescue and restoration. Because of the building of a new marina, which **Catalina** lies across the entrance to, it is essential that she be raised and moved, otherwise she will be scrapped.

2000: First unsuccessful attempt to raise her. Mexican Government agreed that once the ship was afloat, ownership would pass to the SSCPA.

2003: Proposed to be used in the film *Sea of Glory* playing the part of the troopship **U.S.A.T. Dorchester**, which was torpedoed and sunk in the North Atlantic on February 3 1943.

2004: October: Film project delayed indefinitely because of problems with the scriptwriter not producing a script with sufficient historical accuracy. The problem at the moment is returning the ship to the United States. Once she is there, she will qualify for various grants which are not available while she lies in Mexico.

2005: July: $1.2-2 million still required to raise **Catalina** and return her to the USA, which Raising the SS Catalina Association is trying to do. Ownership cannot be transferred until she is raised.

2007: Retired Lt-Com. Richard MacPherson of Orange County, Ca., announced plans to restore **Catalina** as a nautical museum in California. It would take $2 million to raise her and $6 million to restore her.

Latest unconfirmed reports are that the City of Ensenada is interested in using **Catalina** as a tourist facility of some kind. There have also been plans to sink her as an artificial reef for divers. It is hope that she can be saved and restored to active service.

PARAGUAY

TSS PARAGUAY

Paraguayan gunboat *Paraguay* on the River Parana. (C. Mey)

Length: 70.15m   **Tonnage:** 856 displacement
Propulsion: Twin Screw   **Engine type:** 2 Turbines, 3,800hp
Built: 1930
Body of water: steam gunboat   **Home port:** Asuncion
Frequency of operation: possible charters
Website address: www.histarmar.com.ar/ArmadasExtranjeras/Paraguay/ARPParaguay.htm
Builders: SA Cantieri Navale Odero, Genoa
Engine builders: Parsons, Newcastle upon Tyne
Owner: Paraguayan Navy
Former name: *Comodoro Meyo*

1930: Built as the gunboat **Comodoro Meyo** for the Paraguayan Navy.

1931: May: Delivered to Buenos Aires.

1975: Modernised.

2004: A travel agent has mooted the possibility of using **Paraguay**, which has been laid-up for some time, on charters. She has not seen service in recent years because of boiler problems, and there has been talk about eventually dieselising her.

PERU

SS OLLANTA

Ollanta at Puno, 1999. (B. Worden)

Length: 79.00m   **Gross tonnage:** 750
Propulsion: Single Screw   **Engine type:** Compound
Built: 1930   **Rebuilt** (most recent): 1997
Passenger capacity: 712 day; eighty berths
Body of water: Lake Titicaca   **Home port:** Puno
Frequency of operation: Charters
Website address: www.heinz-buehler.ch/peru/titicaca/index.htm
Builders: Earles, Hull
Owner: Peruvian Railways
Former names: *Gran Mariscal Andres de Santa Cruz* 1998, *Ollanta* 1989

1930: Built in the UK and shipped out in sections to Mollendo, Peru by sea, and then 250 miles by rail to Puno. Built for the Peruvian Corporation, to work with Peruvian Railways on a weekly international ferry service from Puno to Guaqui, Bolivia.

1931: 18 November: Launched at Puno.

1932: June: Ran trials, and entered service. Originally she was fitted for sixty-six first-class and twenty second-class passengers and up to 1,000 tons of cargo.

1975: Peruvian Railways nationalised.

Mid-1980s (?): Withdrawn from service.

1989: Renamed *Gran Mariscal Andres de Santa Cruz*.

*c.*1995: Named *Ollanta* again.

1998: Reportedly was sailing about once a month, or less often, on cargo sailings.

2000: Peruvian Railways taken over by Sea Containers/Orient Express group, headed by Jim Sherwood.

August: Operated one passenger sailing in connection with a railtour by Trains Unlimited Tours, USA.

2004: Drydocked for a major refurbishment.

A plan to convert *Ollanta* for use on three-day tourist cruises on Lake Titicaca in connection with the Orient Express train has been abandoned.

Ollanta is a remarkable survivor of that is essentially a Victorian passenger/cargo steamer. Also at Puno is *Coya*, built by Denny of Dumbarton in 1892. Laid-up on the beach for many years she is now reportedly in the process of being converted to a static restaurant ship at Puno. Also at Puno is the venerable *Yavari*, built in 1862 by Cammel Laird and brought over the mountain to the lake by mule. She has been restored and is still a museum. Her steam engine was replaced in 1913 by a Bolinder semi-diesel, which is itself now very historic.

The Amazon steamer *Jhuliana*, one of two which was used in the film *Fitzcarraldo* in 1982, survives in service at Iquitos, although it is beloved she has now been dieselised.

Epilogue

IS THERE ANYTHING ELSE OUT THERE?

While the listings of steamers in this book are believed to be comprehensive, it is possible that there may be a more to be 'discovered'.

These might include small steam launches, which may offer public trips at steam rallies, but are normally used privately be their owners. Most of these are modern craft, and there are groups of steamboat enthusiasts in many countries throughout the world.

There may possibly be survivors in remote areas of the world, such as the River Zaire in the Congo, where the sternwheeler **Luama** was featured in the BBC 'Great Rover Journeys' series about twenty years ago, the River Niger, where there used to be stern wheel steamers run by the United Africa Co., or the Rover Brahmaputra in India, where a paddle steamer featured in the 1980 ITV series *The Commanding Sea* presented by Clare Francis.

Bill Worden snapped several apparent steamers at Cairo in 1996, including an unidentified one pictured here. It is assumed these are in use as houseboats, but there may be one or more which could possibly return to service at some stage.

A friend snapped a steam ferry, pictured, across the Irrawaddy at Rangoon/Yangon in 1987. Does it still survive? Short of anybody going out there and looking, who knows? Such vessels are too small to feature in Lloyds Register.

Up to around 1990 Indian Railways operated a paddle steamer ferry across the Ganges at Patna, using ferries such as **Yamuna**, pictured. Were they scrapped after the service ceased, or do they survive rotting in some creek or another?

Throughout the compilation of this volume I have 'discovered' a number of passenger-carrying steam vessels previously unknown to me. I am sure there must be more out there.

If you know of any other passenger-carrying steam vessels, or any which are awaiting or undergoing restoration, please let the author know, c/o the publishers or at Alistair@deayton.freeserve.co.uk. They can then be incorporated in any future edition.

Above left: The Indian Railways paddle steamer *Yamuna* crossing the Ganges at Patna, 1977. (Roderick Smith)

Above centre: An unidentified paddle steamer laid up at Cairo, 1996. (B. Worden)

Above right: An unidentified steam ferry on the Irrawaddy at Yangon, 1987. (Roderick Smith)

Appendices

I

Longest 10

UNITES STATES	301.80m
PACIFIC SKY	240.31m
OCEANIC	238.44m
INDEPENDENCE	208.01m
THE TOPAZ	195.10m
MAXIM GORKIY	194.72m
THE EMERALD	182.1m
IVORY	159.26m
MARINE STAR	150.28 m
AMERICAN VICTORY	133.2m
LANE VICTORY	133.2m
RED OAK VICTORY	133.2m

Longest 10 reciprocating-engined steamers

JOHN W BROWN	128.80m
AMERICAN QUEEN	127.40m
JEREMIAH O'BRIEN	127.30m
BADGER	125.15m
MISSISSIPPI QUEEN	116.40m
LOMONOSOV	102.30m
CATALINA	86.90m
DELTA QUEEN	86.90m
GOETHE	83.25m
SHIELDHALL	81.69m

II

Largest 10 (by tonnage)

UNITED STATES	53,329
PACIFIC SKY	46,087
OCEANIC	38,772
THE TOPAZ	32,327
THE EMERALD	26,431
MAXIM GORKIY	24,220
INDEPENDENCE	23,719
MARINE STAR	12,773
IVORY	12,609
AMERICAN VICTORY	7,612
LANE VICTORY	7,612
RED OAK VICTORY	7,612

Largest 10 reciprocating-engined (by tonnage)

JOHN W BROWN	7,176
JEREMIAH O'BRIEN	7,176
AMERICAN QUEEN	4,700
MISSISSIPPI QUEEN	4,500
BADGER	4,244
CATALINA	1,766
SHIELDHALL	1,753
DELTA QUEEN	1,650
SANKT ERIK	1,441
NATCHEZ	1,384

III

Oldest 10

TUDOR VLADIMIRESCU	1854
JURA	1854
SKIBLADNER	1856
FORTUNA	1857
GONDOLA	1859
HJEJLEN	1861
MAYFLOWER	1861
ENGEBRET SOOT	1862
TOMTEN	1862
DOMNARFVET	1863

Oldest 10 in regular scheduled service

SKIBLADNER	1856
GONDOLA	1859
HJEJLEN	1861
MAYFLOWER	1861
GERDA	1865
ENGELBREKT	1866
ADELAIDE	1866
BJOREN	1867
FORSVIK	1867
FREJA AF FRYKEN	1868

IV

British-built surviving steamers, by yard

Ailsa Shipbuilding, Troon
MEDWAY QUEEN 1924

Alley and McLellan, Glasgow
NILE PEKING 1908

C. Bathurst & Son, Tewkesbury
KING 1905

J. Bond, Maidenhead
THAMES ESPERANZA 1899

Bow McLachlan & Co., Paisley
BENARES 1896
NYANZA 1907
KAVIRONDO 1912
USOGA 1912
SUDAN 1921
JOHN OXLEY 1927
JOHN H AMOS 1931

Breaker, Bowness on Windermere
LADY ROWENA 1926

John Brown & Co., Clydebank
NAHLIN 1930

Burgoyne, Windsor
WINDSOR BELLE 1901

E.W. & W.E. Cawston, Reading
ECLIPSE 1901

E Clarke & Co., Brimscombe
NUNEHAM 1898

Denny, Dumbarton
SIR WALTER SCOTT 1900
DELTA QUEEN 1926
KIWI 1930

Ditchburn & Mare, London
RIGI 1848

R. Dunston, Hull
TOMMI 1943

Dunston, Thorne
VIC 32 1943

Earles Shipbuilding, Hull
OLLANTA 1931

John Elder & Co., Govan (later became Fairfield, Govan)
IBIS 1883
THE TOPAZ 1956
INKILAP 1961
KANLICA 1961
TEGMEN ALI IHSAN KALMAZ 1961
TURAN EMEKSIZ 1961

Fellows, Morton and Clayton, Saltley
PRESIDENT 1919

Ferguson Brothers (Port Glasgow) Ltd
LYTTLETON 1907
TE WHAKA 1912
SPIRIT OF THE TAY 2004

Fleming and Ferguson, Paisley
SALIN 1921

Alexander Hall & Co., Aberdeen
EXPLORER 1955

W. Harkness & Son Ltd, Middlesbrough
LA PALMA 1912

Harland and Wolff, Belfast
NOMADIC 1911

Harland and Wolff, Govan
PORTWEY 1927

Hawthorn Leslie, Newcastle
GUZELHISAR 1911

T.W. Hayton, Bowness on Windermere
KITTIWAKE 1898

J., S. & W. Horsham, Bourne End
ALASKA 1883

A. & J. Inglis, Pointhouse
EXEQUIEL RAMOS MEJIA 1911
ROQUE SAENZ PENA 1911
WAVERLEY 1947
MAID OF THE LOCH 1953

Jones Quiggin, Liverpool
GONDOLA 1859

Kingfisher Marine, Leeds
SIDNEY 1993

Glyn Lancaster Jones, Port Dinorwic
MELISANDE 1985
LIBERTY BELLE (Vitznau) 1987

Lobnitz & Co., Renfrew
WILLIAM C DALDY 1935
LYTTLETON 1939
SHIELDHALL 1955

Simons-Lobnitz Ltd, Renfrew
SEVA 1963

Lytham Shipbuilding & Engineering, Lytham
KARIM 1917
MISR 1918

Philip & Sons, Dartmouth
KINGSWEAR CASTLE 1924

Pimblott & Co., Northwich
AULD REEKIE 1943

Rennoldson, South Shields
PIETRO MICCA 1895

Henry Robb & Co., Leith
SOUTH STEYNE 1938

Salter Bros, Oxford
STREATLEY 1905

Scott & Co., Bowling
CAROLA 1898

Neil Shepherd, Bowness
OSPREY 1902
SWALLOW 1911

Smiths Dock, Middlesbrough
SOUTHERN ACTOR 1955

Stephen, Linthouse
MEDEA 1904

Stothert & Marten, Bristol
MAYFLOWER 1861

Tranmere Bay Development Co. Ltd
DANIEL ADAMSON 1903

Vickers Sons & Maxim, Barrow in Furness
LAURINDO PITTA 1910

Brian Waters
MONARCH 2003

J.S. White, Cowes
ELFIN 1933

Wootten, Cookham
FIREBIRD 1954

Yarrow, Poplar (later moved to Scotstoun)
WAIMARIE 1900
MYAT YADANA 1947

Unknown yard in the UK
AFRICAN QUEEN 1912
FORTUNA 1857
SEGWUN, as NIPISSING 1887
MEMNON 1904
GONCA 1910

Sometimes a planned trip to sail on a steamer can be unfruitful, like when I attempted to sail on *Gallant* in 1997.

V

Steamers, sorted by type of propulsion

	side paddle	stern paddle	quarter wheeler	single screw	twin screw	quadruple screw	Total
United Kingdom	6			25	3		34
Denmark	1			2			3
Estonia				1			1
Finland				76	1		77
Norway	1			22	1		24
Sweden	1			68			69
Austria	3			3			6
Czech Republic	3						3
France		1					1
Germany	13			22	7		42
Netherlands	2			23	2		27
Switzerland	21			7			28
Poland				1			1
Romania	3						3
Russia	5			1			6
Cyprus					1		1
Greece					2		2
Italy	3			1	1		5
Monaco					1		1
Spain				2	1		3
Turkey				2	5		7
Egypt	3	1	1		1		6
Kenya				2	1		3
South Africa				1			1
Bangladesh	1						1
India	1	1			1		3
Japan				2			2
Myanmar	1			1			2
North Korea	1						1
Australia	20			9	1		30
New Zealand	1	1		7	3		12
Micronesia				1			1
Canada	1			5	1		7

United States	2	15		22	4	1	44
Argentina	2						2
Brazil		1		1	1		3
Chile				3			3
Mexico				2			2
Paraguay					1		1
Peru				1			1
Totals	94	20	1	313	38	1	467

VI

Steamers, by frequency of operation

	cruise-operating	cruise-laid up	overnight passenger	scheduled 4 or more days per week	scheduled 1–3 days per week	scheduled monthly or irregular	rallies	charters (and special non-public trips)	unknown	undergoing restoration	awaiting restoration	Laid-up or currently in static use	under construction	proposed	Total
United Kingdom			1	10	3		3	7		7	1	1	1	0	34
Denmark				1	1					1					3
Estonia										1					1
Finland				6	1	3	47	11		3		6			77
Norway				1	3	2		5		10	3				24
Sweden				16	10	8	14	9	1	7	2	1	1		69
Austria					3	1				2					6
Czech Republic				2							1				3
France				1											1
Germany	1			16	2	9	1	3		5	2	3			42
Netherlands				4	1		13	4		2	3				27
Switzerland				14	1	6		1		1	2	2		1	28
Poland												1			1
Romania								2				1			3
Russia			3							1		2			6
Cyprus	1														1
Greece	2														2
Italy	1				2			1			1				5

Monaco								1							1
Spain	1					1				1					3
Turkey								1	1		1	4			7
Egypt			4	1						1					6
Kenya								1				2			3
South Africa				1											1
Bangladesh								1							1
India								3							3
Japan	1							1							2
Myanmar				1				1							2
North Korea				1											1
Australia			2	7	4		5			6	2	3	1		30
New Zealand				5	1	1	1	1	1	1				1	12
Micronesia			1												1
Canada				1			4	1				1			7
United States		2	4	13	1	6		6	1	3	3	4		1	44
Argentina						2									2
Brazil				1	1			1							3
Chile				2						1					3
Mexico				1								1			2
Paraguay								1							1
Peru						1									1
Totals	6	23	16	100	36	41	78	63	12	53	23	31	3	3	467

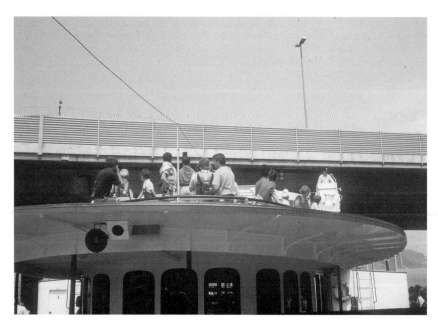

Uri going through the Acheregg bridge on the way to Alpnachstad on Lake Lucerne.

Index